THE PAUL CARUS LECTURES
FIFTH SERIES

TOWARD A PERSPECTIVE REALISM

Published on the Foundation
Established in Memory of
PAUL CARUS
Editor of The Open Court and The Monist
1888–1919

EVANDER BRADLEY MCGILVARY

TOWARD A PERSPECTIVE REALISM

BY
EVANDER BRADLEY McGILVARY
EDITED BY ALBERT G. RAMSPERGER

THE OPEN COURT PUBLISHING COMPANY
LA SALLE, ILLINOIS
1956

Copyright 1956
THE OPEN COURT PUBLISHING COMPANY

Printed in the United States of America
for the Publishers by
Paquin Printers

FOREWORD

My father, Evander B. McGilvary, devoted the last fourteen years of his life to the preparation of this book, which was to summarize his philosophical beliefs. At the time of his death the manuscript was still growing and being revised. The family unaided could never have prepared the manuscript for publication because, unfortunately, none of us possesses the necessary technical qualifications. We had almost decided that the book could never be published, and that the labors of over a decade must be for nought. Had it not been for Mr. Ramsperger's devoted efforts, *Toward a Perspective Realism* might never have gone beyond the reams of typewritten sheets that we gathered up in father's study. Mr. Ramsperger was my father's good friend and had often discussed his theories with him.

We, the daughter and grandchildren of Evander Bradley McGilvary, cannot possibly express our indebtedness to Mr. Ramsperger, but we trust that whoever reads and values this work will appreciate his contribution and will join with us in gratitude for his labors.

MARGARET McGILVARY ZIMMERMAN

Sarasota, Florida
July 1954

EDITOR'S PREFACE

Evander Bradley McGilvary delivered the Fifth Series of Carus Lectures at the meeting of the American Philosophical Association at Columbia University in December 1939. In March 1945 he wrote to his publisher that much had to be rewritten. "However," he said, "I hope to be able to have all my copy in your hands some time this coming summer." But he seems to have underestimated the difficulty of straightening out some of the problems. His method of revision was not to make corrections to a first draft. He would discard one version and write a new one afresh; and, being the perfectionist that he was, he might have labored another lifetime of 89 years, before his work would have satisfied his critical mind.

McGilvary's philosophy, as his title indicates, is a variety of realism; that is, nature is not derivative from spiritual substance nor constructed from mental events. Unlike some other kinds of realism, which encounter difficulty in establishing liaison between subjective experiences and the real world, McGilvary maintains that in the relations (which he calls perspectives) in which living organisms stand to their environment, the real world itself appears to the organism, and in a given perspective the world really has the characters, both physical and non-physical, which appear. This thesis is not supported in a merely general way by saying that observed events are relative to the observer and by mentioning Einstein's theory of relativity; it is worked out in detail, with explicit statement of the postulates that are being assumed, and by the use of Einstein's theory for philosophical purposes only where it is legitimate, that is, in the exposition of spatial and temporal perspectives as elements in the construction of the objective world, which is at once the world of common sense observation and of mathematical physics, for both must build from the same empirical evidence.

Chapters VI through XI are reprinted from previously published articles. They are: Chapter VI: "Relations in General and Universals in Particular" from *The Journal of Philosophy*, Vol. XXXVI, No. 1 and No. 2 (1939); Chapter VII: "Freedom and Necessity in Human Affairs" from *The International Journal of Ethics*, Vol. XLV, No. 4, University of Chicago Press (1935); Chapter VIII: "The Warfare of Moral Ideals" from *The Hibbert Journal*, Vol. XIV (1915–1916); Chapter IX: "The Lorentz Transformation and 'Space-Time'" from *The Journal of Philosophy*, Vol. XXXVIII, No. 13 (1941); Chapter X: "The Paradox of the Time-Retarding Journey" from *The Philosophical Review*, Vol. XL, No. 4 (1931); Chapter XI: "Space-Time, Simple Location and Prehension in Whitehead's Philosophy" from *The Philosophy of Alfred North Whitehead*, edited by P. Schilpp, The Library of Living Philosophers, Evanston (1941). Permission from the publishers to reprint these articles is acknowledged with gratitude.

Thanks are due to authors, and their publishers, from whose works Mr. Gilvary has quoted, especially to the following, who have given permission to use passages from the works mentioned: To The Macmillan Company from Sellars's *The Philosophy of Physical Realism* and from Penfield and Rasmussen's *The Cerebral Cortex of Man*; to McGraw-Hill Book Company from Margenau's *The Nature of Physical Theory*; to Charles Scribner's Sons from Santayana's *Scepticism and Animal Faith, The Life of Reason*, and *The Realm of Spirit* and from C. I. Lewis's *Mind and the World Order*; to Mr. Henry James, Jr. from William James's *Essays in Radical Empiricism* and *A Pluralistic Universe*; to Cambridge University Press from Whitehead's *The Concept of Nature* and Sherrington's *Man on his Nature*; to Harcourt Brace and Company from Russell's *The Analysis of Matter* and Moore's *Philosophical Studies*; to Henry Holt and Company from James's *The Principles of Psychology, Psychology: Briefer Course,* and *The Influence of Darwin on Philosophy*; to Columbia University Press from Woodbridge's *Nature and Mind*; to University of Chicago Press from Carlson and Johnson's *The Machinery of the Body*.

A. G. RAMSPERGER

July 1954

CONTENTS

	PAGE
FOREWORD by Margaret McGilvary Zimmerman	vii
EDITOR'S PREFACE	ix
I INTRODUCTION: SOME POSTULATES AND DEFINITIONS	1
II CONSCIOUSNESS	41
III MIND, BODY, AND EXPERIENCE	73
IV CONSCIOUSNESS IN OTHER PHILOSOPHIES	123
V PERSPECTIVES	154
VI RELATIONS IN GENERAL AND UNIVERSALS IN PARTICULAR	226
VII FREEDOM AND NECESSITY IN HUMAN AFFAIRS	255
VIII THE WARFARE OF MORAL IDEALS	275
IX THE LORENTZ TRANSFORMATION AND "SPACE-TIME"	297
X "THE PARADOX OF THE TIME-RETARDING JOURNEY"	312
XI SPACE-TIME, SIMPLE LOCATION, AND PREHENSION IN WHITEHEAD'S PHILOSOPHY	338
XII CONCLUSION	367
INDEX	373

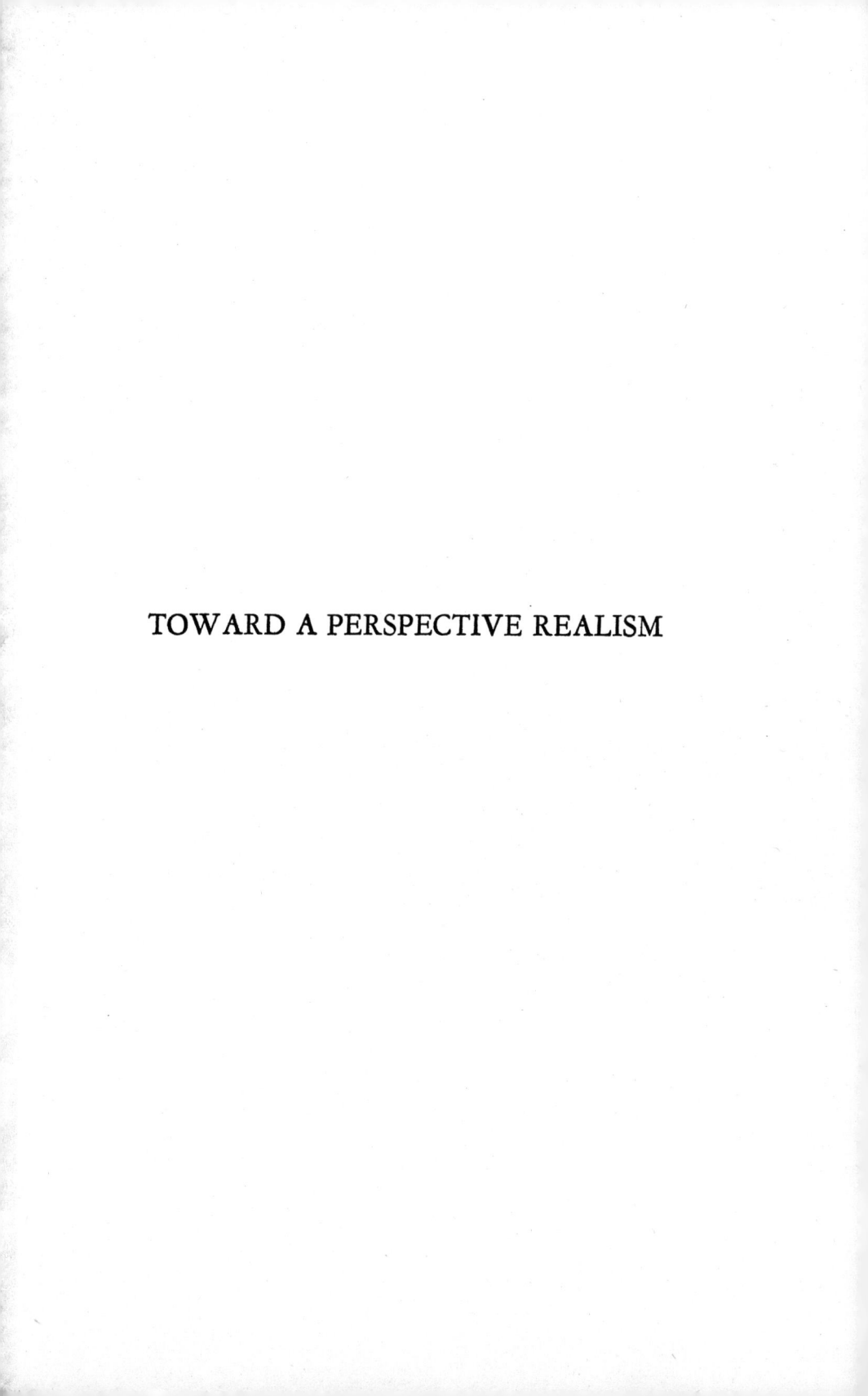

TOWARD A PERSPECTIVE REALISM

Chapter I

INTRODUCTION
SOME POSTULATES AND DEFINITIONS

Every philosophy is the universe as it appears in the perspective of a philosopher. It is a *Welt angeschaut* and not *die Welt an und für sich*. Whether the world is anything for itself is a question the discussion of which would plunge us into a futile debate into which it is not the purpose of these lectures to enter. The perspective realist makes no claim that he can speak for the universe as it is for *itself*. He does not consider himself as an outsider looking on, a stranger, as it were, from some supernatural realm, passively contemplating a world of nature with whose goings-on he has no active business. On the contrary, he is a natural organism responding to natural stimulations and acquiring thereby such knowledge as nature thereupon puts at his disposal. This knowledge, so far as he can integrate it into a system, is his philosophy. As this knowledge and the integration of it develops, his philosophy develops. His philosophy therefore never reaches maturity. It ever enjoys all the prerogatives and suffers all the growing pains that are the lot of adolescence. It never is but always to be blest. A mature philosophy for him is an ideal never realized. He sees in part, he knows in part, he prophesies in part; and that which is perfect never comes, except as a goal that lies afar off before him.

Ideals properly cherished are indispensable for any but a random success in the conduct of life. Properly to cherish an ideal is to recognize its function and therewith its limitation. Its function is to guide, not to be acquiescently attained. It is sometimes the furthermost point on the horizon in the direction in which our interests are driving, and it is not always the part of wisdom to make straight for that point. The lie of the intervening land should be taken into account, and with every important move a new horizon appears. At other times an ideal is what the North Star is to the mariner without compass. He steers his course thereby without ever entertaining the thought that he is ultimately to arrive at Polaris. It might not be there where he now sees it, even if he could get there; and if he could it would be a disastrous journey's end. A lodestar is not a future abode. Thus the limitation as well as the value of an ideal is to be found in its relevancy to the situation in which it is employed. An absolutely unchanging ideal in a world of change is an unnaturalizable alien in an uncongenial land.

These remarks are intended as a commentary to the title your lecturer has chosen for this series of Carus Lectures. Absolutes, whether logical or ontological, he has none, and what he will give you may prove to be a thing of shreds and patches after the critics have had their way with it. All he can say of it is that it has been of help to him of late years by giving some semblance, retrospective and prospective, of continuity of direction to his philosophical meanderings.

A philosophical friend some time ago raised the question why the view to be presented is called a *realism*. It was a pertinent question, and the point was well taken. There are abundant signs that the war between idealism and realism is all but over. Neither side has won a smashing victory or suffered an overwhelming defeat. This is because the issues involved have been changing with the course of time till now it is difficult to tell a realist from an idealist. They differ from each other very much as Democrat and Republican differed from each other in some presidential campaigns: they wore different party labels, but these labels were largely meaningless except as badges that gave title to seats in party conventions. The reason I had for choosing to call the view here to be presented by the name "perspective realism" is that it has been reached from an earlier position that was unquestionably "realistic" as judged by earlier standards. The continuity of development to which reference was made a moment ago—call that movement progressive or retrogressive as you will—has resulted in the keeping of a realistic residue. Perhaps, for the sake of appeasement, it would have been better to drop the old realistic label. "Isms" of whatever sort are in somewhat bad repute these days, and it would have been politic to follow the example set by physicists when they adopted "relativity" rather than "relativism" as their name for the doctrine now current among them; thus we should dub our view "perspectivity" and call ourselves "perspectivists." But having committed myself in announcing these lectures in the printed program of our meeting as "Toward a Perspective Realism," I let the "realism" stand, but claim the privilege of calling the view "perspectivity" as well. Roses and skunk cabbages do not get their characters from the names they go by; neither do philosophical systems. At any rate, it will soon be seen that in "perspective realism" the emphasis is on "perspective" rather than on "realism." What is thus emphasized is of course at the service of the philosophic public, including those who may prefer to call themselves idealists; realists may claim no monopoly here.

What then is this philosophy toward which I am inviting you to grope your way with me? In one sense it is nothing new. It is almost as old as philosophy itself. We are all familiar with the dictum of Protagoras that "man is the measure of all things: of the things that are, that they are; of the things that are not, that they are not." Whether or not Protagoras used this as a basis on which to build a philosophy of thoroughgoing scepticism has of late been a matter of dispute among commentators; but in the philosophical tradition that goes back at least as far as Plato the acceptance of Protagoras's "Man the Measure" has been regarded as the great philosophical betrayal. If there is to be anything that deserves the name of knowledge it must rest, so this tradition would have it, on something absolute, something ecumenically established. Philosophy was regarded, if not as a "quest for certainty" in *all* things, at least as a quest for certainty in *some* things. There was a soul of certainty in things uncertain, would men discerningly distil it out. Without some certainty, without something that is known as absolutely true, it was dogmatically assumed that there could be no advance to knowledge of anything else. There must be "first principles" which are "self-evident" and therefore unquestionable, and they remain such, world without end. Each of them could say with Brahma,

>They reckon ill who leave me out;
>   When me they fly, I am the wings;
> I am the doubter and the doubt,
>   And I the hymn the Brahmin sings.

Through the centuries this position found powerful support in the geometry then current, which reasoned to its theorems from axioms then unquestioned. What had not been questioned was taken as unquestionable. If the most exact science thus had at its disposal in those earlier days unquestionable first principles, it is not surprising that philosophy, too, in her earlier days, while aspiring to be the queen of the sciences, should have had equally indubitable first principles, the very first of the first. Let us not be too hard on the philosopher of those earlier days. In more recent times it was the *mathematician* Descartes who was "the founder of modern philosophy" and also of modern dogmatism. Spinoza, whose *Ethica* has been the admiration of succeeding ages, worked out his system *more geometrico* at a time when the *mos geometricus* was that of Euclid, and as yet Lobachevski, Bolyai, and Riemann had not been born. And Kant had the implied backing of the mathematicians of his day when he pronounced the Aristotelian logic to be perfect as it came from the hands of Aristotle. That logic authorized the syllogism based on the three laws of Identity, Contradiction, and the Excluded Middle, whose exclusive validity was acknowledged in the geometry then current. Great was the mood of *Barbara*, and the mathematician was its prophet. And what was true of mathematics was naturally true also of mathematical physics. Newton's first principles were based, so at least he thought, on Absolute Space and Absolute Time. Read his *Principia*.

If philosophy is a human enterprise and if science is a communal enterprise, it is natural that the scientific spirit of any age should be pervasive. The great philosophers were human beings and did their work in the community of human scientists. It could not be expected that they should be less infallible than their scientific compeers.

But the *Zeitgeist*, even in science, undergoes changes, and the nineteenth century brought with it a radical change in the foundations of mathematics. There are in mathematics no longer any "axioms" of universal sweep. They have been replaced by "postulates." Instead of starting from self-evident premises geometry now starts from "assumptions," and many different assumptions are eligible. And a similar position is now taken by many arithmeticians in their work.[1]

Philosophers are beginning to follow again the lead of science. The mood of absolutism is evaporating, leaving relativism as a deposit in many quarters. And relativism works from postulates and not from principles enjoying the sanction of self-evidence. This relativism differs from that attacked by the earlier tradition of absolutism. It is not a relativism that results in general scepticism. What scepticism there is is one of caution and not of despair. For instance, in Mr. Santayana there is reliance on healthy "animal faith." In Mr. Dewey and Mr. Bertrand Russell, in spite of their great differences, there is a confidence in the postulational method of science. Postulates, the former tells us, "are not arbitrary or mere linguistic conventions. They must be such as control

---

[1] Professor A. N. Whitehead goes so far as to question the "uniform truth-value" of the proposition: "One and one make two." "There is no difficulty," he tells us, "in imagining a world . . . in which arithmetic would be an interesting fanciful topic for dreamers, but useless for practical people engrossed in the business of life" (*Process and Reality*, New York and Cambridge, 1929, p. 303). Of course, in this passage Mr. Whitehead has express reference to applied, not to pure, arithmetic. The foundations of pure arithmetic, however, are a still moot problem among the experts.

the determination and arrangements of subject matter with respect to achieving enduringly stable beliefs. Only after inquiry has proceeded for a considerable time and has hit upon methods that work successfully, is it possible to extract the postulates that are involved. They are not presuppositions at large." Such postulates guide "inquiry," and "judgment may be identified as the settled outcome of inquiry." And Mr. Dewey accepts the judgments thus reached as having "*direct* existential import."[2]

Mr. Russell's "causal theory of perception," which will be examined in detail later and which is perhaps his most distinctive contribution to philosophy, has two parts:

> The first of these tends toward scepticism; the second tends in the opposite direction. The first appears as certain as anything in science can hope to be; the second depends upon postulates which have little more than a pragmatic justification. It has, however, all the merits of a good scientific theory—i.e., its verifiable consequences are never found to be false.[3]

There is here an interesting combination of scepticism with tempered certainty. That which tends toward *scepticism* is as *certain* as anything in science can hope to be. The difficulty is removed by resort to "pragmatic justification." Thus many are the ways of surmounting scepticism; and perspective realism offers itself as one of the possible ways.

But what is perspective realism? No single sentence, or even two or three sentences, can adequately epitomize any theory, but so far as this can be done, perhaps perspective realism (or "perspectivity," as it shall be alternatively called) can be provisionally defined as a philosophical theory that regards every experience, including the experience of a philosophical theory, as the *real objective world* appearing in the perspective of an experiencing organism. There are several words in this definition that themselves need definition, but this need will be met, so far as it can be met, only as we proceed. Not every word can be defined by

---
[2] John Dewey, *Logic: The Theory of Inquiry*, New York, 1938, p. 18.
[3] Bertrand Russell, *The Analysis of Matter*, New York and London, 1927, p. 197. By permission of Harcourt Brace and Co.

genus and specific difference. Professor C. I. Lewis has well said:

> All points have their positions eventually in terms of the array of all space: no point or set of points has any primal position in any other fashion; we merely choose as an arbitrary basis of reference some set which is convenient or marks the place where we happen to be. All terms or concepts similarly have their meaning eventually in the array of all meanings, and no member of this array is intrinsically primal or privileged.[4]

But do we all have the same array of meanings, by reference to which any single meaning can be identified? I think that it is obvious that in many respects we do not. Bergson has somewhere called attention to the necessity of putting ourselves on the same "plane" of meanings with another in order to understand him. We have all perhaps had the experience of wondering what a man—and not necessarily a philosopher—is talking about. His words don't make sense. But hoping that we shall arrive at an understanding, we continue to listen. After a longer or shorter time it all "clicks." We have succeeded in reaching his plane, and on this plane his several meanings now mutually fit and thus define each other. For many of us philosophers this progress from mystification to understanding has taken place (if indeed it has) in our converse with Hegel or with Bergson or with John Dewey. Patience was needed, and confidence that the philosopher in question knew what he was saying and was not a mere purveyor of words, not just a verbalizing freak. A new philosophy is like a new suit of clothes; it must be tried on before one can learn whether it fits, and it must be worn in order to find out whether it wears well.

Perspective realism offers itself for this trying on and this wearing; but, as has been already intimated, it does not offer itself as something brand-new. Very few recent philosophies have neglected the use of perspectives in their make-up. Perhaps the most thoroughgoing use of perspectives is to be found in Mr. Russell's philosophy; and perspectives play an important part in Samuel

---

[4] *Mind and the World Order*, New York, 1929, p. 83. By permission of Chas. Scribner's Sons.

Alexander's *Space, Time, and Deity*; in Professor Whitehead's "philosophy of organism"; and in George H. Mead's *Philosophy of the Present*.[5] Thus perspective realism is not introducing a new concept into philosophical discussion. All that it claims to do is to make it central in the array of philosophical concepts, and, as will be seen later, it is different from that current in many present-day philosophers. It restores to the word "perspective" the meaning it has in popular thought.

Before proceeding to lay down some of the postulates on which we shall operate, it is necessary to say that in addition to these there will be without question other postulates that should be listed. All that can be reasonably expected of any philosopher is that, in addition to those he explicitly employs, he shall, when called on, avow unexpressed postulates which he is shown actually to have used. The omission of such postulates from our list is of course a technical defect. But I do not make any claim to technical perfection such as the pure mathematician has as his ideal. And there will doubtless be found another kind of defect. The postulates do not claim to be independent of each other, but at any rate they seem to be compatible with each other. It must be remembered that I am only working *toward* a philosophical system, and if my views are viable it will remain for others to develop them.

There is another cautionary observation it is desirable to make here. In the course of my discussion I shall cite many passages from other philosophers and criticize the views therein expressed. The criticisms will be made not always in the belief that the views are untenable. I believe that almost any philosophy that has gained wide support is not only respectable but also tenable if only its assumptions are laid bare and explicitly recognized as assumptions. Like Kipling's tribal lays, there are nine-and-thirty ways of writing philosophy, and all of them are right in the sense that they are logically justifiable on the basis of assumptions they

---

[5] References will be given later. Among other perspectively minded thinkers may be mentioned Dr. Irwin Biser (*General Scheme for Natural Systems*, 1938) and Professor Andrew Ushenko (see especially "A Theory of Perception," in the *Journal of Philosophy*, Vol. XXXVII, p. 141 ff). And this is not a complete list.

make, but often make unwittingly. No one philosopher or school of philosophers has discovered the only solution for the riddle of the universe. There are many more key words for this riddle than the words "Perspective Realism," and at first blush they may seem as unpromising for the unlocking of doors as Ali Baba's "Open Sesame" must have seemed for his doors. What is magic and what is natural can be learned only by systematic inquiry. The magic of medieval transmutationists has developed into the physics of our present day, and a daring and unsupported guess has been itself transmuted into science by methodical labor.

Therefore when I criticize another philosopher I do not do this in the magisterial spirit of one who knows what is what and what is not. A criticism worth making in philosophy points out what is a defect *from the point of view of the critic,* and thus helps to *the understanding of the critic's view.* In earlier drafts of copy for this volume I scrupulously inserted the words "from the perspectivist's point of view" in every stricture. Most of these qualifications have now been elided. Too many "I think's" savor not of modesty but of egotism. At best they soon begin to bore and cease to penetrate. The reader will please reinsert them where he is tempted to condemn me for dogmatism.

An expositor must resort to all sorts of devices to make himself understood, and among them the use of contrast by adverse criticism often seems advisable. But fortunately something more positive is available. For while in many respects we find ourselves unable to get on the same plane of meanings on which others take their stand, it is obvious that in other respects and in our unphilosophical moments we are all of us, with some unhappy exceptions, already on the same plane when we speak of "reality." We live in a common world where the ground on which we walk, the houses in which we live, the food we eat, the clothes we wear, the bodies of ourselves and of our fellow men, the words we use in our communication with each other—in short, the larger part of what we experience—we naively take to be real; not real in the sense that we can agree on a definition of reality in terms of genus and specific difference, but real in terms of common acceptance. Was it Carlyle who, to a lady on her preposterous remark that she "accepted the universe," bluntly replied: "Egad, you'd better"? I am naive and preposterous enough to accept the universe now that it has accepted me, and I feel the better for this reciprocity. All of us find that in the common things of life it is the same universe we accept.

Professor Dewey has said:

> Of all affairs, communication is the most wonderful. That things should be able to pass from the plane of external pushing and pulling to that of revealing themselves to man, and thereby to themselves; and that the fruit of communication should be participation, sharing, is a wonder by the side of which transubstantiation pales."[6]

This is the observation of the philosopher and not of the common man in Mr. Dewey. The man in the street would find it indeed wonderful if he suddenly were unable to communicate with others. I remember once hearing as a boy the story of a sane man turned into a raving maniac when his companions entered into a conspiracy to deny everything he said. He was not to be a man but a loathsome snake; his hands were not to be real hands but imaginary excrescences from his serpentine coils, and so on; till what he took at first to be a coarse joke played on him gradually became a doubt and finally a horrible certainty. I do not vouch for the truth of the story, but neither should I like to have such a conspiracy plotted against me. I might stubbornly resist for a while, but I rather suspect that if every stranger I met, as well as my former friends, were to back up the conspirators and insist on refusing to communicate with me on my own plane, I could not in the end maintain my stance on that plane. It would be hard to believe that every one except myself is crazy as a loon, or devilishly malicious. We all maintain our mental poise only as we find support in the common poise of our fellows. As many of us as have "realities" in our experience bring them and lay them down at the feet of others, and distribution is made to every man

---

[6] *Experience and Nature,* Chicago and London, 1926, p. 166.

according as he has need. Even the solipsist continues to have social moments when he tries to convince others of the correctness of his views, and would probably become as mad in behavior as he is in theory if the social denizens of his world were persisently to deny that they and he are what he and they seem to them and to him to be.

Echoing Mr. Santayana, I would say, and I wish that I could have said it as splendidly by myself:

> I have a great respect for orthodoxy; . . . for a certain shrewd orthodoxy which the sentiment and practice of laymen maintain throughout . . . I am animated by distrust of all high guesses, and by sympathy with the old prejudices and workaday opinions of mankind: they are ill expressed, but they are well grounded . . . . What novelty my version of things may possess is meant simply to obviate occasions for sophistry by giving everyday beliefs a more accurate and circumstantial form. I do not pretend to place myself at the heart of the universe nor at its origin, nor to draw its periphery. I would lay siege to the truth only as animal exploration and fancy may do so, first from one quarter and then from another, expecting the reality to be not simpler than my experience of it, but far more expansive and complex. I stand in philosophy exactly where I stand in daily life; I should not be honest otherwise. I accept the same miscellaneous witnesses, bow to the same obvious facts, make conjectures no less instinctively, and admit the same encircling ignorance.[7]

And with Mr. Santayana, but without the malice of a lifelong bachelor, I would say:

> The philosophy of the common man is an old wife that gives him no pleasure, yet he cannot live without her, and resents any aspersions that strangers may cast upon her character.[8]

These two estimates of the philosophy of the common man, mutually contradictory as they may seem, are reconcilable on the assumption that this philosophy is a complex of beliefs, some sound, and some mere old wives' fables. The philosopher who banks on common sense should remember that it is like a river in the region of its delta: it has many banks. On which bank does

---

[7] George Santayana, *Scepticism and Animal Faith*, New York, 1923, p. v–vi. By permission of Chas Scribner's Sons.
[8] *Ibid.*, p. 11.

the philosopher rest his philosophical structure? The choice he here makes is all-important. After he has begun to build on whichever bank he selects, he may find it necessary to tidy it up a bit here and there, not leaving it in the wild state in which he found it. As the work goes on he may even find it necessary to extend his operation over the whole delta. He blasts and excavates and fills, blocking some of the river's mouths, and opening others. He even works up the stream, dredging, straightening, dyking, backward toward its source, fabulously hitherto reported to gush forth from the throat of some mythical monster or from the fiat of some benign god. The more the whole land changes under his operations the more it remains the same old *terra firma* of common sense, if all his work is not to be in vain. Every philosopher knows this, and when his work is done he points proudly to its conformity to the workaday opinions of mankind when those opinions have been properly adjusted to what he has accomplished! For instance, read "the good Bishop Berkeley."

The bank of the river of common sense on which the perspectivist chooses to land in starting his work of philosophical construction is the conviction that the world lying before him in sense-experiences is the real world. What he sees, handles, feels, and remembers, is "the real thing," and he himself is a part of the real thing. All this not in the sense that it is the whole of the real thing, but that it is the paradigm and prototype of whatever *more* there is of reality. That there is more is evidenced to him by the fact that each day *brings* him more of it, to be seen, handled, felt, and otherwise dealt with as best he can. Parts of this real world are his fellow men, whom he sees and can touch and must deal with for better or for worse. He can communicate with them by speech and gesture and learn from them what they too have seen and touched and felt. In his earliest memories he finds that he was already in communication with them. He does not remember having begun thus to communicate. But he does remember how his congenial if not always genial environment has grown in his changing perspectives. It may have been early or it may have been late that he began to philosophize, but his philosophy *now* as a logical structure rests upon and consists of what he *now* finds his world to be and to have been, and what in consequence he expects it to be in the future. As Mr. Santayana has said:

> A philosopher is compelled to follow the maxim of epic poets and to plunge *in medias res*. The origin of things, if things have an origin, cannot be revealed to me, if revealed at all, until I have travelled very far from it, and many revolutions of the sun must precede my first dawn.[9]

But when Mr. Santayana continues: "The light as it appears hides the candle," the perspectivist demurs. It is the candle as well as other things that he sees in the light. To return to our own metaphor, the structures our traveler rears upon the river's bank rest at any time during their construction upon that bank as it is *at that time*: the same bank indeed that previously he discovered, but same with a difference. And the materials he uses at any time are the materials as they are at the time of using. They have had, of course, a history; and a knowledge of that history is of value in this building because it casts light on what they are when he comes to use them. And so it is in their own way with the materials the philosopher uses in his building. These materials have had a history, and whatever present knowledge he has of that history is of value in his present use of them; but that knowledge of their history need not debar him from using them as they now are. And the only direct evidence he has as to what they now are is the evidence of his senses. Therefore the perspectivist does not hesitate to use as his first building stone "sense-experience" as containing a factor of "peripheral" origin in contrast to other factors of "central" origin. It gives him no pause when he is told by Mr. Dewey:

> It requires ... a highly technical apparatus of science to discriminate the exact place and nature of a peripheral stimulation, and to trace its normal course to just the junction point where it becomes effective for redirection of activity and thus capable of perception. "Peripheral origin" marks an interpretation of events, a discrimination scientifically valid and important, but no more an original datum

---
[9] *Ibid.*, p. 1.

than is the spectrum of Betelgeuse. The same thesis holds good, of course, of the "consciousness" corresponding to the centrally initiated processes .... The theory that certain kinds or forms of consciousness intrinsically have an intellectual or cognitive reference to things present in space is merely the traditional theory that knowledge is an immediate grasp of Being, clothed in the terminology of recent physiology ... physiology and psychology merely afford a vocabulary with which to deck out an unconscionable survival.[10]

But *all* philosophy is only "an interpretation of events," Mr. Dewey's as well as any other, and the fact that an interpretation is based upon a "discrimination scientifically valid and important," a discrimination originally made by common sense and backed up and refined by the use of "a highly technical apparatus of science," does not debar it from use as a fundamental assumption in a philosophical theory. On the contrary it is the best kind of credential obtainable. Scientists use just such "products of discrimination" as postulates. For instance, Einstein's special theory of relativity is an interpretation of events based upon the postulate of the constancy of the velocity of light *in vacuo*, a constancy discovered by scientific reflection upon results of experiment.

However, even a credential is to be interpreted with caution. In any theory a postulate is to be interpreted as part of the theory, and its meaning and sweep are to be understood in the light of the other postulates used; and in any discussion of a theory, the theory as a whole is the context which controls the interpretation to be given to any postulate and even to single words. For instance, the word "experience" has meanings importantly different in the philosophies of Royce and James. A reader would be ill-advised who should try to fit all the assertions either one of these thinkers made about "experience" into the framework of the other's philosophy of experience. A "dollar" in Mexico or Canada does not mean the same thing as it does in the United States; and so with "experience" in different philosophies. Any one who has attempted to understand various systems of philosophy has probably learned that it is better to start with the assumption that the

---

[10] *Experience and Nature,* p. 334.

ordinary words employed in any system have their ordinary meanings and then to let these meanings change as context after context may suggest any changes. When finally he identifies for any word a meaning that will fit all contexts from beginning to end, he probably has the meaning in which the word is used in that philosophy, even though that meaning be very different from that which he assigned to the word at the beginning. To come by this method to understand a philosopher is to "follow" him in his argument, and any one who attempts to write philosophy may well offer at least a silent prayer that his readers will "follow" him in this way.

When therefore the perspectivist lays down his first explicit postulate, which has been implicit in what has been already said, he hopes that, until further postulates are likewise laid down, his words shall be understood for the present in their vernacular meanings.

Postulate 1. In our sense-experience there is presented to us in part the real world in which we all in common live and move and have our being.

By "us" here I mean *you* and *me* and *others* like us. Whatever else we are it is here assumed that we are *organisms* that under suitable physical conditions can see and touch and hear and otherwise sense each other. What seeing and hearing may be defined to be remains to be discussed. But the *fact* that we do see and hear is taken for granted; i.e., it is assumed that something on occasion occurs in connection with your organism and in connection with mine that is called seeing and hearing. For the present let us confine ourselves to seeing. *You* see with *your* eyes, and *I* see with *mine*. Your eyes are in your body and mine in mine. And our bodies are spatially external to each other, and yet parts of the same real world. All this is included in the meaning to be given to our postulate. But this is not all that is included. The more than this that is important just here is that under appropriate conditions I can see the *very eyes* with which you see, and you can see my eyes with which I see: not, indeed, the *whole* of your eyes or the *whole* of my eyes. But what I see of your eyes are actually parts of your eyes, not merely a picture or a symbol or representation in my brain, or in my "mind," of *something else* spatially external to the picture. The denial of the "picture theory" of vision, combined with the assertion of a part of what has been called the "spectator theory," is included in the meaning of our postulate. But in adopting a part of the spectator theory as a postulate in his perspectivism, the perspectivist is under no obligation to adopt the whole of it as it has been set forth by those who will have none of it. The choice open to him is not between all or none. He will take *some* of it; just how much will appear in the sequel; but, to prevent misunderstanding, it must be repeated here that what he will *not* take is the suggestion that as a spectator he is looking on the real world from outside of it. He is a participant as well as a spectator. Like Tennyson's Ulysses he is a part of all that he has met—or, rather, a part of its *context*. Spectation is never divorced from action; but even the partisans of indissoluble marriage have never gone so far as to assert that oneness of flesh precludes such differences between man and wife as analysis may reveal.

Before affirmatively laying down our next postulate let me first state in the words of a distinguished philosopher the position that is the diametrical opposite of that which our postulate will assume:

> Particulars have this peculiarity, among the sort of objects that you have to take account of in an inventory of the world, that each of them stands entirely alone and is completely self-subsistent. It has that sort of self-subsistence that used to belong to substance, except that it usually only persists through a very short time, so far as our experience goes. That is to say, each particular that there is in the world does not in any way logically depend upon any other particular. Each one might happen to be the whole universe; it is a merely empirical fact that this is not the case. There is no reason why you should not have a universe consisting of one particular and nothing else. That is a peculiarity of particulars.[11]

As the words here stand we have Mr. Russell's *ipse dixit*, utter-

---

[11] Bertrand Russell, "The Philosophy of Logical Atomism," in *The Monist*, vol. 28, p. 525. It is to be noted that what is said here is not limited to "logical atoms." It deals with the "inventory of the world."

ing an unmitigated dogma, jealously declining to admit any other than itself. Thou shalt not have any other dogma than mine. Here Mr. Russell has reverted, it would seem, from "modern logic" to "the logic practised by the classical tradition," of which he says:

> In that logic . . . it is decreed in advance that reality must have a certain special character. In modern logic, on the contrary, while *prima facie* hypotheses as a rule are admissible, others, which only logic would have suggested, are added to our stock, and are very often found to be indispensable if a right analysis of the facts is to be obtained. The old logic put thought in fetters, while the new logic gives it wings.[12]

The perspectivist prefers wings to fetters, and essays flight on the postulate which he labels

Postulate 2. Every particular in the world is a member of a context of particulars and is what it is only because of its context; and every character any member has it has only by virtue of its relations to other members of that context.

This is to say that every character of every particular is a "relational character." This postulate does not even labor under the disadvantage of being one that only logic could have suggested. On the contrary it is suggested to logic by our everyday experience. It is true that this suggestion has not been adopted by all philosophers, but it is there to the hand of any one who chooses to operate with it. It does not require great temerity to assert that, with a single set of exceptions, no one has ever experienced any particular that was the whole universe.[13]

Even Mr. Russell admits that this is an "empirical fact." Not only are particulars in general found in contexts, i.e., in relations to other particulars, but it is a familiar fact that many of their empirical characters vary with the varying relations in which they

---

[12] *Our Knowledge of the External World as a Field for Scientific Method in Philosophy,* Chicago and London, 1915, p. 58–59. Later references to this volume will be by the abbreviated title, *Scientific Method in Philosophy.* It might be remarked by the way that this volume was published three years before Mr. Russell relapsed into the dogmatism expressed in his characterization of "particulars."
[13] The exceptions belong to the class which William James called "pure experiences." These will be considered later.

are found. The tables and chairs and trees and mountains we see have different seen shapes and sizes according to the distances and directions in which they stand to us. Until some nagging dialectician raises the question it never occurs to any of us that these different shapes and sizes of any particular are incompatible with its particularity. In fact one of the means whereby we identify a particular is the set of relations in which it stands to other particulars, as well as the characters it has in these varying relations. And what is true of the particulars recognized by common sense is also true of scientific objects, such as electrons, protons, and neutrons. A lone electron, constituting all by itself a universe, could not have the opportunity of being an electron, since there would be no other electrons for it to repel or protons for it to attract. And a neutron could not be a neutron if there were no other particles to which it could be neutral. Neutrality, whether of particles or of nations, has meaning only in relation to what is going on in a larger world. Neither an international politician, nor an experimental scientist, nor a hod carrier, nor an abstract logician, could get his teeth into any sort of particular that was what it was all by itself. All deal with objects whose characters are relational and whose relational characters vary with their varying relations. Our postulate therefore has the support of unreflective experience, of experimental science, and of any logic that can go from somewhere to somewhere else. It is not an assumption *ad hoc*; it is *ad omnia*. Using this assumption and such logic, whether "new" or "old," as he has at his disposal, the perspectivist attempts solutions of philosophical problems "with results [he hopes] that do not merely embody personal idiosyncrasies." These results invite— not "must command"—"the assent of all who are competent to form an opinion."[14]

Another distinguished philosopher, in most respects a polar opposite of Mr. Russell, takes on this point a position similar to Mr. Russell's. He writes:

---
[14] Russell, *Scientific Method in Philosophy*, p. 59.

Some Postulates and Definitions

But in every event there is something obdurate, self-sufficient, wholly immediate, *neither a relation nor an element in a relational whole,* but terminal and exclusive. Here, as in so many other matters, materialists and idealists agree in an underlying metaphysics which ignores, in behalf of relations and relational systems, those irreducible, infinitely plural undefinable and indescribable qualities which a thing must *have* in order to be, and in order to be capable of becoming the subject of relations and a theme of discourse. Immediacy of existence is ineffable.[15]

For perspectivity whatever obduracy any event has it has as an element in an obdurate universe. But no other event has exactly the same relations within the universe. Every event is "terminal" in that it is a *term of the relations* in which it stands. It is "exclusive" in that it does not share its whole complement of relations with any other event. But it is not "self-sufficient," else how can it be that "in the end what is unseen decides what happens in the seen"?[16] And by the same token how can it be "*wholly* immediate"? Mr. Dewey at times would have us believe that he himself believes and has all along believed that there have been events that were not experienced at the time of their occurrence. What does total immediacy mean of these events at the time of their occurrence? Of events that are "enjoyed," that are unquestionably experienced for what they are, I can understand what immediacy may mean. Even of the other kind of events just mentioned I can understand what is meant by *their* immediacy, if what is meant is that for me now or for you they did occur. But even here they are elements in a relational whole one of whose constitutive relations is time, and one of whose terms is you or I.

And now as to qualities, it is to be observed that the only known qualities that pre-experiential *events* had at the respective times of their occurrence[17] are those that mathematical physics deals with; and of these qualities it cannot be said that they are undefinable and indescribable. There is no empirical evidence that

---

[15] Dewey, *Experience and Nature*, Chicago and London, 1926, p. 85. The first italics are mine; *"have"* is italicized in the original text.
[16] *Ibid.*, p. 43.
[17] There is in this expression an ambiguity that will be discussed later.

such "things" as pre-Cambrian rocks had *during* the pre-Cambrian period "irreducible and infinitely plural qualities . . . in order to be," *at those* times, and "in order to be capable of becoming . . . a theme of discourse" *now*. Of course when a geologist now discourses of them it is because he has seen what has been left of them. These relics, when seen, have visual qualities for whose *precise* respective nuances we have no several names, and in that sense they are ineffable. But were these ineffable qualities necessary for the existence of the rocks in the pre-Cambrian age? Of immediacy of existence I shall have something to say later, ineffable though it be.

The belief that anything has absolute, i.e., non-relational, characters or, as Mr. Dewey puts it, something that is "neither a relation nor an element in a relational whole" is without question widespread. It is so inveterate that even Mr. Dewey, who in general has no use for absolutes of any kind, clings, as we have seen, to absolutes of this kind. Of other certainties for which men quest he will not have any. But here is a certainty which he does not seek: he already has it. Why is he, together with so many others, joined to this idol of the market? For such I think this belief to be. Pointing to the source of any ecumenical dogma is always fraught with peril, but I nevertheless venture a conjecture: From the earliest times the magic of names seems to have exercised a fatal fascination over men. Give anything a name and have the name generally accepted, and presto! the thing is the name and the name is the thing. Deny that the name is absolutely appropriate and you have denied that the thing is what it really is! "Give a dog a bad name and you hang him."

Now it probably was in social communication that names were first given to things; and the function of names in the first instance was their function of securing identification by others of what you were talking about and what you were saying about it. Fortunately for ordinary purposes of communication and practical co-operation, men could agree as to the characters of many things that they knew and had to deal with in common. Some roses were red and violets were blue for everybody—or almost everybody—and it was taken as a matter of course that this unanimity of finding was due to the fact that the characters found and named were, as we now say, "intrinsic," a word meaning, as the dictionary tells us, "belonging to the inmost nature or essential constitution of a thing." The perspectivist recognizes a certain element of soundness in this, so that we are correct in saying that this rose *is red*; things *are* their characters; and the complement of the characters of anything is that thing, so that what is red and has besides certain other characters is a rose. What from the point of view of the perspectivist was lacking in this earlier view was the recognition of the relativity of all the characters of things; and this lack was itself due to a natural and healthy reliance of early man on the consensus of his fellows. Men not only acted in concert but also felt and thought in concert. Had they not had common emotions and opinions they would not have overtly acted together for any common cause; and conversely they got community of emotions and opinions by acting together. The thoroughfare that connects the overt and the introvert is not a one-way lane. A community in which each man has a right to his own *private* views and feelings has been slow in coming about; and in fact where do we even now find such a community in full blossom? Some Hellenic communities in the middle centuries of the first millennium B. C. flowered for a time into something like this, but even in them the individual had only precarious hold on the right of freedom of thought. Even in the Golden Age of Athens, although a man might go about for years challenging traditional communal views in the open streets and gathering around him a group of devoted young followers, the popularity of Aristophanes and the fate of Socrates prove that the risk was great. And no wonder. Once grant that conformity must give way to idiosyncrasy, that absolutes must yield to relatives, and what do you get? In company with or in sequence upon revered Protagoras and inquiring Socrates, Greece *did* get Thrasymachus and a brood of devastating sceptics. It required the eloquence of Plato with his absolute ideas, and the security of Aristotle with his self-contemplating and immovable "prime mover," to keep philosophy from disintegrating into nihilistic scepticism. The habit, acquired in discourse, i.e., "in the market place," of believing that anything must have characters in its own absolute right had become inveterate; and like all veterans enjoyed the inalienable privilege of pensions even after they had ceased to be of active service. Plato and Aristotle, each in his own way, made great contributions to the common fund, but the authority which each in later generations acquired was based in large measure not on what they gave but on what they took—and this they took from the common agoraphilic prejudice in favor of absolutes.

When the time came for challenging their authority the challenge was not at first directed against their absolutism but against what they took to be absolutes. A new set of characters of things was brought into prominence on which men by exercising due caution could find agreement. Men might differ interminably on what was good or bad, what wise or unwise, but not on the sizes, shapes, and durations of events. And even if for a time there might be some variance here, a method was discovered for eliminating "the personal equation." Now at last it was given to men to "settle the hash of the universe." The hash gradually became very fine—molecules, atoms, and finally electrons, all measurable. Such measures were accepted as absolute. With such absolutes, gradually becoming smaller, physicists and chemists worked successfully for many decades. Even the result of Michelson and Morley's experiment, which at first baffled the mathematical physicists, was brought into line by Einstein's Special Theory of Relativity. The objective world of physics was a world of measurable quantities, of which the velocity of light *in vacuo* in inertial systems was assumed to be constant; i.e., its measured value was assumed to be identical from system to system even though the lengths of moving objects and the simultaneities of events varied from system to system. And such variations as remained furnished

Some Postulates and Definitions 23

no difficulties since the Lorentz transformation offered a means for passing with assurance from one table of measurement to another.

But this state of affairs was not destined to remain satisfactory to those who demanded an absolute. Since measures of spatial lengths and measures of lapses of time between events varied from system to system, neither space nor time can be considered to have physical objectivity, so they argued. Space by itself and time by itself are to sink into shadows, and only a sort of union of the two is to be regarded as physically objective and therefore as absolute. Absoluteness belongs only to such a union. Science, as these mathematical physicists conceived it, demands invariance, and Einstein's "postulate of relativity" must therefore be replaced by the "postulate of the absolute world," or a "world-postulate" for short.[18]

Einstein agreed that his principle of relativity must be widened, and that *"the laws of physics must be so fashioned as to be valid with respect to whatever reference frames are in relative motion."*[19] This is a "requirement" exacted of a "description of nature" *(Naturbeschreibung)* and is called the "requirement of universal covariance which *deprives space and time of the last vestige of physical objectivity."*[20]

It is significant that, for those who take this attitude to invariance, what varies from person to person loses physical objectivity. The totalitarian absolute "liquidates" the relative. Absolutes have a way of doing this eventually if not immediately.

In another chapter I shall discuss the logic of the procedure that led these mathematical physicists to this conclusion. Here I wish to emphasize the implications of the conclusion. If space and time have no vestige of physical objectivity, what shall be

---

[18] H. Minkowski, "Raum und Zeit," an address delivered at Cologne, September 21, 1908, and reprinted in *Das Relativitätsprinzip: eine Sammlung von Abhandlungen,* 5te Aufl., Leipzig, Berlin, 1923. This volume of reprints will be referred to in these lectures by the abbreviated title, *Relativitätsprinzip.*

[19] A. Einstein, "Die Grundlage der allgemeinen Relativitätstheorie," reprinted in *Relativitätsprinzip,* p. 83.

[20] *Ibid.,* p. 86. The italics are mine. Einstein's own words are: "diese Forderung der allgemeinen Kovarianz, welche dem Raum und der Zeit den letzten Rest physikalischer Gegenständlichkeit nehmen. . ."

said of the laboriously acquired technique of physical measurement, which in the last analysis is measurement of spatial and temporal quantities? If the values thus obtained are not, any of them, physical, can any combination of such values be treated as physical? Of course, one may not place too much reliance on any metaphor used by the advocates of a theory under discussion; but, with due allowance for this restriction, one may at least indicate the difficulty one finds in the theory by taking advantage of such a metaphor. May one attribute to any union of "shadows" a self-sufficient reality—a *Selbständigkeit*, to use Minkowski's word—competent to cast the shadows?[21] Or to put the question more literally, may a mathematical expression, no term in which has the least physical objectivity, be said as a whole to have physical objectivity? Can a physical world be constructed out of non-physical elements?

Of course, logically this can be done *by definition*. We may define the "physical world" as the name of the mathematical expression. But such a definition does not give "physical objectivity" in any meaning one usually gives to this term.

That Einstein, in giving up the physical objectivity of space and time in favor of an absolute Space-Time, cut the ground out from under his feet can, I think, be made evident by considering his procedure in developing his Special Theory of Relativity. He took "two systems of co-ordinates, i.e., two systems, each of rigid *material* lines, intersecting at a point, and at right angles to each other."[22] In each system he provided measuring rods and clocks exactly alike.[23] And distance in either system was to be measured by the rods in that system, and the time of any event in either system was to be ascertained by the reading of the clock in that

---

[21] "Von Stund an sollen Raum für sich und Zeit für sich zu Schatten herabsinken und nur noch eine Art Union der beiden soll Selbständigkeit bewahren." H. Minkowski in *Relativitätsprinzip*, p. 54.

[22] A. Einstein, in *Relativitätsprinzip*, p. 31. My italics.

[23] *Ibid.*, p. 28. "Von genau denselben Beschaffenheit." This is actually said only of different clocks in the *same system*; but unless it is assumed to hold respectively of all the rods and clocks in both systems, there is no way of comparing time and space measure in both systems.

system at the place of the event. These measurements were "physical experiences."[24] It is significant that Einstein was not satisfied with *mathematical* lines in his reference frames; the lines were to be *material*, and presumably this means physical, since all the observations made during the process were to be considered "*physical* experiences." No one can read the whole discussion without being impressed with the fact that Einstein was dealing with *physical* facts—physical time, physical space, physical velocity. In short the whole discussion was conducted on the plane of physical objectivity, and it was on the basis of this discussion that he built his General Theory of Relativity. If the position taken in the former should be found to be untenable the latter would be baseless.[25] What then is the physical relevancy of the latter if the former has no physical relevancy? And what relevancy to physics can the former have if the space and time it deals with have lost all physical objectivity? We have here in Minkowski's absolute world, adopted by Einstein, a striking example of an absolute which annihilates without remainder all the relative constituents that enter into its constitution, an absolute that is all but not *in* all. Such an absolute Space-Time is less available for scientific purposes than even Newton's absolute space and absolute time. The latter permitted events to be objectively related temporally and spatially *to each other* by taking a place in them, whereas the absoluteness of Space-Time expressly annuls the physical objectivity of all spatial and temporal relations among events.

The viciousness of such an absolute does not consist in the demand that "the universal laws of nature are to be expressed by equations that are valid for all co-ordinate systems, i.e., that the suitable substitutions shall be mutually covariant,"[26] but in the assumption that this demand implies as its corollary that the space and time values thus covariant are thereby deprived of physical objectivity. Such laws are what the mathematical logicians call

---
[24] *Ibid.*, p. 29.
[25] *Ibid.*, p. 82.
[26] *Ibid.*, p. 86.

"propositional functions,"[27] which are neither true nor false until values are assigned to their undetermined constituents. Thus the equation for the "Space-Time interval" in the Special and in the General Theory of Relativity has no "physical objectivity," i.e., it is neither true nor false of the physical world except as *definite spatial and temporal values* are given to its terms. It gets its physical objectivity only in its capacity of being a *summary* formula for all *specific* cases. It is the truth of the formula in *any specific* case that constitutes the universal truth of the formula, and not *vice versa*. If we are to use the metaphor of the relation between an "independent" object and a "shadow" it casts—the perspectivist does not like the metaphor—space and time are the independent objects and "Space-Time" is their "shadow." If we speak more literally of "physical objectivity," space and time have *primary* physical objectivity in specific instances, and Space-Time has only such epitomized objectivity as belongs to the distributive totality of space and time interrelation in *all its specific* instances.[28]

In the preceding pages I have presented some of the views in opposition to which I have laid down Postulate 2, which assumes a universal objective relativity that does not preclude the objectivity of specific relatives. Everything is in the same boat, and the boat in which all things are is constituted of the interrelated things that are in it. The boat is not something into which things that are not a part of it can somehow gain irrelevant entrance. To change the figure, even an alien spy can gain entrance into a closely knit social organization only if the organization he represents is

---

[27] "A 'propositional function,' in fact, is an expression containing one or more undetermined constituents, such that, when values are assigned to these constituents, the expression becomes a proposition. . . . So long as the variables have no definite value, the equation is merely an expression awaiting determination in order to become a true or false proposition." *Introduction to Mathematical Philosophy*, by Bertrand Russell, New York, London, undated, pp. 155–156.

[28] Of course the perspectivist does not attribute independence, *Selbständigkeit*, to space or to time or to both together. As we shall see, he espouses the assumption that space and time are relations, and for him relations are not independent of their terms, nor are the terms independent of the relations in which they stand. It takes relations *and* terms, or rather terms-in-relations, to constitute anything of which any sort of independence can be asserted, and even any relational complex is independent only in a limited sense, since it too is in relation to other relational complexes.

part of a larger world which contains, and is in part constituted by, the two rival organizations. There are many obvious objections—obvious at first blush—that can be raised against this postulate; but they rest upon assumptions that the perspectivist does not make. They do not point out internal inconsistencies in the view criticized; nor do they show that the view objected to is at variance with the facts of experience.

Perhaps the most obvious objection to our postulate is that it makes impossible the "numerical identity" of anything. But "numerical identity" is a weasel word. When used in arguments it is likely to be a question-begging term, as if anything to be numerically identical must be what it is *absolutely*—must be what it is apart from any relation to anything else. But one would think that "numerical identity," when applied to anything that is not a number, should be the same kind of identity that any *number* has. Let us ask whether in mathematics any number has any kind of identity apart from the relations it has to *other* numbers? What, for instance, is the identity of the number 3? A "mere three" without reference to the context of other numbers has no character that any mathematician can lay his hands on. To say that three is just three, and to keep on saying this in the identity equations $3 = 3 = 3 = 3 \ldots$ would reduce the mathematician to an intellectual brother of the mystical if not mythical Indian who is said to contemplate his navel and in ecstasy repeat the mystic word "Ohm, Ohm, Ohm, Ohm . . . ." On the contrary, for the mathematician the only significance of the number 3 is that it can figure in such equations as $3 = 1 + 1 + 1 = 2 + 1 = 6/2 = \sqrt{9}$ etc. The identity of a number consists in the fact that it is precisely distinguishable from other numbers by the fact that it is the *only* number that stands in all the numerical relations in which it stands.

Mathematicians who have delved into the foundation of number theory differ among themselves as to what they find, and this is not the place to enter into a discussion of the controversy that has thus arisen. Let us be content with taking into consideration here the two theories that may be regarded as standing at the two extremes in this debate, that of Russell and that of Kronecker. Two quotations from Russell make evident the relational character of cardinal numbers according to his view: *"The number of a class is the class of all those classes that are similar to it,"* and "A number is anything which is the number of some class."[29] It is "similarity" defined as a *relation* of a certain sort, namely, a "one–one correspondence," that makes any number the very number it is. These definitions bear upon their face the relational status of any particular number and of number in general. Kronecker on the other hand, with more piety than Russell ever exhibits, maintains that "God made the integers and man fabricated the rest." (I am indebted to a mathematical friend for this information.) Here the relational nature of numbers is not explicitly brought out, but it is implied by the fact that these God-made numbers are so interrelated that mathematical induction is justified. There is no evidence, theological or other, that God first made the number 1 and as an afterthought made the number 2 by making a second number 1 and adding it to the first, and so on *ad infin.* And even if he did, no human being could identify the first 1 except by pointing it *out* ostensively, and this means by *singling* it out from the number 2 (for instance) in which the second 1 is found. And this holds of number 1 even if it was not made by God but was constructed by the mathematician. A single number 1, entirely unrelated, is like a single electron all by itself. To use a homely phrase, it would not "have enough guts" to be even itself.

Now if "numerical identity" as it characterizes any *number* is the identity of something whose very nature is to be a term in a relational complex, it seems hardly fair to exact of the "numerical identity" of something that is not a mere number that it should be a "stricter" sort of "numerical identity." What is "numerically" good for numbers should be "numerically" good for anything else.

---

[29] I quote from Russell's *Introduction to Mathematical Philosophy*, pp. 18 and 19. Those familiar with this theory know that "similar" here is used in a technical sense: "One class is said to be 'similar' to another when there is a one-one *relation* of which the one class is the domain, while the other is the converse domain."

There is one caution against a possible misunderstanding of our postulate. It asserts that every character any particular has, it has by virtue of the relations in which it stands. This is not to identify any of these *characters* with the *relations*. Our postulate does not resolve any concrete particular or any sensible quality into mere relations. A man, a tree, a pebble, an "irreducible" shade of red—none of these things itself is any relation, or the sum total of relations in which it stands. It is one thing to be an irreducible shade of red, and it would be *another* thing—if there were such a thing—to be an irreducible shade of red that is *not a term* of some relation. And what is true of "irreducible qualities" is also true of men, of trees, of pebbles. Any of these things, in the very article of becoming, also become terms of relations. Their "*immediacy* of existence" consists in *what* as characters they are in *the relations* in which they occur. Thus our "underlying metaphysics" does *not* ignore in behalf of relations and relational systems those irreducible, infinitely plural, undefinable and indescribable qualities which a thing must *have* in order to be. It recognizes such qualities wherever they occur, and insists, with Mr. Dewey, that they are not relations; but our view is different from Mr. Dewey's in that it regards them as "elements in a relational whole."

Against the position taken in our present postulate it might be and indeed has been plausibly objected that the denizens of our world are like the Scilly Islanders, who are humorously said to "live by taking in each other's washing." This joke had more point in the "horse and buggy age," before it was realized that all of us live in economical interdependence in "*One World.*" We now know that none of us liveth to himself—unless perchance he were a Robinson Crusoe without his man Friday; and even then he could do so literally only if, like Melchisedek, he were without father, without mother, without descent, having neither beginning of days nor end of life.

The objection under consideration should be called the "creator's paradox." No one could create such a world as our theory envisages if he had to bring creatures into being *one at a time*, but each on creation would be what it is only in relation to other creatures not yet created. But there is no earthly reason to suppose that if in the dark backward and abysm of time our world somehow and somewhen got started, its origin was just one damn thing after another. Even according to Genesis it began as a face of the waters, not as a single undifferentiated drop. And even in the more modern version its author, in disclaiming the belief "from which we can see no logical escape . . . that the present order of things started off with a bang,"[30] spoke, it is to be noted, of an "order of things," not of an electron or proton banging itself into a temporarily solipsistic existence. The alternative is not necessarily between things with no beginning and Mr. Russell's "particulars" beginning tandemwise. If beginning we must have—and I see no reason why we must, nor do I see any reason why we may not—why not have a beginning with an order of things? But this is an academic question. Our theory deals with the world as a *going concern,* not as something that is not yet but has to get started.

Let us now lay down another postulate:

Postulate 3. In the world of nature any "thing" at any time is, and is nothing but, the totality of the relational characters, experienced or not experienced, that the "thing" has at that time in whatever relations it has at that time to other "things."

It is to be noted that here I am dealing with "things" *in the world of nature.* What is meant by this phrase will appear later. Meanwhile perhaps the best way to indicate what I mean by "thing" here is to quote from Webster's definition "6" under the entry "thing":

> anything which can be apprehended or known as having existence in space or time as distinguished from anything which is purely an object of thought; as, goodness is not a *thing,* but an attribute of a *thing.*

---

[30] A. S. Eddington, *The Nature of the Physical World,* New York and Cambridge, England, 1928, p. 85.

To make more definite my own denotation of "thing" *as used in the postulate* just laid down, let me add to Webster's example of what a thing is and what it is not: no sense-quality is a "thing," and no elementary relation is a "thing." Thus color is not a "thing," and neither is distance or equality a "thing," but each of these is "something." Examples of what a "thing" *is* are organisms, bricks, molecules, chemical atoms, and electrons—the last when regarded, not as mere symbols in certain mathematical equations, but as "things" in space and time, of measurable "size" and "mass," where "size" and "mass" are not "things," but "attributes" or "properties" or "characters" of "things." One might say that by "thing" is here meant what the man in the street means by "thing," although he may not be able to state exactly what he means, just as he knows what he means by "dog" although he may not be able to give a zoological definition of this word.

In discussing the immediately preceding postulate I protested against Mr. Dewey's view that in every event "there is something obdurate, *self-sufficient, wholly immediate, neither a relation nor an element in a relational whole.*" (I here italicize what I objected to.) Our theory does not recognize any *such* qualities, and therefore does not assume that "a thing must have" such qualities "in order to be, and in order to be capable of becoming the subject of relations and a theme of discourse." On the other hand, our present postulate does recognize that a "thing" must have *some* characters in order to be; the characters, however, are each an "element in a relational whole." But in saying that it must *have* characters we mean that it is the characters which we say that it "has." It "has" characters in the way in which a family "has" members: a family has members in that it *consists of* its members. Etymologically considered, this last assertion is the converse of the assertion that the members *standing together* in certain ways *are* the family: Given the members and their interrelations, nothing more is needed at that time to *constitute* the family, i.e., to *put* the members *together* into a family. A family does not need a family-substance, i.e., a something different from its *constitution* and *underlying* it on which it can *stand*. To mix in another metaphor, it does not need an *inner and self-subsistent core* in which its members must "inhere" before they can become members of a family—"inhere," i.e., stick in, as pins stick in a pincushion. They *co*here without the support of a subsidy supplied by a substance entirely other than themselves. This plethora of words with the Latin prefix, *sub*- (English *under*), calls attention to the crudity and crassness of the traditional concept of substance. If we are to have metaphors, our theory would replace the "sub-" with a "*co-*" or "*con-*", *with*. Unfortunately for our purpose, a substitution of the words "constance" and "consistence" could suggest meanings alien to our requirement; "comport" as a noun is obsolete; "considy" would be too much like the giraffe to the rustic. But we have the perfectly good word "college," not in the sense in which we use it when we speak of Amherst College or Beloit College, but in the meaning the word has in the phrase "the college of cardinals." Let us then say that a family is a college of its members, each member *related* in distinctive ways to other members within the college and also *related* in various ways to other persons and things; and so long as a member of a family lives, be he only a short-lived infant, he is as much a member of the family as is his father or mother.

Just so, a "thing," in our theory, is *a college of its characters* or properties or attributes—these terms being synonymous generic names; "sense qualities" being names of a species. Whatever character a "thing" has at any time *is* in part the "thing" as it is at the time. Thus we discard the traditional doctrine of "substance," which goes back to Aristotle but received its definitive statement in Spinoza's third definition at the very beginning of his *Ethica*: "By substance I mean that which is in itself (*in se*) and is conceived by itself (*per se*); namely, that the concept of which does not need the concept of anything else from which it should be formed." This kind of "substance" is regarded by us as an absent-minded abstraction—an abstract which is mistaken for a more concrete whole within which alone it has any "being." The "being" (οὐσία, *entitas*) of something, whose "being" is being a-characterizing-item-of-a-more-complex-whole, is, by ignoring its relevance to that complex, interpreted as being-an-underlying-support (ὑπόστασις, *substantia*) of the complex whole. If I may be allowed a bad polyglot play upon words, the "substance" of philosophic tradition is a *mis*-under-standing.

But if we interpret the word "substance" with an eye as much to the *temporal* as to the spatial factor of the spatio-temporal context, we can give the word a standing in our theory. Some characters in a "thing" defined as a college of characters may be shorter-lived than others: this is to say, some of the other characters may have constituted a "thing" before a shorter-lived character accrues to that "thing," and may continue to constitute a "thing" after the shorter-lived character ceases to exist. In such a case, we may use the word "substance" to designate the longer-lived characters, especially if without them the shorter-lived character would not occur. What is a *conditio sine qua non* may perhaps be called a "ground," and therefore a "substance," "something that underlies." It will be seen later that in our view there are characters that are continuants and those that are transient.[31] The former are dynamic, the latter are not. Anticipating subsequent discussion of space, time, and space-time, let us say that "substance" as we shall use the term consists of a college of *dynamic* characters *seated in a consistory*—a place of assembly—and that a "thing" *at any time* is such a "substance" together with such non-dynamic characters, if any, as are *at that time* conditioned by dynamic acts then and there taking place. If, on the other hand, what dynamically occurs does not then give rise to non-dynamic characters, then what is denominated a "substance" is then identical with what is called a "thing." To illustrate, I now see a red book lying on the table; the book as a "substance" consists of what is now dynamically occurring where I see the

---

[31] Cf., Roy Wood Sellars, *The Philosophy of Physical Realism*, New York, 1932, p. 274: "The category of substance . . . stands for continuants." But this is also said of the "category of *thinghood*" (p. 143). It is not, however, my purpose here to examine in detail his view of these "categories."

book; it is a set of dynamical characters in dynamical relations. The book as a "thing" is all this together with the non-dynamical character, red. Thus when seen as red, the book as a "thing" *is* red, whereas, qua "substance," it is not red—it has no color at all. (To say that as a "substance" the book is red is like saying that as a geometrical figure the late Gilbert K. Chesterton was an interesting detective-story writer, or that as a well-bearded man G. B. Shaw is now a widower.) Moreover, when *previously* not perceived or thought of at all by anyone, the book as a "substance" and the book as a "thing" are, when *later* thought of, then thought of as identical; i.e., neither had a character which the other had not.

It will have been seen by now that by "the world of nature"—let us call it "nature" for short—I mean the world in which we experience ourselves to be living: a world with all the characters which at any time it is directly experienced at that time to have, and also with those characters which, though not directly experienced, competent scientific investigations have revealed that it has; furthermore with characters not yet revealed and also, let us assume, with characters that may never be revealed to us because of our limitations. Nature, whatever else it is at any time, is always at least a world of physical things dynamically acting on one another; i.e., the world which the physicist investigates by his own methods.

But when we are experiencing it, it is also a world of colors, of noises and of music, of beauty and of ugliness, and in spots also a world of moral values. However, only on reflective analysis do its various characters become sorted into classes. Earliest reflection, we assume, proceeds "spontaneously," i.e., without deliberately tested and adopted method; uncriticized results are deposited and fixed in language; and only slowly are recognized classifications changed and socially adopted. Not until modern times have the characterizing features of a dynamic order in nature been ascertained and expressed in the most precise language yet available. The success of modern civilization in controlling many events in that order, and its failure to control men, have led many theorizers into regarding that order as the only order of nature, thus with a pitchfork expelling from nature another part of nature which is not dynamical. The insight of a great Roman poet knew that this could not be done; nevertheless it has been tried over and over again in all sorts of ways. The plight of much present-day philosophy bears witness to inevitable failure. Our philosophy, on the other hand, avoids this difficulty by assuming that under certain natural conditions a non-dynamical branch grows out from a dynamical stem. In other words, *nature bifurcates itself*, just as a fork that grows out of a tree is nature's own bifurcation. What, however, has recently been called a "bifurcation of nature" is a *dis*furcation of nature. Theorists would lop off a branch that naturally has grown there. This is as if a botanist were to cut off every branch shooting out from the straight stem of a tree on the plea that nothing there is natural except the straight stem! But we must reserve further discussion of this matter for a later chapter. For the present we leave out of account also the "unsubstantial" objects of mathematical theory on the one hand, and on the other the stuff of which dreams and errors are made. For us everything that occurs, including every dream and every error, and of course every relation in which it occurs, is a part of nature, and it is our business to find as well as we can a place for it in our theory. Nothing in nature should be alien to our philosophy. So far as a philosophy is alien to nature, so far is it defective, requiring revision to make good the fault. We make no claim that our philosophy is faultless. It is an attempt, not an achievement. It is presented here in the hope that others may think it worth their while to contribute to its improvement.

The three postulates we have laid down indicate the aim, spirit, and temper of our enterprise. They furnish the groundwork upon which our perspectivist theory is built. By calling our three propositions "postulates," we emphasize the fact that we are not in possession of any self-evident truths, from which these assumptions can be proved to be true. Our postulates are working hypotheses, to be worked for all they are worth, and to be modified if thereby they can be made to work better. They represent an intellectual attitude that is in accord with the scientific spirit of the times. This attitude is relativistic, or, if you prefer, contextualistic. Without the lessons I have learned, successively if not successfully, from Hegel, Einstein, Whitehead, and Smuts, to mention here only four of my masters in relativism, this volume could not have been written. On the other hand, it does not bear the *imprimatur* of any of them. Lessons learned from other masters have given a different turn to this relativism from that which it took in any of the previously mentioned four. Relativism must perforce emphasize relations, and in the next two or three chapters I will call attention to a specific type of relation the integration of which into a relativistic theory is largely responsible for this different turn.

Let us now restate the second part of our second postulate, substituting for "member" used there the word "thing" as it has been used in our third postulate; and let us call this restatement a "corollary" of our postulates without insisting that this is a correct word to use here:

Corollary: Every character which any thing has at any time it has only as it is a term of some relation in which at that time it stands to some other thing.

Any character of any thing and the relation in which the thing has that character may be said to be "correlative" or "correspondent." Thus when we are dealing with some character of a thing and speak of a "corresponding relation," we shall mean the relation in which the thing has that character; and conversely when we are dealing with some relation in which a thing stands and speak of "corresponding character," we shall mean the character the thing has in that relation. In many cases characters and their respectively corresponding relations are in ordinary speech designated by identical or cognate words. Thus when we say, "Chicago is west of New York," the adjective "west" denotes a character predicated of Chicago, and the corresponding relation is often called by the same name, or we may call it "westness," or "westwardness." Unfortunately there is no generally recognized usage in English for naming all the relations that correspond to characters that are named by adjectives. The reason for this probably is that many of these characters are not generally regarded as relational. Mr. Dewey has crude common sense on his side when he speaks of immediate qualities which are not "elements in relational wholes." The colors and odors of roses are "immediate qualities" in that no inference is required for discovering their presence; but it required reflection—just a little bit but not enough of it—to conclude that failure on anyone's part to discover them when everyone else does is due to personal defect and not to absence of these qualities from the roses themselves in relation to others more richly equipped. However, it required the scientific curiosity of a Dalton to discover the fact of color blindness, now known to be a hereditary insensitiveness and therefore a defect of many a female ancestor of his as well as of others. Thus he added a large group of "immediate qualities" to those already regarded by scientists as relational; and even in common-sense circles it is now credibly rumored that where there are no eyes and no ears there are no colors and no sounds. Among scientists it would be hard to find one who does not assume that only in dynamic relation to sense organs do things have the qualities which instrumentalists call "immediate." Our theory adopts this assumption, but because of its present wide prevalence we do not regard it necessary to list it among its distinctive and therefore italicized postulates. However, in our analysis we do not find a dynamic relation sufficient. Still another relation is to be taken into account in dealing not only with sense qualities but with any experience. It is this relation to which we shall later devote our attention.

In a later chapter it will be seen that our analysis reveals two kinds of constituents, namely, "components" and "characters." Components are themselves *things* which can be separated from each other, such as atoms, molecules, grains of sand, and organisms. (Hearts separated out of organisms have continued to beat for many days.) In each case we have wholes physically or chemically divisible into parts. Up to the present, electrons, protons, neutrons, etc., are "ultimate particles." But each of these is characterized by its relations to other particles. The assumption that it has a core of being entirely independent of any relation to anything else is incapable of confirmation by experiment, for the simple reason that any experiment that can be made is *conducted in our on-going complex world*. We cannot abolish the rest of the world and find, say, a single electron all by itself. For this simple reason our first postulate cannot be shown to be at variance with any ascertained findings. We may indeed conceive of it as something all by itself, but we can do so only by ignoring the natural context in which alone it can be found. Hereafter, when we speak of the "constituents" or of the "constitution" of any thing, we shall use these terms to include in their connotation not only the characters of the thing itself but also its separable parts with their respective characters, if it has separable parts.

But before leaving the general topic of a thing's characters and its respectively corresponding relations, let us point out that no character "belongs" to a thing in the same way in which the corresponding relation belongs to that thing. For instance, Franklin D. Roosevelt had the *character* we express by saying that he was the father of Elliott; and corresponding to this character was the *relation* of fatherhood in which he stood to Elliott. The character belonged to F. D. R. *exclusively*, or, to use a mode of expression now current among philosophers, it was exclusively "seated" in him. It was to be found nowhere else than where he at any time happened to be. The corresponding relation also belonged to him, but it was his not as exclusively "seated" in him; having another term, it reached out, as it were, in its own way to that other term, wherever at any time that other term happened to be. The relation was *between* its terms (each kind of relation being its own kind of between), and it terminated in *each* of its terms— this is of course the reason why the terms are called terms. According to our "corollary," every character of a thing is "internal" to the thing, being a constituent of the thing; and, with an important qualification, the relation corresponding to any character a thing has at any time is also "internal" to that thing, since it terminates in a constituent character of that thing. The qualification is that the relation terminates also in at least another thing, and is thus also "external" to the former thing. Thus the words "internal" and "external" when applied to relations are ambiguous, and any discussion as to whether any relation is "internal" or "external" results in confusion until the words are more precisely defined. It is like debating whether a steel bar, spanning the distance between two cement posts and with its two ends respectively imbedded in the posts, is internal or external to either post. In this analogue, the relation involved is spatial; but what holds here holds also elsewhere with due provision made for differences in different kinds of relations: when we say that a relation terminates in its terms the "in" is a different kind of "in" with every different kind of relation, as is shown in the phrases "in the same place," "in the same hour," "in the same family," "in the cardinal-number series."

We may now bring this introductory chapter to a close by laying down another postulate needed to offset the apparent lopsidedness of our previous postulates. So far we have emphasized the indispensability of relations in assuming that all characters are what they are only as they are terms of relations. This emphasis on relations might possibly suggest to readers that in our view relations enjoy what we may call a priority in nature as against characters, as if there might be relations which are what they are without characters as their indispensable terms. To protect ourselves against such a possible misunderstanding we lay down:

Postulate 4. In the concrete world of nature every relation is a relation between terms that are characters, such characters not being wholly analyzable into relations.

There are indeed relations which upon analysis are found to be complexes of relations. But these complexes of relations, of which mathematics affords us numerous examples, are themselves abstracted within nature, where in the first instance they are relations between terms that are not analyzable into vacuous relations. To adapt F. H. Bradley's striking metaphor, nature is not a ballet of bloodless relations. It is replete with infinite variety, its fundamental pluralism being the inextinguishable dualistic difference between relations and characters which are not relations. And the fundamental monism of nature is the fact that every part of it, no matter how minute, is in some relation to some other part. Nature is not a seamless whole; its seams are of its very texture. Its joints and articulations join and articulate part with part. As James the pluralist correctly said, "a joint in a bamboo is [not] a break in the wood . . . the joint is a part of the bamboo."[32] When we speak of "*relational* characters," we do not mean characters that are themselves relations, but characters that have being only as terms of relations. If there was a beginning, in that beginning was the relational complex; and as it was in the beginning, nature is now, and ever shall be a relational complex of relational complexes, neither relations alone nor characters alone but characters in relations and relations between characters.

---

[32] William James, *The Principles of Psychology*, New York, 1890, Vol. I, p. 240.

Chapter II

CONSCIOUSNESS

"Does 'consciousness' exist?" And if it does, what is it? In view of the wide diversity of answers among present-day philosophers to these questions it is well for one who believes that there is such a thing as consciousness to identify what it is. Where is consciousness to be found, and how is it to be found there? Let us begin with Woodbridge's forthright assertion:

> It seems clear enough to us today as it was clear enough to the ancients, that being conscious, if it requires further specification, is seeing, hearing, tasting, smelling, feeling; thinking about what we see, hear, taste, smell, and feel; and expressing the result in language of some sort. That is what being conscious is, and no philosopher has ever delivered anything more, be he ancient, mediaeval, or modern.[1]

This specification might be enlarged; and if so, perhaps the most important additions that would suggest themselves would be remembering and willing. Now it is one thing to point by words to situations in which consciousness is to be found, and it is another thing unmistakably to identify what it is that is to be found there. No one who understands and uses English ever hesitates to use—and to use correctly—some of the words in Woodbridge's specification; and I venture to say that every one knows in a way what is meant when he hears someone else say, "I see a boy," "I hear a footstep," and "I slept so soundly last night that I was not conscious of anything till the alarm clock woke me." The last

---

[1] "The Problem of Consciousness Again," first published in the *Journal of Philosophy*, Vol. XXXIII (1936), and reprinted in *Nature and Mind: Selected Essays of Frederick J. E. Woodbridge*, New York, 1937. I quote from this reprint, p. 420.

assertion, for instance, is taken to mean: "I did not see or hear or taste or smell or feel or remember or think about anything till . . . ." And when anyone hears that John Smith was knocked unconscious, he understands this to mean that John Smith for the time stopped seeing, hearing, and so forth. The use of the words "conscious" and "unconscious" here seems to imply that there is something alike in what is meant by seeing, hearing, smelling, remembering, and thinking, or, to use the current terminology, that all such processes have "something in common." What kind of a thing is this something-in-common? The answer any one gives to this question is his answer to the question: "What is consciousness?"—when the word is used to name the abstract *character* denoted by the adjective "conscious."

In answering this question the perspectivist *postulates* what common sense these days seems to take for granted as self-evident, that inanimate things do not see, hear, feel, and so forth; i.e., that they are not conscious. He does not undertake to say dogmatically how far down in the scale of animate things a conscious character is to be found. He prefers to start with human beings. *They* at least are at times conscious. And when they see, they see *something;* when they hear, they hear *something;* when they remember, they remember *something*; when they think, they think-of *something*. Now scientific physiology leaves little room for reasonable doubt that no one ever sees or hears or remembers or thinks except in response or reaction to a stimulus. Such a stimulus may be external or internal, but stimulus there always is when any one is conscious. Calling a physiological reaction to a stimulus a "doing" or an "act" on the part of the reagent, one is tempted to say that seeing and hearing and thinking are "doings" or "acts" or "physiological functions" of the person who sees and hears and thinks. Now the perspectivist does not question that when any one sees, or hears, or thinks, he is acting or doing. But if seeing is *only* an act, and if there is no such thing as temporally retroactive causation, it would seem to follow that we can see only what is in our bodies, where the physiological act involved in seeing is taking place.[2]

No one has stated this argument more clearly than Mr. Bertrand Russell:

> Common sense holds—though not very explicitly—that perception reveals external objects to us directly; when we "see the sun," it is the sun that we see. Science has adopted a different view, though without always realizing its implications. Science holds that, when we "see the sun," there is a process, starting from the sun, traversing the space between the sun and eye, changing its character when it reaches the eye, changing its character again in the optic nerve and the brain, and finally producing the event we call "seeing the sun." Our knowledge of the sun thus becomes inferential; our direct knowledge is of an event which is, in some sense, "in us." This theory has two parts. First there is the rejection of the view that perception gives direct knowledge of external objects; secondly, there is the assertion that it has external causes as to which something can be inferred from it. The first of these tends toward scepticism; the second tends in the opposite direction. The first appears as certain as anything in science can hope to be; the second, on the contrary, depends upon postulates which have little more than a pragmatic justification.[3]

This theory that when we "see the sun" there has been a physical process, starting from the sun and finally producing the event we call "seeing the sun," Mr. Russell calls "the causal theory of perception," and of it he says:

---

[2] To avoid ambiguity I shall try always to use the word "act" so as to correspond with the word "action" as this latter word is used in physics "to denote energy multiplied by time. That is to say, if there is one unit of energy in a system, it will exert one unit of action in a second, 100 units of action in 100 seconds, and so on; a system which has 100 units of energy will exert 100 units of action in a second, and 10,000 in 100 seconds, and so on" (*The ABC of Relativity,* by Bertrand Russell, N. Y., 1925). Here of course "energy" is used in its technical physical sense. With this meaning of "action," a physical object is said to *act* when it exerts energy. Thus "the physiological act involved in seeing" denotes only the physiological exertion of energy taking place in the brain when an organism is seeing. Now on our theory there is no seeing without consciousness, and consciousness is not an act but a non-dynamic relation. But neither is there any seeing without the physiological exertion of energy in the brain, which is not consciousness but is a dynamic act. Seeing is neither the one alone nor the other alone: it is the natural combination or concretion of the two. Similar integrations of act with consciousness constitute other so-called "mental processes" such as hearing, remembering, and thinking.

[3] Bertrand Russell, *The Analysis of Matter,* New York and London, 1927, p. 197.

Whoever accepts the causal theory of perception is compelled to conclude that percepts are in our heads, for they come at the end of a causal chain of physical events leading, spatially, from the object to the brain of the percipient. We cannot suppose that, at the end of this process, the last effect suddenly jumps back to the starting-point, like a stretched rope when it snaps. And with the theory of space-time as a structure of events . . . there is no sort of reason for not regarding a percept as being in the head of the percipient. I shall therefore assume that this is the case, when we are speaking of physical, not sensible, location.

It follows from this that what the physiologist sees when he examines a brain is in the physiologist, not in the brain he is examining. . . . Thus a percept is an event or a group of events, each of which belongs to one or more of the groups constituting the electrons in the brain.[4]

Now the perspectivist agrees with Mr. Russell in postulating a "causal theory of perception"; and, without going into matters that here are irrelevant, he is willing to accept what in the third sentence of the first quotation above Mr. Russell says science holds with regard to the *physical* processes that cause our "seeing the sun." But in interpreting this scientific tenet, the perspectivist again prefers the wings that modern logic puts at his disposal to the chains that keep Mr. Russell bound to a traditional interpretation. One cannot but suspect that Mr. Russell may have been misled by the grammar of language. "See" is a "transitive" verb, and grammarians and lexicographers tell us that a transitive verb is one that expresses "an action that passes over to an object."[5] Therefore if it is a *physical* star that I see when at night I see Sirius, and if the seeing is only a physiological action on the part of my organism, then my *action* in seeing, which occurs at the end of a long space-time chain of physical processes, must "suddenly jump back to the

---

[4] *Ibid.*, p. 320.
[5] One of the outstanding grammarians of recent times gives as a first, off-hand definition: "Verbs are called Transitive when their action *goes over* to an object . . . *Intransitive* when their action *does not go beyond.*" There follows a Remark: "Properly speaking, a Transitive Verb in Latin is one that forms a personal passive, but the traditional division given above has its convenience, though it does not rest upon a difference of nature, and a verb may be trans. or intrans. according to its use" (*Gildersleeve's Latin Grammar*, by B. L. Gildersleeve and Gonzales, 3 ed., N. Y., pp. 150–151). But the "difference of nature" is not brought to light when circularly we are told: "The Passive Voice denotes that the subject receives the action

starting point" over a spatial distance of more than eight light years and a temporal interval of more than the same number of years! But of course this is "absurd." The physiological act involved in seeing cannot produce a physical effect upon a star *as it was* eight years ago. Ergo, whatever it may be that I see, it cannot be the star Sirius. Q. E. D.!

But let us see. We are told that a disastrous fire "followed" the San Francisco earthquake of April 18, 1906. But that must be a mistake, for, if it were true, then the *action* of the fire must have suddenly jumped back to the somewhat earlier earthquake "like a stretched rope when it snaps." It should not take much discrimination to discover that the word "followed" here expresses not an action (or at least not an action alone) but a relation of temporal sequence, and that it is this relation which (if you wish to use a striking metaphor) jumps back with all the suddenness that characterizes the occurrence of the sequent event. Now let us consider a case where "following" is asserted not of a fire, but of a person acting physiologically. "Mary's entrance into the room followed Jane's by a few minutes." Unless Mary was a paralytic wheeled in by a nurse, her entrance was a physiological act of hers; but Mary's *act* in following Jane's entrance did not "pass over" to Jane's act in her entrance. Mary's act concerned Jane's, not in the way of reaching it physically, but in the way of *ex post facto* making Jane's entrance a *term of a relation* in which that entrance did not stand at the time of its occurrence. Here the verb "followed" expresses not only a physiological act (which does not pass over

---

of the Verb" (p. 64). Cf. *Webster's New International Dictionary* under the entry "transitive": "*Gram*. Passing over to an object; as, a *transitive action*; expressing an action not limited to an agent or subject; as, a *transitive* verb form or construction (he *holds* the book)." But under the entry "resemble" we read: "*Transitive:* 1. To be like or similar to; . . . as, these brothers *resemble* each other." What is the transitive *action* here? The verb form or construction here expresses an inactive relation. Our excellent dictionary of course recognizes transitive and intransitive relations, giving the verbs "precedes" and "implies" as examples of the former, and "disagrees with" and "likes" as examples of the latter. But even intransitive relations *obtain between their* terms. I still like the word "transist," which I once invented for expressing the function of all relations that are physically inert. Such a relation is consciousness as my analysis reveals it in the situations in which it occurs.

to its "object") but also a relation that arises with the act and *does* reach its "object." And this relation is not necessarily even a relation of intention or purpose. Mary may not have known that Jane had entered the room. Grammars and dictionaries to the contrary notwithstanding, the transitiveness of the transitive verb "follow" does not consist in the fact that the *action* it names passes over to what is named by its grammatical object.

Now the perspectivist takes the verb "see" as analogous to the verb "follow" as the latter was used of Mary's entrance just a while ago; analogous but with difference. The relation involved in seeing is of a different kind from that involved in following. But so is the relation expressed in the assertion that the number 3 follows the number 2 in the series of cardinal numbers a different kind of relation. To repeat, "see" names an occurrence analyzable, as I think, into a physiological process or act, *and* a relation of its own specific kind; and the grammatical object of the verb "see" does not name an object to which the *physiological act* physically passes over. It names a *term of this relation* whose other term is named by the grammatical subject of the verb. A relation of the same kind is found in occurrences that are named by the verbs "remember," "think," etc. In each of these cases there is also a physiological process or "act." This *act* does not "go over" to what is denoted by the grammatical object of the verb, but the *relation does* "go over" in the way in which any relation "goes over" from one term to another in relating the terms.

In thus analyzing the occurrences or events expressed by these verbs we can secure a theory of perception and of thought that, as we shall see, reconciles what Mr. Russell tells us is a tenet of science with the common-sense conviction that when one sees a star it is the "real" star one sees—a star away out there in the heavens and not something in the perceiver's physical head. Of course if anyone prefers to put all the heard choir of heaven and seen furniture of earth in his physical head and keep it there no one else may say him nay. But the perspectivist does not like this sort of physical big-headedness; he feels uncomfortable when he plays with the thought that his own physical head is bigger than all seen out of doors. Of course he might get used to it if he had to; and in time he might even take pride in the fact that his head is so large as to house the whole perceived universe, just as the fellow who has come to believe that he is Napoleon seems to plume himself over his military competence. But the perspectivist had rather not indulge himself in the belief that by taking scientific thought he can add untold trillions upon trillions of seen cubits to his stature. For him no such megalocephalomania, if you please! Therefore he lays down

Postulate 5. Consciousness, a natural event, occurs in the course of natural events when and only when an organism is physically reacting to physical stimulation from without or from within itself; and it is analyzable (but not separable) into a character ("conscious character") of a specific kind and a corresponding asymmetrical non-dynamic relation also of a specific kind ("conscious relation"). So long as any consciousness lasts, its constituent character is a character of the reacting organism: "the organism is conscious"; and its constituent relation is a relation which the organism has to something or other: "the organism is conscious of that something or other." The converse of a conscious relation is a relation of appearing: when an organism is conscious of anything that thing appears to the organism; and conversely, when anything appears to an organism the organism is conscious of that thing.

The organism as having the asymmetrical relation is the "subject" of consciousness, and that to which the subject has that relation is collectively the "field" of consciousness and distributively its "objects."

Our present postulate has been stated in very general terms; more specification will be supplied as we proceed; and first let us observe that consciousness as it is used here names not a specific kind of character (or quality) alone, not a specific relation alone, but both together in an indissoluble union. Whenever an organism has a conscious character, it also has a conscious relation, and *vice versa.* In the discussion that follows we shall generally concentrate our attention upon consciousness as a *relation;* but the reader should always bear in mind that the subject of consciousness is also a *conscious* subject, where "conscious" is used in the sense it has in ordinary non-technical speech as when we say that John Smith is conscious. The view that consciousness is a relation seems strange to many; this is at least partly because it is interpreted as meaning that consciousness is *not also* the kind of character or "quality" that the word is ordinarily used to name. There is good reason to believe that when we first begin to analyze what we experience, the characters or qualities that things have are first discriminated; and things are identified by the qualities they are experienced as having. Things are seen to be red, warm, similar, different, near or far, still or moving. What grammarians call adjectives and verbs as "parts of speech" were in all probability not first used as *parts* of speech: they were *wholes* of speech. Our occidental grammars are analyses of quite fully developed languages, but the analyses represent a logic by no means fully developed. The logic was controlled by the structure of the languages analyzed, and recent logicians have found this logic rudimentary. It is the logic of *"predication,"* and fails to deal with *relations* in any competent fashion. It is relations, however, with which present-day extensional logic, including that of mathematics, deals; and since present-day physics is a mathematical science, it is relations with which it too deals. Extensional logic, the logic of relations, has the field now almost to itself, although there is important work done in intensional logic. It is the opinion of the present writer that each implies the other, and that either to the exclusion of the other is a one-sided logic. Our second postulate is the assumption of this mutual implication.

Now the adjective "conscious" in the first instance names a character which something is recognized as having, and the abstract noun "consciousness" names this same character treated abstractly. In this respect it is like the abstract nouns "similarity," "equality," "difference," and "distance." But further analysis of the situations in which these characters are found reveals the fact that these characters imply each a distinguishable relation, and the relevant relation is grammatically expressed in English by a preposition: to be similar or to be equal is to be similar *to* or to be equal *to,* and to be different or to be distant is to be different *from* or to be distant *from.* The same prepositions have to be supplied respectively with the abstract nouns "similarity," "equality," "difference," and "distance." But it is to be observed that neither of these prepositions *by itself* adequately identifies the relation meant in the instances in which they are severally employed. For instance, the "to" in "similar to" and the "to" in "equal to" express entirely different relations, each being also an entirely different relation from that expressed by the "to" in "adverse to." When we name these relations in the abstract we should, if we are meticulous, call them the relations "similarity-to," "equality-to," etc. But this is too awkward, and logicians by tacit convention now call these relations "equality," etc., omitting the appropriate preposition. Thus the same abstract nouns have come to denote sometimes abstract characters and sometimes abstract relations. This verbal ambiguity is not apt to lead to misunderstanding when speaker and hearer keep in mind that, for instance, similarity as a character is indissolubly connected with similarity as a relation; the context will show whether the speaker is dealing with the character, with the relation, or with the two together.

The perspectivist treats "consciousness" as in this respect analogous to "similarity" or "distance." The word names both a specific kind of character or quality and also the specific kind of relation implied by the character. As we have said before, no one is ever conscious without being conscious *of* something. This preposition "of" (like "to" and "from") taken by itself names many different kinds of relations, and it gets its specificity of denotation only from the context: the relation is specified when, for instance, I say "my consciousness of heat," "my consciousness of pain," "my consciousness of a contradiction in a theory," etc. Here the relation is the relation "consciousness-of"; and adopting the tacit convention above mentioned, I call it "consciousness" for short, and say that consciousness is a relation. But since I *am* conscious when I have (i.e., am in) a consciousness-relation to something, consciousness is also a character that I have when I have that relation. I have the relation in the sense that I am a term of the relation. In what follows I shall without more ado treat consciousness as a relation except where there is indication to the contrary.

But before proceeding further I wish to call attention to two points on which in the formulation of our present postulate we have been intentionally vague. The first concerns the physical reaction of an organism to a physical stimulation which conditions the occurrence of consciousness. There is good if not conclusive scientific evidence that in human organisms such a reaction involves processes in the cortex of the brain; and although we cannot orally question other vertebrates to ascertain whether they are conscious, and if so whether their consciousness occurs only when their central nervous systems are stimulated, still so far as we have evidence that these vertebrates are conscious the same evidence points to the occurrence of consciousness in them only when their brains are involved in their reactions to physical stimulation. I therefore *assume* that this is the fact. Since I do not wish to complicate my discussion of consciousness with the question how far down in the scale of evolution consciousness is to be found, I have left the formulation of our postulate noncommittal on this point. In this chapter I am dealing in the first instance only with *human* consciousness.

The other point on which the formulation of our present postulate has been noncommittal concerns the "objects" of consciousness. All sorts of things appear to us; in other words, we are conscious of all sorts of things. Whether what appears, or conversely stated what the organism is conscious of, is the stimulus or something else is a matter for further investigation, and therefore our postulate is for the present silent on this question.

In any case, it is a *physical, biological organism* that is conscious, not a "mind" considered as a sort of entity entirely different from such an organism. This is not categorically to deny that there is such a "mind," but it is to say that our theory finds no need to assume that there is such a "mind." All we need is that there shall be an organism which is conscious, i.e., has conscious character, by virtue of the fact that it is a subject-term in a specific sort of relation denoted by "consciousness."

Consciousness is an *asymmetrical* relation. It is the organism that is conscious of the object, and not the object that is conscious of the organism. This is not to deny that when in seeing I am conscious of an object the object may also see me. But in such a case there are two different consciousnesses, and not just one consciousness considered in two ways: first considered as the relation of myself to the object, and then conversely as the relation of the object to me. We have an analogy in the case of duellists killing each other. Here there are two different killings. It is only superficial observation that would lead anyone to consider the two killings as one. *A*'s killing *B* starts with *A*'s pulling the trigger of his gun and ends with *A*'s bullet in *B*'s heart. And *B*'s killing *A* starts with *B*'s pulling the trigger of *his* gun and ends with *B*'s bullet in *A*'s heart. Likewise, my seeing you starts with the stimulation of *my* eyes by light from *you* and ends with *my* physiological reaction which conditions *my* visual consciousness *of you;* whereas your seeing me starts with the stimulation of *your* eyes by light from *me* and ends with *your* physiological reaction which conditions *your* visual consciousness of *me*.

When it is said that in consciousness there is a relation of *a specific kind*, what is meant is that, although this relation resembles other relations in the ultimately indefinable way in which all relations resemble each other, yet it is a relation specifically different from relations of any other kind, such as time-relations, space-relations, and equality-relations, just as these relations are specifically different from each other. We therefore call the conscious relation a relation "of its own kind." In the last analysis the character of this specific difference is indefinable except ostensively.

At best one can only state the conditions under which a relation of this kind occurs, and ask others whether they do not find under these conditions something that can without violence but with advantage be considered as a relation different in kind from other kinds of relations. Ultimate similarities and ultimate differences between all sorts of things are the *ne plus ultra* of logic; this holds of relations more importantly even than of qualities such as colors.

One cannot indisputably prove to others that the conscious relation is a relation, any more than one can prove that temporal or spatial distance is a relation. As we shall see later, there may be such a thing as Newton's "Absolute Space"; but if it can be shown that everything which is urged as proving the absoluteness of space can be dealt with as well on the assumption that space is a complex of relations, and if in addition it can be shown that the relational theory of space can deal more satisfactorily with spatial problems than the absolutist theory can, then the relational theory obtains a preferred status in science. It gets a priority rating from William of Ockham, who by fairly common consent has become the Counsellor of the Office of Scientific Management.

When consciousness is treated as a relation an organism does not lose its specific *character of being conscious* any more than when time is treated as a system of relations an event in that relation loses its specific character of being a temporal event. Without ceasing to be conscious a conscious organism by being in a conscious relation becomes more consonant with common sense, which believes that a man can see what is distant in space and remember what is distant in time even though he may not be able to *act* immediately *upon* the spatially distant and cannot act physically at all upon an event that has *already occurred*. The best he can do is to do something *about* it, not something *to* it as it was *when it was occurring*. A relation is not tied down to and exclusively housed or confined in only one of its terms. And of the conscious relation we can say with Mr. Santayana's poetic license what he so eloquently says of spirit:

... barriers of space and time do not shut it in; they are but boundary-stones of field and field in its landscape. It is ready to survey all time and all existence if, by establishing some electric connection with its seat, time and existence will consent to report themselves to it ... and as it arises only when and where nature calls it forth, so it surveys only what nature happens to spread before it.[6]

But to descend from the heights of Parnassus to the drab plains of logic, let us not take literally such a personification of consciousness. Consciousness, as we have seen, is not itself conscious of the term which is called the "object of consciousness." Let us again employ an analogy. A person in Madison is, say, ninety miles distant from Milwaukee; and when, using the abstract noun "distance," he speaks of his distance from Milwaukee, he does not think of the distance as being itself distant from Milwaukee. It is *he* and not his distance that is distant from Milwaukee. So when, being in a conscious relation to some object, say the State Capitol in Madison, I speak of my consciousness of that object, I do not mean that my *consciousness* is conscious of the object. It is *I* who am conscious; it is *not my consciousness* that is conscious. Thus *consciousness* does not "survey" anything, nor is it "ready to survey" anything. But *I*, when in a conscious relation to the State Capitol, am *ipso facto* "surveying" that object. Nor is my consciousness literally connected with me as its seat, as if it had some sort of independent being requiring some electric connection to bring it to me in order to become my consciousness. When it arises, it arises as *itself* the specific kind of relation between me and the Capitol, namely, the specific kind of relation that corresponds with my character of being conscious. I am its "seat" in the sense that I am a term of the relation it is, but not in the sense that it abides in me, any more than the relation of distance from Milwaukee abides in me. Just as in its own fashion the relation of distance reaches out from me to Milwaukee but does not abide in me, so the relation of consciousness also in its own way succeeds in reaching from me to the Capitol a mile away, and thus does not abide in me.

---

[6] George Santayana, *Scepticism and Animal Faith*, New York, 1923, pp. 162–163. By permission of Chas. Scribner's Sons.

The view that all consciousnesses are of the same differential kind, whether the consciousness be that in seeing, hearing, thinking, remembering or willing, needs explanation.[7] Is it not true, it may be asked, that the consciousness involved when I feel a sharp pain, or am in a blind rage, or am resolutely pursuing some difficult course of action, is different from the kind of consciousness involved when I am dispassionately discussing some trivial subject at an afternoon tea? Are there not varietally "different forms of consciousness?" Before giving my answer to this question I wish to emphasize the fact that this answer, even if it be found to be unpalatable or even untenable, does not prejudice the tenability of the postulate we are now discussing, since this postulate is compatible with other possible answers. The question whether there are different varieties of conscious relations may be answered affirmatively or negatively by both Aristotelian and Platonic universalists, or it may be answered differently by the two. But whatever be these answers they do not prejudice our postulate. It happens that the present writer is a nominalist of sorts, and that he also finds no reason to believe that there are differential varieties of consciousness. This may, if you please, be set down to personal idiosyncrasy. Nominalism he discussed some years ago in a paper, now reprinted as a chapter in this volume,[8] and now he will try to develop the view that, to use a traditional expression, consciousness is an *infima species* of relations. No further analysis he can make results in differential varieties of consciousness. This is not to say that there are no differences discoverable between seeing something and remembering something, or between hearing something and feeling a pain or being consciously in love or consciously tackling a difficult problem. There are differences here, but the differences he finds to be in the *terms,* not in the relation.

---

[7] What is meant by such expressions as "the consciousness in seeing" must be distinguished from expressions such as "the consciousness of seeing." The former names a relation to be found in every instance of seeing, whereas the latter names another instance of this relation, a consciousness whose term is the seeing. This latter is discussed on pp. 59–62 of our text.

[8] See Chapter VI.

Analysis always is a distinguishing of factors or elements or moments—as William James said, "call them what you will"—in an integral whole more "concrete" than the factors distinguished. *Abstractive* analysis, unlike chemical analysis, does not *break up* the whole into elements that can exist each *apart from* the rest. Two wholes, found after abstractive analysis to be quite different "in some respect or respects," do not lose these differences even if in some *other* respect they are found to be "exactly alike" except as to singularity, or, as we often say, except "numerically." Now let two integral wholes which reflection offers for analysis be describable as "I-seeing-a-typewriter-against-a-background" and "I-in-a-dentist's-chair-with-my-eyes-closed-and-feeling-a-pain." These two descriptions may not be exhaustive, but they are sufficient for the present purpose. Each describes what some of us perhaps now remember to have lived through in the course of some hour or so. It is the same "I" in both integral wholes, but an "I" undergoing decidedly different physiological processes in reaction to equally different stimuli. Just as different, too, were the objects that appeared to the "I" on the two occasions; for instance, the typewriter as compared with the pain. Not many objects can differ from each other more than these two. And yet, in spite of all this, the nicest discrimination I can make discovers no difference whatever in kind between the factor of *appearing* in the one case and that in the other. There were, of course, two appearings, one at one time and the other at another; at one time a typewriter appeared at one place, and at another time a pain appeared at another place. But the *appearings* were indistinguishably alike. Expressed conversely, not as appearings but as consciousnesses, my *consciousness* of the typewriter in the one case did not differ at all except numerically from my *consciousness* of the pain in the other. There are no more varieties of consciousness than of the *relation* called "sibship," which in certain instances is called "brotherhood" and in others "sisterhood," the difference of names indicating differences of sex in the *terms* of the relation but not in the relation itself, when the *relation is distinguished from its terms.* Brotherhood is the sibship of *males,* and sisterhood is the sibship of *females,* the abstract sibship itself being neither male nor female. It is only when "brotherhood" names a group of brothers, i.e., brothers collectively, and not the abstract relation of brotherhood, and "sisterhood" names a group of sisters, that difference of sex is found between brotherhood and sisterhood. Only because in familiar language the biological relation is not sharply distinguished from its terms have scientists found it necessary to resuscitate the old Anglo-Saxon word *sib* and give it a meaning which distinguishes the *kind* of relation involved from its terms, the kind being precisely alike in all instances whereas the terms vary from instance to instance. Sibs are sibs solely by virtue of their being offspring of the same parents, and sibship is precisely the same relation—whether male or female—arising from this relation in which each stands to the common parents of all. *Sibs* may vary in all sorts of ways within the same family, but sibship is of exactly the same kind whenever found, differing only numerically.

It is the same sort of undifferentiated sameness of *kind* that our nominalism postulates with regard to consciousnesses where they occur. This assumption, we think, is borne out by examination of such a succession of experiences as James described when he said:

> You can hear the vibration of an electric contact-maker, smell the ozone, see the sparks, and feel the thrill, co-consciously as it were or in one field of experience. But you can also isolate any one of these sensations by shutting out the rest. If you close your eyes, hold your nose, and remove your hand, you can get the sensation of sound alone, but it seems still the same sensation it was; and if you restore the action of the other organs, the sound coalesces with the feeling, the sight, and the smell sensations again. Now the natural way of talking of all this is to say that certain sensations are experienced, now singly, and now together with other sensations, in a common conscious field. Fluctuations of attention give analogous results. We let a sensation in or keep it out by changing our attention; and similarly we let an item of memory in or drop it out.[9]

---

[9] William James, *A Pluralistic Universe,* New York, 1909, p. 268. James's note in this passage is worth quoting, since it represents a retraction from an earlier position: "I have myself talked in other ways as plausibly as I could in my *Psychology,* and talked truly (as I believe) in certain selected cases; but for other cases the natural way invincibly comes back" (p. 343).

Here what James called "the common conscious field" consists of what I regard as the objects of consciousness; and what James called "sensations" I would call sense-qualities, also regarded as objects of consciousness. Let us now translate James's statement of the facts into the language that the perspectivist finds more literally expressive of the facts as he himself views them. Sounds, smell, sparks, and thrills are together the terms of a conscious relation in which I stand to them; i.e., they are in my "field of consciousness." My organism, which is the "I" here, is in the same kind of asymmetrical conscious relation to all these objects. Here we have a relation which may be a one–one relation or a one–many relation. The character of this *relation* does not change when I close my eyes and the sparks drop out of the field, or when I hold my nose and the smell drops out, or when I remove my hand and the vibration drops out, leaving only the sound in the field. If now I reverse the process and open my eyes, sparks return to the field, and so on. Through all these changes the character of the *consciousness* remains the same. What has changed is to be found in the *objects* in the field, and also in my *physiological reactions. Specifically the same sort of relation* seems to be involved in the formation of the successive fields; the *conscious relation* in sight seems indistinguishable in kind from that in hearing, etc., just as my ownership relation to a certain fountain pen, a certain pocket knife, a certain watch, and some suits of clothes is of the same kind in all these cases. The articles form a group which I call my possessions. Similarly, the *same sort of relation* to a camera, consisting in the fact that certain objects send light with sufficient intensity to effect certain changes in its film, constitutes these objects into the field of the camera. Take almost any kind of "field" you can think of and you will find, I think, that it is constituted by some kind of relation, and if different fields are of the same kind then the relations involved are of the same kind, however different the objects in the fields may be.

Consciousness can therefore be defined as the specific kind of relation in which an organism stands to what is called its field of experience or field of consciousness.

When a person says that he is dimly conscious of something, what is dim is the *object* of consciousness, not the conscious relation in which the speaker stands to the object. But an adverb that grammatically qualifies the adjective "conscious" may, on the other hand, name a character or attitude of the subject *other than* the character of being conscious, as when one says: "I am gratefully (or humbly) conscious of your favor"—which on analysis is seen to mean: "I am conscious of your favor *and* am grateful (or humble)."

But not only does what James says suggest that all conscious relations are of the same kind; it further suggests, when translated into terms appropriate to our theory of consciousness, that the consciousness of sound, the consciousness of thrill, the consciousness of sight, the consciousness of smell, all may *coalesce* into *one* consciousness of sound-thrill-sight-and-smell, and that when this occurs the one consciousness and the many coalescing consciousnesses can be numerically distinguished if attention is directed to these distinctions. Here a one–one relation becomes a one–many relation. Thus, to go back to what James said, if I am asked whether I now feel as well as hear, see as well as smell, I can answer truly that I do. Instead of the word "coalescence," which James used, let us use "integration," which, since the publication of Professor (now Sir) Charles Sherrington's *The Integrative Action of the Nervous System* in 1906, has established itself in physiological usage. Just as the various distinguishable physiological activities that occur in different parts of a well-integrated nervous system are integrated into one comprehensive activity, so, if each of these activities when occurring separately conditions a consciousness, all such activities when occurring simultaneously in a well-integrated organism condition a *single* integrated consciousness, whose field is a single conscious field distinguishable into different objects.[10]

---

[10] In cases of multiple personality there is a lack of such singleness of consciousness; but the lack is presumably due to a lack of physiological integration.

What we have to say of a single integrated consciousness whose single conscious field consists of events in temporal succession we must reserve for Chapter VI.

Not all relations have this integrative character, but at least temporal and spatial relations have. If A, B, and C are points in that order on a straight line, the distance from A to B and that from B to C are numerically distinguishable distances within the distance from A to C. The segment AC remains a single unbroken segment even though B is recognized as a point within that segment. We speak in geometry of a line as being "intersected" at a point by another line; but such intersection is not a cutting into *separate* pieces. A line that is intersected by another line remains the integral whole it was to start with. Geometrical linear intersection is not an interruption, a bursting apart. For this reason, among others, mathematicians call space a continuum and have developed precise definitions of continuity. This is not the place to deal with these technical concepts, which are logical refinements of what we all find in experience when only crudely analyzed in "common sense." Take for instance a smooth board of wood which a carpenter plans to saw in two. Before he begins to saw he marks off with a pencil on its "continuous" surface two successive feet. This continuity of its surface is the fact that the "parts" thus marked off still *hold together* next to next in a single whole (as the etymology of the Latin word *continuus* indicates: *con-tenere*). From left to right, the second part begins *where* the first part ends, with no gap between. The marking off is not a severance; the whole board, with two feet marked off, remains as yet intact. And as he can distinguish the marked-off parts of the board without sawing them apart, so *if called on* he can distinguish his seeing the second part, both seeings being integrated in the seeing of both parts together. The *seeing* of the one part holds together with the seeing of the other.[11] There is as much integration in his seeing as in what he sees. And what is true of the consciousness

---

[11] Was it something like this that Aristotle had in mind when he spoke of a faculty, δύναμις, which was not only κριτική but also σύμφυτος, born together?

in vision is true of the consciousness in vision-and-audition-and-memory-and-thinking, when a normally integrated organism sees, hears, remembers and thinks at the same time. He is in a *single* integral conscious relation to all that he is then conscious of, but this integrity of consciousness is an integrity of *distinguishable* but not always *distinguished* consciousnesses.[12]

In all this it must be borne in mind that each different kind of relation integrates in its own way, and that therefore the integration characteristic of any kind of relation is different from the integration characteristic of any other kind. Each kind of integrative relation is integrative in its own fashion. Now, analogies are not identities. A perspectivist uses them, not to *prove* that what he says of any kind of relation is correct, but to prove that there is no *logical* reason why it should not be correct. Whether it is correct or not can be ascertained only by recourse to experience. If an assertion has no logical reason against it and has experience in its favor, nothing more can be asked of it than the question, "What of it? Does its acceptance help solve any remaining problem?" We shall see that in the case of consciousness it does, but meanwhile let us be on our guard against drawing unwarranted conclusions from the analogy between the integrity of consciousness and that of space. Such conclusions have been drawn.

For instance, Woodbridge, whose view of the nature of consciousness will be considered in some detail in Chapter IV, regarded consciousness as "a type of existence" whose

> three most noticeable instances, . . . other than consciousness, are things in space, events in time, and individuals in species. . . . Some suggestive conclusions may be drawn from this fact which throw a clarifying light on several controverted questions. . . . We do not

---

"According to Aristotle, each sense . . . is, as regards its proper αἰσθητόν, a δύναμις σύμφυτος κριτική with the faculty of distinguishing and comparing all διαφοραι, belonging to that αἰσθητόν. Thus ὄψις discerns black and white and all the colours between these. Such a measure of synthetic power Aristotle grants to each individual sense." (*Greek Theories of Elementary Cognition from Alcmaeon to Aristotle*, by John I. Beare, Oxford, 1906, p. 276.)

[12] As we saw in the preceding note, Aristotle attributed such a singleness to another faculty, κοινὴ αἴσθησις, which was later translated into *sensus communis*. But of course the English term "common sense" has acquired a different denotation.

ask how things get into space, so we should not ask how objects get into consciousness, if we thereby imply, in any way, the previous separate existence of the two. . . . Finally, one who has recognized that in consciousness we have simply an instance of the existence of different things together, will not engage in the controversies which are suggested by such terms as "automatism," "interactionism," "parallelism," "agnosticism," and their kindred. Indeed, he will have to renounce many so-called metaphysical pleasures.[13]

But from the fact that anything that is ever in space never existed first out of space, it does not follow that everything that is ever in consciousness never first existed out of consciousness. And if some things did first exist out of consciousness before they got into consciousness, there *is* a question how they did get into consciousness; and it is not merely a metaphysical pleasure but a metaphysical duty to tackle this problem. Woodbridge himself later not only recognized the existence of this problem, but went to the other extreme in saying: "I find no other problem of consciousness than the genetic one."[14]

Another conclusion that Woodbridge drew was that "consciousness has other characters, such as infinity, which are common to all continuums."[15] Just what he meant by this infinity of consciousness he did not say, for he mentioned it only in passing. Opposed as he was to the eternal consciousness of Thomas Hill Green and other neo-Hegelians, he could not have meant that our finite consciousnesses are parts of an eternal consciousness in the same way in which finite space and finite time were supposed, before the advent of physical relativity, to be parts respectively of infinite space and infinite time. But of course a philosopher who renounces metaphysical pleasures evades many metaphysical obligations. The perspectivist does not have to evade this problem. For him every consciousness is assumed to be finite. This means that no one is ever conscious of everything in detail. Even when anyone is conscious of (i.e., is thinking about) the universe as a whole, this whole as it appears in his consciousness is woefully

---

[13] F. J. E. Woodbridge, *Nature and Mind,* pp. 308–309.
[14] *Ibid.,* pp. 421–422.
[15] *Ibid.,* p. 308.

sketchy; the only infinity that can be asserted of it is the infinity of details that are *lacking*. It cannot with any meaning even be said of his consciousness that it is "finite but boundless." The only meaning that can be given to a boundary of a relation is to be found in the terms of the relation, and every particular relation terminates in its terms.

Some pages earlier it was emphasized that consciousness does not survey anything, that it is not consciousness that is conscious of objects but some organism that is conscious. Applying this principle to the much discussed problem of the consciousness of consciousness, we can say that no particular conscious relation is conscious of *itself*, just as no distance-relation is distant from *itself* and no priority-relation is prior to *itself*. No particular instance of a relation of any kind relates *itself to itself*; it relates its *terms to each other*. Keeping this in mind, we can see that if consciousness be considered a relation it is absurd to speak of a consciousness of consciousness with the implication that the two different words "consciousness" in this combination denote identically the same *particular* instance of the relation and that therefore any consciousness is conscious of *itself*.

Although no particular instance of any relation functions as a term of itself, there are *particular* instances of relations of some kinds that may function as terms of *other particular* instances of relations of the same kinds. For example, there is a particular temporal relation, r_1, between the beginning and the ending of the Peloponnesian War—B. C. 431–404, the relation with its terms constituting a particular relational complex, c_1. There is another particular temporal relation, r_2, between the beginning and the ending of our Civil War—A. D. 1861–1865, this relation with its terms constituting another particular relational complex, c_2. There is a third particular temporal relation, r_3, between c_1 and c_2, this relation with its terms constituting a third particular complex, c_3. Relation r_3, in relating c_1 and c_2, also relates r_1 and r_2 (which are respective constituents of c_1 and c_2); it integrates them into a whole of a unique kind, of which r_1 and r_2 are parts.

This sort of temporal integration of temporal relations is a factor in constituting the *unity* and *continuity* of time. A similar hierarchy of relations and relational complexes can be found in some social organizations—similar but of course with a difference that goes with the specific difference between time and society.

Now, the perspectivist finds a similar integration occurring in the matter of consciousness—similar, but again with characteristic differences. While I am seeing and thus am in a conscious relation (r_1), and also am smelling and thus am in a conscious relation (r_2), I am sometimes also in conscious relations (r_3) to the seeing and the hearing. In such a case the particular conscious relations, r_1 and r_2, are terms of a particular conscious relation r_3 which integrates its terms into a single consciousness, r_3, in which I am not at the time conscious of r_3, but of r_1 and r_2. But although the perspectivist attempts in this way to give a logical account of the situation in which, *while* one is conscious, one is also conscious of thus being conscious, he emphasizes the fact that such situations occur only occasionally. To be conscious is not *ipso facto* to be conscious of being conscious. In this respect the perspectivist disagrees with most of those earlier psychologists and philosophers who maintained that there is such a thing as being conscious of being conscious; he disagrees with them because they also held that to be conscious is *ipso facto* to be conscious of being conscious. They thus exposed themselves to the charge that their contention involves an infinite regress: being conscious is being conscious of being conscious of being conscious of being conscious, and so on. The dialectics of this charge we need not stop to consider, any more than naturalists have to defend themselves against Dean Swift's witticism:

> So, naturalists observe, a flea
> Hath smaller fleas that on him prey;
> And these have smaller still to bite 'em;
> And so proceed *ad infinitum*.[16]

---

[16] I quote from *Familiar Quotations*, by John Bartlett, 11th ed., revised by Christopher Morley, 1937, p. 190, where also will be found De Morgan's more familiar lines.

A distinction must be made, of course, between an assumption which by its own terms implies an infinite regress and a report on a discovered regress containing a limited number of steps. In a storeroom one may find a box lying on another box, a third box on the second, and so on, say for ten layers. Or one may count the number of times one has counted the entries in some contested race. There is nothing in the nature of either case to suggest, much less to imply, an infinite regress. And so with any actual instance of a consciousness of consciousness. There are in it as many consciousnesses as there are, and no more.

Of late it has become the fashion among psychologists and philosophers to deny that there can be any such a thing as a consciousness of consciousness if the two consciousnesses are simultaneous. Those who take this position maintain that the traditional view is due to the failure to discriminate between the dates of the two consciousnesses; and they would correct this alleged mistake by saying instead that while there may be such a thing as a consciousness of consciousness, this would be a case of being conscious of *having been* conscious. Thus one sees without being conscious of seeing, and later is conscious of having seen. Then again one sees, and again is conscious of having seen. If this alternation is sufficiently rapid, it may erroneously appear as a single occurrence. It was perhaps William James who was responsible for the widespread acceptance of this view. Only a very careless reader of his psychological works would need to have his attention called to the fact that James was interested in avoiding two extremes, one of which was British empiricism. This offered no connecting link other than a temporal one between one perception and another. But without some such link there is no "explanation" for the fact that some perceptions follow one another "co-consciously," i.e., belong to the same self, while others belong to different selves. The other extreme James was intent on avoiding was Continental transcendentalism, which, as he understood it, explained co-consciousness by insisting that:

The awareness that *I think* is ... implied in all experience. No connected consciousness of anything without that of *Self* as its presupposition and "transcendental" condition![17]

Interpret "experience" in this sentence as connected consciousness and "I think" as "I am conscious," and then this insistence becomes the insistence that awareness of consciousness is implied in all connected consciousness. James took this to be a claim that no one is ever conscious without at the same time being conscious of being conscious; and he regarded it as an instance of the psychologist's fallacy—as indeed such an insistence would be. The course that James charted for himself here in sailing between the Scylla of British empiricism and the Charybdis of transcendentalism shows that even the most daring and resourceful navigator pioneering in intellectual waters always carries with him something from what he would leave behind. He proposed to treat

> successively of *A*) the self as known, or the *me,* the "empirical ego" as it is sometimes called; and of *B*) the self as knower, or the I, the "pure ego" of certain authors.[18]

Among the constituents of the me is "the material me," of which the "*body* is the innermost part,"[19] but this is not the I.

> The I, or "pure ego" ... is that which at any given moment *is* conscious, whereas the Me is only one of the things which it is conscious *of.* In other words, it is the *Thinker;* and the question immediately comes up, *what* is the thinker. Is it the passing state of consciousness itself, or is it something deeper and less mutable?[20]

His reply to this question is that

> *If there were no passing states of consciousness,* then indeed we might suppose an abiding principle, absolutely one with itself, to be the ceaseless thinker in each one of us. But if the states of consciousness be accorded as realities, no such "substantial" identity in the thinker need be supposed. Yesterday's and today's states of consciousness

---

[17] *The Principles of Psychology,* Vol. I, p. 361.
[18] *Psychology, Briefer Course,* 1893, p. 176. In the Preface to this work James said: "In this shorter work, the general point of view, which I have adopted as that of 'natural science,' has, I imagine, gained in clearness by its extrication from so much critical matter and its more simple and dogmatic statement."
[19] *Ibid.,* p. 177.
[20] *Ibid.,* pp. 195–196.

have no *substantial* identity, for when one is here the other is irrevocably dead and gone. But they have a *functional* identity, for both know the same objects . . . . This functional identity seems really the only sort of identity which the facts require us to suppose. Successive thinkers, numerically distinct, but all aware of the same past in the same way, form an adequate vehicle for all the experience of personal unity and sameness which we actually have.[21]

These "successive thinkers" are each a "pulse" of consciousness, which

dies away and is replaced by another. The other, among the things it knows, knows its predecessor, and finding it "warm" . . . greets it, saying: "Thou art *mine,* and part of the same self with me."[22]

Thus James at this period carried over from the past the British empiricists' notion of the "passing states of consciousness" as the only selves, but he accorded to them the synthetic "function" that had belonged to the "substantial" transcendental selves—or transcendental Self—of the Continent. In retrospect this now seems a strange procedure on the part of a thinker who at the same time adopted as his working hypothesis

the simple and radical conception . . . that mental action may be uniformly and absolutely a function of brain-action, varying as the latter varies, and being to the brain-action as effect to cause.[23]

With this hypothesis it would seem more natural to regard the *organism* whose brain-action is "the immediate condition of a state of consciousness" as "the thinker" who "owns" the consciousness, rather than have each "state of consciousness" born owning its predecessor. One reason for James's failure to take this position was perhaps the fact that he had not yet hit upon the conception that consciousness is a relation. As we shall see in the next chapter, it is to James that the perspectivist owes this conception. (We shall also see there a change in James's view of what "the self" is.)

Appropriating this conception we are now in a position to define the perspectivist's *mind* as an organism whose dynamic brain-

---
[21] *Ibid.,* pp. 202–203.
[22] *The Principles of Psychology,* Vol. I, p. 339.
[23] *Psychology, Briefer Course,* p. 6.

action is conditioning, or giving rise to, a nondynamic conscious relation of which it therewith becomes a term. Mind is an organism if and when the organism is conscious of some object; or, more briefly, *a mind is a conscious organism.* Thus being a mind is like being a husband or a wife. A man is not actually a husband except when he is in a matrimonial relation to a woman; just so, an organism is not actually a mind except when it is in a conscious relation to an object. At other times it can only be said to be "potentially" a mind; and when we say this we should have due regard to the meaning of "potentiality," a matter we shall discuss more fully when we take up the problem of time. Meanwhile the perspectivist would say that an unconscious organism is "potentially" a mind in the sense that *some* but not all of the necessary conditions for the occurrence of consciousness are to be found in the organism. The expectancy of "mentality" during "nonmental" intermissions is so great that it has become the fashion to speak of much that goes on in an organism in intervals of unconsciousness as "subconscious"—which is as if we were to speak of a widower's acts as "submatrimonial" when they are such as under further conditions would give rise to marriage. In our theory, what the psychiatrist calls the "subconscious" is *purely physiological* since the subject is not conscious of it. It is a physiological diathesis, in many cases blocking the occurrence of physiological processes that would otherwise be conducive to "normal" behavior. In other cases it is but another instance of what a German author called "learning to skate in summer and to swim in winter."

But if all consciousness is of the same kind, what shall we say of attention? Is there no difference between an attentive mind and one that is woolgathering? Of course there is a difference, but it is not a difference in the kind of consciousness involved; it is a difference (1) in what is physiologically occurring in the organism, and (2) in what consequently appears to the organism. Let us first consider the physiology of attention; and here again we quote a distinguished physiologist whom as laymen we may adopt as scientific mentor in matters physiological:

> We are each . . . at any moment a pattern of active doing; a single pattern of pieces all subordinate to one keypiece. No other part of the pattern is allowed to disturb the keypiece of the pattern. Should it do so, then the pattern changes and the disturbing piece becomes usually the keypiece of a new pattern which supplants the previous. The keypiece is the crown of the unified doing of the moment . . . . In the great array of motor acts done by animate things there is one class of act which differs in no wise from others except that for its time being it, so to say, grips the individual as a whole, and nothing else going on in the individual may impede it. It is this one main doing which has the accompaniment of mind. As it gives way to the next main act the mind, so to say, leaves it and accompanies that next one.[24]

However, I do not suppose that our author means that all such "one main doings" have the "accompaniment of mind." Usually within every twenty-four hours in the life of a normal human adult there is a period in which the one main doing can be characterized physiologically as recuperation. He is resting from his workaday wakeaday labors, and if he is lucky what he is then doing has no "accompaniment of mind." One might, of course, say that he is then attending to the business of sleeping; but the perspectivist prefers to restrict the word *attention* to "the one main doing which has the accompaniment of mind," or rather, as he prefers to say, which gives rise to consciousness and therewith to mind, just as the legal ceremony of marriage gives rise to a lawful married husband and a lawful married wife out of two "single" persons.

When consciousness does arise, the one main doing, the keypiece of the pattern, *is* attention on its *physiological* side; it is the *act* of attention. However, at the same time there are "subordinate pieces." Thus if the main thing doing is, say, my eating when I am very hungry, a subordinate piece may be the reaction of my auditory mechanism to sound waves. This reaction may not

---

[24] Sir Charles Sherrington, *Man on His Nature*, New York and Cambridge (England), the first half of the quotation being from p. 173, and the other from p. 205. By permission of Cambridge University Press.

"disturb the keypiece of the pattern" or "impede it." But it may result in my being *conscious* of sounds as well as of the food I am eating. As we say, I am "set on" eating and am not "distracted" by what I hear. Among all the things that appear to me *the food stands out*; it appears *prominent*—not prominent*ly*, because what is prominent is not the appearing but the food—while the other things are in the background at lower levels. It is this outstandingness—this prominence of something that appears in contrast to something else that appears—that is the nonphysiological factor in attention, which however is conditioned by the physiological "keypiece of the pattern"; and the fact that the other things which appear take as it were a back seat is conditioned by the physiologically "subordinate pieces." Just as in a physiologically integrated individual all the physiological pieces constitute one integral *act,* so all the appearings "coalesce" into one integral appearing; and because of this integrality of the appearing, all that appears constitutes *one field of consciousness,* which—again to change our metaphors—has one or more outstanding peaks, sloping away in different directions into more and more obscure valleys. As Tennyson has put it,

> . . . all experience is an arch wherethrough
> Gleams that untravelled world, whose margin fades
> Forever and forever as I move.

In our present postulate consciousness is said to be a nondynamical relation, and by this is meant that it is not measurable in *dynamic* units such as ergs, watts, and footpounds. These are units of work done by a physical body upon another physical body per unit of time; i.e., they are units of what in physics is called "kinetic energy." In classical physics—here it is not necessary to go into complications introduced by relativity—there is an expression which, when translated into what seems at first blush to be the vernacular, reads: "one half the product of the mass of a body by the square of its velocity"; and this by definition is "the kinetic energy of the body." But "mass" is no longer quantity of matter, as it is in ordinary speech. Without going into details, it will be found that in the last analysis the "ultimate units" in terms of which energy is defined are indeed spatial and temporal units. However, it is not these units combined in *any* sort of way, but *in a definite way*, that constitute a unit of energy, i.e., a dynamic unit. When therefore it is said that consciousness is not measurable in dynamic units, there is no denial that consciousness is measurable in time units—or even in spatial units if suitable specifications are laid down as to what is meant by the spatial dimensions of consciousness. Consciousness being intermittent, any particular instance of it begins at a certain time and ceases at a certain time; and there is no reason why its temporal dimension should not be measurable, with allowance made of course for "error." The spatial dimensions of consciousness can also be measured if we stipulate that by this term we mean the dimensions of its *field*. For instance, take the conscious factor in vision. When shut up in a lighted room at night with one eye open and for a time at rest, there is a limited spatial volume within which lie all the things I can see. If we call what consciousness thus "spans" the spatial dimension of the consciousness then involved, there is no reason why it should not be measured in spatial units. Now if I go out of doors and look at the starry heavens above me, there is again a spatial volume involved in what I see. But how large is it? Does it extend, in the different directions of the stars I see at the same time, over the respective distances at which the different stars lie from me, and if it does, what about the black I see between the stars? How far out does that reach? Such questions make it clear that any one who maintains that consciousness is *a relation* and is also spatial, has on his hands the problem of measuring consciousness in spatial units. (I am not here considering the view that everything I see is in my physical head.) But let us grant at least for the sake of argument that this problem can be satisfactorily solved. With this concession, consciousness has both spatial and temporal dimensions. But does it therewith have *mass*—"mass," i.e., as this term is used in physics?

As has already been said, it is not my purpose here to go into details; but I venture the following definition of physical mass as sufficient for my present purposes: Mass is a "quantity," i.e., a measurable character of an object, ascertainable by subjecting that object to conditions under which it is *accelerated*, and by comparing its accelerations with those of a *standard* object, i.e., a "unit of mass," under similar conditions. It is thus discovered that the ratio of the two accelerations under similar conditions is constant. The inverse of this ratio is the ratio of the *masses* of the two objects. One of these objects being the unit of mass, the numerator of the inverse ratio is the *mass of the other* object. This definition is admittedly and intentionally vague; for instance, "under certain conditions" leaves the "conditions" undefined. However, the point I wish to emphasize is that in physics no object can be intelligibly said to have mass unless it is *accelerable*, i.e., unless its velocity (zero velocity included) is subject to change, and unless its accelerations under similar conditions are comparable with those of a unit of mass, say, the gram or the kilogram. Now, it is unquestionable that objects do appear to me in succession, sometimes rapid and sometimes not; and in this sense it can be said that not only are the objects in the field of consciousness accelerable, but also their *appearings*—and, conversely, the successive consciousnesses of them—are accelerable. Do we then have two masses, or rather one *set* of masses—those of the appearing *objects*, on the one hand, and the mass of *consciousness* on the other? If we do, then does the relation of appearing act upon *what appears*, or on *the one to whom* the appearing occurs, in the same way in which there is action and reaction among the objects that appear, and action of the appearing objects upon the physical organism?

Let us take a specific instance. I wake from deep sleep and begin to see various objects; they appear to me, I am in a conscious relation to them. They have mass, my organism has mass, and the physical light which acts upon my eyes has mass. Does also the conscious relation have mass—a mass distinguishable from the other masses? This question asked, not about consciousness as a relation but about *mind* defined in various ways by various philosophers, has since the time of Descartes been answered differently by various philosophers. I do not mean that the question has been expressly formulated in terms of mass, but that the answers given—namely, interactionism, psycho-physical parallelism, epiphenomenalism, etc.—have involved mass either positively or negatively. So far as I know, this question has never as yet been asked expressly of *consciousness as a relation* between a *physical organism* and the *"objects"* of its consciousness. The reason is obvious: there has seldom been an explicit recognition of consciousness as such a relation. But any one who seeks to gain such a recognition for it has to face this question and give an explicit answer. For myself, in view of the analysis I have made, which I think discloses consciousness as such a relation, I must report that I find nothing in consciousness that qualifies it for treatment as measurable in units of mass, any more than I find any physical "massiveness"—if I may use such a word here—in the relation of cousinship. If you ask me whether first cousinship or second cousinship has the greater mass or whether they have equal physical massiveness, I can only answer by saying that the question is as meaningless as to ask whether a nova is more or less morally virtuous than an atom of helium. Each cousin has mass, but the cousinship has none.

Not only does consciousness, the relation, lack physical massiveness, but sense-qualities too lack massiveness. The seen red of a plate, the heard pitch of a sound, the felt ache of a tooth, all these are massless.

But although consciousness is not physically massive, *mind as we have defined it*, has mass, for the reason that such a "mind" is a *physical organism* — when-it-is-in-a-conscious-relation — and any such organism does not forfeit its mass on becoming a term of a conscious relation, any more than a first-born child forfeits his mass on becoming a brother of the second-born child.

Chapter III

MIND, BODY, AND EXPERIENCE

Since the view we are trying to develop considers the biological organism as one factor in mind, it is necessary for us to state the position we take as to biological organisms. The perspectivist, being a philosopher and not a biologist, must here depend upon biological experts, and is fortunate in having at hand a recent work of a distinguished neurophysiologist, Sir Charles Sherrington, who serves our purpose well in that he keeps clear the distinction between scientific physiology on the one hand and theories about mind on the other. This author offers as a "man on the street" his own theory as to the nature of mind and of its relation to the physiological organism.[1] For reasons that will appear soon I cannot accept this theory; but being myself an arrant layman in his own biological field, I gratefully avail myself of his masterly guidance as I wander therein, recognizing, of course, that expert biological opinion is not unanimous on points discussed in the passages I shall quote from him. There are still vitalists in biology. Like all other present-day scientists of the first water, he is fully aware that scientific theory proceeds on the basis of assumptions and not on "self-evident principles."

Let us begin with his own formulation of his basic assumption, which, after treating of "Life in Little," he lays down at the close of a chapter on "The Wisdom of the Body."

> Evidently the physics and chemistry of the cell can do much. Can they account for all that the cell does? That is, in short, can they account for life? Chemistry and physics account for so much which the cell does, and for so much to which years ago physical science

[1] Sir Charles Sherrington, *Man on His Nature*, New York and Cambridge, England, 1940, p. 290. By permission of Cambridge University Press.

could at that time offer no clue, that it is justifiable to suppose that the still unexplained residue of the cell's behavior will prove resoluble by chemistry and physics.[2]

This supposition holds not only of unicellular organisms but also of "compound organisms" or "individuals" as Sir Charles calls them, for we are later told:

> At first approach we might have thought, and some did think, that the integration of the individual, the making of such an individual as one of ourselves, or for that matter of our friend the dog, is a synthesis by mind. But the evidence is against that; it is the integration of the individual which brings with it the finite mind.[3]
>
> A healthy man is a set of organs of interlocking action regulating each other, the whole making a self-regulating system. It is practically a chemical system, and its means of interaction between organs is largely chemical. . . . Internally secreted substances distributed by the circulation co-ordinate the work of different organs and bring them into co-operative union. They, in a sense, integrate the many-organed creature, or body, into one working chemical organization. . . .
>
> Chemistry builds. All of that impressive growth and development which produces a child from an egg-cell is in the main chemical building, operated, regulated, co-ordinated and unified chemically. The new-born infant may indeed be said to be a product of chemical integration. . . .
>
> The motor acts of the individual [however] require co-adjustment of a swiftness and spatial precision not needed elsewhere. . . . The nervous system supplies it. . . .
>
> Integration by the nervous system is *sui generis*. . . . [It] is worked by living lines of stationary cells along which run brief potentials which, at certain places, excite or repress others. Finally, reaching muscle, they activate it. It is not surprising that this integration has the features of speed, nicety and gradation. . . . All is purely mechanical. As mechanized as is . . . the release of a spring-hammer which then releases another, and that a next, and finally a stronger spring which instead of being a bell is a muscle. . . .
>
> The mechanism is purely physical, but is not so rigid as Descartes' wheels, weights, etc. It is a network of nerve-paths, composed of branching nerve-cells, and the contact-points between the cells are nodes in the network, and these nodes introduce variability of reaction. . . . In short, nerve unifies the motor animal and gives it solidarity.[4]

---

[2] *Ibid.*, p. 135. Note that this is a supposition, an hypothesis.
[3] *Ibid.*, p. 205.
[4] *Ibid.*, pp. 208–211.

As we shall soon see, this is not all that Sir Charles has to say of the "acts" of individuals; but what has been quoted so far is purely mechanistic. He uses such terms as "mechanical" and "mechanism" to include electrical processes. I will follow his example, and even go further than he expressly does, and include in these terms whatever modifications the new "quantum *mechanics*" has introduced into mechanical theory. With this understanding I lay down

Postulate 6. Every act of every organism is mechanical and therefore expressible in purely mechanical equations.

This, of course, does not mean that any one can now write such equations, or ever will be able to do so. Where something cannot as yet be done, it is permissible to suppose that it can be done, unless some indubitable fact can be adduced that is incompatible with the supposition. Sir Charles, as we have seen, is willing to proceed on the supposition that "the still unexplained residue of the cell's behaviour will prove resoluble by chemistry and physics"; i.e., that all the acts of any single cell are mechanical. He also supposes that "all the growth and development which produces a child from an egg-cell is in the main chemical building"; and that where chemical integration fails, electrical "integration by the nervous system" supplements it. Up to and including this point, "all is purely mechanical."

> There remains, however [he finds] among the happenings met with in such a compound organism as ourselves and our like a certain residue seemingly not thus resoluble. Neither by the biologist with his analysis, nor, and even more definitely negatively, by the physicist with his analysis.
> The residual phenomena left unaccounted for by each of these analyses are the same. Since they are phenomena which seem all of one category, we may class them together. They come under the one word "mind." Energy acts, i.e., is motion. Of mind a difficulty is to know whether it is motion. . . . But in so saying we use "mind" in the meaning "recognizable mind." Mind as in everyday parlance we understand it. Mind presupposing of it what each of us experiences as "mind," feeling, knowing, wishing, and so on. . . . Both in time and space there seems a surplus of life without it. In the sense of recognizable mind, it seems a relatively novel terrestrial fact.[5]

---

[5] *Ibid.,* pp. 204–205.

But is this "recognizable mind" a stage in an evolutionary development? It is not possible here to examine in detail Sir Charles's reply to this question. The whole of Chapter IX, "Brain Collaborates with Psyche," may be regarded as an attempt to answer this question, and what I take to be the answer is given in the following sentences:

> Has the evolution of the brain produced mind out of no mind? But we have seen evolution does not create. All it does is, out of something which was, to reconstruct something further. The fundamental is still unchangeably there. Mind we think of as *sui generis*. Admittedly it seems not physical energy. The energy-concept of Science collects all so-called "forms" of energy into a flock and looks in vain for mind among them. But mind has evolved. What has mind evolved from? Has the evolution of the brain compassed the evolution of the mind or how has the evolution of the mind accompanied that of the brain? It is as though the elementary mental had never been wanting; as though evolution in dealing with the brain had taken that elementary mental and developed it until it has blossomed into evidence.
> Somewhat in that sense "emergence" is sometimes used for the evolution of mind.[6]

But however it may be with "mind near its lower limit," where it is not recognizable, Sir Charles finds himself unable to accept the view "that finite mind [another term which he uses as synonymous with 'recognizable mind'] is a product of the individual's energy system," a view according to which "the mental would in fine be a form of energy."

> Speaking for myself [he continues] I experience no inherent aversion to such a view. It has for me a certain attraction because bringing life as a whole under one monistic rubric. . . . But against that rises the difficulty that mental phenomena on examination do not seem amenable to understanding under physics and chemistry. I have therefore to think of the brain as an organ of liaison between energy and mind, but not as a converter of energy into mind or vice versa.[7]
> No attributes of "energy" seem findable in the process of mind. . . . For myself, what little I know of the how of the one does not, speaking personally, even begin to help me toward the how of the

---
[6] *Ibid.*, p. 266.
[7] *Ibid.*, p. 318.

other. The two for all I can do remain refractorily apart. They seem to me disparate; not mutually convertible; untranslatable the one into the other. . . . How can a reaction in the brain condition a reaction in the mind? Yet what have we sense-organs for, if not for that? This difficulty with sense is the same difficulty, from the converse side, as besets the problem of mind as influencing our motor acts.

I would submit that we have to accept the correlation, and to view it as interaction; body → mind. Macrocosm is a term with perhaps too mediaeval connotations for use here; replacing it by "surround," then we get surround ⇌ body ⇌ mind. The sun's energy is part of the closed energy-cycle. What leverage can it have on mind? Yet through my retina and brain it seems able to act on my mind. The theoretically impossible happens. In fine, I assert that it does act on my mind. Conversely, my thinking "self" thinks that it can bend my arm. Physics tells me that my arm cannot be bent without disturbing the sun. Physics tells me that unless my mind is energy it cannot disturb the sun. My mind then does not bend my arm. Or, the theoretically impossible happens. Let me prefer to think the theoretically impossible does happen. Despite the theoretical I take it my mind *does* bend my arm, and that it disturbs the sun.[8]

I have quoted so fully from Sir Charles because we have here a forthright statement from an eminent brain physiologist of a problem that faces every mechanistic biologist but is often evaded. There is no burking of it by Sir Charles. For him what occurs is "theoretically impossible"; and rather than gloss over the occurrence or surrender the theory, he surmises, "as a man in the street may guess," that from the materialist standpoint today, the answer to the problem is that

> Thoughts, feelings, and so on are not amenable to the energy (matter) concept. They lie outside it. Therefore they lie outside Natural Science. If you say thoughts are an outcome of the brain we as students using the energy-concept know nothing of it; as followers of natural science we know nothing of any relation between thoughts and the brain, except as a gross correlation in time and space.[9]

Knowledge looking at its world had painfully and not without some disillusions arrived at two concepts; the one, that of energy, which was adequate to deal with all which was known to knowledge, except mind. But between energy and mind, science found no "how"

[8] *Ibid.*, pp. 312–313.
[9] *Ibid.*, p. 290.

of give and take. There was co-existence; that was all. To man's understanding the world remained obstinately double.[10]

Such statements, coming from a man who had with such distinction devoted his scientific life to exploring the mysteries of the physiology of the nervous system, serve, I think, to illustrate the empirical scientific temper at its best; and to me as a man in the street, looking at the scientific structures that line it, such utterances by one who has helped to build them enable me to appreciate in some measure the merit by which he has risen to his high eminence. From long and intimate acquaintance he knows what "Natural Science," operating with the "energy-concept," has done, and he looks forward with confidence that it will do more and ever more. The province of the energy-concept he regards as the realm of the sensible, and over against this is the province of mind as the realm of the insensible; and, since mind thus lies outside the energy-concept,

> Mind, for anything perception can compass, goes in our spatial world more ghostly than a ghost. . . . Stripped to nakedness there remains to it but itself. What then does that amount to? All that counts in life. Desire, zest, truth, love, knowledge, "values," and, seeking metaphor to eke out expression, hell's depth and heaven's utmost height. Naked mind.[11]

Where theory and experienced fact are incompatible, the fault may lie either with the account given of the fact or with the theory as it is stated. Let us first consider the former alternative in the case before us. Sir Charles admits that the mind is a fact of experience: as he puts it, "the mind does experience itself."[12] But he had earlier warned us: "The word *mind* has become in some ways heir to meanings which in the history of language were once, along with others, attached to the word *soul*. It is so here. And using the word *mind* the old point of view is still current."[13] He was at the time referring to "an early tendency to ascribe every act of movement of the body to . . . the soul within,"

---
[10] *Ibid.*, p. 251.
[11] *Ibid.*, p. 357.
[12] *Ibid.*, p. 328.
[13] *Ibid.*, p. 177.

and he would strip the word *mind* of any such suggestion. But even after this stripping he still has left a "mind-energy complex which teases biology."[14] Is it not possible that, without realizing it, he has carried a strip-tease performance too far, with the unusual result that the performer himself is teased as well as his spectators? "Naked mind," that "goes therefore in our spatial world more ghostly than a ghost. Invisible, intangible, it is a thing not even of outline; it is not a thing." The perspectivist finds it hard to believe that such a mind can "amount to all that counts in life." He prefers to view the mind as it was before such an eerie divestment, a mind which like its body

> is redolent of Earth whence it is dug. Its ways affirm it to be so. Its history proclaims it to be so. Our stock is the vertebrate stock; our body is the vertebrate body; our mind is the vertebrate mind. . . . Its activities and proclivities declare it so. Its senses each and all gear into the ways and means of our planet which is its planet. . . . Ours is an earthly mind which fits our earthly body.[15]

The mind of the perspectivist too is all this because it *is* our body—not the body at all times, but the body when it is *experiencing*; i.e., when it is dynamically acting consciously, being a term of a conscious relation which is conditioned by certain dynamic processes occurring in its roof-brain. A mind so defined is, to repeat, a *dynamic* agent, but it is also conscious of whatever appears to it. Such a mind is, I think, the mind of common sense, after that mind has been reinvested with the bodily habiliments of which common sense in one of its atavistic moods has stripped it. At other times common sense, with more sense for the entirety of mind, says, for instance: "I saw him put out his foot and trip me," where it identifies the "I" that saw with the bodily "me" that fell; and to make the identification more unmistakable, it may go on to say: "When I got up, I knocked him down," where the bodily "I" that got up is the same bodily "I" that saw in the first place.

The perspectivist, in reflecting upon what is called "the prob-

---
[14] *Ibid.*, p. 350.
[15] *Ibid.*, p. 164.

lem of the relation of mind and body," takes as his starting point this unreflecting identification by common sense of the body that sees with the body that acts. This is to say that he *postulates* the correctness of this identification; and in his Postulate 6 he assumes that every act of the body is mechanical. He recognizes that there are differences among scientific biologists on this point, but he takes here the position of the mechanists as against the vitalists; and being himself a layman as respects biology, he has quoted Sir Charles as the spokesman for the mechanistic position. Let us quote another passage which states this position summarily; but in such wise as to leave the problem of mind "embarrassing for biology."

> Biology cannot go far in its subject without being met by mind. Biology as its name says is the study of life. And biology is a branch of natural science. Natural science has studied life to the extent of explaining away life as any radically separate category of phenomena . . . there is no radical scientific difference between living and dead. Time was when to think and to breathe were on an equality as attributes of life. Now, living, so far as breathing, moving, assimilating, growing, reproducing, etc., amount to life, has by natural science been accounted for—some might say, "explained." There is nothing in them which does not fall within the province of science. They are chemistry and physics. But though living is analyzable and describable by natural science, that associate of living, thought, escapes and remains refractory to natural science. In fact natural science repudiates it as something outside its ken. A radical distinction has therefore arisen between life and mind. The former is an affair of chemistry and physics; the latter escapes chemistry and physics. And yet the occurrence of mind—recognizable finite mind— is confined to a certain particular field of chemistry and physics, namely, that of highly integrated animal lives. "Thinking," in this its limited field of occurrence, appears as a phase of living. If, as is practical, we continue to subsume mind under life, we have to distinguish it as an activity of life selectively and uniquely apart from the rest. The psycho-physical difficulty places us in the position of empirics as to much. By ways which are judged roundabout, we find ourselves at length pragmatically alongside of general common sense opinion. That may be taken either as sanity or superficiality or perhaps both.[16]

---

[16] *Ibid.*, pp. 290–291.

MIND, BODY AND EXPERIENCE 81

This pragmatical attitude differs from that taken in a previously quoted passage where Sir Charles says that we have to view the accepted correlation between body and mind as an interaction which is "theoretically impossible." In the case of vision of a star, if "as to our *seeing* the star" the energy scheme "puts its finger to its lip and is silent,"[17] it cannot at the same time say that it is theoretically impossible. All that it can rightfully say is that if and in so far as seeing is more than an act occurring in the organism concerned, what is more lies entirely beyond its province. There is an alternative that is ignored when our author says in the same paragraph:

> If the energy-scheme exhaust motion and embrace all "doing" then the act of perceiving would seem not to be motion and, it would seem, is not "doing." Otherwise it would be included. So with the whole of mental experience, the energy-scheme leaves it aside and does not touch it.

The alternative is that perceiving is in part an act and in part something else. It is this alternative that the perspectivist adopts as the result of his analysis of perceiving and of what Sir Charles calls "the whole of our mental experience." As the reader has learned by now, I claim to find in every instance in which there is a process of perceiving at least three factors, viz., (1) an organism mechanically reacting, (2) with a conscious character, (3) in a conscious reaction. In the case of visual perception I postulate what the physiologist tells me "the facts assure us," namely, "that without a particular restricted piece of roof-brain vision is not possible,"[18] and this means that without some physico-chemical (i.e., mechanical) "action" taking place in that restricted piece of roof-brain there is no seeing. Now, in seeing a star, or even a typewriter in front of me, I need an optic nerve ending peripherally in a retina and ending centrally in the restricted piece of the roof-brain above mentioned. The retina reacts physically to light from the "seen" object, and a chain of mechanical reactions occurs starting from the retina, running through

---
[17] *Ibid.*, p. 305.
[18] *Ibid.*, p. 251.

the optic nerve to the restricted piece of the roof-brain (and from there through efferent nerves if there is no blockage to muscles). How much of what is expressed in the preceding parenthesis is a *conditio sine qua non* of "seeing" I leave to the physiologist to say; and Sir Charles says that "mind consorts with . . . certain *motor acts* of the nervous system."[19] Now, all this physiological activity, from retina to brain at least, I define as "the *act* of perceiving" in the case of vision; but the act is not an act of *perceiving* unless and until the organism becomes *conscious* of something. By this definition, perceiving is a complex process analyzable into a dynamic factor (namely, the above-mentioned physiological process) and a conscious factor. This conscious factor is, as we have seen, in its turn analyzable into a nondynamic conscious character and a nondynamic conscious relation; these two together we call "consciousness-of," or, more briefly, "consciousness." And what holds of perceiving holds also of remembering, thinking, wishing, willing, etc.: in each kind of case the physiological process, which is part of the whole process, is in some respect different from what obtains in a case of some other kind. In all such cases of whatever kind, we call the whole process, including the physiological processes and the consciousness, a "process of experiencing," or "experiencing" for short. Thus the *verb* "experience" as we shall use it denotes a very complex process, the physiological part of which, and only the physiological part, is an *act*—a physical or mechanical act—whereas the other part, the "consciousness," is not an act and is not mechanical.

With this definition of "experiencing," our previous definition of "mind" can be rewritten: *A "mind" is an experiencing organism when and only when it is experiencing.* When I say "mind" I say in one word what I say in the several words of the above definition.

While I am defining, let me digress somewhat and define the *noun* "experience" as I shall use it. An "experience" thus used

---

[19] *Ibid.*, p. 205, where "mind" is to be understood, he tells us, as presupposing "feeling, knowing, wishing and so on," these last three words evidently including *seeing*. The italics are mine.

is not an experienc*ing*, but it is *what* is experienced *as* it is experienced; i.e., it is the object-term, or any distinguished factor in the object-term, of the conscious relation connoted by the *verb* "experience" as above defined. Thus when I open my eyes the *whole* field of vision is my "experience" at the time I see it; and if in what I see I distinguish a typewriter that typewriter as I see it is also then an "experience" of mine. So, if I feel a pain, that pain is my "experience"; or if I remember a past event, or consciously face a problem, or believe or disbelieve a theory as to the origin of the solar system, that event or that problem or that theory, each *as* I then experience it, is my "experience" at the time I am experiencing it. Thus when I say that I experience an experience I am no more giving utterance to a meaningless tautology than I was when in a guessing game of my childhood I said bashfully, "I love my love with an *S*," hoping that Sally, one of my playmates, would know that I was not giving utterance to a tautology but that I meant *her*.

With the definition of mind given in the next to the last paragraph above we no longer have on our hands a problem improperly stated when we speak of "the problem of the relation of mind and body," any more than in our social system we have an improperly stated problem when we speak of the problem of the relation of man and husband when the man in question is the husband in question. Just as the problem of the relation of man and husband in such a case is the problem of *how* the man while still remaining a man became also a husband, so the problem of the relation of body and mind is the problem of *how* a body while remaining a body becomes also a mind. But we do have another problem; or, rather, we face the probable if not inevitable challenge that our recognition of a conscious relation which is non-dynamic and yet supervenes under dynamic conditions upon a dynamic process, is, if not a contradiction in terms, at least something that has no legitimate place in any evolutionist theory that is scientific. This gauntlet we must take up or else—

Our theory is open to attack from many sides and many are the tactical manoeuvres that are likely to be employed by its assailants. It is not possible here to indicate in detail the tactics available for defense against each of these individual offensive moves. I can consider here only those that seem to be the most dangerous, and these can be grouped together as all of them being attacks upon our recognition of nondynamical factors in a theory which at the same time assumes that every *act* of every organism is a member of the dynamical system. Sir Charles, as we have seen, regarded such an attack against his theory of mind as theoretically unanswerable. " 'Energy' proves itself a closed system, *shutting out 'mind'*," he said.[20] I have italicized the words to which I wish especially to call attention. Our present question is whether "energy" shuts out our nondynamic conscious factor, and if it does, *in what sense* does it "shut out." I have accepted from him as representing what he calls "Natural Science" the view—but modified in my acceptance—that "thoughts, feelings, and so on are not amenable to the energy-concept." But since one constituent of mind, as I have defined it, is the physical body, i.e., is "matter," "Natural Science" obviously does not shut out *that* constituent of mind. Does it shut out the conscious factor, the other constituent? If biologists, as students using the energy-concept, know nothing of it "except as a gross correlation in time and space," is this because of their exclusive attention to that concept, or is it because that concept is logically incompatible with the recognition of something in thought that is not energy? If "biology cannot go far in its subject without being met with mind," is it not rather hasty to assume that its concept "shuts out" mind in the sense of being logically incompatible with mind as we have defined mind? If "the residual phenomena left unaccounted for by the biologist with his analysis and more definitely by the physicist with his analysis" contain "all that counts in life," including knowledge,[21] and if "Natural Science" is knowledge, is it not possible that the gross correlation is itself amenable to

---
[20] *Ibid.*, p. 350.
[21] *Ibid.*, p. 357.

the method of analysis employed so successfully by physical biology—amenable without prejudice to the energy-concept? It is such questions that have prompted the perspectivist to undertake his analysis.

Fortunately he was not without invaluable assistance from a mathematical physicist of no mean standing. "Closed to mind." More than a score of years before Sir Charles employed this expression, there had appeared a volume from the pen of one who was then professor of applied mathematics in the Imperial College of Science and Technology, University of London. In this volume the author said that "in the perception of nature through the senses"

> we are aware of something which is not thought and which is self-contained for thought. *This property of being self-contained for thought lies at the base of natural science.* It means that *nature can be thought of as a closed system whose mutual relations do not require the expression of the fact that they are thought about.* . . . By this statement no metaphysical pronouncement is intended. What I mean is that we can think about nature without thinking about thought. I shall say that then we are thinking "homogeneously" about nature. . . . Natural Science is exclusively concerned with homogeneous thoughts about nature. . . . I will also express this self-containedness of nature by saying that nature is closed to mind . . . that in sense-perception nature is disclosed as a complex of entities whose *mutual relations* are expressible in thought *without reference to mind*, that is, either to sense-awareness or to thought. Furthermore I do not wish to be understood as implying that sense-awareness and thought are the only activities which are to be ascribed to mind. Also I am not denying that *there are relations of natural entities to mind or minds other than being the termini of the sense-awareness of minds.*[22]

I have italicized the words and sentences that state the thesis which is here laid down, and which I adopt as also my own and in adopting adapt to the theory of mind I am trying to work out. I do not wish to be understood as implying that the author would

---

[22] A. N. Whitehead, *The Concept of Nature*, Cambridge, 1920, pp. 3–5. By permission of Cambridge University Press. From these pages I have selected and put together into a single paragraph in the author's own words what he said in the presentation of his thesis.

subscribe to this adaptation. In this adaptation the thesis means that theoretically it is possible to describe completely *the dynamic relations between dynamic events in nature without taking into consideration any other relations or events that may occur in nature.* The subject matter of physics is the dynamic. Physical processes are autonomous, not subject to interference from anything else, natural or supernatural, divine or diabolic. The business of the physicist is to discover the "laws" of that autonomy to the end that he may express or describe in mechanical equations the mutual dynamic relations of events in the physical order. This is not to deny that the same events stand or may stand in other relations not thus describable; but it is to assume that any such other relations, if there be such, may not override by veto the orderly mechanical procedure of nature. The mechanical equations formulated up to any date may be inadequate for *complete* description of the mutual dynamical relations between physical events, and if we may judge from past performance they probably will always be inadequate. Physical relativity and quantum mechanics are the most recent instances of revision of mechanics which physicists have themselves made, and if in turn these prove to be inadequate further revision will be called for. There is no reason, however, to suppose that mathematical ingenuity cannot in the long run keep pace with problems set by discoveries facilitated by improvement in experimental technique.

Now, the perspectivist thinks that he has discovered nondynamical relations among the entities in nature, and he assumes that when such relations occur the dynamical relations continue unimpaired. On this assumption the order of nature is always a dynamical order but at times it is a more complex order. Thus at such times the dynamical order—or the "energy-scheme" as Sir Charles calls it—is "closed" to the nondynamical factors, such closure being such as Mr. Whitehead has defined it; i.e., the mutual dynamic relations then obtaining are "expressible without reference to" the nondynamic relations, notwithstanding the presence of the latter. The former are expressible in dynamic equations; the latter are not. The latter are *dynamically* "irrelevant." The former are "closed" or "indifferent" to the latter. This indifference is *by abstraction*. This is to say that the presence of the nondynamic factors is ignored—and ignored without prejudice to the relation of either kind concerned.

Neither the physicist nor the logician should cavil at such a state of affairs, since a similar state occurs in physics itself without evoking criticism from either. I say "similar," but it is a similarity with a difference to be discussed later. Meanwhile let us consider the similarity, starting with classical physics, which describes physical occurrences in equations of three-dimensional geometry, of kinematics, and of dynamics, all Euclidean. Here the geometry used in the description is "closed" or "indifferent" to the kinematics, and the kinematics to the dynamics. A physicist naturally states the respective relations involved in precisely the same words Mr. Whitehead used in defining his "closure of nature to mind." I quote from an elementary work in physics, in which the author, after treating the subject of kinematics, introduces the discussion of dynamics in these words:

> In the preceding we have considered various cases of motion *without any reference to* the influences that affect that motion of bodies, just as in Geometry we study lines and figures *without any reference to* particular bodies. We must now consider those relations between bodies on which changes of motion depend.[23]

It is to be noted that the "closure" of geometry, i.e., the absence in geometry of reference, to kinematics is one-way closure. Geometry ignores motions. (It is true that Euclid himself used motion in the proof of some of his theorems, but he assumed that figures may be freely moved in space without change of shape or size.[24] This, if I understand them aright, present-day geometers regard as a flaw in the purity of geometry.) But kinematics cannot ignore geometry; on the contrary, it avails itself of theorems of geometry, and in doing so takes them without change. Simi-

---
[23] *A Text-Book of Physics,* edited by A. Wilmer Duff, 3d ed., revised, Philadelphia, 1913, pp. 26–27. The italics are mine.
[24] See the *Encyclopaedia Britannica,* 11th ed., Vol. XI, 1910, p. 677.

larly, kinematics ignores "the influences that affect the motions of bodies," whereas dynamics, in dealing with these "influences," makes use of kinematic theorems without change.

Moreover, although present-day physics is not Euclidean we find in this physics the same principle of "closure" exemplified. Non-Euclidean geometries were developed *without any reference to* their possible uses in physics; and when Einstein tackled the problem of accelerated motion he found Riemannian geometry ready to hand. It had been "closed" to the General Theory of Relativity, but the General Theory was not now closed to it. Generalizing, it is safe, I think, to say that all applied mathematics is the application of closed systems, i.e., of systems developed without reference to possible applications. If the "mathematics" that is applied is not closed to what it is applied to it is not pure mathematics. This is not to say that in the order of temporal sequence the pure mathematics always comes before there is a demand for a mathematics to be applied. Frequently the demand occurs before the supply is available. A notable instance of this temporal sequence is the development of the theory of probability as a "branch of pure mathematics" to meet a demand for a reasonable calculation of risk in games of chance.[25] (Now that we have the mathematical theory, there seems to be as yet no agreement as to the proper technique in the application of the theory.)

What we have been saying is but an echo of Mr. Whitehead's assertion:

> The contributions of mathematics to natural science consist in the elaboration of the general art of deductive reasoning, the theory of quantitative measurement by the use of number, the theory of serial order, of geometry, of the exact measurement of time, and of rates of change.[26]

For the present we are not concerned with mathematics "as an abstract science deduced from hypothetical premises . . . we are

---

[25] *Encyclopaedia Britannica*, Vol. XX, 1911, p. 881, where the reader is "referred to Todhunter's *History of the Theory of Probability* (Cambridge and London, 1905, pp. 7–21)" for a "complete account."

[26] Whitehead, *An Enquiry concerning the Principles of Natural Knowledge*, Cambridge, 1919, p. v.

concerned with mathematics as a physical science." Nor are we concerned with the question how mathematics "is rooted in experience." The fact is that we do have mathematics as an abstract science, and that in physics we have mathematics as a physical science when it is used for the expression or description of certain mutual relations of natural entities without reference to mind.

Now, the subject matter of geometry is spatial relations; and that of kinematics is spatial relations and something more *besides,* namely, temporal relations as they are in a specifically characteristic way integrally united with spatial relations—united, that is, in the fact of motion. Using the prefix "epi-" to mean "with something more besides," we may say that kinematics is *epigeometric.* Likewise, the subject matter of dynamics is that of kinematics integrally united in a specifically characteristic way with something more *besides,* namely, the relations connoted in the definitions of "mass," "momentum" and "energy"; so we may say that dynamics is *epikinematic.* In the same way, the subject matter of the perspectivist's theory of mind is *experiencing* organisms, where "experiencing" connotes an organism's dynamic relations integrally united in a specifically characteristic way with something more *besides,* namely, a conscious relation in which the organism comes to stand and the conscious character it therewith acquires. Hence, he characterizes his theory of mind as *epidynamic* and calls his theory *epidynamicism.*

If I am asked why I should introduce a new word to name my theory instead of adopting one already current, my full reply would be too long to give here; but I can indicate the main reason for my insistent choice of epidynamicism instead of *epiphenomenalism.* This reason is that the latter word is not apt; it does not bring out the distinction between my view and that of those who have been called epiphenomenalists. The two most prominent thinkers whose views have been called epiphenomenalistic are Thomas Henry Huxley and George Santayana. Let us first consider Huxley's view. After discussion, which need not be detailed here, he says:

It may be assumed, then, that molecular changes in the brain are causes of all the states of consciousness of brutes. Is there any evidence that these states of consciousness may, conversely, cause those molecular changes which give rise to muscular motion? I see no such evidence. . . .

The consciousness of brutes would appear to be related to the mechanism of their body simply as a collateral product of its working, and to be . . . completely without any power of modifying that working. . . . Their volition, if they have any, is an emotion indicative of physical changes, not the cause of such changes. . . .

It is quite true that, to the best of my judgment, the argumentation which applies to brutes holds equally good of men; and, therefore, that all states of consciousness in us, as in them, are immediately caused by molecular changes of the brain-substance. It seems to me that in men, as in brutes, there is no proof that any state of consciousness is the cause of change in the motion of the matter of the organism. If these positions are well based, it follows that our mental conditions are simply the symbols in consciousness of the changes which take place automatically in the organism.[27]

In the page headings of the volume from which these quotations are made, Huxley called this hypothesis "Animal Automatism," not "Epiphenomenalism." On the historical record there is no evidence that he adopted or sanctioned the latter name, which was given to it after his death by a hostile critic, James Ward.[28] This author defined Huxley's "Doctrine of Conscious Automatism or Psychical Epiphenomenalism" as maintaining

---

[27] T. H. Huxley, "On the Hypothesis that Animals are Automata, and its History," an address before the British Association for the Advancement of Science, 1874, reprinted in *Methods and Results,* London and New York, 1904, pp. 239–240 and 243–244. I quote from this volume.

[28] In *Naturalism and Agnosticism,* New York and London, 1899, Ward himself did not claim credit for introducing this word into the vocabulary of English psychology and philosophy. On the contrary, he spoke of "epiphenomenon" as "the newly coined phrase" (Vol. II, p. 37), and in another passage he referred to "the dualism now prevalent among scientific men, according to which life and mind are merely concomitants of the physical, epiphenomenal as the latest phrase is" (Vol. I, p. 178). However, the great *Oxford Dictionary* fails to record any earlier occurrence of either word as "applied to consciousness as a by-product of material activities of the brain and nerve-system." I quote from the *Supplement* of 1933, in which epiphenomenalism is defined as "the theory that consciousness is an epiphenomenon, i.e., as a secondary result and by-product of the material brain and nerve system." In the main body of the *Dictionary* "epiphenomenon" is listed as first used in 1706 as a medical term, meaning "something that appears in addition; secondary symptom," and later used in meteorology.

(1) that there can be no causal connection between the psychical and the physical series, and yet (2) that the psychical is a "collateral product" or epiphenomenon of the physical. . . . Mind thus becomes impotent to control matter.[29]

The epidynamicist's insistence that his own doctrine is *not* epiphenomenalism is due to the fact that for him *mind is not impotent to control matter*, whereas in philosophical discussions of epiphenomenalism ever since Ward introduced the word into philosophical parlance it has been taken for granted that what is stated in the last sentence above quoted from Ward is an integral feature of epiphenomenalism. Since the epidynamicist repudiates this doctrine he is justified in repudiating the term "epiphenomenalist" as appropriate for his own view. His *epidynamicism is not epiphenomenalism*, dictionary definitions to the contrary notwithstanding.

Let us next pass to Santayana's view as to the way in which "mind and body" are "so closely bound together," a view that has by its critics also been called "epiphenomenalist."

The mind [Mr. Santayana said] at best vaguely forecasts the result of action; a schematic verbal sense of the end to be accomplished possibly hovers in consciousness while the act is being performed; but this premonition is itself the sense of a process already present and betrays the tendency at work; it can obviously give no aid or direction to the unknown mechanical process that produced it and that must realize its own prophecy, if that prophecy is to be realized at all.[30]

---

[29] *Ibid.*, Vol. II, p. 34.
[30] *The Life of Reason*, New York, Vol. I, 1906, p. 214. By permission of Chas. Scribner's Sons. I do not find in this work any of the words "epiphenomenon" or "epiphenomenal." (But this is by no means a proof of absence. I am a very poor finder of words even when they are there on the page before me.) However, in *The Realm of Spirit* (New York, 1940) the same author says of spirit, which "is ontologically altogether incongruous with . . . energy, motion, or substance," that it "is the *witness* of the cosmic dance; in respect to that agitation it is transcendental and epiphenomenal" (p. 8). "Other names for spirit are consciousness, attention, feeling, thought, or any word that marks the total inner difference between being awake or asleep, alive or dead" (p. 18). Like Huxley, Mr. Santayana generally avoids any technical use of the word "mind" in his later works. For instance, in tabulating "the principal words and ideas that mark the differences, the bonds, and the confusions that exist between matter and spirit," he omits the word "mind" (pp. 14–18). And yet in the same volume "mind" is by implication identified with "spirit," when in the Index we find "Mind, how explained away," with page reference to a passage which deals with spirit and does not mention mind at all.

Here "mind" and "consciousness" are identified, as they are in the whole context from which the passage has been quoted.[31] This identification by Mr. Santayana, following upon Ward's characterization of "epiphenomenalism" as a doctrine that *mind* is "impotent to control matter," led critics, from the very first appearance of this work up to the present, to say that "Santayana holds an epiphenomenalist theory of mind."[32]

If more evidence is demanded for justifying me in declining to accept the term "epiphenomenalism" as appropriate for my theory, on the ground that this term as now often understood among philosophers connotes the theory that *mind* is dynamically impotent whereas on my theory mind is dynamically efficient, I refer the reader to a prominent philosopher who, although not himself an epiphenomenalist, has given the most understanding and most sympathetic presentation of epiphenomenalism that has come to my notice.

> It seems to me [the author says] that the doctrine which I will call "One-sided Action of Body on Mind" is logically possible; i.e., a theory which accepts the action of body on mind but denies the action of mind on body. But I do not see the least reason to accept it, since I see no reason to deny that mind acts on body in volition. One-sided Action has, I think, been held in the special form called "Epiphenomenalism."[33]

I agree heartily in seeing no reason to accept "epiphenomenalism" as Mr. Broad defines it; and since his definition gives the connotation of the term as understood by other competent philosophers, I see no reason for presenting my theory with an accepted label that is likely to lead to needless misunderstanding. A "newly coined word" is preferable to confusion; therefore I insist on calling my theory *epidynamicism*.

We have considered the similarity between the three "states of

---

[31] See for instance p. 212.
[32] See Professor Eliseo Vivas's excellent paper in *The Philosophy of George Santayana*, edited by Paul Arthur Schilpp, Evanston and Chicago, 1940.
[33] C. D. Broad, *The Mind and its Place in Nature*, New York and London, 1925, pp. 117–118. The passages in which he discusses epiphenomenalism will be found by use of the excellent Index.

affairs," (1) motion involving space, (2) energy involving motion, and (3) mind involving momentum and energy, postponing consideration of a dissimilarity which is crucial. This dissimilarity consists in the innovation found in mind on the one hand and not found in motion or in momentum and energy on the other. All empirical evidence points to what we therefore assume to be a fact, namely, that space, motion, momentum, mass, and energy are coeval; that there never was a time when there was space without any motion somewhere in space, and never any motion without momentum, mass and energy somewhere. All these have always been coexistent. But not so with mind. As Sir Charles says: "In the sense of recognizable mind, it seems a relatively novel terrestrial fact,"[34] and this holds of mind as we regard it as well as of mind in Sir Charles's theory.

Sir Charles takes a glance at the problem of "mind near its lower limit. What of a mind . . . which is perhaps merely a blind urge toward food, or a call toward light, or into shadow?"[35] If by "blind" be meant "without conscious character in conscious relation," our definition of mind rules out any such "mind." At what point in organic evolution, then, did mind first come into being; or, more precisely stated, at what point did organisms become minds? I do not undertake even to guess. But I do assume that at some point this happened, and I agree that—as Sir Charles goes on to say—"mind as we know it has for this present its acme in the mind of man." And this agreement brings us face to face with the question he then poses: "Has the evolution of the brain produced mind out of no mind?" Our answer to this question is not the answer he gives, viz., "But we have seen evolution does not create." Here he refers to an earlier passage in which he has said:

> I would be clear as to what we mean by "new" evolving from "old." "New" signifies here no more than a fresh arrangement, a reconstruction, a novel combination, of parts, the parts themselves not other than those existent before. . . . There, as is usual where "crea-

[34] Sherrington, *Man on His Nature*, p. 205.
[35] *Ibid.*, p. 266.

tion" is spoken of, he [Bergson] means that something new springs into being *de novo*. On the contrary, any [evolution] is in fine after all a reshuffling.[36]

Our theory differs from Bergson's as much as does Sir Charles's, and for this reason we dislike the expression "creative evolution," which has acquired from Bergson as well as from older sources a connotation alien to our theory. For Bergson creative evolution is primordial; the *élan vital* is an *élan originel*, and not a relatively novel terrestrial fact. The mechanical order is a construction, or rather perhaps a misconstruction, by the intellect, a fabrication by *homo faber* interested in smithing and not in intuiting the real. One cannot, however, do justice to Bergson in a few words. The words that he himself uses to express his views are misunderstood if an attempt is made to understand them intellectually. They must be understood by sympathetic imagination, not by reflective analysis; and since the perspectivist obtains his own theory by reflective analysis he can contrast his own views with Bergson's only by presenting his own in terms that Bergson could not have accepted rather than by presenting Bergson's in terms that Bergson would have regarded as doing them justice. Therefore I contrast my views with Bergson's by saying that in the order of time that was not first which was conscious (even in the form of instinct) but that which was purely mechanical; and afterward that which is conscious. Since this is not the temporal order in *l' évolution créatrice*, I prefer not to call my view of evolution by the name of "creative evolution." Nor do I wish to adopt the term "emergent evolution" which has become current among philosophers.[37]

The word "emergence" suggests, unintentionally no doubt, a coming to the surface of what has previously been in being but submerged and latent, hidden. For this reason "emergent evolution" seems a rather unhappy choice for a name of a theory that

---

[36] *Ibid.*, pp. 138–139.
[37] See *Emergent Evolution*, by C. Lloyd Morgan, New York and London, 1923, where an account of the history of the word "emergent" in philosophy is sketched in Lecture I.

something, the like of which has never occurred before, occurs in the course of evolution. Let us therefore call our theory "innovative evolution," and let us call this sort of a novelty as well as its occurrence an "innovation."

The same reason for declining to use "emergence" may of course be urged against the word "evolution," which etymologically implies the unrolling of what has been already there but folded up. However, the latter word has become so firmly rooted in our language since the publication of *The Origin of Species* that the very refusal of any one to use it would almost inevitably lead to more confusion than clarification, if the refusal were also accompanied with the acceptance of Darwin's main thesis; whereas "emergence" in the sense that it now has in philosophical discussion is itself a more recent innovation. Lamarckians, Weismannians, DeVriesians, Bergsonians, emergentists, and who not — all agree as to the meaning of the general concept of "evolution," however they may differ as to the "methods" involved; and even theological "fundamentalists" use the word "evolution" in the same meaning, although they will have none of it. It is too late to object to the word as naming what Mr. Whitehead has perhaps more aptly called "the advance of nature."

Sir Charles Sherrington is not alone among scientists when he says: "All [evolution] does is, out of something which was, to construct something further. The fundamental is still unchangeably there."[38] Here "to construct" means to rearrange according to the "old principles"; and if it is a matter of chemistry, to rearrange according to "the old chemistry, still the same chemistry as was in essence before life came"—a chemistry which admits of "a rich extension of endless variety within certain limits. The old principles comprise it." But it "shows no *fundamental* departure."[39] In our theory, too, there is no fundamental *departure* so far as concerns chemistry and physics; we travel the same old chemico-physical road, firmly metalled as before, but because we

[38] *Man on His Nature*, p. 266.
[39] *Ibid.*, p. 139.

who course it are minds we contribute what in us dynamically lies to what is dynamically occurring, while at the same time innovating *values* that but for us and our likes would never be. All this by magic if you will; but the magic is nature's magic, no whit supernatural. If you insist on something super, call it super*material*.

Thus in our epidynamicist theory, too, evolution shows no *fundamental departure*, since in an organism, when by innovation it becomes a mind, the same *kind of chemical and physical processes* still occur, *uninfluenced dynamically* by the innovation. They are "closed to mind" in the sense and only in the sense that theoretically they are still "expressible" in dynamical equations "without reference to" *the innovation* wherewith the organism becomes a mind. There is no *departure from* chemistry and physics, but there is *addition to* chemistry and physics. The addition, so we claim, is not one that our analysis unwarrantably foists upon nature but one that *naturally occurs in the orderly process of nature*—if we may be allowed the redundancy. We are not multiplying entities beyond necessity; we are only recognizing nature's own multiplication. It is not for any empiricist to say to nature: "You can't do that: only thus far and no farther can you go." If personifyingly we talk to nature in that way, she is likely to talk back and say: "I can go as far as I damn please, and you will go with me or be scientifically damned."

Before proceeding further, let us name other innovations than consciousness, further analyzable into conscious character and conscious relation. One important group of innovations consists of innumerable "sense-qualities" such as seen colors, heard sounds, and pains. These occur when an integrated organism is reacting to specific physical stimuli acting physically upon specific receptors. The *physiology* of the whole process is, on our assumption, purely physical. It belongs to what Sir Charles calls the energy-scheme. But at some stage during the course of this reaction something occurs which is not physical. Take the case of a retina of a "normal" human being, a physiological receptor organ reacting to physical light of a certain wave frequency. As we are told, "it is misleading to call the organ a sense-organ" except as it becomes "a gateway to the mind."[40] But this way of describing what occurs is in terms appropriate only to such a theory of mind as Sir Charles's. In terms of our theory we should say, "except as the organism becomes conscious of a color, say red, specific to the physical stimulus that initiated the physiological process." A red, occurring under these conditions, we call a "sense-quality." (For the present we leave out of account the spatial and temporal characters sensed when we sense a red.) Were the wave frequency acting on the receptor different, the organism would be conscious of another sense-quality, say, blue. Neither the red nor the blue is a member of the energy scheme; it has no momentum; it has no mass; it has no energy. It is, additional to all that, supervening upon events in the energy scheme but not dynamically acting upon what is dynamically occurring. In short, it does not break or interrupt the continuity of dynamic processes. On the other hand, the abstract "scheme" of which it is a member has no continuity of its own—no continuity that is other than temporary, lasting it may be through a livelong day but ceasing entirely with a deep sleep, during which abated physiological processes still carry on over the intermission of the flux of sense. "Great nature's second course" is part of her only continuous course, antedating the course of sense; sense-qualities are a dessert, served now and served then as physiological occasions give the cue.

But to prevent misunderstanding let me hasten to say that I have been speaking of "the order of genesis," not of "the order of discovery"; of the *ordo essendi*, not of the *ordo cognoscendi*; or, as I should prefer to say, of the *ordo existendi*, not of the *ordo experiendi*. What is first experienced by any human organism is in all probability either affects or sense-qualities, with the greater likelihood that it is affects, or perhaps both together, but not at the time distinguished.

---

[40] *Ibid.*, pp. 179–180.

I refer here to what Sir Charles calls "the bodily phenomena of affect," which "pertain" to "an ancient piece of brain, of no great size, which relatively modern parts have outgrown and overgrown," the "old brain of 'affect'." (This little piece of brain is known in anatomy as the *cerebellum*.)

In his article on the physiology of the brain contributed to the 11th edition of the *Encyclopaedia Britannica*, Vol. IV, 1910, Sir Charles had said: "Consciousness . . . does not seem to attach to any portion of the nervous system of higher animals from which the fore-brain has been cut off." "In the lower vertebrates [however] it is not clear that consciousness in primitive form requires always the co-operation of the fore-brain." He goes on to say: "The behaviour of some Insects points strongly to their possessing memory, rudimentary in kind though it may be. But in them no homologue of the fore-brain of vertebrates can be indisputably made out. . . . Though, therefore, we cannot be clear that the head ganglia of these Invertebrates are the same structure morphologically as the brain of vertebrates, they seem to hold a similar office . . . including psychosis of a rudimentary kind." His reason for this conclusion is that their "behaviour . . . points strongly to their possessing memory, rudimentary in kind though it may be" (p. 404). But in all this he assumes that what is often called *organic memory* (See Webster, "Memory," 8b) carries with it *conscious memory*.

In the thirty years that had elapsed between 1910 and 1940 endocrinology made enormous advances, if indeed it might not be said that it began as a special science during this period. This fact accounts for any differences between what Sir Charles said in the sentences above quoted and what he says in *Man on His Nature*:

> It would seem that to [the cerebellum] pertain the bodily phenomena of affect. Emotion comprises motor behaviour and mental experience. . . .
> When the roof-brain is gone, the emotional storms generated by this same ancient piece of the brain produce emotional effects which are spoken of as pseudo-affects. . . . Exhibition of "rage" breaks forth

and subsides like a summer shower; it seems a mere motor presentment of rage stripped of mental counterpart. That such divorce can be is certain, after yet deeper mutilation. With this focal part of the brain still active it may be that emotion is back again at something like its primordial essence. A drive, an urge, an added tension; perhaps that is all, but yet a physical reinforcement of its motor act.

To say that this is an ancient piece of brain is to say that it is part of our brain which still continues that of man's animal ancestral and related stock of long ago. It has meant in them, and still does so, fear, rage, and passion; it does so also with man. . . . But over it the roof-brain is a new brain so developed in man as to be the "human feature." It stands for knowledge and reason.[41]

Note the admirable reserve with which the author speaks. While recognizing that emotion comprises *motor* behavior and *mental* experience, yet when the roof-brain is gone, an exhibition of "rage" *seems* "*mere motor presentment* of rage stripped of mental counterpart"; *perhaps* that is all, but yet a physical reinforcement of its motor act. And yet when in man the roof-brain is there, it stands for *knowledge and reason*. It is there that " 'thought' gets into touch with motor behaviour and the intent of the motor act with the motor act itself."

The perspectivist would adopt this same attitude of caution. No one can know with any degree of assurance whether an animal whose roof-brain has been disconnected from its cerebellum has "mental experience" or a "mere motor presentment of rage stripped of mental counterpart," and I can think of no way in which this question could be put to the test.

James called a human babe's first experience "one big blooming buzzing Confusion."[42] Whether during an organism's prenatal life it has experiences, and if it does when its experiencing begins, are questions we must leave to physiologists within whose province any probable answers lie. We have already quoted Sir Charles as saying that science has found no how of give and take between energy and mind, although biology cannot go far in its subject matter without being met by mind. It would seem therefore that

---
[41] *Ibid.,* pp. 231-232.
[42] *Psychology, Briefer Course,* p. 16.

biology should be able to tell us (if any science can) when recognizable mind is met in its study of a human organism's physiological development.

Confining ourselves to limits within which evidence of some sort is available, let us assume that the part which the cerebellum plays in conditioning the consciousness of affect-qualities is analogous to that played by receptors in conditioning the occurrence consciousness of sense-qualities. Thus specific hormones chemically acting specifically upon "the old brain" and through it *upon the roof-brain* are the specific dynamic stimuli that give rise to what we call fear, anger, "pep," etc., just as light waves of different frequency are the specific dynamic stimuli that give rise to what we call red, blue, green, etc., *only if* the roof-brain is in its turn stimulated.

There is another possible misunderstanding of epidynamicism that is to be expected and needs to be forestalled. Epidynamicism does not imply, as a critic may charge, that if there were no consciousness in the world the dynamical course of nature would run precisely as it does in our actual world, in which there is consciousness. Such a conclusion foisted upon the epidynamicist might be allowed to pass if his only assumption were that the mutual dynamic relations of dynamic events are closed to consciousness. But he also postulates that if and when certain specific dynamic events occur in any organism's brain the organism becomes conscious. From this assumption it follows, as every logician knows, that if any organism does not become conscious those specific dynamic events assumed to condition consciousness do not occur. Therefore it is an integral part of the epidynamicist's theory that if no organism ever became conscious, i.e., *if there were no consciousness in the world, the dynamical course of nature would not run precisely as it does in our actual world in which there is consciousness.* The two courses differ by the absence, from one of the courses, of the specific dynamic events that in the other course are assumed to condition the occurrence of consciousness;

and the points at which the differences would be first found are the points at which *consciousness is found* by the epidynamicist's analysis in the actual world.

In saying this, the epidynamicist is not dogmatically asserting that his analysis and his theory based on that analysis are not open to question; he is merely safeguarding his theory against an anticipated misunderstanding by pointing out that such a misunderstanding could result only from the identification of two theories diametrically opposed to each other—an identification made possible only by a flagrant commission of a notorious fallacy.

Of course it is possible to suppose a world in every dynamical respect like the world the epidynamicist postulates, but unlike his world in that there is no consciousness in the former anywhere and at any time. The epidynamicist himself has to suppose such a world in order meaningfully to repudiate it as not being the world he assumes. He even can and sometimes does with interest suppose the world of the Arabian Nights, in which by contrast there is consciousness but not the dynamic order of his assumed world. He finds delight in supposing with Lewis Carroll the Wonderland of Alice, beautifully organized logically but with a dynamics in many respects the reverse of that assumed in his own world. He entertains as guests any of these suppositions and, as we shall see, tries to find a place for them in his assumed world; but when one of them tries to usurp by cuckoo-birthright a place that belongs to a permanent member of his philosophical family he draws the line.

With the above discussed misunderstanding cleared away, let us turn our attention to the argument from survival value as it applies to our theory:

> Nothing is clearer [says Sir Charles] than that in her process of Evolution [Nature] evolves in living creatures characters which, largely as they spell advantage or disadvantage to the individual life, tend to survive or disappear. . . . Since life is a system of energy a character to be of advantage or disadvantage to that system must influence that system. Nothing is clearer than that mind has evolved. Mind therefore has had survival value. Mind it would seem then

has an influence which Nature finds can count for advantage to the energy-system colligate with it, the body.[43]

The epidynamicist agrees in substance; but since for him any mind is a dynamic organism when it is experiencing, he distinguishes between the admitted relevance of this argument to the *dynamic constitution* of the organism, and its questioned relevance to the organism's *nondynamic consciousness*. The brain, often called "the organ of mind," has had by and large an inestimable survival value. Insect, spider, and man—not one of these would have survived without the kind of brain it has to integrate its reactions to its environment in which food was to be found, a mate to be copulated, and enemies to be conquered or avoided. Had the energy that went to the building of the brain in any species or genus been expended in the development of something less conducive to success in "the struggle for existence," the result would have been a tactical if not a strategic defeat. This is because the quantity of energy available in any organism is finite: the more there goes to the development of any organ, the less is left for something else. But such give-and-take transactions occur *within the energy-scheme*. If anything occurs meanwhile that is by assumption not part of the energy-scheme, by that same assumption it is irrelevant to the give-and-take of energy within that scheme. Since energy is expended only within that scheme no energy goes to the production of any nondynamic event. To put down in black and white for purposes of ready reference, let us lay down in explicit terms

Postulate 7. A dynamic event (i.e., a member of the energy scheme) may be a condition of the occurrence of a nondynamic event without transference or "transformation" of any of its energy into the nondynamic event which it conditions.

To elucidate the position here taken, let me use a frequently mentioned analogy between the work of a mathematical physicist and that of a financial accountant. A correct balance sheet of a

---

[43] Sherrington, *Man on His Nature*, p. 351.

corporation summarizes its financial transactions consisting of its receipts and expenditures, without taking into account the joys or griefs that may accrue to its stockholders from the net profit or net loss disclosed. The abstractness of accountancy is no bar to the successful accomplishment of the accountant's task. Financial matters and financial matters alone are his concern. He may suspect the presence of nonfinancial matters, such as for instance the president's infatuation with a beautiful blonde; but such presence is neither here nor there for him, except as it may bring to light unrecorded withdrawals of funds or records of financial transactions that did not occur. If he discovers no evidence of anything of this kind the balance sheet is correct, whatever may be the weal or woe entailed. Weal or woe is, to coin a hybrid word, epifinancial. So the mathematical physicist is a physical accountant concerned with physical transactions reported to him by experimental physicists as occurring in nature. Physicists, mathematical and experimental, work on the assumption that

energy can be neither created nor destroyed (except as it can be changed into matter under certain extreme conditions, and produced from matter), but it can appear in any of a dozen or more forms.[44]

Any philosopher whose concern is with "recognizable mind" as well as with the physical world may indeed decline to adopt this assumption. But the perspectivist does not, for he has great respect for expert opinion on any subject with regard to which he is himself a mere layman. Expertness is of course not infallibility; but when the methods by which expertness has been acquired are those which he assumes to be the best available he chooses to go along with the experts. In the case before us he has no criticism to make of the methods employed by physicists; consequently he adopts the assumption on which they proceed. But as I have pre-

---

[44] George Russell Harrison, *Atoms in Action*, Revised edition, New York, 1941, pp. 8-9. Even the exception here "proves the rule"; it is regularized by use of units of energy-mass and not of energy alone. In my account above I have for simplicity's sake ignored this recent revision of the older assumption of the "conservation of energy." I am glad to be permitted to quote from a competent physicist this succinct translation into the vernacular of the assumption of present-day physicists, which of course they technically phrase in mathematical language.

viously emphasized, the assumption here adopted is to be construed literally as concerning only the mutual relations of the *dynamic* events in the *energy* system: no measurable amount of *energy* arises *ex nihilo dyamico* or lapses *in nihilum dynamicum*. The assumption is not to preclude the arising or the lapsing of anything that is *not* dynamic. Of anything not dynamic it is "silent," as Sir Charles says. It has no veto power any more than the financial auditor's assumption that the assets and liabilities of a corporation must balance has veto power over the happiness or unhappiness of the shareholders. In fine, in subscribing to the Constitution of the energy system, the epidynamicist stipulates that the powers not delegated to the energy system by its Constitution, nor prohibited by it to Nature, are reserved to Nature. And in the interpretation of that Constitution he is a strict constructionist. He agrees (but with a reservation to be noted later) when Mr. Whitehead says:

> We may not pick and choose. For us the red glow of the sunset should be as much part of nature as are the molecules and electric waves by which men of science would explain the phenomena. It is for natural philosophy to analyze how these various elements of nature are connected. . . . We are instinctively willing to believe that by due attention more can be found in nature than that which is observed at first sight. But we will not be content with less. What we ask from the philosophy of science is some account of the coherence of things perceptively known.[45]

But while thus agreeing heartily that the red glow of the sunset should be as much part of nature as are the molecules and electric waves, I find it impossible to regard it as a part of nature without bringing into consideration "the synthesis of the knower and the known," which Mr. Whitehead "leaves to metaphysics."[46]

> The philosophy of a science [he tells us] is the endeavor to express explicitly those unifying characteristics which pervade that complex of thoughts and make it a science.

According to this definition *mathematical* physics is the philos-

---
[45] Whitehead, *The Concept of Nature,* p. 29.
[46] *Ibid.,* p. 28.

ophy of the science of physics, which the British often still call "natural philosophy."

When the Michelson and Morley and other similar effects were discovered, physicists unified them with previously discovered physical phenomena by means of the mathematics of the physical theory of relativity. When quantum effects were discovered, unification with previously discovered physical phenomena was achieved by means of mathematics, this time by matrix algebra. Meanwhile chemistry, which had been more or less independent of physics and had as its unifying characteristic the mutual behavior of atoms, has been undergoing correlation with physics by mathematical treatment of electrons. Biological phenomena also have been subjected to similar mathematical treatment, and so with phenomena studied in other "special" sciences. In this movement we find "the endeavour to exhibit all sciences as one science," and so far as it is successful we have what Mr. Whitehead calls "the philosophy of the sciences," or "the philosophy of science." This philosophy gives some account of "things perceptively known"; i.e., of things with such extensively measurable properties as mass and momentum—a unification, however, only with respect to such properties.

But what has all this to do with the red glow of the sunset, "the greenness of the trees, the song of the birds, the warmth of the sun, the hardness of chairs, and the feel of the velvet"?[47]

"The molecules and electric waves by which men of science would explain" these phenomena and thus unify our experiences into one nature unbifurcated do not belong to *nature as Mr. Whitehead defines nature*: namely, "Nature is that which we observe in perception through the senses." This is to say that nature is the terminus of sense-awareness.[48] That the former proposition is intended as a definition of nature is evident from the context:

> What [he asks] do we mean by nature? We have to discuss the

---
[47] *Ibid.*, p. 31.
[48] *Ibid.*, pp. 3–4.

philosophy of natural science. Natural science is the science of nature. But—what is nature?
Nature is that which we observe in perception through the senses.

On the following page he "repeats the main line of this argument, and expands it in certain directions":

> Thought about nature [he tells us] is different from the sense-perception of nature. Hence the fact of sense-perception has an ingredient or factor which is not thought. I call this ingredient sense-awareness. It is indifferent to my argument whether sense-perception has or has not another ingredient. If sense-perception does not involve thought, then sense-awareness and sense-perception are identical. But the something perceived is perceived as an entity which is the terminus of sense-awareness, something which for thought is beyond the fact of that sense-awareness.

The expansion of the author's argument in this direction therefore makes it clear that when he defines nature as "that which we observe in perception through the senses," he means that *nature is the terminus of sense-awareness.*

Now this definition, like every other definition, not only tells us what is meant by the defined term, but also what is not meant. So, just as the definition of a plane triangle tells us that what is not a plane figure bounded by three lines is not a plane triangle, so the above definition of nature tells us that what we do not observe in perception through the senses is not nature. Now, I submit that we de not observe either electric waves or electrons in perception through the senses. They are not "termini of sense-awareness," and therefore not what the author calls "natural entities."[49]

---

[49] *Ibid.*, p. 13: "Thus there are three components in our knowledge of nature, namely, fact, factors, and entities. Fact is the undifferentiated terminus of sense-awareness; factors are termini of sense-awareness, differentiated as elements of fact; entities are factors in their function as the termini of thought. The entities spoken of are natural entities. Thought is wider than nature, so that there are entities for thought which are not natural entities."

My argument here is that, *with Mr. Whitehead's definition of nature,* since only such termini of sense-awareness, when they become entities for thought, are natural entities, and since electric waves and electrons are not termini of sense-awareness, undifferentiated or differentiated, they are entities for thought which are not natural entities.

"This is surely a muddle," as Mr. Whitehead said of the bifurcationist view he was opposing. We no longer indeed have two natures of which "one is the conjecture and the other is a dream." The former nature, consisting of "the entities such as electrons which are the study of speculative physics," is shorn away with one devastating clip of a definition, leaving as the only nature what in the opposed theory our author called "the byplay of the mind."[50] With the roles thus reversed there is no progress toward unification. To call this result a "bifurcation" would be an understatement. It is dis-furcation. Nature is dis-furcated of her main enduring stem.

But, as Horace discovered long ago, nature has a way of coming back with a vengeance:

> Namely the *immediate fact* for awareness is *the whole occurrence of nature*. It is nature as an event present for sense-awareness, and essentially passing.[51]

What I have italicized calls attention to the overstatement here as contrasted with the understatement of the definition which we have been considering, and which we must now consider to be an inadvertence. There *is* a wholeness about nature such that it includes all conjectures and all dreams as well as all sense-awareness and all valid thought. But this wholeness is not an immediate fact for sense-awareness, although *for thought* nature is disclosed in sense-awareness. To say that for sense-awareness, defined as an ingredient in sense-perception that is not thought, the immediate fact is the whole of nature is at the very least to commit the psychologist's fallacy. What subsequent reflective analysis recognizes as red spatially-extended-and-passing is, for example, "recognized in reflection as an immediate fact for sense-awareness," an "undifferentiated terminus of sense-awareness." For the perspectivist "the concept of nature" is a slowly developing achievement, in which a sense-awareness, sense-perception, memory, imagination, reflective analysis, inference, and

[50] *Ibid.*, p. 30.
[51] *Ibid.*, p. 14.

even abstract thought, have played a part; and *nature*, now resultantly conceived by him, *is a whole including everything that occurs and every relation in which any occurrence stands*. (The present tenses of the verbs used in the definition are *general*, not specific.) It is from nature *thus defined* that "we may not pick and choose." Nature thus defined embraces in its tolerant bosom every intolerance and every tolerance, every sin and every virtue, every error and every truth, every devil and every god, every nightmare, however frightful and every daydream however futilely entrancing—in short, nature, being catholic and ecumenical, is everything.

One often hears nowadays the objection raised against such an all-inclusive term that in meaning everything it means nothing, there being nothing to distinguish it from—as if the totality it means cannot be distinguished from the parts it includes! We need some term to denote any "universe of discourse," and this is true even if the universe of discourse happens to be the universe of all discourses about nature. Mr. Whitehead's philosophy of nature is "the philosophy of the thing perceived," and he insists that it "should not be confused with the metaphysics of reality of which the scope embraces both the perceiver and the perceived."[52] But he finds "a definite factor in nature . . . an event in nature which is the focus in nature for that act of awareness."

> I call it [he says] the "percipient event." This event is not the mind, that is to say, not the percipient. It is that in nature from which the mind perceives. . . . This percipient event is roughly speaking the bodily life of the incarnate mind.[53]

From this it is clear that he has himself a definite "metaphysics" —definite at least to the extent that for him mind is not a part of nature, although roughly speaking it is "incarnate in the bodily life" of an organism that is a part of nature. "Sense-awareness" is an "act" of the mind, which has a *locus standi* in nature but is not a part of nature. "Percipience in itself" as an act of mind

---
[52] *Ibid.*, p. 28.
[53] *Ibid.*, p. 107.

he "takes for granted." He "considers indeed the conditions for percipience, but only so far as those conditions are among the disclosures of perception,"[54] leaving, as we have seen, "to metaphysics the synthesis of the knower and the known." Thus he states the problem of "the philosophy of nature" from the point of view of a metaphysics which excludes mind from nature. From this point of view,

> Objects are elements in nature which do not pass. The awareness of an object as some factor not sharing in the passage of nature is what I call "recognition" . . . the non-intellectual relation of sense-awareness which connects the mind with a factor of nature without passage.
>
> An object is an ingredient in the character of some event. In fact, the character of an event is nothing but the objects which are ingredient in it and the ways in which those objects make their ingression into the event.[55]

All this, be it remembered, is part of Mr. Whitehead's philosophy of nature, a philosophy that leaves "the synthesis of the knower and the known . . . to metaphysics." The Cambridge blue of a coat, like the red glow of the sunset, is a part of nature, but a part that "does not share in the passage of nature";[56] it is recognized as such a part by "the non-intellectual relation of sense-awareness which connects the knower [i.e., the mind] with a factor in nature without passage"! If this is not metaphysics, "a synthesis of the knower and the known," what is? Although the author does not in this volume give the name of "eternal objects" to his "sense-objects," he is with an innocent surreptitiousness resorting to a Platonic metaphysics to bring blues and red into nature by the process of "ingression" or "ingredience." The red of a sunset is not an event: it does not occur; what occurs is only its ingression!

It is not my purpose here to try to do justice to the "concept of nature" presented in the volume under consideration. There is much in it of great value that any one interested in the philosophy

---
[54] *Ibid.*, p. 28.
[55] *Ibid.*, pp. 143–144.
[56] *Ibid.*, p. 149.

of science should not ignore—very much more than the quotations I have made from it would lead any one to suppose. When all there is in it is seen in its interrelations, what has been quoted appears in a new light. What I have been trying to do is to show that if "the philosophy of science is the philosophy [only] of the thing perceived, and [if] it should not be confused with the metaphysics of reality of which the scope embraces both perceiver and perceived,"[57] then Mr. Whitehead's philosophy of science resorts to another kind of metaphysics, that of Plato, than which no metaphysics is more metaphysical. Its scope embraces the ingression of "objects which are neither new nor old,"[58] an ingression which my sense-awareness at least has never disclosed as occurring. If "to travel beyond the entities which are disclosed in sense-awareness" is to be metaphysical, I prefer to travel in the direction of a metaphysics whose scope embraces both perceiver and perceived, since I have a prejudice in favor of treating as natural entities not only the perceived but also the perceivers. I rather suspect that many a "perplexity concerning the object of knowledge can be solved by saying that there is a mind knowing it."[59] Among these perplexities is that concerning the glow of the sunset which I perceive as here red and there violet with other shades between, whereas my neighbor reports that he is aware of none of these. Again, natural scientists have convinced me that nature throughout enormous slabs of its duration embraced nothing of what we know as percipience and as perceivers; but those earlier slabs, as objects *of present knowledge*, involve me in bewildering perplexity when I am told that those very scientists *as percipients and as thoughtful* are not parts of nature, that "thought is wider than nature, so that there are entities for thought which are not natural entities." What is this thought that now is and apparently formerly was not? Has it also, like sense-objects, made ingression into nature, being like them

---
[57] *Ibid.*, p. 28.
[58] *The Principles of Natural Knowledge*, p. 98.
[59] *The Concept of Nature*, p. 28.

"neither new nor old"? If so, why does it not, like them, become part of nature? Why "pick and choose" here? The perspectivist is "instinctively willing to believe that by due attention, more can be found in nature than that which is observed at first sight." But on this point he "will not be content with less." What *he* "asks from the philosophy of science is some account of things" *scientifically* as well as "perceptively known."

If "science is not a fairy tale,"[60] we know at least in outline a past in which, as yet, the conditions for thinking as well as for perceiving, such as *our* perceivings and *our* thinkings are, were not in existence. This is to say that in scientific geology the temporal direction in which the things thought about lie from the scientist is opposite to that of "Time's Arrow," which points in the direction that dynamical processes are assumed always to take.[61] Time as a process "flows" always from earlier to later. To say this is to utter a tautology, as we shall see when we take up in detail the topic of time, whose direction is irreversible. An event A that is earlier than some other event B never becomes later than *that* event B. There may conceivably occur a still later event A' *exactly* like event A in every character and in every relation *but one*, so that we may have the temporal sequence $A\ B \ldots A'\ B'$; but the fact that A' comes after B whereas A came before B differentiates A' from A as events. We have something like this occurring on the dial of a clock every twelve hours, where the minute and the hour hands come respectively into coincidence with the same numerals twice every twenty-four hours; but the afternoon coincidences, occurring twelve hours later than the forenoon coincidences, are not identical events, being differentiated by the very fact that the afternoon events occur later than those of the forenoon. Entire identity requires precise similarity not only of all characters but also of *all* relations; similarity of all relations *but one* is not enough. What goes by the name of a "recurrence" of an event

---

[60] *Ibid.*, p. 40.
[61] The expression "Time's Arrow" is of course taken from Sir Arthur Eddington.

is not the occurring again of *that* event.[62] Nietzsche's "Eternal Recurrence" is a temporal *sequence* of temporal sequences, one *after* another and therefore none of them identical with any other.

If this irrevocability of the past is not conceded by the reader as an "axiom," he will please regard it as an *assumption* made by the perspectivist. It is an assumption that is made by every physicist in his dynamical theory. It can be expressed by saying that no dynamical effect can dynamically react upon its cause in such wise as to make that cause *have been at the time it occurred* other than it actually was at that time. It can only make it be *at a later time* other than it *had been before*. If any one is disposed to doubt the tenacity with which physicists hold to this assumption, let him read what Sommerfeld says about the case where if anywhere an effect can act *temporally* back upon its cause. As is well known there is a spatio-temporal region, in the theory of relativity, where an event e_1 is, in the calendar of S, one of two relatively moving systems, earlier than event e_2, whereas it is later than e_2 in S', the other system's calendar. Why then may not a dynamic emission from e_1 reach e_2, which in S is, as we have seen, later than e_1 in S', and if this is possible then in S' it has reached e_2 before its emission from e_1, and in reaching it *dynamically* effect it? Laue's reply is that such an emission would have a velocity of propagation greater than the velocity of light, which according to the principle of relativity is impossible. Sommerfeld's reply is that in the theory of relativity one can define processes geometrically—I presume he means in *abstract* geometry—with velocities greater than light; but such processes cannot "serve as signals"; i.e., one cannot at will start a signal which "sets going a relay" earlier at the point of reception. Each of these authors, like any other physicist, knows that if in the physical theory of relativity a later dynamic process could effect a change

---

[62] An instance of a crushing exploitation of such a recurrence is the witty reply of the head master of a school to his subordinate: "My friend, in reality you haven't had 20 years' experience. You have had one year's experience 20 times." *Reader's Digest*, June 1945, p. 114. The editor called this "Broken Record"; shouldn't it be *Un*broken Record?

in an earlier process while that process was still earlier, the doom of the theory would be sealed.

Let us put this assumption more briefly by laying it down as our *Postulate 8. No physical action is mechanically retroactive.*

Here "action" is used as synonymous with *change*, and the "retro" in "retroactive" is to be interpreted in the temporal sense, *backward from later to earlier.* The temporal direction of physical action is from temporal antecedent to temporal consequent. Applying this to the dynamic reactions of organisms to physical stimuli, we say that all such actions proceed futurewards. We occasionally hear something in the dynamic order called "physiological memory" or even "chemical memory"; but according to our present postulate this is only a striking figure of speech, a psychomorphism. There is no more memory here than in the automobile which runs more smoothly now that it is broken in, or in a ship that has found herself. Any one may call such present frictionless or balanced ease of action a "result of learning from experience" if he will—he may call anything by any name that pleases him—but only on penalty of confusion. If "experience" is to mean anything else than a series of actions more or less alike but showing a progressive lack of mechanical resistance; if "learning" is to mean anything more than the progressive dynamic resultant of previous reactions, such that the character of the performance becomes in some respect more and more pronounced, then a forest fire as it sweeps over a larger area is learning from experience: the higher the temperature the more rapidly it burns whatever it reaches. To call this "learning from experience" is to rob the phrase of any distinctive meaning. The epidynamicist's analysis reveals that dynamically and thus biologically we live forwards in time, but that in sensing, perceiving, and remembering, and often in thinking, we are conscious backwards; and that only as we thus sense, perceive, remember, and think do we ever understand either forwards or backwards.[63] But none of this can we

---

[63] Cf. "a saying of Kierkegaard's to the effect that we live forwards, but we understand backwards." James, *Essays in Radical Empiricism*, p. 238.

do if sensing, perceiving, remembering and understanding are nothing but dynamic actions, since the direction of consciousness is from conscious subject to the object of consciousness. We can do all this only if in the doing of it there is besides a dynamic factor also a nondynamic factor, which in being nondynamic is not limited to the uniform direction from earlier to later which all dynamic processes take—if, in short, although we are never retro*active*, we are often retro*spective*, notwithstanding. But retrospection is literally a looking backwards, conditioned by what is dynamically going forwards in the brain. Unless therefore there is in looking backwards a factor that is not dynamic, there is no such thing as retrospection, since all dynamic processes march only forwards.

This is why the epidynamicist rejects all forthright and exclusive "scientific" materialisms, all "under-the-hat theories of mind"[64] and of consciousness, and any exclusively "instrumental theory of knowledge." To be more specific, he rejects any "scientific materialism" because it is a totalitarianization of the energy scheme of modern physical science, unmindful of the fact that the knowledge of this scheme has been acquired by scientists who retrospect. We must distinguish between the energy scheme and any *knowledge* of such a scheme. By observing under controlled conditions, by *remembering,* and by making records by observation later *interpreted as records of past*, by analyzing and reasoning, scientists have acquired knowledge that that scheme existed and operated long before there were any men to know. The words italicized in the preceding sentence bring to attention some of the retrospection involved both in the data used and in the conclusion reached by physical scientists. The under-the-hat theories of mind are rejected for the same reason. It is not possible here to examine these theories in detail; but we may take Mr. Roy Wood Sellars's "philosophy of physical realism" as an outstanding representative of such theories. If I mistake not, the key words in his theory

---

[64] See *The Philosophy of Physical Realism,* by Roy Wood Sellars, New York, 1932, pp. 411 ff. Quotations from this work by permission of The Macmillan Co.

of perception, conception and judgment are "polarized pattern" and "directed activity."

> That there is ... biological configuration in perception seems to me undeniable [he says]. ... And to me the field of consciousness always *expresses* organic pattern. The polarization of the one is prefigured in the polarization of the other. ... I take it that projicience, or projection as Lloyd Morgan uses these terms must not be taken literally as a kind of shooting out of anything into the external world. Rather it is a clarification of spatial pattern, as is notably the case with vision and audition, with a sense of the organic self polarized in the background. In projicience, we have a spatially organized field deepened with motor and attitude meanings. *In short, it is around sensory presentations that the sense of external thinghood develops.* In prospective reference, we have a development of temporal pattern in terms of images, meanings, and anticipatory attitudes. ... As I see it, a percipient organism falls into a percipient attitude towards the external thing being perceived. This attitude involves a polarization which appears in consciousness as sensory presentation deepened in meaning and terminating what we experience as *interested awareness*. Thus projicience is really a functional configuration resting upon an objective situation.[65]

The "objective situation" here is the physical action of a physical object, say an apple, upon a physical organism, which thereupon reacts to the stimulus. In the brain, meanwhile, there occurs as a link in the chain of physical processes a physical event, "intrinsic" to which ("but more the quality of the event than simply equatable with it") is a "sense-datum," say red. This red is "given," but the physical apple is not "given." However, though the physical apple is not given, it is *perceived* as red, since "perceiving is a directed activity," and the direction of this activity conforms to the direction of "the response of the organic percipient which is towards the object." Thus the vector or directional configuration in the field of consciousness *expresses* the vector or directional configuration in the physical field of organic response. And what holds for perception "holds equally for conception and judgment."[66] Stated in terms of "meanings," Mr. Sellars's view is that we consciously mean the things to which our organisms are

---
[65] *Ibid.*, pp. 87–88.
[66] *Ibid.*, pp. 412, 148, 69, 68.

physically responding. When our minds mean something physical they intend, or refer to, but do not in experience reach what they mean; for

> the feature of meanings is that they are logical contents which are realized only in acts of thought. Being on the inside of our mind, we become aware of meanings as understood contents while all this awareness is intrinsic to, and inseparable from, the configurated pulse of consciousness sustained by brain activity.[67]

Thus in perception sense-data play a double role. On the one hand, they "are literally in the brain," but "as qualitative events in the brain and not qualities of the brain." On the other hand, they "are enveloped in a directed complex of meaning in the perceptual experience."[68]

Barring the way to the acceptance of this view by any physical realist who also accepts the dynamical theory of physicists, I find two incontestable facts—at least I cannot contest them. The first concerns the spatial direction of organic responses, not all of which are directed spatially *toward* the objects to which the organisms are responding. Responses which are recoils or flights from physical objects play an important part in human and other animal life. How, for instance, would Mr. Sellars with his theory account for the response to the perceived color of burning gas in an explosion? We do indeed speak of the percipient organism as reacting *to* the physical stimulus; but physically the spatial configuration is reaction from. The perceptual configuration here fails to "reflect" the physical. The second bar to the acceptance of Mr. Sellars's view is that the *temporal* vector in the physical response of an organism to stimulus is always forwards, whereas in the "mental operation" of perceiving it is backwards. In vision things in our immediate neighborhood are perceived so soon after the stimulation occurs that the difference between before and after escapes attention. Only after experiment had disclosed that light from object to eye and the physiological process coursing along the optic nerve from retina to brain—to which according to Mr.

---
[67] *Ibid.*, p. 343.
[68] *Ibid.*, pp. 412, 143, 202.

Sellars the sensed color is intrinsic—have finite velocity did it become known that the time of perceiving is later than the time of the object seen. With this knowledge it has become impossible to maintain that the temporal configuration of the "mental operation" of seeing reflects that of the physiological response involved in seeing. Literally, in seeing we always look backward in time and react forward. The perspectivist, facing this difficulty and yet attempting to maintain a realistic position with regard to perception that accords with all that is known of physical operations, finds it necessary to assume that in perception there is something more than physical processes—something vectorial, of course, but with its vector opposite in direction to that of the physical vector involved, and yet not *dynamically* opposed. The only kind of thing that he can conceive of as having these requisites is an asymmetrical nondynamic relation. Being asymmetrical it is vectorial; being nondynamic it is not dynamically opposed to the physical vector. "Consciousness" as we have defined it conforms to these specifications. It has, as we have seen, a nondynamic relation of a specific sort in its connotation.

This assumption of consciousness as having a nondynamic relation in its connotation is not *ad hoc*; it applies to *memory*, realistically interpreted, as well as to perception. Consciousness in memory is directed toward the past. It applies to *thought*; we think about a past we have never perceived. How much would be left of scientific geology and of the scientific doctrine of evolution if scientists did not think about the Archeozoic and other prehuman eras? Or, for that matter, what would become of fundamentalist theology if theologians and their lay followers did not think about "the beginning," when God created the heaven and the earth some days before he made man? So far as human records go man has always thought about a prehuman past, starting from Chaos and Dark Night or from some other beginning or quasi beginning. The assumption applies to *emotions*: men resent past insults, pride themselves on past achievement, and regret past follies. The assumption even finds application in jurisprudence;

in some jurisdictions we have what are called "retroactive laws." But what is dynamically "active" here is subsequent, i.e., prospective, *enforcement*; and what is "retro" here is retro*spection* upon a past when the law was not upon the statute book. This is, of course, a very sketchy account of what occurs when any one—be he legislator, tax collector or payer, judge or juror—is concerned with a "retroactive" law, and has any ideas about it as a law that deals with the past. Such a one has dynamic processes occurring in his brain, whose action is forward in time while those ideas being directed backward are thereby shown to be not dynamic.

So far our attention has been centered on the retrospective feature of consciousness, but of course consciousness may be and perhaps more often is directed forward. When it is thus prospective, its temporal direction is the same as that of the dynamic process in the brain which conditions it. But this is not the whole story. Prospective consciousness has a temporal reach as well as a temporal direction. When I plan to do something twenty-four hours from now, in some sense that time tomorrow is in my mind now. For our theory this sense is that tomorrow is the terminus of the conscious relation which is a distinguishable factor in mind. As we shall see in a later chapter, time for us is itself a complex relation one of whose components is the relation of before-and-after. To anticipate dogmatically what I hope to develop more fully later, let me say that since tomorrow is not yet in being, today *is not yet* before tomorrow. We are *consciously* foreseeing a tomorrow which dynamically is not yet, and which only when it eventuates will supply the forward dynamic terminus "tomorrow" for the relational complex, today-dynamically-before-tomorrow.[69] But when twenty-four hours from now, say 9 A. M., January 2, will have automatically elapsed, then and not till then *will* 9 A. M.,

---

[69] When Sir Charles Sherrington speaks of the mind as "providing us with time" (*op. cit.*, p. 316), he is speaking a truth but only a half truth. Mind provides us with a future, to plan for and talk about before in the natural course of events it automatically eventuates. Time past and present is a discovery of the mind; and if "invention" is discovery of what is not yet but will be, then time future is "an invention of the mind" (p. 271).

January 2 *have become* dynamically twenty-four hours earlier than 9 A. M., January 3. It cannot have become twenty-four hours earlier till the twenty-four-hour lapse has been completed.

Thus since *elapsing* time, time *ongoing*, is one of the relations constituting the dynamic order, at any time this order extends temporally forward only so far as time in its dynamical ongoing is reaching. As Bergson suggests—but not as he interprets it—impatience is a measure of the difference between the dynamical process of living and life's conscious order in which alone anticipation occurs. No purely dynamic event predicts what will come to pass. But a mind, i.e., a conscious organism, which has learned from its own past experience and from that of others the "how" of the dynamic order, can and does predict because it can and does look before and after. Its consciousness, "outstripping the hours," in its own way reaches—often falteringly and faultily—the issue first, while what is physical in the organism keeps step with the hours and has therefore to bide its time. (But even to speak of *its* biding its time is to commit the pathetic fallacy.) The very errors of any mind are proof of the immateriality of the factor in mind that makes errors possible. No purely material process ever errs, but neither is it ever inerrant. Errancy and inerrancy imply a path *already* laid down *to be* followed, whereas any purely physical process lays down its own path as it goes along. This is usually expressed by saying that the "laws of nature" are not prescriptions that "nature" has to obey. Thus what Bergson says of time as lived[70] the epidynamicist says of the time of dynamic processes. It is only for a mind that anything that has not yet happened, as for instance an eclipse, will happen. The epidynamicist cannot stress too strongly or too frequently that for him memory and mind involve a factor which shows itself to be nondynamic in that it temporally overreaches what anything dynamic can do at the time.[71] This temporal overreaching is mind's

---

[70] *Creative Evolution*, translated by Arthur Mitchell, New York, 1911, pp. 9–10.
[71] *Time and Free Will*, tr. by F. L. Pogson, London and New York, 1910, pp. 181–183. Bergson's error lies in his assumption that "mathematical time," i.e., time as it appears in the equations of physics, is "spatialized" or "spread out instan-

"transcendence" of the dynamic—a transcendence which is epidynamic in that the mind which in its *conscious* reach transcends the dynamic is at the same time a *dynamic organism*.

The recognition of this fact, that the mind while it is conscious is also dynamic, is its declaration of emancipation from the "oppression to the heart and paralysis to imagination" which affect those who contemplate "a picture of a world of things indifferent to human interests because it is wholly apart from experience."[72] The world of "scientific objects," as it is viewed by the epidynamicist, is not disconnected from "the affairs of primary experience"; neither is it "fixed and final." It is a world of things dynamically going on, of which he himself is one. He is a dynamic part of all that he dynamically meets, reacting to the dynamic action of things upon him, and in turn acting upon such of them as are within his dynamic reach. He has physically thrown his weight about, sometimes happily as when he helped push his car out of the mud with the aim to keep an appointment; but sometimes unhappily, as when he fell down the stairs while rushing to get a screw driver in the basement. In the former case he got what he wanted; in the latter he got a sprained ankle, which was not what he wanted, and he did not get the screw driver. But in both cases the result was presumably describable in dynamical equations, although no one knows enough of what was taking place in his brain to enable him to write the equations. However, he suspects that no opponent of epidynamicism knows enough to justify him in denying dogmatically that the consciousness accompanying the dynamic processes then occurring were nondynamic. What is important for our theory is that it is the same organism, the same "I," that is dynamically acting in both cases, at one time willingly, at the other time unwillingly. If the "I" that desires and hopes

---

taneously in space." This is not the place for tarrying to belabor this error. Suffice it to say that the spreading out of time symbols, such as t_1, t_2, t_3, on a page no more proves that the times symbolized are thus spread out in space than the fact that the word "red" is printed in black on a page proves that the author thinks of red as black.

[72] John Dewey, *Experience and Nature*, 2d. ed., Chicago and London, 1926, p. 11.

and fears were merely a spectator he would indeed be powerless to affect the course of events. But what reason is there to suppose that an "I" thus disconnected from the world of scientific objects, from material nerves and muscles and glands, could exist in this world of ours, or that if it could it would desire and hope and fear as we human organisms do? Everything we scientifically know about our emotions and imaginations justifies the assumption that they are conditioned by what takes place in our nervous systems; and a philosopher is playing both ends against the middle when he supposes a world "wholly apart from experience," whose goings on can oppress human hearts and paralyze human imaginations.

The only unquestionable access that anyone has to another's mind is through his body, whether it be by physical words and cheerful mien or by the more drastic method of injection of such a drug as sodium pentothal.[73] Similarly, the only means by which discussion can be carried on by any one who seeks to secure agreement on a disputed point is physical. Of course the debaters must understand each other's language, but this understanding has been acquired by previous "conditioning" of the disputants to the meaning of the words employed. This conditioning is in principle similar to that by which Pavlov's dog came to salivate in reaction to sound waves from a bell. Mr. Dewey's argument in the passage last quoted from him can secure the result desired by him only if by "ideo-motor action" the reader becomes oppressed in heart and paralyzed in imagination on contemplating the picture he paints; and the present writer in his reply uses similar physical means to overcome that effect. Whichever of us can secure the desired brain reaction in his reader will win the argument. Each is acting with aim, but the aiming is conditioned by brain action.

This is not to say that there is no such thing as logic. Logic is consistency of conclusion with premise. But consistency is one thing; consciousness of consistency is another. Anyone who has

---

[73] See the *Reader's Digest*, July, 1945, p. 89.

taught logic to a rather dull student remembers the pains he has taken to exhibit instances of consistency and inconsistency; this exhibition was by use of *physical* symbols. All teaching, whether of logic or physics or the appreciation of music, in the last analysis is by use of physical means which act physically upon the brains of pupils. He is the best teacher who can best bring about the brain reactions that in their turn condition the desired conscious processes.

Chapter IV

CONSCIOUSNESS IN OTHER PHILOSOPHIES

Since a philosopher does not bombinate in a vacuum but is always indebted to those who have gone before, as well as to his contemporaries, it is fitting that a philosophy which in any way differs from its predecessors should be seen in historical perspective. This is especially true of a view that accentuates perspectivity. In what follows I shall largely confine myself to consideration of the philosophers of our own century to whom I have been most indebted in arriving at the identification of consciousness as a relation of a specific kind.

Let us begin with Mr. G. E. Moore, whose "Refutation of Idealism" appeared in 1903. He sums up his analytic findings in one paragraph:

> The true analysis of a sensation or idea is as follows: The element that is common to them all, and which I have called "consciousness," really *is* consciousness. A sensation is, in reality, a case of "knowing" or "being aware of" or "experiencing" something. When we know that the sensation of blue exists, the fact we know is that there exists an awareness of blue. And this awareness is not merely . . . itself something distinct and unique, utterly different from blue; it also has a perfectly distinct and unique relation to blue, a relation which is *not* that of thing or substance to content, nor of one part of content to another part of content. This relation is just that which we mean in every case by knowing." . . . To be aware of the sensation of blue is . . . to be aware of an awareness of blue; awareness being used, in both cases, in exactly the same sense . . . though philosophers have recognized that *something* distinct is meant by consciousness, they have never yet had a clear conception of *what* that something is. They have not been able to hold *it* and *blue* before their minds and to compare them in the same way in which they can com-

pare *blue* and *green*. And this for the reason . . . that the moment we try to fix our attention upon consciousness and to see *what*, distinctly, it is, it seems to vanish: it seems as if we had before us a mere emptiness. When we try to introspect the sensation of blue, all we can see is the blue: the other element is as if it were diaphanous. Yet it *can* be distinguished if we look attentively enough, and if we know that there is something to look for. My main object in this paragraph has been to try to make the reader *see* it: but I fear I shall have succeeded very ill.[1]

This analysis results in finding "consciousness" to be a *term* of a relational complex, whose *other term* is the "object of consciousness," and whose *relation* is a "distinct and unique relation," indicated by the preposition "of," but given no name. In contrast with this analysis is that of a perspectivist, who considers *consciousness* to be itself a unique and distinct asymmetrical relation, whose terms are an organism on the one hand and the "object of consciousness" on the other. If this latter analysis is correct, the reason why Mr. Moore's effort to make the reader "see" consciousness may have "succeeded very ill" is that he has not told the reader *what* it is that he should look for. The reader should look for a relation in which he, an organism, stands to what he sees, or hears or remembers or thinks about—a relation in which he does not stand when he is said to be unconscious, as for instance when he is in deep sleep. (What Mr. Moore called the diaphaneity of consciousness is characteristic of many relations; for instance, of the relation of distance in which a seen object stands to me. I see through the distance between it and me.)

Let us now turn to William James's view of consciousness:

I believe [he wrote] that "consciousness," when once it has evaporated to this estate of pure diaphaneity [as in Mr. Moore's account],

---

[1] *Mind*, N. S., 1903, pp. 449–450. This essay was reprinted in *Philosophical Studies*, New York: London, 1922, where the passage above quoted will be found on pp. 24–25. Attention however should be called to the comment the author makes on the paper in the Preface to the *Studies*: "This paper now appears to me to be very confused, as well as to embody a good many downright mistakes; so I am doubtful whether I ought to have included it. But in this case I have another excuse: namely, that it is a paper to which a good many allusions have been made by contemporary writers on philosophy; and I was told that, for some readers at all events, it should be reprinted along with the rest, if only for the sake of reference." As will very soon appear, this is also my excuse for quoting from the paper.

is on the point of disappearing altogether. It is the name of a nonentity, and has no right to a place among first principles. Those who cling to it are clinging to a mere echo, the faint rumor left behind by the disappearing "soul" upon the air of philosophy. During the past year, I have read a number of articles whose authors seemed just on the point of abandoning the notion of consciousness, and substituting for it that of an absolute experience not due to two factors. But they were not quite radical enough. . . . It seems to me that the hour is ripe for it to be openly and universally discarded. . . . Let me . . . immediately explain that I mean only to deny that the word stands for an entity, but to insist most emphatically that it does stand for a function. There is, I mean, no aboriginal stuff or quality of being, contrasted with that of which material objects are made, out of which our thoughts of them are made; but there is a function in experience which thoughts perform, and for the performance of which this quality of being is invoked. That function is *knowing*. "Consciousness" is supposed necessary to explain the fact that things not only are, but get reported, are known. . . .

My thesis is that if we start with the supposition that there is only one primal stuff or material in the world, and if we call that stuff "pure experience," then knowing can easily be explained as *a particular sort of relation* towards one another into which portions of pure experience may enter. The relation itself is a part of pure experience; one of its "terms" becomes the subject or bearer of the knowledge, the knower, the other becomes the object known.[2]

If asked what pure experience consists of, the reply, he says, is easy:

Although for fluency's sake I myself spoke early in this article of a stuff of pure experience, I have now to say that there is no *general* stuff of which experience at large is made. There are as many stuffs as there are "natures" in the things experienced. If you ask what any one bit of pure experience is made of, the answer is always the same: "It is made of *that*, of just what appears, of space, of intensity, of flatness, brownness, heaviness, or what not. . . . Experience is only

---

[2] "Does 'Consciousness' Exist?" in the *Journal of Philosophy*, Vol. I, September 1, 1904, and posthumously reprinted in *Essays in Radical Empiricism*, by William James, New York, etc., 1912. The passage quoted in the text will be found on pages 2–4 of this volume, but without the italics in the last paragraph. This volume contains reprints of twelve articles all together, eleven of which had been "written consecutively within a period of two years"; thus, as Professor Ralph Barton Perry noted in the "Editor's Preface," they "form a connected whole." (In a footnote Dr. Perry is credited with being "frankly over the border" in having already discarded "the notion of consciousness" as having a place among first principles.) The reader should note that the word "Consciousness" in the title of the paper under consideration is in quotation marks, a fact sometimes ignored by critics.

a collective name for all these sensible natures, and save for time and space (and, if you like, for "being") there appears no universal element of which all things are made.[3]

None of these bits of pure experience *"has any such inner duplicity"* as to admit of analysis into consciousness and content; *"and the separation of it into consciousness and content comes, not by way of subtraction, but by way of addition*—the addition, to a given concrete piece of it, of other sets of experiences."[4]

When we reflect upon our experiences we may freely say that

> at the outset nothing was there in us but a flat piece of substantive experience like any other, with no self-transcendency about it, and no mystery save the mystery of coming into existence and of being gradually followed by other pieces of substantive experience, with conjunctively transitional experiences between.[5]

Consciousness is one type of these conjunctively transitional experiences. A pure experience is, as it were, a single undivided cell, which proliferates—the metaphor is James's own[6]—and consciousness is a connective tissue that comes into existence between different experiential cells when the process of cell-division has advanced to a certain stage. In this metaphorical way of putting the matter, each cell, being an "undivided portion of experience," is of course thought of as atomic.

Any "one self-identical thing," such as a room that appears in your "personal biography,"

> has so many relations [which are "transitional experiences"] to the rest of experience that you can take it in disparate systems of association, and treat it as belonging with opposite contexts. In one of these contexts it is your "field of consciousness"; in another it is "the room in which you sit," and it enters both contexts in its wholeness, giving no pretext for being said to attach itself to consciousness by one of its parts or aspects, and to outer reality by another. . . . As a room, the experience has occupied that spot and had that environment for thirty years. As your field of consciousness it may never

---

[3] *Essays in Radical Empiricism*, pp. 26–27.
[4] *Ibid.*, p. 9. On the same page the author speaks of a "given undivided portion of experience."
[5] *Ibid.*, pp. 57–58.
[6] *Ibid.*, p. 87: "That one moment of [experience] proliferates into the next by transitions which, whether conjunctive or disjunctive, continue the experiential tissue, can not, I contend, be denied."

have existed until now. . . . As a room, it will take an earthquake, or a gang of men, and in any case a certain amount of time, to destroy it. As your subjective state, the closing of your eyes, or any instantaneous play of your fancy will suffice.[7]

But in whatever context we take it, a room, or anything else that is recognized in the philosophy of radical empiricism, must be directly experienced, for

> To be radical, an empiricism must neither admit into its constructions any element that is not directly experienced, nor exclude from them any element that is directly experienced. For such a philosophy, *the relations that connect experiences must themselves be experienced, and any kind of relation experienced must be accounted as "real" as anything else in the system.*[8]

But what of a room when it is not directly experienced by you or by your neighbor?

> The beyond must, of course, always in our philosophy be itself of an experiential nature. If not a future experience of our own or a present one of our neighbor, it must be a thing in itself . . . that is, it must be an experience *for* itself whose relations to other things we translate into the action of molecules, ether-waves, or whatever else the physical symbols may be. This opens the chapter of the relations of radical empiricism to pan-psychism, into which I can not enter now.[9]

If the reader were to object that the very expression, "an experience *for* itself," implies an inner duplicity, James would, I think, have said that the objection rests upon a fallacious attribution to the experience of a distinction which only the objector recognizes: the objector commits the psychologist's fallacy. In the "experience for itself," *what* is experienced and *its experiencing* constitute "an undivided whole," and it is the objector that divides or distinguishes the two "factors." The experience itself does not. The two "phases," distinguished by the objector (and also by James himself when he philosophizes) so "interpenetrate" in the "experience *for* itself," that no "points, either of distinction or of identity, can be caught."

---
[7] *Ibid.*, pp. 12–14.
[8] *Ibid.*, p. 42.
[9] *Ibid.*, pp. 88–89. Cf. pp. 94 and 188–189.

But our present interest is not in this phase of his philosophy; we are now interested only in his "pure experience," which is the basis on which his philosophy of radical empiricism was based. Is there anything in his ostensive definition of "pure experience" which may equally well serve as an ostensive starting point for our definition of "consciousness"? Like James, the perspectivist asks you, the reader, to take your own experiences in order to see what he means.[10] Is "any one bit of pure experience" which "is made of just what appears" and is "directly experienced" ever experienced by you except as it appears *to you*? Note that James said there is nothing *in us* but "a flat piece of substantive experience." But let us go on with James:

> Only new-born babes, or men in semi-coma from sleep, drugs, illnesses, or blows, may be assumed to have an experience pure in the literal sense of a *that* which is not yet any definite *what*. . . . Pure experience in this state is but another name for feeling or sensation. . . . Its purity [after the flux of it has come] is only a relative term, meaning the proportional amount of unverbalized sensation which it embodies.[11]

But when "sensation" is used as a name for a "sensible nature," such as "brownness," or let us say a pain, can you, taking your own experiences, point back to any brownness or any pain that did not at the time of its occurrence appear to you? If you are a psychologist you may answer: "It is true that I *now in retrospect* regard a pain as having been my pain; but at the time of its occurrence the pain was just there, but not there as *my* pain; nor was it there as an *appearing* pain. If in claiming to describe it *as* it was experienced when it occurred I were to describe it *otherwise than* as it was experienced when it occurred, I should be committing what James called '*the psychologist's fallacy*,' no matter how much I now know about what else occurred then and how these additional occurrences were related to what was *experienced* then." If you say this, you will be bringing up a nice problem which must be discussed, and will be discussed, more fully at a

---
[10] *Ibid.*, p. 11.
[11] *Ibid.*, pp. 93–94.

later time. Meanwhile let us note that in the papers we are examining, James was writing not as a psychologist but as a philosopher who only a few years later called philosophy "a Weltanschauung, an intellectualized attitude toward life." [12] As such a philosopher he was recognizing pure experience "in the literal sense of a *that* which is not yet any definite *what*." But when he added, "full both of oneness and of manyness," he was not describing a "pure experience" as it is when it is experienced: he made this clear when he went on to say, "but in respects that don't appear." When he said this he was speaking as a philosopher for whom experience was *then* flowing "as if shot through with adjectives and nouns and prepositions and conjunctions," and for whom, as he tells us in the immediately following paragraph, the flux of experience, "both as a whole and in its parts, is that of things conjunct and separated."

Now, whatever may have been the origin of the use of words by human beings, "later reflection with its conceptual categories"[13] recognizes the category of relation, to which James gave much clarifying attention. Let us quote again:

> The conjunctive relation that has given most trouble to philosophy is *the co-conscious transition,* so to call it, by which one experience passes into another when both belong to the same self. About the facts there is no question. My experiences and your experiences are "with" each other in various external ways, but mine pass into mine, and yours into yours in a way in which yours and mine never pass into one another. . . . Personal histories are processes of change in time, and *the change itself is one of the things immediately experienced.* "Change" in this case means continuous as opposed to discontinuous transition . . . and to be a radical empiricist means to hold

---

[12] *Some Problems of Philosophy*, New York, 1911, p. 6. In the preceding sentence he had said: "Any very sweeping view of the world is a philosophy in this sense, even though it may be a vague one." What the sentence quoted above in the text adds is that this view, to be a philosophy, is an intellectualized attitude, one— and now he quotes Mr. Dewey—"of conjoined intellect and will." Of course "intellect" and "intellectual" must be understood here in James's meaning for these terms.

[13] " 'Pure experience' [said James, *Essays in Radical Empiricism,* p. 93] is the name which I gave to the immediate flux of life which furnishes the material to our later reflection with its conceptual categories." Again: "The instant field of the present is at all times what I call the 'pure experience.' It is only virtually or potentially either object or subject as yet" (p. 23).

fast to this conjunctive relation of all others . . . to take it at its face value [which] means first of all to take it just as we feel it, and not to confuse ourselves with abstract talk *about* it, involving words that drive us to invent secondary conceptions in order to neutralize their suggestions and to make our actual experience again seem rationally possible.[14]

The perspectivist agrees; but in agreeing he would italicize some other words also, thus calling attention to something in James's definition of this conjunctive relation which James slurs over in *this* passage: this relation is the transition "by which one experience passes into another *when both belong to the same self.*" This belonging "to the same self" is part of the very essence of the co-conscious transition. But what *is* "the same self"? As we saw in the preceding chapter, James had given one answer to this question: the self is a pulse of cognitive consciousness which, born knowing its predecessor and finding it "warm," greets it, saying: "Thou art mine, and part of the same self with me." This was written by James the psychologist as of 1890. Now let us quote from James the psychologist as of 1904:

> There is no direct evidence that we feel the activity of . . . "consciousness" as such. . . . The individualized self, which I believe to be the only thing properly called self, is part of the content of the world experienced. The world experienced (otherwise called the "field of consciousness") comes at all times with our body as its centre, centre of vision, centre of action, centre of interest. Where the body is is "here"; when the body acts is "now"; what the body touches is "this"; all other things are "there" and "then" and "that." These words of emphasized position imply a systematization of things with reference to a focus of action and interest which lies in the body; and the systematization is now so instinctive (was it ever not so?) that no developed or active experience exists for us at all except in this ordered form. So far as "thoughts" and "feelings" can be active, their activity terminates in the activity of the body, and only through first arousing its activities can they begin to change those of the rest of the world. . . . The body is the storm centre, the origin of co-ordinates, the constant place of stress in all that experience-train. Everything circles round it, and is felt from its point of view. The word "I," then, is primarily a noun of position, just like "this" and "here." Activities attached to "this" position have prerogative

---

[14] *Essays in Radical Empiricism,* pp. 47–48.

emphasis, and, if activities have feelings, must be felt in a peculiar way. The word "my" designates the kind of emphasis. . . . The "my" [of "my" activities] is the emphasis, the feeling of perspective-interest in which they are dyed.[15]

The perspectivist here takes his stand with James, with such change of statement as is involved in the difference between us as to what the "field of consciousness" proves itself to be for one who makes "an unusually obstinate effort to think clearly." Here as elsewhere in James's philosophical writings the perspectivist finds the makings of his own philosophy, needing only to be organized under some such postulates as I have already laid down. James's works are one of the richest mines a philosopher can find to delve in. But it needs to be mined. When the ore is brought to the surface and treated by one process it yields one type of philosophy; when treated by another process it yields another. Otherwise put, the making of a philosophy is not altogether unlike Kipling's "nine-and-thirty ways of writing tribal lays." The theme may be the same but the finished results are different, and each may at least to a certain extent be right. Each of us deals with what James called "the content of the world experienced," but with different assumptions or presuppositions; or, if you like, with different prejudices. The perspectivist with his "prejudice" gets, like James, "the individualized self"—the body, an organism—as the center of "the field of consciousness," "center of vision, center of action, center of interest." He gets the field of consciousness as "just what appears." He gets consciousness as a relation. So far he is Jamesian. But he gets this relation, not as a relation between what are already experiences on their own account—which is James's way of getting it—but as a relation which makes an experience out of anything. Anything becomes an experience only when it appears—to an organism. Conversely stated, anything becomes an experience only when an organism becomes con-

---

[15] "The Experience of Activity," the President's Address before the American Psychological Association, December, 1904, first published in the *Psychological Review*, Vol. XII, 1905, and now here quoted from a reprint in *Essays in Radical Empiricism*, pp. 169-171, and from *The Pluralistic Universe*, pp. 379-380.

scious—of the thing. This is the fundamental difference, the difference which underlies perhaps all the other differences between James's radical empiricism and our perspectivism. And perhaps this fundamental difference can best be brought out by italicizing and putting in brackets only four words which James used in the following paragraph and which the perspectivist would delete:

> The puzzle of how the one identical room can be in two places is at bottom just the puzzle of how one identical point can be on two lines. It can be, if it be situated at their intersection; and similarly if [*the 'pure experience' of*] the room were a place of intersection of two processes, which connected it with different groups of associates respectively, it could be counted twice over, as belonging to either group, and spoken of loosely as existing in two places, although it would remain all the time a numerically single thing.[16]

In one case the connection is by *dynamic* relations; in the other case by a *conscious* relation. Less than four months after James had published his paper, "Does 'Consciousness' Exist?" Professor Woodbridge read a paper before the American Philosophical Association on "The Nature of Consciousness," in which he expressed himself as

> in hearty agreement with many recent discussions of consciousness, especially with that of Professor James, which aims to take consciousness out of the realm of terms and put it into the realm of relations. But there are some points of disagreement which I should like to note. These recent views aim to define consciousness as, in some way, a function within experience whereby experience itself becomes differentiated into the objective and the subjective, into the physical and the psychical, into the objects of the outer world and the events of a personal biography. That such a differentiation arises in the course of experience is, I suppose, beyond question. But I have been unable to discover that the differentiation throws light on the nature of consciousness. The differentiation simply divides the field of consciousness into two parts, but does not isolate a separate field in which alone consciousness is found. Physical objects just as much as personal histories may be objects of consciousness. Both are known. And to know the physical world does not convert it into autobiog-

---

[16] *Essays in Radical Empiricism*, p. 12. For James and for us the two groups are "the physical and the mental"; and, for both, the latter group is "your field of consciousness," or mine, or, some one else's. But for us "consciousness" would be declared to be a specific type of relation occurring between terms which, before it occurred, were not as yet experiences.

raphy. . . . Furthermore, the term "experience" which appears so frequently in recent discussions, appears to me so shot through with the implications of consciousness, that it obscures the problem at issue. Objects, when in consciousness, may be regarded as elements of experience, but this experience . . . can hardly be regarded as the fabric out of which it is itself composed.[17]

The publication of this address was followed within some ten years by a number of papers by the same author dealing with consciousness, which, all together, form a connected whole. The objects of consciousness, he said,

> may be varied and as variable as you please . . . but all, without exception, stand out as the objects *of which* there is consciousness, but never as the consciousness itself. . . . There is thus a distinction between consciousness and its objects. . . . It is the distinction involved in the existence of things together.

Again the perspectivist agrees, but the difference begins with what follows.

> . . . Consciousness should . . . be defined as the same general type of existence as space, time, or species. Its nature is akin to theirs.
> When things exist together, that which constitutes their being together is some sort of continuum. Consciousness may be defined, therefore, as a kind of continuum of objects. . . . In this form [of continuity] they become grouped and systematized in a manner quite different from their grouping in any other form. They become representative of each other. Note that it is *of each other* that they are representative, but not of anything else.[18]

In a later paper, first published in 1909 and therefore of the same period, he sums up the result of the earlier papers by saying

> that if we directly question reflective experience as to what consciousness is, we get the answer that it can not be identified with the objects of that experience, but is to be identified with a relation between them, and that this relation is the relation of meaning or implication,

---

[17] "The Nature of Consciousness," published in the *Journal of Philosophy*, Vol. II, 1905, and reprinted in *Nature and Mind: Selected Essays of Frederick J. E. Woodbridge*, New York, 1937. Twelve of the essays in this volume deal with consciousness and cognition. Of these the first appeared in 1902, nine others in the decade 1904–1913, and the last two in 1932 and 1936. The quotation in the text above is made from *Nature and Mind*, pp. 313–314. Subsequent references to any of these essays will be to the reprinted form as it appears in the volume. Quotations by permission of Columbia University Press.
[18] *Nature and Mind*, pp. 308–310.

in short, the logical relation. In other words, I have taken the fact of meaning to be the fact of consciousness, and urged, consequently, that consciousness is just the existence of logical relations. . . . These conclusions were based on a direct analysis of reflective experience without considering the relation of the organism which is said to be conscious to its surroundings.[19]

This, then, is what Woodbridge at that time presented as an "analytic expression" of the nature of consciousness, before proceeding in the same paper to develop "a biological expression" of its nature and to correlate the two expressions. His biological expression was evidently based on the central thought of *The Integrative Action of the Nervous System,* which Professor (now Sir) Charles S. Sherrington had published in 1906 and which had already been received with acclaim by physiologists throughout the world. This central thought was what Woodbridge called "a striking difference" between the sense organs and the nervous system, a difference "in structure and function."

> Thus the sense organs appear to be constructed and differentiated in relation to specific differences in the stimuli which may affect them while the nervous system appears to be constructed and unified in relation to co-ordinated activity by the organism. While the sense organs put the organism in diversified interaction with its surroundings, the nervous system prevents this diversification from resulting in disintegrated and isolated reactions. It is thus apparent that the nervous system secures to the organism individuality and unity of life in spite of the very great diversity of stimuli and environment. We have in these considerations, I believe, the means of stating the relational view of consciousness in biological terms. An organism so situated that it should be in differentiated interaction with the specific differences in the world about it, but which should, none the less, react in a unified manner no matter how it might be stimulated, might well be defined as a conscious organism. Its consciousness would be a relational system integrating and unifying its differentiated interaction with its surroundings.[20]

Woodbridge's papers from which I have quoted and others of the same period I cannot now but regard as most important contributions to a satisfactory view of "the nature of consciousness."

---

[19] *Ibid.,* p. 365.
[20] *Ibid.,* pp. 366–367.

Whatever may have been my reactions to them at the time, they kept me on the way on which James had set me—a way by which after many years and many turnings I have reached my present view. This view, however, differs widely from the view presented by Woodbridge. But in spite of such disagreement there is agreement on two points, namely (1) that consciousness is a *specific kind of relation*, and (2) that it is not a relation between terms which, as James maintained, are *experiences on their own account before the relation occurs*.[21]

But when Woodbridge asserts that the specific kind of relation that consciousness is is the relation of *meaning*, and that the terms of the relation of consciousness are the so-called "objects of consciousness," the agreement ceases. I find that the conscious relation is as different from the relation of meaning as spatial or temporal relations are, and that the terms which any consciousness relates are *some organism* on the one hand and the "objects" of that organism's consciousness on the other. It is the *organism* that is in a conscious relation to the "objects of consciousness"; these objects are not *ipso facto* in a conscious relation *to each other*.

The objects of any consciousness are indeed in a relation to each other, but that relation is not a conscious relation (unless they happen to be conscious organisms). It is what I once called an "indirect relation," i.e., a relation conditioned by another relation. They are together in a certain way in virtue of the conscious relation in which some organism stands to them, or, conversely, in virtue of the relation of appearing in which they stand to some organism. The difference between Woodbridge's view of consciousness and our view can perhaps best be brought out by emphasizing his assertion that "consciousness should be defined as the same general type of existence as space, time, and species. Its nature is akin to theirs." But objects are in space in that they are in spatial relations *to each other*; and they are in time in that they

---

[21] This, I take it, is what Woodbridge meant when he said: "The term 'experience' which occurs so frequently in recent discussions, appears to me so shot through with the implications of consciousness, that it obscures the problem at issue."

are in temporal relations *to each other*; they are in species in that they are in certain respects similar *to each other*. If the nature of consciousness is akin to the nature of space, time, and species, then objects are in consciousness in that they are in conscious relations to each other; i.e., are *conscious of each other*. This is Woodbridge's view, but it is not ours. And Woodbridge identified these conscious relations with relations of meaning, not finding any other identification plausible. But this way of treating consciousness seemed to have left out of account any "conscious organism." This omission he attempted to make good, as we have seen, by saying that an organism so situated as to be in differentiated interaction to specific differences in the world and at the same time to be reacting in a unified manner to that world "might well be defined as a conscious organism."

This seems to the perspectivist to be putting the cart before the horse. It is as if a genealogist were to start with the relation of brotherhood between two children as the primary relation and were then to define the relation of parenthood as that in which a particular male and a particular female stand in common to the brothers. In genealogy, treated realistically, i.e., biologically, linear descent is primary, and collateral relation is a corollary.[22] So, in treating consciousness as a natural relation that occurs in connection with biological facts the perspectivist regards as secondary and collateral the relation to *each other* in which the objects stand in the field of consciousness of any organism, since this relation is corollary to the primary relation of consciousness in which the organism stands to these objects.

Ignoring details, we may say that what in effect Woodbridge's view of "the nature of consciousness" amounted to is this: (*a*)

---

[22] It is quite true that in a purely conceptual system of relations such as Euclidean geometry, it is a matter of convenience which relations we start with as implying the others, since as a matter of fact we start with the assumption of mutual implication. But in the *temporal order of nature,* parenthood does not come after brotherhood. Even if all the children any couple had were born simultaneously there would still be biological considerations that would give priority to parenthood. Brothers do not beget their parents. Neither do objects in a conscious relation to each other give rise to a subject conscious of them.

There is a relation of *meaning* obtaining between what are called the objects of consciousness, and this relation is consciousness; (*b*) the sense organs of an organism react, each specifically to a specific kind of stimulus, while the organism as a whole reacts in a unified and co-ordinated manner to *all* the stimuli acting upon it; and (*c*) these two facts, namely (*a*) and (*b*), justify us in defining such an organism as a conscious organism. Thus the organism's *consciousness* is its *integrated physiological reaction* to its surroundings. This summary brings out clearly the difference between Woodbridge's view of the nature of consciousness and the perspectivist's view. According to the latter, (*a*) an organism's consciousness is a specific kind of relation which arises between an organism and its "surroundings," and this relation is not the relation of meaning; and (*b*) the occurrence of a relation of this kind is conditioned by but not identical with the organism's integrated physiological reaction. The difference between the two views is not a matter of arbitrary definition. One may, if one chooses, define "consciousness" as Woodbridge defined it; but if one does, one has left out of account something that is present, so the perspectivist finds, in every instance of seeing, hearing, remembering, thinking, etc., and it is this omitted something that the perspectivist calls "consciousness." Any theory of vision, audition, memory, or thought, that leaves out this specific type of relation—call it what you will—is as defective, as one-sided, as a theory that should leave out the integrative physiological reaction of an organism.[23]

A little over a year after the publication of Woodbridge's "The Nature of Consciousness," Professor Dewey undertook "to do his little part in clearing up the confusion" that had appeared in "criticisms made upon that vital but still unformed movement variously termed radical empiricism, pragmatism, humanism,

---
[23] There is a difference between what is here said with regard to vision and what I said in the paper contributed to *Contemporary American Philosophy*, ed. by George P. Adams and Wm. Pepperell Montague, London: New York, 1930, Vol. 2, p. 112 ff.; and this is not the only change that my philosophical views have undergone.

functionalism." Recognizing that "the *fundamental* difference is not so much in matters overtly discussed as in a presupposition that remains tacit," he undertook to "make his own presupposition explicit." He chose the name "Immediate Empiricism" for the position he took in this movement—a position which he defined by the postulate "that things—anything, everything, in the ordinary or non-technical use of the term 'thing'—are what they are experienced as."[24] This paper was soon followed by his now more famous paper, "The Experimental Theory of Knowledge,"[25] and this again by many others in the course of nearly a score of years, until the unformed movement took definite form in his Carus Lectures.

In this volume Mr. Dewey recognized and rejected three views as to what consciousness is, and presented his own. The first of the rejected views, with his summary criticism of it, is thus identified by him:

> When the word "consciousness" is — as it often is — used for a short name for the sum total of such immediate qualities as actually present themselves, it is the end or terminus of natural events. As such it is also gratuitous, superfluous and inexplicable when reality is defined in terms of the relational objects of science.[26]

The other two views which he rejects are the "current idealistic" and the "counterpart realist doctrine" contrasted with his own in the following passage:

> Consciousness, an idea, is that phase of a system of meanings which at a given time is undergoing redirection, transitive transformation. [This is his own view of the nature of consciousness.]

---

[24] Dewey, "The Postulate of Immediate Empiricism," first published in the *Journal of Philosophy*, Vol. II, 1905, and "reprinted, with very slight change," in *The Influence of Darwin on Philosophy*, New York, 1910. The above quotations are from this volume (pp. 226–227).

[25] In *Mind*, Vol. XV, N.S., 1906, and reprinted "with considerable change" in *The Influence of Darwin*.

[26] *Experience and Nature*, Chicago, 1925, 2d ed., 1929, p. 104. (Only when the two editions differ shall I hereafter mention the edition to which I refer.) Cf. p. 303: ". . . on the psycho-physical level, consciousness denotes the totality of actualized immediate qualitative differences, or 'feelings.' " Mr. Dewey, as we have seen, regards any immediate quality as "neither a relation nor an element in a relational whole" (p. 85), and therefore as not amenable to treatment as a "relational object."

The current idealistic conception of consciousness as a power which modifies events is an inverted statement of this fact. To treat consciousness as a power accomplishing the change is but another instance of the common philosophic fallacy of converting an eventual function into an antecedent force or cause. Consciousness *is* the meaning of events in course of re-making; its "cause" is only the fact that this is one of the ways in which nature goes on. . . .

There is a counterpart realist doctrine, according to which consciousness is like the eye running over a field of ready-made objects, or a light which illuminates now this and now that portion of a given field. These analogies ignore the indeterminateness of meaning when there is awareness; they fail to consider a basic consideration, namely, that while there exists an antecedent stock of meanings, these are just the ones which we take for granted and use: the ones of which we are not and do not need to be conscious.[27]

The "basic consideration" here is that we take for granted and use an antecedent stock of meanings, which themselves *are not undergoing transformation* during the time when some other meanings are. The meanings which do not undergo transformation are "the ones of which we are not conscious and do not need to be conscious." Why? We are not conscious of them because by Mr. Dewey's definition consciousness *is* the meaning of only the events which are in the course of *re*making.

We can best contrast our view of consciousness with Mr. Dewey's view, just quoted above, by seeing what he says of "appearance"; because, in our view, to say that an object *appears* to an organism is to say that the organism is *conscious* of the object; and when we discover what Mr. Dewey means when he says that an object appears, we can compare his meaning with our own. By consulting the Index in *Experience and Nature* we see that he defines "appearance," and recognizes a connection between it and "consciousness." There we read: "Appearance, defined . . . and consciousness." In the text to which the Index refers us for a definition of appearance, we find:

> To call [any immediate object] "appearance" denotes a functional status, not a kind of existence. Any quality in its immediacy is doubly an appearance. In the first place, it appears; it is evident,

[27] *Ibid.*, pp. 308–309.

conspicuous, outstanding, it is, to recur to language already used, *had*. A thing appears in the sense in which a bright object appears in a dark room, while other things remain obscure, hidden. The affair is one of physical and physiological limits of vision and audition, etc. . . . The difference between the appearing and the unappearing is of immense practical and theoretical import, imposing upon us need for inference, which would not exist if things appeared to us in their full connections, instead of with sharply demarcated outlines due to limits of perceptibility. But the ground of the difference is as physical as that between solid, liquid and gas. The endings of organic events, seeing, hearing, etc., are for the time being, or immediately, endings of the history of all natural events. To re-establish a connection of histories within a longer course of events and more inclusive state of affairs, requires delving, probing and extension by artifice beyond the apparent. To link the things which are immediately and apparitionally had with one another by means of what is not immediately apparent and thus to create new historic successions with new initiations and new endings depends in turn upon the system of mathematical-mechanical systems which form the proper objects of science as such.

The empirical basis of the distinction between the apparent and the non-apparent thus lies in the need for inference.[28]

Here we have the difference between knowledge and immediate experience stated in terms of physical and physiological "grounds" that differentiate "the appearing and the unappearing." The author, however, evidently felt that the treatment he had given of "appearance" here and elsewhere in this volume needed elaboration, for in the interval between the two editions he published a paper, "An Empirical Account of Appearance," the importance of which has not been generally recognized. What he accomplished in this paper he tells us in his conclusion:

The general notion of "appearance" we have broken up into a number of meanings, each distinctive in a particular contextual situation. The elimination of traditional misconstruction is procured when we keep these meanings definite, each in its proper place, and do not transfer and mix traits of one with those of another.[29]

This "breaking up" is of course a process of *reflective analysis*, but it is not a separation of the different meanings from each other, such that where some one meaning is present all the others

---
[28] *Ibid.*, pp. 137–138.
[29] In the *Journal of Philosophy*, Vol. XXIV, 1927, pp. 449–463.

are absent: we shall see later that when for instance the fourth meaning is under consideration, the first meaning is taken for granted. But there may be "appearance" in the first meaning without "appearance" in the other meanings. It is this first meaning to which the author devotes the first section of his paper, and to which I wish now to direct attention:

> The primary, innocent neutral meaning of appearance may best be expressed participially by the word "appearing." . . . Land disappears after a ship has got a distance at sea; another land appears after an interval of days. What is indicated by the term "appearance" is coming into view, sensibly or intellectually—as when . . . the clue to a desired invention presents itself to an Edison. Appearance signifies conspicuousness, outstandingness, obviousness, being patent, evident, in plain view. Its contrast is being obscured, hidden, concealed, absent, remote. . . . When a thing appears, its hereness and nowness is emphatically realized. . . . From any point of view we must say that appearance marks a stage in the history of some object having different phases, owing to various relations to other things. . . .
>
> It may, however, be objected that the epistemological aspect of the matter can not be so easily disposed of. It will be contended that since an appearance is always to somebody, it involves dependence upon the mind or consciousness in or to which a thing appears; for this reason, I suppose, appearances are often called presentations, and presentations are then either identified with states of mind or at least with things modified by mind. But appearance does not denote a total or pervasive character, an intrinsic quality, but a relation which is additive. A lad appears in school; he answers present when the roll is called. . . . This presence . . . marks a phase of his biography determined by his relations to school, class, and teachers, just as his absence marks a phase determined by other relations. . . . So a presentation marks the existence of a thing in relation to an organism; the table before me is in view. If I close my eyes, it disappears from view:—a particular relationship ceases, namely to a certain part of my organism.
>
> This relation is physical, existential, not epistemic. Its establishment is, indeed, a necessary condition of knowing, but it does not constitute knowledge. . . . The sun is efficaciously present to the soil it warms, the plants whose growth it effects. . . . Or, taking the case of the organism, its appearance may . . . operate as a signal to begin the round of daily duties. . . . In short, while the appearance is a recondition [precondition?] of knowing, it is not a case of knowing.[30]

[30] *Ibid.*, pp. 449–451. This view as to the nature of appearance is the view that I have adopted and, as I have said more than once before, for me consciousness is

One matter may be mentioned here before we proceed further. The context shows that the word "participially" in the first sentence of what is here quoted is an inadvertence. A participle is grammatically an adjective, whereas the "-ing" words, "coming into view," "being patent," which in later sentences of the same paragraph are mentioned as synonyms of "appearance," are gerunds, i.e., verbal nouns, and not participles. They are abstract nouns.[31] I mention this here because in what I shall say later I shall assume that wherever the word "appearance" occurs in the first section of Mr. Dewey's paper, from which the above long quotation is made, the gerund "appearing" can be substituted for it. Thus "an appearance" means an *appearing*; "the appearance" means the *appearing*; "its appearance" means its *appearing*; in short, "appearance" (also called "presence" and "presentation"), wherever used in this first section of the paper under present consideration, is "a relation which is additive."

Moreover, Mr. Dewey's empirical account of appearance in its primary, innocent neutral meaning challenges comparison with "*experience* in *its* primary integrity," or "experience in first instance and intent," as these terms are used in his writings of this period. This is obvious to anyone who reads the present paper in light of what Mr. Dewey says in *Experience and Nature*. But let the reader also look back, say, to "The Experimental Theory of Knowledge," where he is invited to "suppose a smell, just a floating odor. . . . The smell, *imprimis*, is there; the movements it excites are there; the final plucking experienced. . . . We may take, in short, these experiences in a brutely serial fashion. . . . Nowhere is there looking before and after; memory and anticipation are not born. Such an experience . . . [is not] acquaintance.

---

the converse of this additive relation of appearance. The paper from which I have been quoting is to me one of the most important metaphysical achievements of Dewey, but unfortunately the author was not consistent in the development of his thesis. Some years ago I wrote a paper of considerable length criticizing it. Some time after the appearance of the volume on which I am now working I may publish my paper. I now regret that I did not publish it before Dewey's recently lamented death.

[31] See *Webster* under the second and third entries, "-ing."

Acquaintance is presence honored with an escort; presence is introduced as familiar, or an associate springs up to greet it. . . . If one is acquainted with the smell of a flower it means that the smell is not just smell, but reminds one of some other experienced thing which stands in continuity with the smell. There is thus supplied a condition of control or purchase upon what is present, the possibility of translating it into terms of some other trait not now sensibly present."[32] Note here the words "is there," "is experienced," "is present," "sensibly present." Do not these words unmistakably identify the "experience," namely, a smell which "*imprimis* is there," with a smell which *appears*, where "appears" is used in its primary meaning? *It is this fact that makes this account so important when we come to deal with Dewey's Carus Lectures, especially in its 1929 edition.*

When, in the last paragraph quoted on p. 141, the author says: "This relation is physical, existential, not epistemic," there is nothing in the preceding paragraph to suggest that by "this relation" he does not mean *appearance* in its neutral meaning, best expressed gerundively by the word "appearing." On the contrary, the suggestion is that, in the case of a table "before me in view," its "coming into view sensibly"—"an additive relation"—*is* its particular "relationship . . . to a certain part of my organism," and that its disappearance from view is the cessation of this particular physical relationship. The additiveness of the relation of appearing is, for all the context suggests, the occurrence of this physical relation which has not occurred before. Now, there *is* here, of course, a physical relation; the table now before me in view reflects physical light to my physical eyes which react physically to the physical light. All *this* is as physical as when "The sun is efficaciously present to the soil it warms, the plants whose growth it effects." And when, in the very next sentence, he takes "the case of the organism" and says that the sun's "appearance may . . . operate as a signal to begin the round of daily duties," there is nothing—except the word "signal," which we shall con-

---

[32] *The Influence of Darwin*, pp. 78–83.

sider later—to indicate that its "appearance" is anything but a relation of the same physical kind as the sun's "efficacious presence to the soil it warms."

But is there only one relation occurring when a table comes into my view, only the physical relation we mentioned a moment ago? The author himself answers in the three sentences that conclude the last paragraph, already quoted in part. In quoting these sentences I will introduce italics.

> Furthermore, we must note that the relation which *determines* the thing *to appear* is definite, specifiable, not wholesale. A table disappears—not absolutely, but with respect to sight; when the eyes close, it may still be present to the hand. Failure to bear in mind the definite character of the organic relation that *conditions an appearance* is largely responsible for treating it as if it involved a unique problem.

Can a physical relation determine *itself* or condition *itself*? Of course Spinoza, in the very first sentence of his *Ethica*, speaks of a *causa sui*. But Spinoza was a rationalist; and, besides, he defined *"causa sui"* in such a way that he and his followers regarded the term as compatible with the rest of his rationalistic system. But Mr. Dewey is an empiricist, employing "the empirical method." Does this method, as he understands and uses it, recognize a *conditio sui*, a relation that conditions *itself*, a relation that determines *itself*? If not, it should go without saying, but apparently it must be said, that the physical "organic relation that conditions an appearance" *is not* and *cannot be* the additive relation of *appearing* which it determines. "Failure to bear in mind" that *appearance, an additive relation, is additive in that it is* other than *the physical processes that bring it about,* "is responsible for" Mr. Dewey's *not* "treating it as if it involved a unique problem"—"unique" in the sense that appearance is not a *physical* problem.

We have so far been considering sensible appearance; let us pass to intellectual appearance. "Things which appear are present [Mr. Dewey says] in sense-perception; the eye, ear, hand are the media of their determinate presence. Inferred objects that define their meaning . . . are on the other hand, qua inferred, objects of thought."³³ It is such objects that have been subject to "epistemological misconstruction."

> Deferred inference, or relation to a missing signified object, is expressed in such propositions as . . . . "The rails seem to converge; the stick appears bent; the coin seems elliptical." . . . The propositions just stated refer to the way in which the object used as evidence presents itself. They state the appearing object as it appears—in our first neutral sense. But they state it with a purpose—that of defining the exact nature of the evidence at hand. "The stick seems bent in water" does not mean that the appearing object *seems* bent. It means that what appears *is* something bent, though not necessarily the stick; perhaps light.
> The first step is to put ourselves on guard against depending upon the vague term "seems," "appears." We must specify the respect in which it appears, to eye, ear, touch, smell. If I say that a straight stick rising out of water *looks* bent (implying relation to the eye) I but state an objective fact, verified by a camera, and explained by well-known physical principles . . . there would be a problem only if it were not so. . . . But the force of the substitution is to call attention to a specific relation, to that particular part of the nervous organism which is involved as a condition, a physical or causal condition, of the appearance of the thing which is to serve as a sign. The propositions under discussion make explicit the exact nature of the thing to be used as evidence, before it is used. . . . If we say "There is present to the eye an elliptical form" we describe the nature of the appearance (in our first sense) preliminary to making inferential use of it. . . . As actual existences all "appearances" stand on the same level; as signs some are better than others, just as what one witness says is better evidence than what another says, although the utterances of each are equally actual occurrences.³⁴

Here again we have a physical occurrence stated as "a condition," but this time more explicitly as "a *physical or causal* condition, of the appearance of the thing," where again we are told that "appearance" is used "in our first sense,"³⁵ namely, as denoting an

---

³³ "An Empirical Account of Appearance," p. 458.
³⁴ *Ibid.*, pp. 459–461.
³⁵ I do not know whether, when it is said that "the force of the substitution is to call attention to a specific relation, to that particular part of the nervous organism . . ." the comma after "relation" is another misprint; if it is, then what is said to be "the physical or causal condition of the appearance" is definitely stated to be "the specific relation." If the comma should stand, then attention is called to two things: (*a*) "the specific relation," not further defined here, and (*b*) the particular part of the nervous organism. But the fact that "appearance" is twice on the same page here declared to be used "in our first sense," i.e., in sense of the "additive

"additive relation." And what is said of appearances where what appears appears as evidence is universalized: "As actual existence all 'appearances' stand on the same level." And here again the previous question arises—but now in more specific form—"Can a physical relation be a physical or causal condition *of itself?*" To use an epithet Mr. Dewey himself uses of those he criticizes, the perspectivist answers this question by saying: An affirmative answer from one who employs the empirical method employed in natural science is absurd.

Reviewing what has been said of the contributions made by three outstanding leaders of American philosophical thought to the problem of the nature of experience and of consciousness, we find that James, in 1904, abandoning, as Dr. Perry had abandoned, the notion of consciousness as an "aboriginal stuff or quality of being," championed the view that "knowing can easily be explained as a particular sort of relation towards one another into which portions of pure experience may enter," and identified "pure experience" as "just what appears." But he said nothing that could cast light upon what is meant by the verb "to appear." James called his view "radical empiricism." Woodbridge expressed agreement with the view that consciousness is a relation; but, finding it confusing to regard it as a relation between experiences since "the term 'experience' is shot through with the implications of consciousness," he identified the relation of consciousness with the relation of *meaning*. Mr. Dewey, also taking

---

relation" *of appearing*, leaves no doubt as to the author's meaning: the previous treatment of this first sense has already defined the specific relation as "the organic relation which conditions the appearance." Since this relation was expressly declared to be "physical," it is *ipso facto* "a physical or causal condition" of the appearance. (Of course the word "causal" has to be interpreted in accordance with the author's meaning of "cause" as "the fact that this is one of the ways in which nature goes on," *Experience and Nature*, p. 308). The whole "empirical account of 'appearance' " would have been easier to understand if the author had mentioned another denotation of the word "appearance," namely, "*the appearing object as it appears*" or "*what appears*" (expressions he uses on pp. 457–458), and had expressly stated that the word "appearance" in his paper is not to be understood in this sense. The appearing object appears *as* red, or as hot, or as sweet. Such sense qualities are also conditioned by "the particular part of the organism which is involved as a condition, a physical or causal condition of the appearance," i.e., of the *appearing*.

part "in the unformed movement" represented in James's radical empiricism, attempted to clear up the confusion by laying down "the postulate and criterion of *immediate empiricism*"; but after an interval of more than twenty years found it desirable to give "an empirical account of appearance"—in terms of which James had identified "pure experience"—treating it as "an additive relation" conditioned by a physical organic relation. But with unhappy inadvertence he identified this additive relation with the physical relation that conditioned it.

If Mr. Dewey had discovered what his own analysis had uncovered, he might have made many more changes in the second edition of his Carus Lectures than we find in it. As it now stands printed, there is nothing in it that even hints at his paper on appearance. This is perhaps the reason why that paper has received so little attention. For all the clarification that it gave to his view of experience, it might as well not have been written. Let us look at some of the changes that might have been but were not made in the following issue of his most important work of that period, if he had taken account of "appearing" as a "relation which is additive" and is conditioned by and therefore distinguishable from the response-relation of an organism to its physical environment. First we find:

> To a truly naturalistic empiricism, the moot problem of the relation of subject and object is the problem of what consequences follow in and for primary experience from the distinction of the physical and the psychological or mental from each other.[36]

That is to say that there is nothing more to the problem of the relation of subject and object than the problem of the consequences that follow from the distinction of the physical and the psychological. Nothing at all is said of the fact that the object *appears to* the subject, and that appearing is a relation which is additive to and conditioned by the physical. This has dropped entirely out of sight and out of mind. On the two immediately preceding pages we can see how this happened. "We begin [so the

---

[36] *Experience and Nature*, 2d ed., p. 10.

author tells us] by noting that 'experience' is what James called a double-barrelled word," whose "congeners [are] life and history."

> It is significant that "life" and "history" have the same fullness of undivided meaning [that "experience" has]. Life denotes a function, a comprehensive activity, in which organism and environment are included. Only upon reflective analysis does it break up into external conditions—air breathed, food taken, ground walked upon—and internal structures—lungs respiring, stomach digesting, legs walking. The scope of "history" is notorious: it is the deeds enacted, the tragedies undergone; and it is the human comment, record, and interpretation that inevitably follow. Objectively, history takes in rivers, mountains, fields and forests, laws and institutions; subjectively it includes the purposes and plans, the desires and emotions, through which these things are administered and transformed.

Here we have the objective and the subjective, but nothing is said of any additive relation of appearing in which the objective stands to the subjective. The subjective consists solely, so far as the present account goes, of the administration and transformation of the objective through "the purposes and plans, the desires and emotions." This ignoring of the relation of appearing with its converse—call this converse what you will; the perspectivist calls it the conscious relation—is responsible for what Mr. Dewey says of "the moot problem of the relation of subject and object" as it concerns experience. Once recognize this relation, and the object is *what* appears, the subject is *that to which* the object appears, and the relation of object to subject is the relation of appearing. Or conversely stated, the subject is that which is conscious, the object is that of which the subject is conscious, and the relation of subject to object is the conscious relation. But if one ignores this relation, what remains of "the moot problem of the relation of subject and object" is what Mr. Dewey says it is.

Again it is the same ignoring that is accountable for the confusion that clouds his discussion of *experience*. He calls this a double-barrelled word, but as he treats it, it is four-barrelled, and the reader is often in a quandary as to which barrel the author is shooting with. It is (1) a "what," (2) a "how," (3) "the one who," and (4) "a primary integrity" which recognizes "no division between act and material, subject and object, but contains them both in an unanalyzed totality."[37] This "both" is troublesome, especially as the paragraph in which it occurs begins with the assertion that the author's previous "general statement must be made more definite." "Object" and "material" apparently are used synonymously; are "subject" and "act" also so used? Is the "subject" nothing but "the act," with "the one who plants and reaps, who works and rejoices, hopes, fears, plans," etc., now lost sight of? Is the answer to this question to be found in the following quotations?

> As was remarked in the introductory chapter one can hardly use the term "experience" in philosophical discourse but a critic rises to inquire "Whose experience?" The question is asked in adverse criticism. Its implication is that experience by its very nature is owned by some one; and that the ownership is such in kind that everything about experience is affected by a private and exclusive quality. The implication is as absurd as it would be to infer from the fact that houses are owned . . . that possessive reference so permeates the properties of being a house that nothing intelligible can be said about the latter. It is obvious, however, that a house can be owned only when it has existence and properties independent of being owned. The quality of belonging to some one . . . is additive; it marks the assumption of a new relationship, in consequence of which the house . . . acquires new properties. . . .
> Substitute "experience" for "house," and no other word need be changed. Experience when it happens has the same dependence upon objective natural events, physical and social, as has the occurrence of a house. It has its own objective and definitive traits; these can be described without reference to a self, just as a house is of brick . . . irrespective of whom it belongs to. Nevertheless, just as for some purposes and with respect to some consequences, it is all important to note the added qualification of personal ownership of real property, so with "experience." In first instance and intent, it is not exact nor relevant to say "I experience" or "I think." "It experiences or is experienced," "It thinks or is thought" is a juster phrase. Experience, a serial course of affairs with their own characteristic properties and relationships, occurs, happens, and is what it is. Among and within these occurrences, not outside of them nor underlying them, are those events which are denominated selves. In some specifiable respects and for some specifiable consequences, these selves, capable of objective denotation just as are sticks, stones, and

---
[37] *Ibid.*, p. 8.

stars, assume the care and administration of certain acts in experience. Just as in the case of the house, this assumption of ownership brings with it further liabilities and assets, burdens and enjoyments.

The cogent line of defence [the author says in the second following paragraph] is that it promotes prudence, accountability, ingenuity and security, in the production and administration of commodities and resources which exist independently of the relationship of property. In like fashion, *not all thoughts and emotions* are owned either socially or personally; and either mode of appropriation has to be justified on the basis of distinctive consequences.[38]

Now "thoughts and emotions" are for Mr. Dewey "*processes of experiencing*" which are "discriminated by reflection out of primary experience,"[39] and when he says: "In first instance and intent, it is not exact nor relevant to say 'I experience' or 'I think,'" he evidently refers to "primary experience." Furthermore, presumably such a "primary experience" contains in its "unanalyzed totality" a self "who rejoices, hopes, fears, plans," i.e., who has "emotions and thoughts." But to use the "juster phrase" is to *analyze*, since "thought" is one of the "products discriminated by reflection out of primary experience." If one is analyzing, one's analysis should be as thorough as possible before any conclusion can be drawn from the "products"; and Mr. Dewey himself finds that "among and within these occurrences [constituting 'experience, a serial course of affairs'], not outside of them nor underlying them, are those events which are denominated selves." Are any thoughts and emotions also found there, but lying loose and unowned till these selves begin by an "adoptive act" to "assume the care and administration of certain objects and

---

[38] *Ibid.*, pp. 231–234. The italics are mine. To save the curious reader unnecessary trouble, he may as well be told that he will not find "in the introductory chapter" of the *second* edition the remark mentioned at the beginning of the long quotation made above. He will find it on p. 4 of the first edition.

The reader will have noticed a decided similarity of phrasing between the last sentence of the first paragraph quoted above and the sentence, "So a presentation marks the existence of a thing in relation to an organism," previously quoted from Mr. Dewey's paper on "Appearance." This suggests that in writing the later sentence he had in mind the same situation he was discussing in the first edition of *Experience and Nature* when he spoke of a house as assuming a new and "additive" relationship—a discussion reprinted without change in the second edition—and said that the assumption occurs in the case of "experience."

[39] *Ibid.*, 2d ed., p. 8.

acts in experience"? Of course, in human society often a "self as a centered organization of energies identifies itself (in the sense of accepting their consequences) with a belief or sentiment of independent and external origination"; but in such a case all the evidence I can find points to a previous ownership of the belief or sentiment by some *other* self or selves. Again, of course, there is many a thought whose "source and author" is unknown; but this does not prove that any such thought first came into being unowned, *nobody's* thought but nevertheless a thought floating about ready to be picked up and become the property of the first claimant.[40]

If in reply to our criticism Mr. Dewey should call attention to the fact that he has been dealing with experience "in first instance and intent," in which often a person has emotions and thoughts that are not experienced as being *his own* emotions and thoughts, we should willingly admit his contention; but in our turn we would call attention to the fact that the critic whom he has in mind as asking the question "Whose experience?" asks it in "philosophic discourse." Philosophy for Mr. Dewey as for us is one of the "forms of reflective analysis,"[41] and he himself begins his consideration of method

> with the contrast between gross, macroscopic, crude subject-matters in primary experience and the refined, derived objects of reflection. The distinction is one between what is experienced as the result of a minimum of incidental reflection and what is experienced in consequence of continued and regulated inquiry. For derived and refined products are experienced only because of the intervention of systematic thinking. The objects of both science and philosophy belong chiefly to the secondary and refined system. . . .
>
> That the subject matter of primary experience sets the problems and furnishes the first data of the reflection which constructs the secondary objects is evident; it is also obvious that the test and verification of the latter is secured only by return to things of crude or macroscopic experience—the sun, earth, plants and animals of common, everyday life. But just what role do the objects attained in reflection play? Where do they come in? They *explain* the primary

---

[40] What appears in quotation marks in the above paragraph and has not been already located by specific reference will be found in the text of *Experience and Nature*, 2d ed., in the context of passages previously identified.
[41] *Ibid.*, 2d ed., p. 19.

objects, they enable us to grasp them with *understanding*, instead of just having sense-contact with them. But how?[42]

Precisely. Now, among the "gross, macroscopic, crude subject-matters in primary experience" all evidence seems to indicate that experiencing selves were among the first objects attained in "a minimum of incidental reflection." In fact, even now "myths are rife and the world is peopled with fabulous personages and is the home of occult forces."[43] "Animism, the attribution of desire and intent of inanimate things," and also of thoughts and emotions as well, seems to have been omnipresent in the early history of mankind, not requiring much reflection to get such a firm hold. We may agree that "it is a misinterpretation of a natural fact, namely, that significant things are things actually implicated in situations of shared or social purpose and execution."[44] And yet we may question whether there is ever an experience, significant or not, that is not *some one's* experience, and whether there is ever any process of experiencing that is "not owned" by some one in the sense that when it occurs there is some one who is undergoing that process—some one who "desires and enjoys, sees, believes, imagines," etc., whatever the process may be. If the method of philosophy is not to diverge from that of "the natural sciences," which "not only draw their material from primary experience, but . . . refer it back again for test,"[45] what shall be said of a philosopher who describes "primary experience" as containing in its unanalyzed totality a "subject"—apparently a subject that "rejoices, hopes, fears, plans," etc.—and who nevertheless asserts against critics that "not all thoughts and emotions are owned either socially or personally"? Is it any worse to "begin with results of a reflection that has already torn in two the subject-matter experienced and the operations and states of experiencing" than to begin and end with results of a reflection that has already torn in two "the operations and states of experiencing" and the *one who ex-*

---

[42] *Ibid.*, 2d ed., pp. 3–5.
[43] *Ibid.*, p. 348.
[44] *Ibid.*, pp. 180–181.
[45] *Ibid.*, 2d ed., p. 4.

periences? Is not his problem of getting again what has been sundered as impossible of solution as that of "the king's men," who "started with the fragments of the egg and tried to construct the whole egg out of them"?[46] His problem is even more hopeless of solution, for, to turn against him the analogy he himself uses in the immediately preceding paragraph, life, a "congener" of experience, finds a "what" already existing, a *ground* to walk upon, but it does not find the operation of *walking* already going on without *legs* walking—an operation to be "appropriated" by legs when, forsooth, they "assume care and administration of the acts" of walking! And so in history, the other "congener," there are already "rivers, mountains, fields and forests" before there are "deeds enacted" in and on them, but who has ever heard of historical deeds enacted that were not enacted either socially or personally, or of "tragedies undergone" that were not undergone either socially or personally? By the same token, who among truly naturalistic empiricists has ever *credibly* heard of thoughts or emotions that were not somebody's or somebodies' thoughts or emotions? It is true that once upon a time an occidental philosopher wrote:

> Fire and Water and Earth and the mighty height of Air, dread Strife, too, apart from these and balancing every one of them, and Love among them, their equal in length and breadth. Her do thou contemplate with thy mind, nor sit with dazed eyes. It is she that is deemed to be implanted in the frame of mortals. It is she that makes them have kindly thoughts and work the works of peace. They call her by the names of Joy and Aphrodite. Her has no mortal yet marked moving among the gods, but do thou attend to the undeceitful ordering of my thoughts.[47]

But while Empedocles was a towering figure among the naturalistic philosophers of his day, that day was some twenty-four hundred years ago, and any "truly naturalistic empiricism" (with its evolutionism) of the present day is the outcome of many strides from that of the author of the *Poem on Nature* and of the *Purifications*.

---

[46] *Ibid.*, 2d ed., p. 9.
[47] I quote from *Early Greek Philosophy*, by John Burnet, London and Edinburgh, 1892, p. 222.

Chapter V

PERSPECTIVES

In view of the many meanings in which the word *perspective* has long been and is now currently used, a philosopher and especially one who calls himself a perspectivist should make as clear as possible the meaning in which he uses the word. And this meaning should be understood in light of the system of postulates under which he is operating. Therefore it is desirable here to restate some of the postulates in connection with which the present writer uses that word. I assume that nothing in the world exists all by itself: everything exists only as a member of a world consisting of other members, and every character that anything has it has by virtue of its relation to some other member or members. Some relations are dynamic, some are not. Among the latter is "consciousness," a specific relation in which a physiological organism at times comes to stand to something else called the "object" of consciousness, the organism being called the "subject." The object of consciousness is at times, but not always, a *physical object*. The converse of "consciousness" is the relation "appearing" (used as a verbal noun as in the expression "his appearing before an audience"). When an organism is a term in a consciousness relation to something else it acquires in this relation a character it does not have at other times, and this character also goes by the name of consciousness, and the organism is said to be conscious of that thing; and in the case in which the thing is a physical thing, that thing conversely appears to the organism, i.e., becomes a term in a relation of appearing, and as such it acquires in this nonphysical relation one or more nonphysical qualities.

Let us now confine our attention to human organisms—to you and to me, as instances which we know best so far as consciousness is concerned. If we are fortunate enough not to be hopeless insomniacs, for some hours out of the twenty-four we are unconscious of anything so far as any positive evidence goes, and in the absence of evidence to the contrary I assume that this is true. But for the rest of the time we see, hear, remember, anticipate, and perhaps think, i.e., in all this we are conscious of something. Now when we see, what is it that ordinarily we see? We live in a world that to a large extent is usually familiar—a familiar environment, the same houses on the same street, the same rooms in our respective homes, and so on. When we leave home in the morning to go to our work we return in the evening to the same home and later go to sleep in the same bed as we rose from in the morning. Such are the things we usually see: concrete things, colored things, in spatial relations one to another. Any such seeing is an instance of *perception*, technically distinguished from *sensation*, which analysis discovers to be a factor in perception. We *sense* the color of what we see, and we *sense* spatial relations in which the colored thing is perceived to stand to any other colored things perceived. But as James said in the passage quoted in the last chapter in another connection: "Only newborn babes, or men in semi-coma from sleep, drugs, illnesses, or blows, may be assumed to have an experience pure in the literal sense . . . [which] is but another name for feeling or sensation."[1]

But we are not now dealing with such exceptional cases. We are dealing with "normal" experiences occurring when we look out upon a nearby scene, some of the objects in which are at rest and some in motion, ourselves moving about among them. During such a movement the perceived spatial relations between objects change. What was first *sensibly* perceived as lying to the right of another object now is perceived as lying to the left, and

---

[1] *Essays in Radical Empiricism,* New York, 1912, pp. 93–94.

the sensed shapes of many objects change as we move; and so do the *sensibly* perceived sizes of objects change as we approach or recede from them. All such changes are "perspectival" changes; and any field of such objects *sensibly* perceived by an observer from any one of the positions his eyes may occupy is his *perspective* from that position, and any object in that field is "in that perspective."[2]

This denotation of the word *perspective* we have been discussing has the sanction of long usage, the great Oxford *New English Dictionary on Historical Principles* citing an instance of this use in 1620 in the meaning, "A visible scene, a real view or prospect, esp. one extending in length away from the spectator and showing distance." According to this definition, the position of the observer's eyes—called the "center" or the "station-point" of the perspective—is *not in* the perspective, which is the real visible scene stretching *before* his eyes off into a distance. Since the perspective is here defined as what the observer sees with his eyes, and since usually the observer does not perceive his own eyes, his perspective consists of "external objects" where *external* means spatially outside the observer's eyes. His eyes are not *in* the perspective, nor is the perspective seen as *in* his eyes. Thus the word "center" in the expression "center of perspective" has a different meaning from what it has in the expression "center of a circle." The center of a perspective is the point of view *from* which a thing is *seen*, not the point *at* which it is seen *to be*. In our theory, these perceived objects are in the normal case *physical* objects which in the nonphysical relation of appearing to the observer now acquire each a new quality, a "sense quality" which is not physical. That a physical object should acquire a nonphysical quality is something a hard-and-fast dualist regards as a contradiction in terms, but on the postulates we have laid down

---

[2] I have italicized "sensibly" in the expression "sensibly perceived" to call attention to the fact that here I am speaking of the *sensed* factor in perception. And I speak of the position occupied by the eyes (rather than an eye) of the observer who senses the *third* dimension of a perspective as *stretching outward* from him, because normally it is only in binocular vision that this third dimension is distinctly *sensed*.

there is nothing contradictory about it. On these postulates there is a clearly definable distinction between the physical and the nonphysical, but there is no unbridgeable chasm between the two.

Why the physical should take on nonphysicality can no more be told than why there is the physical at all. But taking the world as we find it we can, I think, discover *how* it happens: i.e., the conditions under which it occurs. Perhaps this discovery can be facilitated if we examine another denotation of the word *perspective*, the earliest recorded use of which in English is found by the Oxford Dictionary to have been twenty-two years earlier (1598) than that of the definition we have adopted in this chapter. This earlier definition is formulated in that dictionary in these words:

> The art of delineating solid objects upon a plane surface so that the drawing produces the same impression of apparent relative positions and magnitudes, or of distance as do the actual objects when viewed from a particular point . . . the drawing is such as would be made upon a transparent vertical plane *(plane of delineation)* interposed in the proper position between the eye and the object, by drawing straight lines from the position of the eye (point of sight) to several points of the object, their intersections with the plane of delineation forming the corresponding points of the drawing.

This definition of *perspective*, more specifically of *linear* perspective, presupposes *perspective* as we have defined it, namely, a visible scene lying before the artist, a scene a drawing of which he is engaged in producing. But nothing is said here of the physics involved. This omission was due to the fact that the art here defined was practised before there was even a hint that light is a form of energy. The first hint of this was by implication given by Römer when in 1675 he published his discovery that the eclipses of Jupiter's satellites were seen at intervals varying in length with the varying distance of Jupiter from the earth; and he explained this functional relation by assuming that light is propagated with finite velocity. But this great discovery was ignored till Bradley, another astronomer, published in 1727 his discovery of a periodic change in the observed positions (parallaxes) of the fixed stars, accounting for this change by assuming, as did Römer, that light has a finite velocity. It was in the half-century between these two great discoveries that Leibniz, apparently oblivious of Römer, endowed each of his monads with a "perspective" of the whole universe, and thus, as Whitehead has pointed out, introduced the idea of perspective into philosophy.[3] But Leibniz's monads were "without windows," and thus without energetic communication with each other. They were perspectives by the grace of God, the monad of monads, not by virtue of any dynamic interplay among themselves.

Since perspectives are spatio-temporal phenomena it is necessary, before we proceed further, to deal with space and time, and in doing this let us lay down

Postulate 9. Space and time are relational. Space, as it appears in direct experience, is a three dimensional system of relations of distances and direction. Time is a system of distances and one dimensional direction. In either case a direction has two "senses": from here to there and from there to here in the case of space, and from earlier to later and from later to earlier in the case of time. Furthermore, the relations and directions in space and in time are not definable by genus and species; they can be identified only by examples.

As has been frequently remarked by physicists, in the physical world every event has its position in both space and time. No event occurs anywhere except at a certain time and no event occurs at any time except at some place.

In the vernacular the three spatial directions are to the left or right, upward or downward, and outward or inward with reference to anyone who is using the terms. Of course, actually there is a complex of these three directions so that we have an infinity of directions some of which appear in the terminology of the magnetic compass. In the case of time it is a question whether it should be said, as we have just said, that time has only one direction for not only are events either earlier or later one than another, but there are events that are neither earlier nor later

---

[3] *Science and the Modern World*, New York, 1926, p. 102.

with respect to each other but are said to be at the same time or simultaneous with each other. This latter fact has led to the recognition that in one meaning of the term *dimension* time has a second dimension which in mathematical physics is called the zero dimension and which Dewey expresses by saying that "time is thick."

In sensed vision the mutual spatial directions of objects relatively to the observer are determined by the respective directions in which light from the objects reaches his retina, and the third direction (outward and inward) is for the most part sensed only in binocular vision. The mutual spatial relations in which the different objects are seen at the same time as standing to each other constitutes the "linear perspective" of the objects in the percipient's field of vision.

However, not all perspectives arise under usual conditions. There are such things as mirrors in our familiar world, and light reflected from mirrors may reach a percipient's eyes. In such a case the spatial relations to an observer of a seen object are determined by directions from which the reflected light reaches the retina. It must be emphasized that the seen directions here are just as much physically determined, and therefore just as physical, as in the usual cases above mentioned. Considered in its physical relations, the object seen when reflected light reaches the eye has exactly the same status as the object seen under usual conditions. If, as the perspective realist assumes, the objects seen in normal vision are physical objects the objects seen by reflected light are also physical objects. In both cases it is the direction from which light reaches the retina that determines the direction in which any object is seen. And so it is when the light which reaches the eye is refracted on the way to the observer. We are all familiar with the fact that a spot at the bottom of a cup containing clear water is not seen in the same direction as it would be seen if the cup were empty. Here again the difference in the seen direction is determined by physical conditions. Thus we see *correctly* in either case; correctly, that is, when considered with reference to the *physical* presence or absence of water in the cup. Nature, if we may personify her, does not lie to us here. She tells us a truth but not the whole truth. We cannot reasonably expect the latter, since sensing is a primordial stage of human experience to be followed by pretersensory knowledge (or erroneous belief as the case may be).

Nor do we expect it in other cases of sense data. When for instance in sensing she gives the datum round-yellow we do not in return give her the lie because, forsooth, she does not also give us the further fact that there is an orange there with a blemish on the other side. Why then charge her with deceiving us in not reporting visually the fact that light rays from the bottom of a cup take a curved path in reaching our eyes? And what holds in the case of the speck at the bottom of the cup holds also of the more drastic "displacement" of any object seen in a mirror. We see the speck and also, as we said above, the direction from which the light that comes from it reaches the eye. In both cases we see the object but see it in *visual perspective* just as under more normal conditions we sense any object that we sense. Because sensing is a primordial stage in our experience it needs to be supplemented by what occurs additionally in perception, in memory, and in rational thought. This supplementation is what Mr. William M. Ivins, Jr. called "The Rationalization of Sight." Such rationalization can be successful in giving us such knowledge of physical nature as we have in present-day science, only if what we sensibly see has its place in the physical world. An important physiologist has recently said that men "were always aware that vision provides their closest link with the external world."[4]

In what has been said above it should be remembered that what is given correctly in sensory vision is the *direction* of what is seen. The part played by sensory quality will be discussed later.

It is well known that the wave theory of light found perhaps its strongest support in the behavior of light when reflected or

---

[4] George Wald, "Eye and Camera," in *Scientific American*, Vol. 183, No. 2, August 1950, p. 32.

refracted, and that without photography a present day physical scientist, whether dealing with the microscopic or the sub-microscopic, would be without an indispensable instrument. Now a single camera always takes pictures from a perspectival point of view.

While George Wald, writing as physiologist, has correctly emphasized the comparison between the mechanism of vision and that of the camera a philosopher of my stripe must call attention to the fact that a camera presumably does not see. It takes pictures of what is seen and of what we cannot see because of the limitations of the mechanism of vision, and it also has the advantage of the durability of the reports that it makes. A photograph is an image, that is, a likeness, of the object photographed. According to the philosophy submitted in these lectures what is visually sensed is not an image. It is the object itself from which the light comes that, on stimulating the optical neural mechanism, gives rise to vision of the object in perspective. To state the contrast here more definitely as it is conceived by the present writer, what is visually sensed is not a *picture* such as what a camera, placed where the eye is, would photograph. It is the object itself *in propria persona*, but that object in perspective. There is a belief shared by many physiologists who deal with the subject that what is sensed in vision is the image on the retina which is literally an image analogous to the image formed on the film when a photograph is taken. That image in either case is not the object that is photographed or seen. But we shall return to this subject later.

Up to the present we have been dealing only with spatial perspectives and it is these that are usually discussed where the subject of perspective is under consideration. But since, in present day physics, there is nothing in space that is not also in time it is necessary to take up here the problem of temporal perspective, because the time that it takes light from an object within my manual reach, or even one across the lake, to reach my eyes is negligible. Such is not the case with astronomical objects. Take the instance of the seen eclipse of the sun. The light from the sun has taken some eight minutes to reach our eyes whereas the light from the moon has taken less than a second and a half. If we wish to be captious we might be tempted to say that the eclipse is over by eight minutes before we can see or even before we can photograph it. But very properly the practicing astronomer is not bothered by such a paradox. The date of the solar eclipse is by convention taken to be the date at which it can be seen or photographed on the earth. But it is one thing to date by convention such an event; it's another thing to ignore the spatio-*temporal* character of a solar eclipse. To be accurate we should recognize three different dates, the conventional date of the eclipse, the date of the sun involved as some eight minutes earlier, and the date of the moon as something more than a second earlier: all this with the three corresponding spatial locations involved. Just as the spatial distance between the sun and the moon is foreshortened to zero, so the temporal interval between the sun involved and the moon involved is foreshortened to zero.

To return to the case of the speck at the bottom of the cup filled with water, present day critics of the correctness of what we see fail to suggest any way in which what for them would be a correct visual sensation could be produced physically. They judge from the point of view of Newtonian *absolute* space and, furthermore, they are merely echoing the Greek skeptics who were ignorant of the fact that light has a finite velocity. Now, if its velocity were infinite it could very well be maintained that what we see is erroneous, especially if space were Newtonian. But since light has a finite velocity it has a path, and the arrival of light at any point in this path could be sensed only when the light arrives at the eye; thus all its successive arrivals at intermediate points can be sensed only as simultaneous with each other. To repeat what I've said before, our visual sense gives us physical facts but now it is necessary to add that it does not claim to give us all the facts. For further facts not given by our various senses we must go to other sources: namely, memory, experimentation, and thought, the last operating from sensory bases. In what we have recently said about vision we have spoken only of "the eye," and binocular vision is more complicated.

> Neurologically, the basis for man's binocular vision is found in the arrangement of the optic nerve fibers and the optic tracts, connecting retinal units with specific regions of the visual cortex. Activation of any point on the right-hand side of either retina is transmitted to the right occipital cortex. . . . Furthermore, for every point on one retina . . . there is a so-called *corresponding point* upon the same side of the other retina. . . . Simultaneous stimulation of the two points gives rise to a single sensation. Presumably, this is because the optic nerve and tract fibers from these two points terminate in the same point in the occipital cortex, where only the single sensation rises into consciousness. A flat object, then, made of innumerable points emitting light, will stimulate a pattern of corresponding points on the two retinae, and the whole object will be perceived as single.[5]

Note the word "presumably"; apparently the tracing of the nerve fiber to the point of coincidence in the occipital lobe has not been accomplished. But the assumption here is neurologically tenable.

Returning now to the fact that the notion of perspectives was introduced into philosophy by Leibniz, it is to be observed that this notion did not originate with Leibniz but had long been familiar with the painters of the Renaissance. Strange as it may seem, "Although the Greeks worked all around the problem of perspectives, . . . they seemed never to have realized that there was such a thing as a mathematical problem of perspectives."[6]

---

[5] A. J. Carlson and V. Johnson, *The Machinery of the Body*, Chicago, 1948, pp. 469–470.

[6] William M. Ivins, Jr., *On the Rationalization of Sight with an Examination of Three Renaissance Texts on Perspective*, The Metropolitan Museum of Art, New York, 1938, p. 8. Cf. the article on painting in the *Encyclopaedia Britannica*, 11th ed., p. 465. This monograph deals, as its title indicates, with two different but connected subjects. To a "hasty account" of the rationalization of sight the author devotes only seven pages (pp. 7–13), while the examination of the three Renaissance texts takes up the rest of the paper (pp. 14–53). Although this second part is naturally of more importance to the members of the Metropolitan Museum of Art, one gets the impression that to the author his treatment of the rationalization of sight is more important from the fact that it gives its name to the leading title of the work, and it is of greater importance to philosophers. By the rationalization of sight is here meant the process, mathematical and technological, by which, "from

It was the painters of the Renaissance who succeeded for the first time in history in making pictures on canvas or wall that represented faithfully the appearance of three-dimensional objects in the field of sight. However, although this technique succeeded gloriously in the great paintings of the Renaissance, there was a failure in theory to connect the physical field of vision with the physical picture produced by this technique. What was lacking was the knowledge that light is a physical process having finite velocity. Had Leibniz known this fact it is possible that he might not have developed his theory of monads, each having in its perspective what was occurring simultaneously in the perspective of other monads without any dynamic connection between them. For this reason one might perhaps say that Leibniz was born before his time.

It would be fortunate if we could proceed without more ado to attack the problem of perspectives with the aid of the present-day theory of light reinforced by the results brain neurologists have gained largely within the present century; but unfortunately many if not most contemporary physiologists still maintain the tradition that what anyone senses when he says that he sees an external object is not external to his organism but is an inverted image of an external object on his retina, re-inverted in projecting it "to the actual source of stimulation out in space." In their view:

> the capacity to project correctly retinal images . . . is acquired by training and practice. We learn by experience that, when an image is formed on the left side of either retina, we must reach to the right to grasp that object, or walk to the right to approach it. We learn to project visual stimuli properly just as we learn to project

---

being an avenue of sensuous awareness for what people, lacking adequate symbols and adequate grammars and techniques for their use, regarded as 'secondary qualities,' sight has become the principal avenue of the sensuous awarenesses upon which systematic thought about nature is based." The beginning of this process occurred with the emergence of the idea of perspective; and the author submits the thesis that this beginning "was the most important event of the Renaissance" (p. 13). This is of course a startling claim, but if it were toned down by replacing the words "the most important event" by the words "one of the most important events" I should be inclined to think he had made good his claim. I wish to express my obligation to my colleague James S. Watrous, Chairman and Professor of the Department of Art History, University of Wisconsin, who not only called my attention to this significant monograph but also lent me his copy.

other subjective sensory data; for example, we must learn that stimulation of a specific sensory area in the cerebral cortex means that the index finger of the left hand is being touched.[7]

This "interpretative phenomenon," as the authors call it, presupposes that before anyone can project retinal images correctly he must see his retina and also see on which side of his retina images are formed. But we know from our experience of human babies that before they have become one year of age they have acquired the ability to reach correctly for seen objects in their immediate neighborhood; and it is surely an extravagant assumption that in acquiring this ability each was guided by the knowledge of the side of his retina on which the image of the object in any case is seen.[8] And what holds of the present day infant also holds with even greater force of human adults who for some million years must have succeeded quite well in reaching out correctly for food and other objects necessary for the preservation of their lives. As a matter of fact the knowledge that images are formed on retinas in any case of vision is something that has been learned in comparatively recent years and so far as I can discover it wasn't learned by anyone who saw images on his own retina. Personally I doubt whether anyone ever saw either of his own retinas; at least I've never been able to see anything that I might properly call a retina of mine. My doubt is reinforced by the following remarks by Wald:

> As for the inverted image on the retina, most people who learn of it concede that it presents a problem, but comfort themselves with the thought that the brain somehow compensates for it. But of course there is no problem, and hence no compensation. We learn early in infancy to associate certain spatial relations in the outside world with certain patterns of nervous activity stimulated through the eyes. The spatial arrangements of the nervous activity itself are altogether irrelevant.[9]

---

[7] Carlson and Johnson, *The Machinery of the Body*, p. 465. On the preceding page the authors say, "the problem is really one of cerebral interpretation of sensory data."
[8] Arnold Gesell, "Infant Vision," in *Scientific American,* Vol. 182, No. 2, pp. 20–22.
[9] Wald, *op. cit.,* p. 32.

What I agree with in this quotation is the complete rejection of the "problem" supposed to be involved in "seeing the inverted image upright." The sentence that begins "We" is a rather sketchy statement of what is brought out more fully by Gesell, and the last sentence of the quotation is so unqualified in its curtness that as it stands I find it better to refrain from further comment.
Gesell tells us that

> the child is born with two eyes partly yoked in a single organ—"a physiological binoculus." Accordingly the newborn infant is able to move his eyes conjugately, and to fixate momentarily and monocularly. Sustained fixation of a nearby object occurs in the first week, fixation of more distant objects at the end of the first month. Binocular convergence comes later.
>
> The infant takes hold of the world with his eyes long before he does with his hands—an extremely significant fact. . . . The young infant when awake lies in an asymmetric attitude simulating a fencing position, with the head averted to one side, the arm on that side extended and the opposite arm flexed at the shoulder. This tonic-neck-reflex posture is fundamental in the patterning of eye-hand behavior.[10]

Although as we have seen the infant is born "a physiological binoculus," his first true looking is monocular.

> He fixates the near object of interest by aligning the active eye and relaxing or closing the subordinate eye. At a later stage the monocular fixation alternates rapidly between the two eyes with a rhythmic excursion of the head from right to left to right. This eventually leads to teaming of the two eyes, which at about eight weeks of age simultaneously converge upon an object of interest. . . .
>
> The basic patterns and sequences are untaught, for they are the functional expression of gene effects operating at appropriate stages of maturity. Ocular prehension precedes manual. A 20-week-old infant at the test table unquestionably can pick up a white pellet, seven millimeters in diameter, with his eyes. He doubles his age before he picks up this pellet with his fingers. At 44 weeks he plucks it with precise finger prehension and neat thumb opposition.
>
> As the child grows older his visual tasks become increasingly symbolic, although they always retain a concrete core. He has to associate visual experiences with words. He "learns," as we say, to build a tower, a wall, a bridge with his blocks. . . . All of which reminds

---

[10] Gesell, *op. cit.*, p. 21.

us again that the ability to see really depends upon the total behavior equipment.

At birth the visual system of the child is very incomplete; it continues to develop throughout infancy, preschool and school childhood into the adolescent years. The intricacy of this development indicates that the refractive condition of the eyes is only one factor in the total effectiveness of the child's visual behavior. Superimposed upon a basic delimiting refractive state there is a margin of adaptability which is under the dynamic controls of the cerebro-spinal and automatic nervous systems. The total visual apparatus has three closely interacting components: skeletal, visceral and cortical. . . . Nowhere else in human behavior do we see such an intimate linkage between postural, viscero-sympathetic and cerebral reactions. The cortex functions as the master tool of synthesis and integration. It funnels and mediates the electrodynamic forces that culminate in adaptive visual behavior. . .

All this becomes somewhat understandable when one thinks of the eye not as a camera but as the most direct corridor to the vast networks of the brain cortex, where billions of neurones engender and organize the energies that issue in vision. The seeing eye is a reaching, groping, grasping organ—a teleceptive prehensory apparatus. In league with the growing brain it manipulates visible objects, cues and symbols. At every stage of growth during infancy, childhood and youth the visual mechanism undergoes changes which serve to reorient the evertransforming individual. For him the space-world is not a fixed and static absolute. It is a plastic domain which he manipulates in terms of the growing powers of his total behavior equipment.[11]

This account of the visual development of human infants gets confirmation in a report from the Yerkes Laboratories of Primate Biology (Orange Park, Florida) where, since human babies obviously could not be subjected to the chosen experiments, the experiments were made on chimpanzees.

The chimpanzee was chosen, because its behavior, like man's, is dominated by vision, and because it is intelligent and tractable. In 1945 . . . two newborn chimpanzee infants, a male and a female respectively named Snark and Alfalfa, were housed in a completely darkened room. During the first 16 months the only light these infants experienced was an electric lamp turned on for intervals of 45 seconds several times daily for their routine care and feeding. When they were first tested for visual perception at the age of 16 months,

---
[11] *Ibid.*, p. 22.

both chimpanzees showed extreme incompetence. Their reflex responses indicated that their eyes were sensitive to light—the pupils constricted; sudden changes of illumination startled the animals; they responded to a slowly waving flashlight with jerky pursuit movements of the eyes and side to side following motions of the head.[12]

These jerky pursuit movements are apparently vestigial refixations of the eyes but not of the eyes alone; they were carried by the side to side motion of the head. Under the conditions described they could not have been learned from experiences to be expected of infants in the early weeks after birth. The 16-month lack of practice and experience had succeeded only in arresting the natural process of maturation and incapacitated them for further development at a normal rate. As the author says on the following page: "The lack of light . . . is not the whole explanation. . . . Moreover, we now have clear evidence from further experiments with chimpanzees that not merely light itself but stimulation by visual patterns is essential to normal visual development." I will not quote from reports on further experiments but merely indicate that what the author means by visual patterns is later instanced in "a moving person," "a moving feeding bottle," and "a stationary person." If I understand the author correctly a visual pattern is what in traditional psychology would be called an object of visual perception discriminated from other such objects—a discrimination in which other receptors play their part as Gesell has pointed out.

It is to be noted that Gesell recognizes the refractive condition of the eyes as one factor in the total effectiveness of the child's visual behavior. This is to say that the retinal image produced by refracted light plays a part in vision, although in his article he does not state what that part is. We shall take up this question later. All through the article Gesell never hints that what the child sees is not the physical object that his hand grasps. In an article published in 1933 I assumed

---

[12] Austin H. Riesen, "Arrested Vision," in *Scientific American*, Vol. 183, No. 1, p. 17.

as a *postulate* that, *unless* there is reason to the contrary in any specific case, *the seen spatial characters of objects in monocular perspectives are physical characters that belong to physical objects*; however, they thus belong *not absolutely, but with respect to the physical conditions under which the perspectives obtain*. If such a view is to have a distinctive name, I would suggest as the most appropriate name "perspective realism."[13]

This is a position that I still take but there is something lacking in this paper. It was written three years after a paper, "A Tentative Realistic Metaphysics,"[14] in which I define my position in regard to Vision, a position that I still held in the above named later paper. I said:

> Vision is not an *act* of the organism or of a mind; it is the converse of the relation in which the objects just identified stand to the organism. If vision were an *act* of the organism, it would indeed be difficult to understand how an organism could see *now* what antedates the seeing. But if vision is the relation in which an organism stands to what initiated (or reflected) the light that on arriving at the eyes of the organism sets up changes in it, it is difficult to understand how vision could fail to be later than the objects (or events) which initiated the light. . . . When I say "I see physical objects," the verb "see" does not name any act I perform on the objects that I say I see, any more than my having a great-grandfather is an act I perform toward him.[15]

If that were all that vision is, then the relation of which vision is here said to be the converse, being a physical relation, vision itself would also be a physical relation. Furthermore, vision, whatever else in addition it may be, involves an act, or in other words is an activity of the seeing organism. It was this view of vision that was carried over to the paper on "Perceptual and Memory Perspectives."

Some years later, I do not remember how many, I came to the conviction that vision, while being an activity of an organism, is something more besides, and that that something more is itself

---

[13] "Perceptual and Memory Perspectives," *The Journal of Philosophy*, Vol. XXX, p. 313.
[14] In *Contemporary American Philosophy*, Vol. II, edited by George P. Adams and Wm. Pepperell Montague, New York, 1930.
[15] *Ibid.*, p. 113.

a relation but not a physical relation. It is a nonphysical effect of the activity of the organism initiated by the physical stimulation of the eyes by light from the object seen. If vision were nothing more than the physiological response of the organism to the action of light upon the retina, then by the same token the formation of the image on the retina, being a physical response to stimulation of light from a photographed object, might properly be said to be a vision of the object, and I could not but believe that common sense was justified in declining to say that the camera sees what it photographs. Wald has said:

> The more we have come to know about the mechanism of vision, the more pointed and fruitful has become its comparison with photography. By now it is clear that the relationship between the eye and the camera goes far beyond simple optics, and has come to involve much of the essential physics and chemistry of both devices.[16]

Before I had read Wald's paper what little I knew of the physics and chemistry of the eye in seeing appeared to me to furnish no understanding of seeing. It is only when seeing is postulated as an instance of consciousness and consciousness as an epiphysical relation between the organism and the object seen that one can understandably believe that one can see objects in space outside the eye at such distances from the organism as the sun and other stellar objects. With this postulate seeing can be defined as a certain activity of the brain integrated with the relation of consciousness as its result. We are familiar with many relations that obtain between objects distant in space and in time. If consciousness is a relation in which an organism with a functioning brain comes to stand to distant objects then we can understand how we can be sensorially conscious of a tree out in the yard, or of the planet Venus in the night skies, or even of Sirius or Vega, many light years distant.

With consciousness a relational factor in vision, I can adapt to my present purpose one of my favorite passages from Santayana, beautiful and challenging:

---

[16] Wald, *op. cit.*, pp. 32–33.

It is as if Vision [Santayana wrote Substance] said to Knowledge: My child, there is a great world for thee to conquer, but it is a vast, an ancient, and a recalcitrant world. It yields wonderful treasures to courage, when courage is guided by art and respects the limits set to it by nature. I should not have been so cruel as to give thee birth, if there had been nothing for thee to master; but having first prepared the field, I set in thy heart the love of adventure.[17]

Until of late, 1951, the assumption named above was not so far as I knew supported by experimental evidence. Now, however, we have at our disposal a monograph which is to all intents and purposes an official report from the Montreal Neurological Institute of Investigation that its director had been conducting with the assistance of associates for nineteen years.[18] Even those of us who have been following from afar the work that has been done in the last quarter of a century by brain neurologists have known that remarkable experiments have been made by electrically stimulating patients whose cerebral cortex was exposed by craniotomy. But unfortunately reports of these experiments were generally published only in technical journals leaving the layman no general conspectus of the findings. What interests the philosopher from the very first page of this monograph is that the brain neurologists whose work is reported therein emphasize the fact that consciousness is of paramount importance to them, but they do not tell us what consciousness is. Their patients lie fully conscious on the operating table, and what they report on the effects of electrical

---

[17] *Scepticism and Animal Faith*, New York, 1923, p. 191.
[18] Wilder Penfield and Theodore Rasmussen, *The Cerebral Cortex of Man: A Clinical Study of Localization of Function*, New York, The Macmillan Company, 1950. George W. Gray in an article in the October 1948 issue of the *Scientific American* referred to this work as a "forthcoming monograph." From what by report I knew of the authors I delayed writing the final draft of my present chapter till I could see this study. It was my friend, Dr. Hans H. Reese, professor of neuropsychiatry in the Medical School of the University of Wisconsin, who not only called my attention to the actual publication of this volume but also kindly lent me his own copy till I could secure one of my own. I owe much to a discussion I subsequently had with him on some of the problems involved; but of course he is not to be held responsible for any erratic, if not erroneous, use I make of what I learned from him. The work itself contains 235 pages of text amply illustrated with Figures (drawings and photographic reproductions), in addition to Preface, Bibliography, Case Index, and General Index. In the text a description of routine operative procedure in osteoplastic craniotomy is given on pp. 4–7. A layman could not readily find a technical work of such importance and yet so easily intelligible.

stimulation on their cortices constitutes an important source of material.[19]

Since we are at present concerned with vision let us turn to Chapter VII of *The Cerebral Cortex of Man*, which deals with vision. In the course of the approximately four hundred craniotomies under local anesthesia "22 of the patients reported gross visual sensation as the result of [electrical] stimulation." The small number, 22, may seem surprising but it must be remembered that practically every region of the brain at one time or the other is exposed for therapeutical purposes. It was only when clinical symptoms indicated the necessity of treating some limited region of the brain that craniotomy was practiced; thus the opportunity to stimulate the occipital cortex with the consent of the patient occurred only when it was this part of the cortex that had been exposed. As we are told in the Preface: "These surgical procedures are not experiments, for we are dealing with human beings. But from time to time conditions present themselves which would satisfy the most exacting requirements of a critical investigator."[20]

Now, in every case in which gross visual sensation was reported by the patient as the result of stimulation, the "stimulation point was found to be on the cortex of the occipital lobe." This of course was not surprising to our neurologists; it would not have been surprising even to William James sixty years earlier.[21]

"These visual responses are elementary sensations of light, darkness, and color, in gross shapes."[22] To be somewhat more specific, some of the descriptions which the patients used as to what they

---

[19] *Ibid.*, p. ix.
[20] *Ibid.*, p. ix.
[21] The pathologists who have discussed the pathological lesions that turn up "conclude that the occipital lobes are the indispensable part for vision in man. Hemiopic disturbance in both eyes comes from lesion of either one of them, and total blindness, sensorial as well as psychic, from destruction of both." (*The Principles of Psychology* by William James, Vol. I, p. 47.) What is interesting is that out of some four hundred cases of electrical stimulation of the cerebral cortex visual sensation was reported only where the stimulation was applied to the occipital cortex.
[22] Penfield and Rasmussen, *The Cerebral Cortex of Man*, p. 135.

saw are: "Red, green, and yellow lights," "Diamonds," "Wheels," "Blue, green, and red colored discs," "Colors advancing," "Colorless star," "Star moving," "Things larger than the stars moving from ipsilateral to contralateral sides," "Shadow moving up and down," "Undulating black wheel."[23]

It should be kept in mind that of course the patients were not newborn infants. The sensations here are not what James called "the *immediate* results upon consciousness of nerve-currents as they enter the brain and before they have awakened any suggestion or association with past experience. But it is obvious that *such immediate sensations can only be realized in the earliest days of life.*"[24] But it can be said that what is here reported as having been seen was not seen by the operating surgeon or any of his assistants. The same thing can be said of the visual responses to stimulation in CASE K. H. for instance:

> Two stars seemed to go from the midline a little across to the right. Stars lower than the bridge of my nose and over to the right.
> My left eye twitched again, and I saw something, I don't know what it was—it was lighted like a star and not colored.
> I saw something much larger than the stars I have seen before. It was like a board, starting in the left eye and it went over to the right, opposite the cheek.
> A star came down toward my nose.[25]

None of what is seen here or in the cases earlier quoted is physical in either the popular sense of the word or the sense in which present day physicists use it, but in all these cases what is seen is the result of physical stimulation of the occipital cortex. The object of sensory vision in each of these cases is "epiphysical" in the meaning that I have given to this term, namely, something that is not physical but is the result of a physical event.

Just a while ago I said that the authors of this monograph do not tell us what consciousness is but they use expressions in which consciousness occurs, expressions that accord with the meaning

---
[23] *Ibid.*, pp. 140–141.
[24] James, *Psychology, Briefer Course*, p. 12.
[25] Penfield and Rasmussen, *The Cerebral Cortex of Man*, p. 145.

in which I have been using it, although they do not necessitate the adoption of this meaning. In the very chapter on vision from which we have been quoting they speak of "the images of things seen that ordinarily reach consciousness" and again, "the final image that reaches consciousness during normal vision."[26] In a later passage, which deals with pain sensation, we are told "that the pathway of pain conduction reaches the thalamus and consciousness without essential conduction to the cortex."[27] It is to be noted here that a distinction is made between the thalamus and consciousness, and yet the implication seems to be that in reaching the thalamus the same sensation reaches consciousness. A natural interpretation of this is that stimulation of the thalamus produces consciousness and this interpretation is borne out when we find in another passage that the dorsomedial "portion of the thalamus, or other areas in the diencephalon most closely related to it, contains the essential neuronal mechanism upon the integrity of which depends the very existence of consciousness."[28] Here the thalamus is by implication said to be an area of the diencephalon.

> Popular tradition [we are told], which seems to be largely shared by scientific men, has taken it for granted that the cortex is a sort of essential organ for the purposes of thinking and consciousness, and that final integration of neural mechanisms takes place in it.[29]

Our authors do not follow this tradition. Earlier in the monograph our authors assume that "the control of the synthesis of cortical motor and cortical sensory processes is to be found in the diencephalon and mesencephalon," but this "will be hypothetical."[30]

Our authors also tacitly or by implication assume that consciousness depends for its existence upon the functioning of the highest level of integration and they find this, as we have seen, in the

---

[26] *Ibid.*, pp. 145 and 146.
[27] *Ibid.*, p. 233.
[28] *Ibid.*, p. 227.
[29] *Ibid.*, p. 205.
[30] *Ibid.*, p. 19.

diencephalon, including the thalamus, and the mesencephalon. For this reason I suppose they are not following the popular tradition since the occipital cortex is obviously a way station and not a terminal of nerve impulses.[31] But while sensory and motor cortical areas are not integrating agents their "activity forms just one part of an activity which is taking place also in the subcortical structure to which it is most closely related."

> But the various functional areas of the cerebral cortex play, each of them, an integral role in the activity of what might be called the different departments of the diencephalon. The cortical projections serve to elaborate afferent and efferent mechanisms. Through these interconnections memories are stored in neurone patterns within the temporal cortex, and the frontal cortex is utilized in the elaboration of thought.[32]

If I remember correctly, here we have one of the few instances in the monograph of the use of the word "projection," but the context here, taken with the anatomical discussion of "Cortex and Diencephalon" on pages 204 and 205 where projection is also used, makes it clear that by projection is meant proliferated outgrowths. If I understand the authors correctly they take no part in the widely held theory that what appears sensorially in the brain is literally projected out into space. Whether this view of consciousness as depending upon the integrating activity of the old brain will find general acceptance among brain neurologists it is too early to say. To an outsider the arguments for it, spread throughout the whole final chapter, seem very strong.

Whether a philosopher accepts this view here expressed, or whether he accepts the tradition that consciousness depends upon cortical activity, there is nothing in the view of consciousness presented in my present lectures that should be found fundamentally incompatible with either view. To confine our attention for the present only to what has been reported as seen by the patients electrically stimulated at their occipital cortices there is nothing there that does not jibe with the assumption that consciousness

---
[31] *Ibid.*, pp. 232–233.
[32] *Ibid.*, p. 235.

is a relation of its own kind in which an organism comes to stand to what appears to it, and that this relation is *epiphysical*.

A similar result is obtained by electrical stimulation of "the temporal lobe of either side close to the fissure of Sylvius." With such a stimulus applied to this part of the exposed temporal lobe the patient gets sensations of sound such as "Ringing sound like doorbell," "Low-pitched sound 'like a motor,'" "Continuous clicking like crickets at night," "Rushing sound like a bird flying." Here we find reported, just as in the case of the electrical stimulus of the occipital cortex, sensed objects that are epiphysical for they are presumably not sensed by other persons present.[33]

Other sensations than visual and auditory have been reported by patients whose other specified cortex was electrically stimulated. It is not necessary here to go into detail, but it might be well to note here "that the *sensation of movement*, when no movement occurred in a part, was frequently produced by stimulation in the sensorimotor strip."[34] In these examples we have a similar relation between patient and other observers: the former senses what the latter does not.

(There are eight instances given where electrical explorations produced not what is ordinarily called sense objects but desire to move.[35] But more of this anon.) The localization of sensory responses in general is given in Chapter II, to E, with a diagram called, "Sensory Homunculus" explained in the letterpress under the figure.

In view of the localization of areas in the brain the stimulation of which gives rise to such a variety of so-called secondary qualities that obviously are epiphysical, it appears that one has here a fairly strong basis from which to make the generalization that all so-called secondary qualities appearing under whatever circumstances are epiphysical whereas there appears to be no equally strong experimental basis for the rejection of such generalization.

[33] *Ibid.*, pp. 149–151.
[34] *Ibid.*, p. 132.
[35] *Ibid.*, p. 133.

In 1933 I discussed the question whether the redness of a *physical* apple is a physical quality of that object and answered the question by saying: "The quality of redness does not yield directly to the metrical treatment of an experimental physicist."[36] I now assume that such a quality and all other so-called secondary qualities are epiphysical, thus generalizing the findings of neurologists in the case of patients whose exposed cortices are electrically stimulated. In other words, all sensed sound, sensed heat or cold, sensed odors, tastes, etc. are epiphysical, but how then may they be qualities of physical objects? The answer the perspective realist gives to this question is found in postulate 3, laid down in Chapter I of these lectures, which may be quoted here:

In the world of nature any "thing" at any time is, and is nothing but, the totality of the relational characters that the "thing" has at that time in whatever relations it has at that time to other "things."

Now a physical thing is, and is nothing but, the totality of the physical relational character it has at that time, but thus definition of a physical thing does not preclude such a thing from having other characters in whatever nonphysical relation it stands at that time to other things. The "physical world" at any time is the totality of physical things, and according to the view of most physicists there was nothing but the physical world for many eons of time; and according to the view presented in these lectures when some physical things came to stand in nonphysical relations they acquired certain nonphysical qualities in these latter relations. But these acquisitions were as natural under the conditions under which they arose as the previously existing physical things. The physical world with these natural accruals constitutes the world of nature. I have elsewhere quoted and I now re-quote Whitehead's famous contention:

For natural philosophy [that is the philosophy of nature] everything perceived is in nature. We may not pick and choose. For us the red glow of the sunset should be as much part of nature as are the mole-

---

[36] "Perceptual and Memory Perspectives," *The Journal of Philosophy*, Vol. XXX, p. 320.

cules and electric waves by which men of science would explain the phenomenon. It is for natural philosophy to analyse how these various elements of nature are connected.[37]

According to the assumption we made a while ago red is not a physical character, but it may be, and often is, perceived as a character of a physical thing. It is a natural accrual to the physical thing when this latter becomes a term in the nonphysical relation of consciousness; or, conversely stated, when the physical thing appears as red to some conscious subject. It not only appears as red but it is red in this new relation in which it comes to stand to the conscious subject. And what is true of red in this relation is also true of sound, taste, odors, etc. in similar relations.

All such qualities are called "secondary" and in one sense they are secondary. This is to say that they are not primordial if the view referred to as held by most physicists is to be accepted. There were no such characters until consciousness occurred and with its occurrence expanded the physical world into the world of nature. With this expansion something new occurred but not a new world set over against the physical world with a gulf between the two. There is no such gulf. Let us call what is new in this world the world of mind. This nomenclature accords with our own definition of mind: namely, mind is a physical organism when conscious. Thus the world of mind is not separated by a logically impassable gulf from the world of physics. The connection between the two consists in the fact that certain physical processes in physical organisms give rise to the epiphysical world of mind.

The question may be asked, what bearing has the discussion of these secondary qualities on the subject of perspectives, the title we have given to the present chapter. Graphic artists, who seem to have been the first to introduce the idea of perspectives into the art of the Renaissance, distinguish between linear perspective and aerial perspective. Our earlier discussion of perspective dealt with linear visual perspective, in which the directions between seen objects were determined by the special directions from which

---

[37] *The Concept of Nature*, p. 29.

light from the objects reached the retina. Since linear perspective concerns itself with spatial direction it could be treated geometrically, that is, mathematically. Aerial perspective, which concerns itself with differences in light and shade, was more a matter of pure empiricism, especially in painting, where colors play often a more important part than differences in light and shade. Now, so far as we know there is no mathematical law in accordance with which difference of frequencies in physical light are correlated with differences of color. It is simply a matter of empirical fact that for the normal eye stimulation by vibration within a certain range of frequencies gives rise to vision of red, a certain higher range of frequencies gives rise to orange, etc. But in spite of this lack of subjection of colors to mathematical treatment the effect of colors in a painting is the way of representing the seen colors of physical objects. Painters gave the class name "perspective" to these representations as well as to representations by angular direction, and I question whether they were not justified. At any rate I shall use the word perspective in connection with the vision of colors of physical objects. I shall say that in the perspective of the normal eye a physical object is red.

And now I shall ask your indulgence when I stretch still further the denotation of perspective and speak of past objects in the perspective of memory, and here let us use such guidance as the neurologists give us. We've already seen that a certain part of the temporal cortex is an area whose stimulation gives rise to sensations of sound, but that is by no means the sole function of the temporal cortex, which "differs from other cortical areas in that epileptic discharge and electrical stimulation may activate acquired neuronal patterns within it."[38] All the responses to electrical stimulation and the stimulation of epileptic discharge that we have been dealing with seem to the authors of *The Cerebral Cortex of Man* "to be elementary and, in general, it is fair to say that within the sensorimotor, the visual, and the auditory

---

[38] Penfield and Rasmussen, *The Cerebral Cortex of Man*, p. 157.

areas stimulation is unable to reveal mechanisms other than those which might be called inborn."[39] It is mainly "in the temporal lobe [that] complicated acquired mechanisms are represented."[40]

"Our findings [say our authors] do no more than contribute evidence that such analyses [as the 'psychologists have long used to explain memory'] must be correct." They indicate further that the "synaptic record is established in one temporal cortex, and in some of the adjacent occipital and, perhaps, parietal cortex instead of widely throughout the brain, and that furthermore the record must be laid down in an identical pattern somewhere else, presumably the other temporal lobe."[41]

> It is obvious that within the temporal cortex there are mechanisms which somehow play an important role in the act of remembering and of making comparisons between present sensory perceptions and past experience.
>
> The organization of the temporal cortex is evidently different from that of other areas inasmuch as here alone electrical stimulation and epileptic discharge activate acquired synaptic patterns. The fact that it is only in this region that such stimulation produced complex psychical illusions and hallucinations argues for some degree of localization of intellectual functions.[42]
>
> The mantle of gray matter [our authors tell us] which covers the *temporal lobe* is large. We have referred to it in Chapter IX as a unit related to memory. It is not, however, a unit whose boundaries are distinct. If the temporal mantle were opened up and flattened out like a map, it would be seen that within or adjacent to its periphery are the following representations: (*a*) hearing (first temporal); (*b*) vestibular function (first temporal); (*c*) speech skill (supramarginal); (*d*) hand skill (parietal); (*e*) vision (occipital); (*f*) smell (uncus).[43]

Within such an extended gray mantle we should naturally expect new neural paths to be continually acquired resulting in new integrations of patterns. This is to be remembered in our following discussion.

But it is not only what we call memory that depends upon

---
[39] *Ibid.*, p. 159.
[40] *Ibid.*, p. 160.
[41] *Ibid.*, p. 180.
[42] *Ibid.*, pp. 177–178.
[43] *Ibid.*, p. 225.

activation of the temporal cortex but also perception, dreams, hallucinations, and illusions. The reason for this is that all these "mental functions" may be said, by a perhaps admissible exaggeration, to be forms of memory differing from what James somewhere calls "the conscious phenomenon of memory." In the following passage James quotes with approval what Münsterberg says:

> I may only think of my objects, yet in my living thought they stand before me exactly as perceived objects would do, no matter how different the two ways of apprehending them may be in their genesis. The book here lying on the table before me, and the book in the next room of which I think and which I mean to get, are both in the same sense given realities for me, realities which I acknowledge . . . .
>
> What is true of the here and the there, is also true of the now and the then. I know of the thing which is present and perceived, but I know also of the thing which yesterday was but is no more, and which I only remember . . . .

Of all this and more, James says: "This certainly is the immediate, primary, naïf, or practical way of taking our thought-of-world."[44]

For our present purpose what has been here said in regard to memory is to be emphasized. Until sophistication perverts the report of naïf common sense the man on the street won't say to you that he has a visual image of his child kissing him goodbye in the morning. If you question him on this report and he does not justifiably ignore your impertinence he will probably say, "Why, I can just see her doing it this morning." It is this natural attitude, remembered without a trace of doubt, that I prefer to assume to be the correct attitude. Much unintentional mischief I think has been done to philosophy by those who intend scrupulously to report the facts. It is because they do not see how it is possible for one here and now to be immediately conscious of the there and the then that they misrepresent what they find in their memory experience. Of course memory may be mistaken in the sense that an event remembered may differ from the event as it occurred at the time of its occurrence. Why not use here the

---
[44] James, *Essays in Radical Empiricism*, pp. 18–20.

concept of perspectives? This use is facilitated by the fact that memory arises as the result of the activation of an acquired neuronal pattern. As our neurological authors say: "When memory is reproduced by the stimulating electrode, an acquired neurone pattern is being activated." And they go on to say:

> When a man voluntarily summons a memory which he wishes to examine in detail, the memory may progressively unfold itself before his consciousness, just as it did under the influence of the electrode. It would seem, therefore, that in the voluntary act of recollection there must be neuronal activation of the temporal cortex by means of "voluntary" activity originating within a centrally placed area of gray matter.
> It would seem, also, that the original formation of the memory pattern must be carried out from a high level of neural integration, for a man remembers the things of which he was conscious and especially the substance of his own reaction to them. The same was true of memories evoked by stimulation. They were usually composed of familiar elements, at least to the same extent as dreams are.[45]

To return to our previous suggestion, that in memory a past event should be said to be in the perspective of the subject at a later time, it should not be surprising that the past event appears different in some respects from the event as previously sensed, since this perspective is conditioned by the activation of a neuronal complex with new factors that have entered into the complex since the time of the original experience.

I have treated memory without reference to perception, because our authors, not without reason, have done that. "*Perception* of the significance of things [they say] seen and heard must obviously depend in some manner upon memory."[46] But the memory they speak of here is not the conscious memory that we have been discussing. It is "the *memory* that is stored or 'filed' in the temporal cortex, whether visual picture, musical piece, or significant experience." It is "*the original memory pattern* [that] *was formed in the temporal cortex.*"[47] The italics here are mine. It is upon

---
[45] Penfield and Rasmussen, *The Cerebral Cortex of Man*, p. 234.
[46] *Ibid.*, p. 225.
[47] *Ibid.*, p. 224.

such a memory pattern that the perception of the significance of things seen and heard must obviously depend.

It is significant that brain neurologists find, as we have said, the cortical representation not only of memory and perception but also of dream, hallucination, and illusion in the same temporal lobes, for all these neuronal interconnections are acquired and not inborn and thus they stand as a class distinct from sensations. Just what neuronal connections in the temporal cortex are dominant in any particular case depends upon various factors such as the frequency with which a particular connection has been used, the recency of its use, past and present, emotional condition of the organism, the direction of attention immediately preceding, etc. in their interplay which may be partly summational and partly inhibitory. Our authors tell us:

> We have stumbled unexpectedly upon the location of the neuronal patterns "which dreams are made of" and have glimpsed other mechanisms within the humming loom of the mind.
>
> The epileptic hallucinations reproduce a remembered event more or less perfectly and one that may have been dreamed as well. The epileptic discharge seems to condition the temporal cortex so that the electrode can reproduce the same chain of neuronal activity. But the intermittent epileptic activity instead of always activating the same neurone pattern may reproduce recent memories, memories that are new with each recrudescence of attacks. This suggests that unless a pattern is strongly conditioned by long habit recent memory patterns are more liable to activation by the discharge.
>
> Experience with cortical stimulation brings one to the conclusion that these induced mental states are like dreams. They have in them some reproduction of remembered experience, an experience which is chiefly visual or auditory. It is not a picture or a single sound, but a progressive changing psychical phenomenon. If the electrode is held in place, action goes forward as in a dream and the patient may become frightened and cry out.[48]

A long and careful study of Chapter IX, on Memory, Sensory Perception, and Dreams, with constant pondering over the prob-

---

[48] *Ibid.*, p. 179. One case of total recall (see pp. 164–167), the details of which I need not mention here, was so astounding that Dr. Penfield in a special article called upon all his colleagues in related professions to join in study on the phenomena.

lems presented, has left me wondering whether the so-called mental functions dealt with might not, for the time being at least, be classified into the normal and abnormal with a no-man's land between. Of course I recognize that normality is a rather vague concept when we are dealing with highly complicated organisms. Every human being is more or less abnormal at least in certain of his physiological functions. We all know the story of the Quaker and what he said to his wife about the queerness of people. Nevertheless, not only for practical purposes but also for theoretical purposes it may be well, in spite of the impossibility of defining normality precisely, to classify persons and their physiological functions as more or less normal and to speak, for short, of the more normal as normal, and of the decidedly less normal as abnormal. This leaves the desirable no-man's land between the two. Using these distinctions I think we may with fair safety say that memory and perception are normal. The normal child is not born, presumably, either remembering or perceiving, but he begins to remember and perceive within the first two or three years of his life. Perception is facilitated for him by the fair constancy of many of the objects within his tactile and visual reach and by the acquisition of words which name these objects. The question whether memory or perception develops first perhaps is unanswerable. I rather suppose that they develop together, and here I mean conscious memory and conscious perception. Now as to dreams, who can tell? I prefer to leave them in the no-man's land, between the normal and the abnormal, leaving open the question whether many children do not "normally" live quite frequently in a dream world without distinguishing it from the world of sense perception and memory.

James defines memory proper as *"the knowledge of an event, or fact, of which meantime we have not been thinking, with the additional consciousness that we have thought or experienced it before."*[49] Five pages later James says:

---
[49] *Principles of Psychology*, Vol. I, p. 648.

Such being the *phenomenon* of memory, . . . can we see how it comes to pass? Can we lay bare its causes?
Its complete exercise presupposes two things:
1) The *retention* of the remembered fact; and
2) Its *reminiscence, recollection, reproduction,* or *recall.*
Now *the cause both of retention and of recollection is the law of habit in the nervous system, working as it does in the "association of ideas."*

And for James, so far as association stands for a *cause*, it is between *processes in the brain.*[50] I suggest replacement of the latter part of this quotation by the following:

Its complete exercise presupposes two neurological facts:
1) The establishment and retention of a neuronal pattern in the temporal cortex when "the remembered event" was originally perceived.
2) The reactivation of this neuronal pattern upon the occurrence of which memory arises as its epiphysical effect.

I make these suggestions because I can find no evidence that any remembered fact is ever retained, Bergson and other philosophers to the contrary notwithstanding; and the reactivation of an acquired neuronal pattern is of itself only just that, namely, a physical reactivation of an acquired neuronal pattern. If this were all, there would be no more memory in the sense in which memory is defined than there is in any mechanical brain. There is no more reason for supposing that the synaptic pattern established in a temporal cortex has by itself a whit more of consciousness than the grooves have which are worn in a phonographic record by the needle in the recording machine. All records of any sort made in the physical world by themselves are nothing but physical things; it is only when they come to the attention of a mind, that is, as we've seen, of an organism that's conscious, that they have any conscious epiphysical value. If we look back at the definition that James gave of memory proper we note that it is the *"knowledge of an event, . . . with the additional consciousness that . . ."* It is a conscious relation, resulting from the reactivation of a synaptic record, which is what is called recollection or recall, but

---

[50] *Ibid.*, p. 654.

such a recall is to be distinguished from the kind of recall that occurs when a retired waitress is called back to the table she has been serving. In this latter case, if the recall is successful it is the waitress as of the present time that appears at the table not the waitress as of some minutes earlier. But in memory the "recalled" face of an absent friend is, as remembered, the face as of an earlier time. If then the question be asked how can anyone at present reach back physically into a past and get into physical contact with a vanished hand, the answer is that no one can *physically* do that.

> The Moving Finger writes; and, having writ,
> Moves on: nor all your Piety nor Wit
> Shall lure it back to cancel half a Line,
> Nor all your Tears wash out a Word of it.[51]

Omar Khayyám might have gone further for no one can physically react to the past. Properly speaking, one reacts *from* the past. We must distinguish between reaction and retrospection and in making this distinction we must recognize that physically there is no retroaction. When we speak of retroactive laws consideration should show that in applying them we are treating a person who is in the present in light of what we know of his past and here the knowledge is retro*spective*. However retaliatory or revengeful we may be we cannot wreak our vengeance upon a past person. But although the past is beyond our physical reach, it is not beyond our ken, it is not beyond our retrospect. We can ponder over it, we may dislike it, we may hurl our anathemas at it, but we can do nothing about it. But of course what has resulted from the past is still within our physical reach. But although all this should be so obvious as not to be open to question, it may seem so strange to some as to make it desirable to elaborate. All of us who drive have perhaps had experience of smashed fenders, and when I say that nothing can be done about the smashing of any fender this does not preclude me from trying to do something about the present condition of the fender resulting from a past

---
[51] *Rubaiyat of Omar Khayyam*, translated by Edward Fitzgerald.

collision that cannot be undone. And what is true of a fender is also true of other alterable objects. To alter an object is not to make its past not to have been but it is to act upon its present condition. Perhaps all American philosophers are familiar with the position taken by George Herbert Mead in the first chapter of *The Philosophy of the Present,* edited by Arthur E. Murphy.[52] It was a tragedy that Mead did not live to bring this chapter to a final form satisfactory even to himself. What seems to have been his latest opinion on the subject we are discussing is to be found in these words:

> Durations are a continual sliding of presents into each other. The present is a passage constituted by processes whose earlier phases determine in certain respects their later phases. Reality then is always in a present. When the present has passed it no longer is. The question arises whether the past arising in memory and in the projection of this still further backwards, refers to events which existed as such continuous presents passing into each other, or to that conditioning phase of the passing present which enables us to determine conduct with reference to the future which is also arising in the present. It is this latter thesis which I am maintaining.
>
> The implication of my position is that the past is such a construction that the reference that is found in it is not to events having a reality independent of the present which is the seat of reality, but rather to such an interpretation of the present in its conditioning passage as will enable intelligent conduct to proceed. It is of course evident that the materials out of which that past is constructed lie in the present. I refer to the memory images and the evidences by which we build up the past, and to the fact that any reinterpretation of the picture we form of the past will be found in a present, and will be judged by the logical and evidential characters which such data possess in a present.[53]

The use of the word *independent* in any philosophical discussion is likely to give rise to misunderstanding unless the word is carefully defined. When Mead speaks of "events having a reality independent of the present which is the seat of reality," what is meant by the word "independent"? The natural meaning in the context in which the word appears is what I should call temporal

---
[52] G. H. Mead, *The Philosophy of the Present,* Chicago, 1932.
[53] *Ibid.,* pp. 28–29.

existence of the past as not conditioned by a later present. Now to me it is not evident that the materials out of which that past is constructed lie in the present, and I question whether what Mead calls memory images are images and I question whether these things can be said without ambiguity to be found in a present. Twenty-five years earlier Dewey had said and I think had said correctly:

> Things can be presented as absent, just as they can be presented as hard or soft, black or white, six inches or fifty rods away from the body. The assumption that an ideal content must be either totally absent, or else present *in just the same fashion* as it will be when it is realized, is not only dogmatic, but self-contradictory.[54]

The whole context shows that the words "be presented" have the same meaning as the words "be present." Now by the same token I maintain that things can be present as past or as future and in either or both cases they can be thus present at the same time at which other things are present as present. Now it is obvious that the word "present" here is used in different senses. When Dewey said that "things can be presented as absent" and when I say that things can be present as past or future the words "be presented," or "be present" are synonomous with the word "appear."[55]

James tells us that the sense of time must be due to an element in the brain process which bears "the same inscrutable *sort* of relation to its correlative feeling which all other elements of neural activity bear to their psychic products, be the latter what they may."[56] This relation is of course inscrutable from the point of view of physics and its laws, for these laws are the mathematical description of the way in which physical things behave to each other and to nothing else, and what James calls the "psychic products" are not physical. It is only by a figure of speech that we can speak of memory proper as being stored or filed away in the

---

[54] In *Mind*, Vol. XV, N.S., July, 1906, and reprinted in *The Influence of Darwin on Philosophy*, New York, 1910, p. 89.
[55] Cf. *supra*, Ch. IV, p. 141.
[56] *Principles of Psychology*, Vol. I, p. 632.

neuronal connections within the temporal cortex. Why, when these connections are activated, there should be memory proper is a question that neurology, which is a branch of physics, cannot answer. Neurologists can tell the occasions on which memory proper occurs.

Now, recognizing the physically inscrutable relations between the memory patterns in the brain and memory proper, namely the consciousness of some things as of the past that we had previously experienced as of the then present, we have before us the problem as to how, since various memory patterns in the brain have been laid down on various occasions, it is possible to select the relevant patterns on any particular occasion. To give an example: when I sensuously see a man walking about at a distance how do I know that it is a man or some other animal, for we all know that in sense perception things are not always as they seem. Now, in one sense things are always as they seem, but in spite of that if what we are talking about is a physical object then they are not always as they seem, for what is physically a bear may seem at a distance to be a man. The answer to our question cannot be given with absolute assurance; but if we cannot have reasonable assurance under certain recognizable conditions even physical science would not have a reasonable basis, for, as we all know, what distinguishes physical science is its resort to instrumentation, and yet instruments will be of no value unless we can depend upon the correctness of the readings that they show and they show their readings, generally, only in sense perception. And scientists very properly require that what has been seen instrumentally by one person requires confirmation by others under the same conditions as prevailed in the first observation. Here the question arises as to what constitutes adequate evidence. The first reporter may have been carried away by his enthusiasm or by some other disturbing emotional influence. It is not possible here to go into detail as to the methods whereby dangers due to inaccurate observation may be avoided. Let us say that the training of a scientist is to a large extent training in accurate observation. We have in scientific criticism something analogous to what in law is called rules of evidence, and both in science and in law we have a refinement of tests that common sense adopts in practical affairs. Someone has said that science is only systematized common sense and that is true as far as the rules of evidence go, much more so as regards science than as regards law.

What has been said on the subject of the truth-value of sense perception can be said of the truth-value of memory. Here again in one sense the remembered past was as we remembered and yet I suppose that everyone admits that memory of physical events is justifiably subject to criticism, just as the sense perception is so subject. We find on comparison with others that our memories do not correspond always with that of others who observed the remembered event at the time it physically occurred. We say that one person has better memory than some other person. For this and for perhaps other reasons, in general, we trust more to records made by living witnesses of past events than to their later memories of those events. Autobiographies are more subject to question than records made by their authors at the time of the event recorded. And yet in spite of the so-called fallibility of sense perception and of memory, without the acceptance of the truth-value in general of both sense perception and of memory there could be no physical science and no history. Even worse, there could be no reliable assurance as to anything at all. We may therefore say that knowledge is adequately tested faith, and adequacy is relative to the best tests available at the time.

Let us now turn to another area of the brain, the frontal lobe "(anterior to the precentral gyrus)." Here we must distinguish between lobectomy and lobotomy. Lobectomy is removal of very large areas of this lobe. "Careful study after operation [upon a patient]—both in hospital and in the home—demonstrated no alteration in behavior, except an 'impairment of those mental processes which are prerequisite to planned initiative.' . . . She had not forgotten how to cook but she had lost the capacity of planning and preparing a meal alone." However, in another patient, "Over one-third of the total volume of each frontal lobe was removed . . . No clinical or psychometric deterioration could be detected. Although he may have lacked initiative he managed to find and to hold employment and to satisfy his family."

> *Bilateral lobotomy and gyrectomy.* Much could be said about the effect of cutting across the white matter of the anterior frontal lobes. Physiologically, it is not quite the same as ablation of convolutions, for although the main connections between thalamus and frontal pole are severed, it is difficult to determine how far the untouched convolutions continue to function by means of superficial connections. Also, as these patients suffer from psychoses or neuroses beforehand, it is difficult to make a judgment as to the effect of lobotomy on normal behavior.
>
> A more accurate anatomical conclusion can be drawn from a series of *bilateral frontal gyrectomies* which we have carried out upon such patients (Penfield, 1948). As far as possible the removals were made along fissure lines so that groups of gyri were ablated in homologous areas on the two sides.
>
> *Orbital surface of frontal lobe.* One of the surprising results, in view of recent experimental suggestions as to the importance of the function of the inferior surface of the frontal lobes, was the fact that bilateral ablation of these surfaces had remarkably little effect, in one patient, either upon her anxiety or upon her mental and physical state. She carried on a reasonably intelligent conversation throughout the whole procedure without any alteration being apparent.

Two other cases are reported after which the authors remark:

> The only functional conclusion that could be drawn from the foregoing series of bilateral gyrectomies is the following: There was increasing impairment of capacity for mental performance as bilateral removals were carried farther back into the superior portion of the intermediate frontal cortex.[57]

On the final page of Chapter X, from which we have been quoting, the authors say:

> In this chapter we have made inquiry into the nature of defects produced by therapeutic removals. This method of investigation of function in many cases is less informative than study of the results of epileptic discharge within an area. When a neurosurgeon undertakes the removal of areas of cortex, he is interested to learn whether or not that removal will handicap his patient. He must endeavor to determine what areas may be removed from the cerebral cortex without

---

[57] Penfield and Rasmussen, *The Cerebral Cortex of Man,* pp. 192–196.

producing functional defects. His goal is achieved if he learns nothing at all positive about function! He thus discovers that removal of certain areas produced no defect that he or the patient recognizes. He may even be forced to the paradoxical conclusion that brain removal has resulted in improvement of mental processes when the area removed contained a focus of epileptogenic discharge . . . . The surprising fact is that so large a proportion of the human cerebral cortex may be called *dispensable cortex.*

This does not mean that there are areas of cortex with no function. It means that much of the cortex may be employed by the individual on an optional basis . . . . The man who has lost one occipital lobe turns his attention to the visual field in which he can still see and is often surprised when it is pointed out that he is blind in the other half-field. The patient who has lost one frontal lobe is not aware of, nor initially interested in, the fact that he has lost capacity for effective planning.

It is in man's nature to turn his attention to the sense perceptions and the memories that are available to him and to employ the mental processes which he can command, rather than to concern himself with what is missing. This doubtless accounts for some of the difficulty in discovering the essential function of the "silent areas" of the human cortex.[58]

Some pages back I quoted: "*desire to move* was also a recognized response to the electrical stimulation." Now while there is a distinction to be observed between a desire to move and a will to move, philosophers and psychologists have, correctly I think, regarded desires and volition as instances of a more general class called "conation." Speaking of the fact that "patients sometimes say a certain stimulus causes them to wish to carry out an action," our authors proceed to say, "this suggests that there may be stimulable elements in the cortex which are allied to the mechanism that underlies volitional innovation."[59] And two pages earlier they speak of "motor areas of the cerebral cortex" as activated "by *volitional impulses* from within the brain." But apparently their researches have done little to add to our knowledge of "the mechanism that underlies volitional innovation." There is much in the conscious experience of normal men for which, so far as we know, its neural counterpart has not as yet been found. And

---
[58] *Ibid.*, p. 201.
[59] *Ibid.*, p. 159, footnote.

this is not surprising, for study of localization of function in the brain with methods supplied by recent technique is of course as recent as the technique; but there is still another reason. The higher functions of the mind, that is, of the organism as conscious, are presumably the result of the integrated and coordinated action of many parts of the brain. To adopt and adapt the famous statement of Sherrington's, neurological research of the brain, young as it is, has done so much that we may assume that there is no fixed limit beyond which it may not go. It is therefore with hope and a sense of risk that I assume that all our conscious life is the result of nervous activity in the brain. What differentiates more than anything else my perspective realism is the view of consciousness as an *epiphysical* relation whose occurrence depends upon nerve activity. Just as in sense and sense perception and memory physical objects and events appear to us in perspective, so do they appear to us also in intellectual perspectives and moral perspectives and esthetic perspectives. In none of these cases does the physical object appear to us as it is by itself, for as we've seen, according to our theory, there are no things by themselves; they are all things in relation and the characters that things have vary in some certain respects according to the different relations of which they are terms. The physical characters that physical things have they have as terms in physical relation, and the physical relations which they have vary from time to time. In Newton's physics spatial characters were absolute. The physical size of a physical object was the size of the part of space that the object occupied, that part being absolute. Now in the perspective of the present day physicists the size of an object varies with its velocity with reference to some other physical thing. It has one size in respect to an object that is at rest with it and other sizes with respect to other objects in various relations of motion with respect to it. And so with mass, another so-called primary quality. If we are going to be perspectivists we should be impartial. In the perspective of early man the earth was at rest, and everything else, sun, moon, stars, etc., moved with respect to it. In the perspective of Copernicus it was the sun that was at rest, and real motion of anything was motion relative to the sun. And in the perspective of present day physicists motion is altogether relative. There is no meaning in the assertion that anything is absolutely at rest, that is, at rest without reference to something else, etc. What, at the next stage, will be the view no one can foretell. Now a perspectivist, to be thoroughgoing, should recognize that his perspectivism is itself relative not absolute.

One advantage that can be claimed for this perspectivist view is that it recognizes that other views, even opposing views, are tenable from the respective points of view of those who hold them. In my introductory chapter I emphasized the importance of postulates, or perhaps one had better say of implicit assumptions, and different people have different fundamental assumptions. Since perspective realism in the form in which I am presenting it is based upon the assumption that there is a physical world and that parts of the physical world actually appear normally in the sense, memory, perception, and intellectual theorizings of the perspectivist, he also recognizes that other intelligent human beings starting from different assumptions may also have intelligent views different from his own. And when the fundamental assumptions of various thinkers are different there is no known method by which any one of these thinkers can prove to any other that the other's fundamental conceptions are untenable. Let us take for example the Protestant Christian fundamentalist in his theology. He operates on the assumption that the Bible is the word of God—of an omnipotent and omniscient God. If there are apparent contradictions between different assertions in different parts of the Bible, the fault is with the reader in his interpretation of the word of God. What the scientific geologist teaches with regard to fossil evidence, as proving that eons ago living creatures left their remains embedded in rocks, is erroneous because the Book of Genesis says that in six days God created the Heavens and the earth. If he is asked how comes it then that those fossils are unquestionably found he may reply that God by virtue of his omnipotence can have created those fossils, as it were, at a stroke. If he is told by the scientist that without a horrendous catastrophe the sun could not have stood still at the command of Joshua speaking in God's name until God's people had time to win the victory over God's enemies, his reply again is that an omnipotent God, who in the act of creation established what are called the laws of nature, could easily have suspended these laws. The fundamentalist may go further and quote from the Bible: "To everything there is a season and a time for every purpose under heaven: a time to be born and a time to die; a time to plant and a time to pluck up that which is planted." Thus also there is a time for the orderly course of nature and a time to arrest that course as God wills. Now, what is the matter with this logic once the fundamental premise is laid down from which this conclusion is drawn? And how can you disprove that premise except by drawing your conclusion from a fundamentally different premise? A scientist, if he knew the Bible well enough, might say, "Ephraim is joined to his idols, let him alone, without speaking of his idols." But supercilious vituperation will hardly succeed in converting the fundamentalist to the scientific point of view. It is enough to let him alone unless he interferes with the vital interests of others.

Let us now turn from consideration of theological matters to something recognized by philosophers as more peculiarly philosophical. I am referring now to what calls itself idealism, whether subjective or objective. In both types, especially in their extreme forms, "mind" is primordial and "matter" is secondary and derivative. Such views are traditionally regarded as opposed to modern realism and I have no doubt would be regarded as opposed also to perspective realism if their champions knew that there was such a thing. Opposed to both idealism and realism is the view championed by Arthur O. Lovejoy in his Carus lectures, *The Revolt Against Dualism*.[60] The contestants in this three-cornered philosophical debate apparently believe each that the others can

---

[60] A. O. Lovejoy, *The Revolt Against Dualism*, Chicago, 1930.

be logically proved inconsistent, but I am inclined to believe that this is because neither party lays down explicitly its own fundamental assumptions. If this were done I wonder whether any acknowledged exponent of any one of these three different views might not honestly say with Omar Khayyam:

> Myself when young did eagerly frequent
> Doctor and Saint, and heard great argument
> About it and about: but evermore
> Came out by the same door where in I went.

As for myself when young, I did eagerly frequent great argument but usually I took each door in turn entering by one and making my exit through an opposite door into another chamber, and after this protracted tour I found that I had boxed the compass and like Odysseus I returned to the place of my early years. But the door where through I returned was a wider door and the returning pilgrim is I hope a wiser man. The reason for this happy outcome was that I had become explicitly conscious of the fundamental assumption on which the implicit philosophical faith of my callow years was based.

Tennyson's Ulysses says of himself, "I am a part of all that I have met." Of myself I cannot say this. I should rather say "Much that I have met has become a part of me," and this is true especially of idealism and also of what little I have learned from the physical sciences. No single and simple characterization of any philosophy can of course do it justice, but anyone who has read this present volume up to this point will have learned that I have much sympathy with what has been called "the definitive characteristics of idealism,"[61] "for more than anything else ... the continuity of the idealist tradition is to be found in the recognition of the primacy of 'spirit' in the world." I should rather say "supreme importance" rather than primacy for this latter word is ambiguous: "spirit" is neither first in time nor place in the philosophy I have been trying to work out. Not all idealists, even

---
[61] *Contemporary Idealism in America*, Edited by Clifford Barrett, New York, Macmillan, 1932, p. 16.

not all those who contributed to the volume from which I have just quoted, prefer the word "spirit." One of the contributors says:

> The point of departure for idealism is then the reality, the existence, the spontaneity, the hegemony, of the soul. I use the word soul, in spite of the psychologists, without apology. It is fully as respectable a term as matter, and certainly no more elusive in meaning. When the soul dons academic garb and puts on its dignity its *nom de guerre* is mind, but since it is not merely knower, but the determiner of all other values as well as truth values, both individual and social, the old-fashioned term is the more fitting. The more sophisticated call it the self; those primarily interested in religion prefer the term spirit.[62]

Perhaps the least sophisticated, rather than the more sophisticated, call it the "self." When a growing infant begins to talk he probably refers to himself by the name given to him by others but later he comes to use the personal pronoun "I" as distinguished from "you," "he," "him," etc. He is now a self among other selves and not, at least in English, an *"it,"* and I rather suspect that unless he is brought up in an intensely religious community he learns that he "has a mind" before he learns that he has a soul. But it is not the name preferred by the idealists represented in the volume under discussion that I no longer accept, it is what they say about the thing named. For instance, we are told: "When one speaks of the soul as existent or real, one must mean that it is actually effective in determining facts on the common realm of experience. The universal form that this activity takes is the creation of wholes, in which the whole is always more than the mere sum of the parts." And again: "Thus the soul is the life of the body, but it is more than that, for it is also transcendent of bodily limitations; and the body is the expression in the physical order of the nature of this soul, of this soul made flesh, but it is less than that, for at best it could only represent the soul to date, and that most inadequately."[63]

Of course I cannot disprove any of this; but for years my

---
[62] *Ibid.*, p. 31.
[63] *Ibid.*, p. 35–36.

thinking in these matters has been influenced by the thesis expressed by the title of Sherrington's great work, *The Integrative Action of the Nervous System*. Even when later this author said that "theory has nothing to submit as to how space-time energy and mind stand in some way coupled together," he still had faith that the physics and chemistry of the cell can "resolve the still unexplained residue of the cell's behavior." The author's final word on this problem so far as I know deserves to be quoted in full:

> The demand for discussion of this liaison between two incommensurable factors can be avoided, but at a cost, by adopting either of two other courses. If for instance we start out from the notion of the psychical self and proceed thence to its apprehended world including its apprehended body, the whole scheme is a mental one, and the body-mind incompatibility falls. The self and its world are then one in their nature. Or again, remembering that common sense and physics and chemistry, from their analysis of our body and its cosmical surround reduce these ultimately to a single factor, "energy," *we can suppose that our thinking is likewise an outcome of "energy." Then again the body-mind disparation disappears, because both have become forms of "energy"* [italics introduced]—though in this case by means of an assumption which seems to many an unjustified one.
>
> Of these two views Cajal tells how he was for a time a zealous disciple of the former, and noticed that to his practical life adherence neither to the one nor other seemed to make any difference whatever. I should myself have supposed that the Berkeleian view would impair the "zest" of the waking day, nor can I imagine the achievements of ancient Rome emerging from such a doctrine.
>
> That our being should consist of *two* fundamental elements offers I suppose no greater inherent improbability than that it should rest on one only.[64]

I have italicized some sentences in this quotation in order to raise the question whether the supposition that our thinking is an outcome of energy requires the conclusion that mind has become a form of energy. We may remark that in modern physics it is not energy alone that is the outcome of energy. Mass may also be an outcome, and *vice versa* energy may be the outcome of loss

---

[64] *The Integrative Action of the Nervous System*, 1947. From the Foreword, pp. xxiii-xxiv.

of mass; thus we no longer have the universal law of the conservation of energy. We have the conservation of energy-mass, the result being expressed mathematically in Einstein's now famous equation $E = mc^2$ where all the terms are quantitative. But is there any reason to suppose that the only outcome of an energetic transaction is either energy or mass? When dealing with the physical sciences measurement of phenomena in terms of appropriate units is fundamental, and this is because the effort is to describe any phenomenon in such a way that the description can be tested by others under similar conditions and it is maintained that only metrical descriptions can meet this requirement. But is it necessary or even desirable that everything should be capable of metrical description? For example, pleasures and pain, loves and hates, are important empirical facts no one can ignore without loss or peril, and yet no one has ever succeeded in describing them adequately in terms of metrical units. By and large we can deal with problems that concern pains and pleasures, loves and hates, etc. with some degree of success in spite of lack of metrical units in our dealings. As a wise old bishop once remarked, "Probability is the guide of life," and by probability he probably did not mean something that could be expressed metrically. The problem whether the physical world is purposive has long been discussed, and no general agreement has resulted. In view of the different assumptions on which this discussion has been conducted I should like now to elaborate upon the assumption that consciousness is epiphysical, hoping that with further development this supposition can do much towards solving the mind-body problem, especially in cases where purpose is involved.

If mind is defined as a conscious biological organism when it is conscious, and if the adjective "conscious" is used to denote a character which the organism acquires when it is a term of "consciousness" and consciousness is recognized as a unique relation, there is no reason to suppose that the organism in becoming conscious loses its status as a member of the physical world. An organism in becoming conscious becomes a term of a conscious relation just as a man in becoming a husband becomes a term in a matrimonial relation; and just as a man in becoming a husband does not cease to be a biological, i.e., physical, organism, so a man, let us say, in becoming conscious does not cease to be a biological organism.

In elaboration of this supposition let us take the case of a person who in reacting to red light puts his foot on the brake and brings his car to a stop. On our assumption the same currents of energy starting from the retina stimulated by light-rays give rise to the sensing of red and also to the motor reaction that brings the car to a stop. Both results occur so nearly simultaneously that one cannot be sure which occurs earlier. Here we have a learned reaction, a conditioned reflex, but conditioned reflexes presuppose "simple reflexes" which are inborn or are the outcome of maturation. The process of conditioning in the case we are considering is very complex. It takes a while for a child to learn such motions as he later makes and in that process he is helped by instruction from his elders and by watching their performances. It is a process of forming new neuronal muscular patterns.

Now I assume that each of us begins his life as a purely biological organism. Since in its earlier stages no organism has as yet a differentiated nervous system with a brain as its center, it is in accord with the known facts to assume that it is not yet conscious. So far as we know, the life of the embryo is purely biological and I therefore assume that it is not yet conscious. The different stages in the development of the embryo can be found described in biological treatises. Even when the brain has developed as the center of a nervous system with exteroceptors it is quite well shielded against such stimuli as are specific to these receptors. Just when the organism becomes conscious is largely a matter of pure speculation, and since we have to do with so much speculation later let us not now indulge in it but pass on to consider the newborn babe, which in its very early days is obviously sensitive at least to violent sound stimuli and reacts to them with starts and cries. The muscular activities here are called simple reflexes not because they are so simple but because the neuronal paths leading from the point of stimulation to the muscular processes involved are inborn. All this I think accords with present day biological theory based upon anatomical and physiological facts. Now the question arises, is the babe conscious when he starts and cries? We adults "naturally" suppose that he is, for we generally are conscious when we react to sound waves. But the "natural" answer is not necessarily correct. Neurologically considered in view of the inborn neuronal pathways it is not necessary to say more than that his muscular reactions are caused by the waves of energy flowing from the point of stimulation and activating the muscles involved.

And here the perspective realist applies his theory that consciousness is epiphysical. One might call the conscious factor in hearing a by-product were it not for the derogatory suggestion in that word. Biologically considered it is a by-product, a secondary product, but even in industry, where the word apparently originated, a by-product may become the most important product. Now, can what has been said of hearing when it first occurs in the life of an infant be said also of the sense of pain? Unlike hearing, the sense of pain does not arise from the stimulation of an exteroceptor but of a proprioceptor, and such a receptor is not shielded from possible stimulation before birth.

In addition to inborn neuronal patterns the normal child acquires new neuronal patterns and much of his infantile life is a matter of such acquisition, and also of acquiring inhibitions. In other words he forms habits, as James says:

An acquired habit, from the physiological point of view, is nothing but a new pathway of discharge formed in the brain, by which certain incoming currents ever after tend to escape.[65]

Thus what Pavlov called a conditioned reflex is a special instance of habit. A dog, who by simple reflex salivates upon sight of food, acquires the habit of salivation upon hearing a bell. Going

---

[65] *Psychology, Briefer Course*, p. 134. For a fuller treatment of habit see *The Principles of Psychology*, Vol. I, Chapter IV.

back to the human infant we find that he acquires the habit of speech. The popular way of putting this is that when over and over again he hears his parents use the word "book" and then sees them point to the book the frequent association between the heard word and the seen book results in his saying "book" when he sees a book or when he wants a book. Neurologically considered, and roughly, what happens is that the stimulation of his auditory cortex by the articulated sound waves and of his occipital cortex by the light waves result in the formation of a neuronal pattern, or two-way pathway between the two cortices involved. The conscious factors in the hearing and the seeing are, from the perspective realist's point of view, epiphysical. And when, or at least if, he learns to act upon the spoken suggestion or advice of his parents this learning is an acquisition of a habit. When later a child, say a teen-ager, learns to drive an automobile and has been taught the rules of the road, this learning is also a habit of coordinating movements of arms and legs with visual and auditory stimuli acting upon him from the physical course of the road and from objects approaching him. He becomes a competent driver when his muscular habits have become specific to the physical conditions he meets on the road. All this can be described in purely physiological terms without reference to his visual and auditory consciousness. By this is not meant that during this process he has not seen or heard anything. If he is a normal person he is visually conscious of what stimulates his occipital lobe and auditorily conscious of what stimulates his temporal lobes. According to the assumption that I'm presenting, the description of his muscular responses can be given in physiological terms alone. The consciousness that is involved is epiphysical, and by this I mean that the consciousness is not a causal factor in his physiological behavior.

Up to the present all through my discussions I have purposely avoided the use of the word "cause." I have spoken of physical stimuli as "giving rise" to consciousness knowing that the reader perhaps has understood this as meaning that they were the cause or a partial cause of the muscular behavior. But now I wish to say that on my working hypothesis any consciousness occurring during a physiological process is not a cause of any part of the processes.

This is of course a hard saying and without doubt will require considerable elaboration to make it seem worthy of consideration by the reader, even if he's a philosopher who has followed all the arguments centered upon the word *cause*. To me the most satisfactory expression of causality that I have recently found, the reader will find in a volume by Henry Margenau, Professor of Natural Philosophy and Physics, Yale University.[66] It is not possible here to attempt even a summary of this chapter and fortunately it is not necessary, for the volume is without doubt within reach of anyone interested in the subject. I will quote here only what has bearing upon our present problem:

> Causality is a close relative of the laws of conservation of energy and momentum and also of the principle of relativity. It might be said to be the parent of the former law, a brother of the latter . . . . The causal structure of the laws of nature is always one of the conditions which lead to conservation laws. Precisely what physical quantity will be conserved can be decided only when the laws themselves are known. It is erroneous to say that the principle of causality merely asserts the existence of conservation laws; causality and conservation are not equivalent, but the former is a necessary condition for the latter; it is a weaker statement and lies deeper in the methodological structure of natural science.[67]
>
> The force of the principal of causality is methodological, arising from our success at analysis; the principle is a lesson drawn from and continually reinjected into constructive scientific procedure. It lifts the regularities expressed by laws of nature upon a plane of higher generality but does not make them more certain or more secure.[68]

Now what is conserved according to the conservation laws varies with the varying branches of physics. In classical mechanics what is conserved is the sum of kinetic and potential energy; in electro-

---

[66] Margenau, *The Nature of Physical Theory*, New York, 1950. By permission of McGraw-Hill Book Company.
[67] *Ibid.*, pp. 410–411. The author uses the word "nature" where I should prefer the words "the physical world."
[68] *Ibid.*, p. 407.

dynamics what is conserved is the sum of the energy residing in the volume and of the energy flux across the surface.[69] And we also have of course a conservation of the sum of energy and mass where energy and mass are interconvertible in accordance with the equation $m = E/c^2$ where m is the mass and E is the energy and c is the velocity of light. But whatever be the convertibles they are always quantities expressible in numbers of units. But according to the theory proposed in these lectures the relation of consciousness is not a quantity expressible in a number of units. Whether biology is a causal system with a formulation of the principle of causality different from that used in the physical sciences is to be settled, says our author, "not by consideration of the *problems* of that science but by careful study of their *solution*."

> To settle the problem of causality in biological science, as in physics and everywhere else, attention must be given to those phases of the science which have reached the stage of solution. But when consideration is limited to important recent advances, for example those arising from the work on mutations and general genetics, where specific answers are at hand, the impression becomes strong that such work indicates complete reliance upon the deterministic structure of reality. These accomplishments all proceed from the conviction that the laws valid today will also be valid tomorrow.[70]

The author admits however, that "the interpretation of causality advanced in this chapter, stemming from an analysis of method in the physical sciences, is not natural to the biologist and has rarely been employed in biological discussions." But against those who maintain that biological causation is different from causation in the inanimate world and speak of the unity of "the organismic sequence," the author says, "But it seems that more is required, and we hold the additional requirement to be, not unity of the organismic sequence, but invariability of the laws that govern the sequence.[71]

Although he holds that "causality is not *equivalent* to conservation," he seems to assume that the former implies the latter,

---
[69] *Ibid.*, p. 410, notes 1 and 2.
[70] *Ibid.*, pp. 415–416.
[71] *Ibid.*, pp. 417–418.

and it is the latter in which at present we are especially interested, so much so that we are compelled to repeat that in the newest examples reported in *The Cerebral Cortex of Man* what is called visual and auditory responses to electrical stimuli applied to parts of the cerebral cortex give no evidence of being transformations of energy. In other words, whatever conservation of energy occurs in these experiments is to be found in the currents of energy that flow from the stimulated points through neuronal connections to other parts of the brain. To state this in other terms, the visual and auditory *sensations* are not physical parts of the physical chain of events; they are epiphysical in the sense in which this term has been defined. They are not subject to the causal laws that govern the physical sequence. If therefore the words *cause* and *effect* have the meaning as Margenau maintains, correctly I think, they have in physics, the sensory "reactions" to the electrical stimuli are not the *effects* of the physical stimulations nor are the stimulations their causes. And to elaborate still further, the consciousness in our perception, our memories, and our intellectual theories is the result, so we assume, of brain processes. I use the word *result* here instead of *effect*, having previously limited the denotation of the latter word to physical occurrences.

The problem that the perspective realist has set for himself is to discover and lay down a set of postulates that shall integrate modern physical theory with what he regards as the fundamental conviction of common sense, namely, that in his ordinary experience he has given to him a view of a more or less orderly world which goes on independently of his experience of it, a world consisting of things which he actually sees from time to time and which exist when he does not see them, many of them things upon whose existence, when he does not see them, his own existence depends. Many of these things he believes to be constantly changing, but these changes are such that by taking proper steps he can secure their adjustments to his needs. As an indispensable means to securing this result he must remember how they have behaved in the past. He must be able to rely upon what other human beings tell him, beings who have had more experience than he. He has learned that he has often made mistakes in relying either upon his own memory or upon the reports of others. To use John Dewey's words, the world in which he lives is precarious.

> The visible is set in the invisible; and in the end what is unseen decides what happens in the seen; the tangible rests precariously upon the untouched and ungrasped. The contrast and the potential maladjustment of the immediate, the conspicuous and focal phase of things, with those indirect and hidden factors which determine the origin and career of what is present, are indestructible features of any and every experience. . . . It is a primary datum in any experience.[72]

Dewey, an instrumentalist, had his own way of solving the problem represented. As he says:

> The history of the development of the physical sciences is the story of the enlarging possession by mankind of more efficacious instrumentalities for dealing with the conditions of life and action. But when one neglects the connection of these scientific objects with the affairs of primary experience, the result is a picture of a world of things indifferent to human interests because it is wholly apart from experience. It is more than merely isolated, for it is set in opposition. Hence when it is viewed as fixed and final in itself it is a source of oppression to the heart and paralysis to imagination.[73]

The first of these passages appeared in print in 1925 and remained unchanged in the 1929 edition from the rewritten introduction of which the second passage is quoted. In the first passage as it stands printed we have what seems to be an expression of outright determinism, the view that found expression when leading physicists spoke *ex cathedra*. In the second passage such a view is represented as the result of neglecting the connection between physical objects and the primary affairs of experience. A world of objects fixed and final in itself cannot of course be changed to meet the heart's desire. It is not my intention here critically to examine Dewey's solution of the problem here involved. But I cannot refrain from pointing out that even the determinism of Laplace could not be expressed except by reference to an "intelligence which knows at

---

[72] *Experience and Nature*, pp. 43–44.
[73] *Ibid.*, 2d ed., p. 11.

a given instant all forces acting in nature as well as the momentary positions of all things." Such a definition has been frequently criticized and Margenau's discussion of the subject leaves little to be desired.[74]

The problem of physical causality apparently can hardly be discussed without someone's appealing to the emotions and to the sense of freedom, as when Dewey says that such determination is a source of oppression to the heart and paralysis to imagination. I remember having read an article on Calvinism by James Anthony Froude, in which the author commented on the fact that as a matter of historical fact determinism had no inhibitory effect on the Calvinist's will or his interest in life. Being at that time myself a Calvinist, I was much impressed by this comment, so much so that I still remember it although everything else in the article seems to have gone beyond recall. One might reply to the implication involving the remark by saying with Emerson that "a foolish consistency is the hobgoblin of little minds, adored by little statesmen and philosophers and divines." But such a retort does not go to the root of the difficulty. One might very well be depressed over the ongoings of the world and throw up the sponge.

Dr. Penfield,[75] like many another prominent brain neurologist, may be regarded as carrying on the work begun by Charles Sherrington. In Chapter II of the monograph we find some six pages (13–19) devoted to Sherrington's studies of the anthropoid cortex, and from these pages let us quote:

> In general, it may be said that cortical responses [which Sherrington and his co-workers obtained by electric stimulation from the cortex of the anthropoid ape] are movements which may be called "fractional." Each is a "unitary part of some more complex movement." [The question now arises, where is the integration of these fractional responses accomplished?]

---

[74] *The Nature of Physical Reality*, pp. 397ff. See also Chapter VII, "Freedom and Necessity in Human Affairs," in the present volume.

[75] As we have seen, the monograph, *The Cerebral Cortex of Man*, is the product of collaboration, Dr. Rasmussen's name appearing on the title page with Dr. Penfield, but for brevity's sake from now on I shall refer to views expressed in this monograph as Dr. Penfield's views.

Sherrington and his co-workers carried out ablation of different portions of the stimulable motor cortex on one or both sides. . . . The initial severe limb paresis gradually recovered in each case. . . . By successive removals they found no evidence that the recovery was due to taking over of the function of one part of the stimulable cortex by another except in the face and throat area.

The reasoning of Sherrington and his pupils in regard to substitution for the excised cortex went only as far as the evidence carried them. They did not allow themselves to guess that this function was taken over by subcortical areas.[76] . . . Sherrington and Leyton . . . recognized, however, that the acquisition of *skilled movements* was "certainly a process involving far wider areas of cortex than the excitable zone itself."

Expressed in another way, Sherrington and Leyton stated that in order to produce normal action these cortical movements and fragments of movements must be compounded simultaneously or successively in the greatest possible variety of ways. In order to do this the control must be "within the grasp of the organ which has the compounding of them."

It was typical of Sherrington that he did not print the hypotheses that he must have been constructing. Instead, he recorded only the proven, the verified theses.

We have recorded Sherrington's observations at considerable length because we have been using the same methods that he employed on the anthropoids, upon the cortex of man, i.e., stimulation and ablation. It is true that we have another technique, the one that Jackson employed, i.e., observation of epileptic patterns. We have electroencephalography also. And we have the testimony of conscious patients which opens the whole field of somatic and special sensation to us. And yet, much that we suggest must remain unproven. When we assume that the control of the synthesis of cortical motor and cortical sensory processes is to be found in the diencephalon and mesencephalon, this will be hypothetical. Our aim, however, is to set down the facts and proven observations separately and to indicate clearly the hypothetical nature of the unproven conclusions.[77]

This hypothetical assumption is at variance with popular tradition, of which Dr. Penfield says: "Popular tradition, which seems to be largely shared by scientific men, has taken it for granted that the cortex is a sort of essential organ for the purposes of thinking and consciousness, and that final integration of neural mechanisms

---

[76] The "subcortical areas" in Dr. Penfield's nomenclature are the diencephalon and the mesencephalon, the thalamus being one of the parts of the diencephalon (see p. 227, 1. 10); all this is "the old Brain" (see p. 235, 1. 10 from the bottom).
[77] *The Cerebral Cortex of Man*, p. 17–19.

takes place in it."[78] But integration there of "fractional" responses throughout the cortex presupposes the indispensability of the function of transcortical fibers. However,

> Recent anatomical work indicates that the transcortical association fibers are less important than was formerly thought. . . . Lashley (1944) concluded that transcortical association was unimportant or absent in the learning of maze problems by rats.[79]

Dr. Penfield's hypothetical assumption is elaborated in the final chapter of the monograph and it is possible here to give only some of the arguments he presents for it:

> The study of comparative anatomy suggests that parts of the cerebral cortex have developed as outgrowths of various older portions of the central nervous system. With new functions has come very great elaboration of related areas of cortex. It seems likely that it is this process of corticalization which has made possible elaboration of certain new functions.
>
> [From the work of Walker on the chimpanzee] it is apparent that there are important connections which conduct both ways between areas of cortex and specific nuclei of the diencephalon, and that in the process of encephalization a varying degree of autonomy has been handed over to the large cortical projections. It does not necessarily follow, however, that all function, either new or old, has been handed over in this way nor that correlation between the activities of the different cortical areas is necessarily carried out in the cortex rather than in the diencephalon.[80] . . . One possible explanation of these facts [viz. that "epileptic discharge in the cortex of the anterior frontal region may produce initial unconsciousness, (and that) removal of this area does not abolish consciousness"] is that the epileptic discharge has its paralyzing effect upon centers which are essential to consciousness and which have a direct anatomical connection with this portion of the frontal lobes without being located in them.
>
> The work of Walker and others makes it quite clear that such a connection exists between the anterior frontal cortex and the dorsomedial nucleus of the thalamus. We may consider the possibility that this portion of the thalamus, or other areas in the diencephalon most closely related to it, contains the essential neuronal mechanism upon the integrity of which depends the very existence of consciousness, a mechanism which is able to employ the anterior frontal regions in the process of thinking and to use them in elaboration of thought.

---
[78] *Ibid.*, p. 205.
[79] *Ibid.*
[80] *Ibid.*, pp. 204–206.

[The author proceeds to mention various facts in substantiation of this conception.][81]

Let us now see where Dr. Penfield localizes the integration of the "crude," i.e. fractional, visual and auditory responses and of the crude movements produced by stimulation of the Rolandic convolutions.

> These sensory and motor cortical areas are obviously way stations, not terminals. What we may call the visual cortex and the auditory cortex are stopovers in the afferent stream of visual and auditory impulses. These streams originate in the eye and the ear and they pass through these cortical representations on their way to a higher neuronal level. If the immediately surrounding cortex be removed, sparing only the station itself and its subcortical connections, the individual still sees or hears. Impulses must pass in an afferent direction from periphery to cortex. But from cortex to diencephalon the current is still afferent.
>
> Similarly, the postcentral gyrus is a station in the afferent stream of tactile and proprioceptive impulses. The precentral gyrus forms a station in the efferent pathway of impulses that produce skilled volitional movement. In spite of the close interrelationship of these two central gyri, complete removal of the precentral gyrus does not interfere with the arrival in consciousness of sensory information; nor does removal of the postcentral convolution interrupt the efferent impulses that result in voluntary movement.
>
> Pain sensation has been omitted from this discussion, for no removal of cortex anywhere can prevent pain from being felt and only very rarely does a patient use the word pain to describe the result of cortical stimulation. It is obvious, therefore, that the pathway of pain conduction reaches the thalamus and consciousness without essential conduction to the cortex.[82]

But what does consciousness have to do with all this? Although Dr. Penfield does not give an explicit answer to this question, he uses the existence of consciousness as a test for the fact that the highest level of nervous integration is achieved. That this assumption is made by him is clear from the following passage:

> The anterior portion of the frontal lobe is not essential to the existence of consciousness, as its removal does not abolish it. An epileptic discharge in this portion of the cortex seems to fire directly into the thalamus and thus produce unconsciousness. One may as-

---
[81] *Ibid.*, p. 227.
[82] *Ibid.*, p. 233.

sume, therefore, that the frontal cortex is not the seat of consciousness, as Jackson suggested, but that it is most closely related to the highest level within the diencephalon, perhaps serves the purpose of elaboration of certain forms of thinking.

The "petit mal" seizure of idiopathic epilepsy is associated with a discharge that seems to originate in the thalamus. Consciousness is abolished for the duration of each discharge. Acute injury to the diencephalon also produces unconsciousness. A partial injury in this region may bring about extreme reduction in intellectual activity.

Consequently, it seems fair to conclude that within the diencephalon there are neurone circuits which may be considered the highest level of neuronal representation and re-representation. But much of the function at this level is made possible and is elaborated by the special areas of the cerebral cortex. It is, therefore, inaccurate to say that the cortex belongs to a lower level of activity. . . . The functions which are discharged by some of the major regions of the cortex are indicated, but it must be obvious that when each region discharges its function its activity forms just one part of an activity which is taking place also in the subcortical structure to which it is most closely related.

It is clear that the most important means of coordinating the function of cortical areas is not the association mechanisms within the cortex. Such coordination is provided largely by the integrating action of subcortical centers which must lie within the mesencephalon and the diencephalon.

Therefore, if the term "seat of consciousness" is to be used at all, it must be applied to the old brain, for the diencephalon is "that nervous centre to which . . . the most heterogeneous impressions are brought." From it must go out effector neuronal impulses that are capable of summoning a memory, of causing the lips to speak, or the arm to move.

But the various functional areas of the cerebral cortex play, each of them, an integral role in the activity of what might be called the different departments of the diencephalon. The cortical projections serve to elaborate afferent and efferent mechanisms. Through these interconnections memories are stored in neurone patterns within the temporal cortex, and the frontal cortex is utilized in the elaboration of thought.[83]

The part played by consciousness in this argument indicates the close connection between Dr. Penfield's and Eddington's views and also the difference. Sherrington had said, as we have seen, that not until the physical and the psychical are integrated together

---

[83] *Ibid.*, pp. 234–235.

can we have before us an approximately complete creature. "This integration can be thought of as the last and final integration." Dr. Penfield agrees with this in so far as he uses consciousness, in the way in which we have seen, as a test for the localization of the final integration of the nervous system in the old brain; but nowhere, so far as I can discover, does he retract or even modify the assertion quoted from the first page of the monograph that it is upon the integrated and coordinate action of the many millions of neurones that we must depend for sensation, motion, understanding and consciousness. If we are to use any expression of Sherrington's as adequate for Penfield's view it would be that sensations, feelings, etc. are "adjunct" to the working of the neural machinery.[84]

Not being myself a neurologist and, therefore, not knowing whether there are neurological facts that could be adduced as antagonistic to Dr. Penfield's view, the facts which he adduces lead me to welcome the above elaboration of his hypothetical assumption that "the control of the synthesis of cortical motor and cortical sensory processes is to be found in the diencephalon and mesencephalon." I have long held the position that consciousness depends upon the brain, although I shared the popular tradition that the cortex is the essential organ for the purposes of thinking and consciousness. Dr. Penfield's discussion persuades me in favor of the diencephalon and the mesencephalon, only I wish that he had not used the word "must" in his elaboration.

Dr. Penfield makes little mention of will. We have seen that in Chapter VI *"desire to move* was also a recognized response to electrical stimulation," and in a footnote on page 159 (Chapter IX) he refers to this and says, "this suggests that there may be stimulable elements in the cortex which are allied to the mechanism that underlies volitional innervation." And this to me suggests the interpretation that is to be put upon the statement made on the preceding page that "the somatic areas [may be activated] by

---

[84] Sherrington, *The Integrative Action of the Nervous System*, 2nd ed., p. 355.

Perspectives

volitional impulses from within the brain." This interpretation that I have in mind is that the term "volitional impulses" does not denote impulses activated by will but impulses giving rise to volition just as the term "sensory impulses" does not mean impulses activated by sense but giving rise to sensation.

Let us turn now to time as it is sensed. My readers will all doubtless remember the desperate "confession" made by St. Augustine:

> What, then, is time? If no one asks me, I know; if I try to explain it to one who asks, I do not know; yet I say with confidence that I know. But if nothing passed away, there would be no past time; if nothing were to come, there would be no future time; if nothing were, there would be no present time. Yet those two times, past and future, how can they be, when the past is not now, and the future is not yet? As for the present, if it were always present, and did not pass over into the past, it would not be time but eternity.
>
> [And again.] Even a single hour passes in fleeting moments; as much of it as has taken flight is past, what remains is future. If we can comprehend any time that is divisible into no parts at all, or perhaps into the minutest parts of moments, this alone let us call present; yet this speeds so hurriedly from the future to the past that it does not endure even for little space. If it has duration, it is divided into a past and a future; but the present has no duration.[85]

We have the advantage over this philosopher, one of the great thinkers of the past, in having at our disposal the contributions made by others on the subject in the intervening centuries, and especially by William James, whose central thought here was expressed in the capitalized title of a section, THE SENSIBLE PRESENT HAS DURATION,[86] thus in contradiction to St. Augustine's "The present has no duration." In this section James treats of the "specious present."

A prominent philosopher has said, "I do not find the accounts of the Specious Present given by psychologists very clear, and I shall therefore try to illustrate the matter in my own way."[87] The

---

[85] Quoted from G. S. Fullerton, *A System of Metaphysics*, New York, 1904, pp. 194–195.
[86] *Principles of Psychology*, Vol. I, P. 608.
[87] C. D. Broad, *Scientific Thought*, New York and London, 1923, p. 348.

present writer also finds those accounts lacking in clearness, and proposes to follow Broad's example; i.e., in my own way.

First of all it is necessary to point out how the term *the specious present* got currency in psychological and philosophical circles. James found it in a volume, *The Alternative,* by E. R. Clay, whom he quotes as saying:

> "The relation of experience to time has not been profoundly studied. Its objects are given as being of the present, but the part of time referred to by the datum is a very different thing from the conterminous of the past and future which philosophy denotes by the name Present. The present to which the datum refers is really a part of the past—a recent past—delusively given as being a time that intervenes between the past and the future. Let it be named the specious present, and let the past, that is given as being the past, be known as the obvious past. . . . Time, then, considered relatively to human apprehension, consists of four parts, viz., the obvious past, the specious present, the real present, and the future. Omitting the specious present, it consists of three . . . nonentities—the past, which does not exist, the future, which does not exist, and their conterminous, the present; the faculty from which it proceeds lies to us in the fiction of the specious present." [88]

It is difficult to see how James could say, "the only fact of our immediate experience [of the present] is what Mr. E. R. Clay has well called 'the *specious* present,'" unless it be that just as Clay's specious present is really a part of the past—a recent past—so James's only immediate experience "of present time" also contains a past, an immediate past, a just past, something "just gone" or "gone." For "just past" I will give reference later.

> And since [says James in another passage] . . . our maximum distinct *intuition* of duration hardly covers more than a dozen seconds . . . we must suppose that *this amount of duration is pictured fairly steadily in each passing instant of consciousness* by virtue of some fairly constant feature in the brain-process, to which the consciousness is tied. *This feature of the brain-process, whatever it be, must be the cause of our perceiving the fact of time at all.* The duration

---

[88] *The Principles of Psychology,* Vol. I, p. 609. Not having access to *The Alternative* I quote from James's quotation. The first ellipsis indicates an omission that I have made from James's quotation, while the second occurs in that quotation itself. The context shows that the "faculty" mentioned in the last sentence is that of human apprehension.

thus steadily perceived is hardly more than the "specious present," as it was called a few pages back. Its *content* is in a constant flux, events dawning into its forward end as fast as they fade out of its rearward one, and each of them changing its time-coefficient from "not yet," or "not quite yet," to "*just gone*" or "*gone*," as it passes by. Meanwhile, the specious present, the intuited duration, stands permanent, like the rainbow on the waterfall, with its own quality unchanged by the events that stream through it. Each of these, as it slips out, retains the power of being reproduced; and when reproduced, is reproduced with the duration and neighbors which it originally had. Please observe, however, that the reproduction of an event, *after* it has once completely dropped out of the rearward end of the specious present, is an entirely different psychic fact from its direct perception in the specious present as a thing *immediately past*. A creature might be entirely devoid of *reproductive* memory, and yet have the time-sense; but the latter would be limited, in his case, to the few seconds immediately passing by. Time older than that he would never recall. I assume reproduction in the text, because I am speaking of human beings who notoriously possess it. Thus memory gets strewn with *dated* things—dated in the sense of being before or after each other. The date of a thing is a mere relation of *before* or *after* the present thing or some past or future thing.[89]

In saying that a creature without reproductive memory might yet have the time sense James is obviously abstracting from what human beings experience by grace of reproductive memory. By this abstraction he obtains a time-sense alone and he had told us in the introductory paragraph of this chapter that "in this chapter we shall consider this immediate sense of time alone." There is surely some confusion here which we may do well to avoid, and I hope that what James says in the long passage last quoted will help us to that end. I mean the passage which refers to the "feature of the brain-process, whatever it be, [which] must be the cause of our perceiving the fact of time at all."

Let us now turn over just one page where James asks the question: "*Now, to what element in the brain-process may this*

---

[89] *Ibid.*, pp. 630–631. The italics in "just gone," "gone," and "immediately past" I have introduced, others are James's. In the footnote to the latter page we find that, for James, the assertion " 'No more' and 'not yet' are proper time feelings" is "not strictly true of our feeling of *time per se*, as an elementary bit of duration [but] is true of our feeling of *date* in its events." Moreover, we find on page 611 that elementary *sensations of duration* are units of duration which the time sense is able to take in at a single stroke.

sensibility be due?" meaning the sensibility referred to when he said that *"we are immediately and incessantly sensible"* of the specious present. He gives the answer modestly in "the only conclusion which seems to emerge from a study of [suggestions made by others] and of the facts—unripe though that conclusion be," namely:

> The phenomena of "summation of stimuli" in the nervous system prove that each stimulus leaves some latent activity behind it which only gradually passes away. . . . Psychological proof of the same fact is afforded by those "after-images" which we perceive when a sensorial stimulus is gone. We may read off peculiarities in an afterimage, left by an object on the eye, which we failed to note in the original. We may "hark back" and take in the meaning of a sound several seconds after it has ceased. Delay for a minute, however, and the echo itself of the clock or the question is mute; present sensations have banished it beyond recall. With the feeling of the present thing there must at all times mingle the fading echo of all those other things which the previous few seconds have supplied. Or, to state it in neural terms, *there is at every moment a cumulation of brain-processes overlapping each other, of which the fainter ones are the dying phases of processes which but shortly previous were active in a maximal degree. The* AMOUNT OF THE OVERLAPPING *determines the feeling of the* DURATION OCCUPIED. WHAT EVENTS *shall appear to occupy the duration depends on just* WHAT PROCESSES *the overlapping processes are.* . . . All I aim at is to state the most *elemental* form of the psycho-physical conjunction. I have assumed that the brain-processes are sensational ones.[90]

Justly famous for its splendor, as many other passages are in this chapter, I regard this passage as the masterpiece of them all, not of course because of its beauty, but because of the contribution it makes toward solving the problem of the sense of time alone: the cumulation of brain-processes overlapping one another arises from the fact that these processes occur one after another. Let *a* be the first brain-process under consideration and

---

[90] *Ibid.*, pp. 634–636. Persons familiar with Sherrington's *The Integrative Action of the Nervous System* may remember that he said: "The after-discharge of a reflex may be considered analogous to a *positive* after-image left by a visual stimulus (p. 33). Also see p. 384. Norbert Wiener has an interesting suggestion to account for the retention of impulses in connection with the "specious present"; see *Cybernetics*, p. 143.

let $b\ c\ \ldots\ g$ and h follow a in this order, each when it occurs being at the same maximal degree and each gradually passing away in such wise that a is at its minimal degree when g occurs and has completely passed away by the time h occurs. (By minimal degree is meant just above the threshold of sensation.) All these "lower case" events with their interrelation are purely physical so far as the above descriptions go, but by James's assumption, which we must now mention in accepting it, these brain-processes are "sensational ones," each giving rise to a sensation of some "sensible quality."[91] Let the sound sensed when a occurs be A, the sound when b occurs be B, etc. Now "objects fade out of consciousness slowly," just as the activities of the corresponding brain-processes also "gradually pass away." Thus what has been said of the sensational brain-processes can be said, *mutatis mutandis*, of these corresponding sense qualities; therefore, there is at every moment a cumulation of sense qualities overlapping one another of which the fainter ones are the dying phases of those which but shortly before were sensed in a maximal degree.

James said:

> Objects fade out of consciousness slowly. If the present thought is of $A\ B\ C\ D\ E\ F\ G$, the next one will be of $B\ C\ D\ E\ F\ G\ H$, and the one after that of $C\ D\ E\ F\ G\ H\ I$—the lingerings of the past dropping successively away, and the incomings of the future making up the loss.[92]

Let us change the word "thought" here to "sensation" to make it clear that what we are dealing with here are sensible qualities, and if we ignore, as James does, what has sensibly preceded A our first sensation cannot be the whole durational series $A\ B\ C\ D\ E\ F\ G$ since we cannot sense at the time A is first sensed what follows A because when A is first sensed the brain-processes $b\ c\ d\ e\ f\ g$ which respectively condition the occurrence of $B\ C\ D\ E\ F\ G$ have not yet occurred; in fact, this last series cannot be sensed

---

[91] A sensation being an abstraction, "the object which a sensation knows is an abstract object . . . . 'Sensible qualities' are the objects of sensation." *Psychology, Briefer Course*, p. 13.
[92] *Principles of Psychology*, Vol. I, p. 606.

in its entirety until G is sensed. By the same token, when B is first sensed $C\ D\ E\ F\ G$ cannot yet be sensed and so with $D\ E\ F\ G\ H\ I$ when C is first sensed.

We are all familiar with the fact that any of the longer durations that we deal with familiarly takes time to become the duration it is, thus it takes a month to be a month. If an epigram is permissible, it takes time to be time and time is what time takes. What is true of any of these longer durations is true of a sensed duration with the specific difference that for us human beings those longer durations cannot be sensed as a whole, whereas a sensed duration is sensed as a whole. One of course begins to sense, for instance, the first duration mentioned, $A\ B\ \ldots\ G$, in sensing A and continues to sense it in sensing B, etc. till he senses G, but in any of these forward steps there is a sensing of the relation *after*. Thus, when we sense in the above given series B we sense not B alone but B-as-coming-after-A, and when we sense C we do not sense C alone but C-as-coming-after-B-after-A. And when G is sensed we sense the whole duration with its included sequences whereupon that particular duration is finished—which reminds me of Bob Hope's *bon mot*, a bachelor is an incomplete man and when he is married he is finished. Our conclusion above as to the time we sense the whole of duration thus differs from James's well known position that "we do not first feel one end and then feel the other after it. . . . The experience is from the outset a synthetic datum and not a simple one."[93] Oddly enough C. D. Broad has another way of dating this sensing of a finite duration. To quote: "In general, then, we may say that the beginning of a process of sensing, throughout the whole of which an event of finite duration is sensed, is contemporary with the end of the event in question."[94]

Turning again to James who says: "The units of duration, on the other hand, which the time-sense is able to take in at a single stroke, are groups of a few seconds, and within these units very

---

[93] *Ibid.*, p. 610.
[94] Broad, *Scientific Thought*, p. 359.

few subdivisions—perhaps forty at most, as we shall presently see—can be clearly discerned."[95] Without attempting to reconcile this with what we last quoted from James, I find it true to my experience and also useful for defining the word "moment" as I shall use the term. A moment is any subdivision of a duration singled out for the purpose of dating or for any other practical purpose. Thus when James, in dealing with the sensible present, says, as above quoted, "there is at every moment a cumulation of brain-processes overlapping each other," I understand the word "moment" as meaning any subdivision of any sensed duration. The term "instant" on the other hand is obtained by Whitehead's Method of Extensive Abstraction, applied to "moment" as just defined.

However, a caveat is needed here. In dealing with sensible presents we must remember that they are abstractions recognizable only by those whose conscious fields are wider than the sensible presents they are abstracting. A creature with a time-sense but devoid of reproductive memory could of course not single out any subdivisions for any practical purpose. The account given above of the sensible present as "caused" by sensational brain-processes is obviously conventionalized, stripped of nuances. It is a rough outline omitting many details, a few of which may be mentioned. For instance, for those of us who have reproductive memory "no absolutely sharp line can be drawn" where sensing ends and remembering begins, as Broad says.[96] Again our account assumes that the sensational brain-processes involved have the same maximum intensity which probably would not be true even in the case of the creature mentioned above. It also assumes, or rather suggests, that these processes follow each other at the same rate, as Rosalind says in *As You Like It*: "Time travels in divers paces with divers persons." My intention here has been merely to present only the nub or gist of what I've been dealing with. Perhaps one minutia more should be mentioned because it may

---

[95] James, *Principles of Psychology*, Vol. I, p. 611.
[96] Broad, *Scientific Thought*, p. 348.

have a practical value. On the view of "moment" as presented above no moment has "fled ere we could touch it, gone in the instant of becoming."[97] On the contrary, it endures as long as the sensible present which it initiates.

Earlier in this chapter we dwelt upon the fact that the sense of space gives us a spatial perspective, but at the same time we mentioned the fact that there are temporal perspectives. Before dealing with these let us recall that in vision the sensed spatial relation between any two objects is determined by two physical facts: (1) the respective direction from which rays of light from the object reach the retina, and (2) the spatial relation between the points of arrival of the rays at the retina. If the directions of the points of arrival are respectively the same the objects are seen as spatially coincident. Otherwise stated, the physical distances between objects are projectively foreshortened under the conditions just mentioned.

Now *time* has only the two relations of before to after, and the obverse relation of after to before; and light from objects can reach the retina only after having been emitted before from some object, since light travels with finite velocity. Therefore, all rays of light reaching the eye at any time come from the same temporal direction. Thus, by analogy with spatial perspectives, all the objects relatively at rest from which rays of light reach the retina at the same time are seen as temporally coincident, that is as simultaneous. This fact correlates sensed time with physical time in the same way in which sensed space is correlated with physical space. Now if we assume, as we have assumed, that what we see, when as common sense says we see real objects, outside are physical objects then the fact that all the objects that we see at any time are seen as now existing is no argument against common sense. On the contrary, if the fact were not as we have stated it such a fact would refute common sense. Thus under the condition last mentioned physical time between the emission of light

---

[97] James, *Principles of Psychology*, Vol. I, p. 608.

waves from objects at a distance from the eye is foreshortened to zero.[98]

Since the sensed present is a duration with sensible moments and these moments are sensed as one after another there is a relation of after to before in the sensed present, but for an event to be before another within the sensed duration does not imply that it is past. Pastness is priority to the present, not priority within the present. Grammatically the past tense of a verb refers to something that is no longer present. Just as it is incorrect to say a man who is dying is dead, so it is incorrect to say of something that is passing that it is past. Perhaps this can be made clearer by an analogy with space. Within a limited spatial region, such as my study, there are objects which may be said to be one north of another but of which it cannot be said that they are north of my study. In other words to be north of is different from to be north within and by the same token to be prior to is different from to be prior within. And what has been said with regard to a relation expressed by the preposition *before* can be said *mutatis mutandis* with regard to a relation *after*.[99]

From all that has so far been said about the sensible present you might suppose that the perspective realist maintains that we are always sensing time when awake. Such a supposition, however, would be a mistake. The perspective realist makes no commitment on this point. There may be, as there apparently are, occasions when we do not sense temporal sequence. For instance, when with eyes open we are "in a brown study" there may be no sense of what has been called the flow of time. Light from the same objects monotonously strikes upon our eyes, and there is not enough

---

[98] In the foregoing paragraphs what I have called physical distance is distance in units of long measure, and what I have called physical time is time measured in units of distance covered multiplied by time taken.

[99] [This chapter, up to this point, had been rewritten by Professor McGilvary before he died. The remainder of the chapter is taken from an earlier draft. The rewritten portion is mostly material based on the work by Penfield and Rasmussen, and the reader will have noted that some of it seems more relevant to the mind-body problem discussed in Chapter III than to the problems of perspectives in the present chapter.—Editor.]

change taking place in the stimulations we receive to give rise to a sense of change going on, until some different stimulus brings us back to change in the world of sense. For our purpose it is not necessary in such a case to decide whether we had been sensing temporal flux all along. All that is necessary is to describe what it is that we sense when we do sense change.

But Mr. Santayana claims that we never do sense change, even though he admits that as we "watch a sensible object the evidence of variation is often irresistible. This flag is flapping. This flame is dancing. How shall I deny that almost everything, in nature and in fancy, like the Ghost in *Hamlet,* is here, is there, is gone? Of course I witness these appearances and disappearances. The intuition of change is more direct and more imperious than any other." Mr. Santayana regards as irrelevant the "dialectical arguments, to the effect that change is impossible, because the idea of it is incoherent or self-contradictory." Such arguments are considered by him as irrelevant. But

> The denial of change [he maintains] may rest on more sceptical ground, and may have a deeper and more tragic character. It may come from insight into the temerity of asserting change. [I may remark in passing that the denial of change may be at least equally temerarious, in view of the "irresistible" "evidence of variation."] Why, indeed, do men believe in it? Because they see and feel it: but this fact is not denied. They may see and feel all the changes they like: what reason is that for believing that over and above this actual intuition, with the specious change it regards, one state of the universe has given place to another, or different intuitions have existed? You feel you have changed; you feel things changing? Granted. Does this fact help you to feel an earlier state you do not feel, which is not an integral part of what is *now* before you, but a state from which you are supposed to have passed into the state in which you now are? If you feel that *earlier* state *now,* there is no change involved. That datum, which you now designate as the *past,* and which exists only in this perspective, is merely a term in your present feeling. It was never anything else. It never was given otherwise than as it is given *now,* when it is *given as past.* Therefore, if things are such only as intuition makes them, every suggestion of a past is false.[100]

---

[100] George Santayana, *Scepticism and Animal Faith,* pp. 28–29.

I have italicized the words on which the argument turns. Mr. Santayana argues that no "now" has room within it for an actual earlier and an actual later, because an actual earlier can only be earlier than the "now," and thus be "past." I have already shown, as I think, that this is not *logically* necessary. If I have succeeded, then Mr. Santayana's argument is as futilely dialectical as those that he regards as irrelevant. Why, then, did he not see this? The answer is given in what I have not quoted. Those irrelevant dialectical arguments are not "fortified by a passport countersigned by experience," whereas he evidently is confident that his argument given above has the necessary experiential credentials. From whom did it get them? The only reply I can suggest is that it got them from William James's account of the "only fact of our immediate experience" of time, namely, "the specious present," which is described as a *"duration-block,"* of which he says: "We do not first feel one end, and then the other after it." If, and only if, this is an unquestionable fact of our immediate experience of time, then Mr. Santayana's dialectic *has* a passport countersigned by experience. I have tried to show that the "fact" is questionable. James is correct when he says that our experience of "the *present* moment of time" is "one of the most baffling experiences." Its very bafflingness leaves room for *alternative* accounts of it. Postulates are necessary in such a case. My alternative account is postulational. James's account is dogmatic, and Santayana swallows the dogma, hook, line and sinker, and what he thereupon disgorges is the dogma that "nothing given exists." A dogma that without external assistance develops logically into three such mutually contradictory philosophies as James's discontinuity theory of actually experienced time, Royce's theory of an Absolute Experience of all actual time at once, and Santayana's theory that no actual time is intuited, is surely open to suspicion.

So far in this chapter we have ignored such sensed qualities as color which appear in sense-perspectives, having devoted our attention to perspective chronogeometric characters. Now what are we to do with the sensed qualities? But before answering this question, it is desirable to repeat and emphasize the fact that the perspective realist does not claim to give a first-hand account of the experience of an organism whose only perspectives are those of sense. His account is of what sense-perspectives are when found in his own more inclusive perspectives, such as those of memory and of discursive thought. Thus his account of sensed qualities is an account of them as constituents in his philosophical perspective. Let us take an example. When I see a "white star," it is the star that is white in perspective; i.e., the whiteness is a character the star has in my sense-perspective at the time of my seeing it. In scientific perspective that star is, say, some 500 light years distant from me, and it was 500 years ago, in the physicist's perspective, that the light by which I see it was emitted from the star. But, as we have seen, in the perspective of the perspective realist this time interval is physically foreshortened to zero length. It is in this latter perspective that the star is white, and we must not confuse the two perspectives. Those who would argue that the star was not really white when it emitted the light and that therefore our position is untenable, *do* confuse the two perspectives. They commit the same kind of fallacy as those who should argue that because a coin is round in one perspective it must be round in any other perspective. The whiteness of the star is a character it has in a perspective conditioned by the kind of organism that I have. Had I a different kind of organism, the star in my perspective might have a different color or it might have no color at all. And if I were not on this planet, but on some other planet whose sun were moving toward that star with a velocity nearly equal to that of light, it would not be 500 light years from me but perhaps only a few light minutes from me, and the frequency of the light waves by which on the earth I see it would by the Doppler effect be so increased that I could not see the star at all. If, now, its spatial and temporal distance from me here on the earth and the frequency of the electromagnetic waves it emits are not *absolute* characters of the star, but are real characters that it has with respect to the earth, why may not the perspective realist by the same logic claim that the color it has with respect to my sensing organism is equally real? If you say that it is not equally *physical*, I will grant your contention provided you expressly say that by the "physical" you mean what the physicist can express in his equations. I do not think that it is profitable to engage in terminological dispute. You can have the "nonphysicality" of the seen color, if you leave me its *naturalness* under the natural conditions under which the star is white in my perspective. I do not maintain that anything is ever white except in a perspective at whose station point there is an organism equipped with eyes by means of which it can see white. But I do maintain that under the postulates of my theory, if as the result of sense-stimulation by an object I see it as white, the object is then and there white (the "then" and the "there" and the "whiteness" being all perspective characters): the white is not in my eyes or in my physical brain. And I decline to be downed by what is obviously a fallacy of accident.

Here again I wish to call attention to the fact that perspective realism does not maintain that the seeing organism selects from among characters that an object already has a pre-existing color to be sensed. Even when organisms have previously sensed similar whites in the same object, these whites do not remain as permanent characters of the object in the interval during which no organism is sensing it as white. A lady's gown hanging in a dark closet is not then red; it becomes red again only when it is seen as red, and the red then seen is a different particular from the red seen before the gown was put away. It is only when two organisms at the same time see the same object as white that we can say that the white seen by either one is a character the object would then have if *that* one did not see it, and even then neither could be said to "select" what he sees.

Chapter VI

RELATIONS IN GENERAL AND UNIVERSALS IN PARTICULAR[1]

The only thing that differentiates relations from anything else is that they are relations. In achieving this tautology not much progress has been made except in so far as an intentional tautology may have intended implications that are important. To learn what relations are we must resort to experience, where they are discovered by analysis of relational complexes.[2] Of analysis something will be said later. For the present suffice it to say that when we find relations in experience we do not find just relations: we find relations-between-things; nor do we find things alone: we find things-in-relation. To adopt a happy phraseology from William James, "the unit of composition in the perception" of a relation is a relational complex, which in the first instance can be identified only by exemplification in experience. Whatever may be true of the first flash of experience in the development of a babe, or of the dying glimmer when one is sinking into semicoma, every full-bodied experience is of this, that, and the other, in this,

---

[1] This chapter is reprinted from *The Journal of Philosophy,* Vol. XXXVI, where it appeared as a revision of a paper presented in mimeographed form as topic for discussion at a session of the 39th Annual Meeting of the American Philosophical Association, Western Division, at the University of Illinois, April 15, 1938. The discussion proved of great value in the revision, especially in indicating points needing clarification. A challenge in debate blesses, if not him who gives, at least him who takes.

[2] A commonly given definition of "relation," which is accepted by Webster's *New International Dictionary,* 2d ed., and perhaps is as good as any other, is: "Any aspect or quality which can be predicated only of two or more things taken together." But "two or more things taken together" is a relational complex, and thus relation is defined in terms of a relational complex. The circularity is obvious, but it is also unavoidable. Relation is what recent logicians have called a "primitive notion," and a primitive notion can be "defined" in dictionaries only by synonyms.

that, or the other relation. And even such flashes and glimmers can be treated as experiences only in some other experience, which is itself a relational complex.[3]

In experience no relation (spatial and temporal relations excepted) is external: it is not outside its terms. Neither is it internal: it is not inside its terms.[4] It just *relates* them; and what that means can be learned only by examining its function as it appears in experience. Since the languages with which we are familiar require in certain locutions the use of prepositions to express relations, and since most of our prepositions originally expressed spatial or temporal relations, it seems the part of wisdom to stick to the preposition "between,"[5] from which long usage has worn off the suggestion of spatial and temporal betweenness in such a phrase as "the similiarity between John and James." We therefore say that relations in general are *between* their terms, the betweenness of any relation being after its own kind, to be ascertained from experience. We shall also say that any relation is "in" or "within" the *complex* which, in coöperation with the terms, it constitutes.

What has been said of relations experienced I assume to be true

---

[3] I shall not be constantly calling attention to what is postulate and what is something else in what I shall say. I am not sure that I know which I should prefer to be which. (Even in Euclidean geometry there is latitude in the choice of postulates.) Hence if any one asks for proof of what is not expressly labelled as postulate, he may take as answer that it is either a statement of empirical fact or a postulate or a conclusion from some unexpressed postulates. In any philosophy there are perhaps more assumptions than are dreamt of in that philosophy. Even a wide-awake philosophy does not find all its assumptions automatically marshalled in plain sight. Many of them have to be painstakingly elicited, and some of them probably are never elicited at all.

[4] The *terms* of a relation may be one outside the other, and when such is the case, it is because the terms are spatially or temporally related as well. In what sense spatial and temporal relations are exceptions to the general statement made above in the text is a question that cannot be discussed here. Two or three decades ago the "new realists" were emphatic in maintaining that relations are "external" to their terms, but then "external" was defined so as to have a meaning different from that in which it is used here.

[5] See the *New English Dictionary,* Oxford, where under the entry "Between, V, 19," we find: "In all senses, *between* has been, from its earliest appearance, extended to more than two. . . . It is still the only word available to express the relation of a thing to many surrounding things severally and individually, *among* expressing a relation to them collectively and vaguely."

also of relations not experienced, and this assumes that there are unexperienced relations; for instance, unexperienced similarities, their several terms being experienced or not. In so far as any theory rests on this pair of postulates, does not contradict itself, is not contravened by experience, and answers the purposes for which it is developed, it is impregnable. Objectors may not like it, and of course it is their privilege to say so; but saying so does not invalidate it as a theory. In the realm of theory there are many mansions.

Leaving unnumbered the assumptions just mentioned and such others as we should avow if called upon, let us expressly lay down the following Postulate of the Particularity of Relations:

Postulate 10. Every relation is as particular as the complex it constitutes out of its terms.

If it be asked what is here meant by "particular," the reply is that it is used of anything that may also be indicated as *"this and not that."* I presume that children learn the meaning of "this" and "that"—as well as of all other so-called pronominal adjectives, including "all"—by hearing these terms applied in definite concrete situations, as, for instance, when some one uses these words along with contrasting pointings: *"this* toy and not *that," "this* picture and not *that."* It is to be noted that in this process particular spatial relations between two objects on the one hand and the two intercommunicants on the other are used to identify and differentiate the objects, and also to teach the meaning of "this" and "that." Later, when memory develops, temporal relations are used: "this flash of lightning and not that of a while ago." Again, and perhaps later, other relations are employed: "the mother of your friend John," which particularizes a certain woman, even if she is not one of the child's acquaintances.

Two other facts are to be noted in such a teaching process: (1) If what is indicated by pointing or other means has no recognized characters the indication would be futile. (2) Again, if the child himself had no particular place in the total situation, the indication would be equally futile. The child may not be explicitly aware of his place in that scheme of things, but place he must have to make communication possible. And that he has a place can be brought to his attention—if he is so stupid as not to be able to learn it gradually for himself—by pointing to *him* as "this."

It is by the same process, thus used to identify the particularity of concrete things, that we all learn to identify particular *relations* and particular *characters* of concrete things.

In learning such lessons, each of us sooner or later finds himself in the last analysis to be the center of any frame of reference he may use for identifying anything as particular. (If he does not make this discovery, it is because he has not reflected upon the process.) In other words, for us in our role as knowers, the *principium individuationis* of anything is its complex of recognized characters in its spatio-temporal and other relations to other things, ourselves included. If you ask what, in the order of being as contrasted with the order of knowing, the *principium* is, my reply is that since Nature (please note the capital) has neither kernel nor shell, there is no such principle other than the totality of the characters of the thing in the totality of its relations to other things. Select from this whatever you will, *you* can, if you know enough, identify anything in the manner aforesaid. But Nature makes no selection, unless you prefer to have her behave like the boy we all know, who, when asked to choose between cake and candy, "chose" both.

To exemplify Postulate 10, the equality in weight between the two dimes in my pocket is just that particular equality in weight between *those* dimes, and not the equality in weight between any two dimes you may have, nor even the equality in weight btween one of your dimes and one of mine. Likewise, the distance between New York and Chicago is just that particular distance between those two particular cities and not some other particular distance between some other two places, even if the latter distance be equal to the former, i.e., even if there be a relation of equality between the two distances, in which case the equality is itself another particular relation between its particular terms.

The last instance mentioned illustrates the obvious but important fact that a particular relation, while serving as a *relation* between its terms, may itself be a particular *term* in another particular relational complex without losing its identity because of its dual function.

The tiresome emphasis I have been laying on particularity—particularity of terms, particularity of relations, particularity of relational complexes—raises the question of "universals." Is there an "identical" somewhat, say city, distinct from New York and Chicago, that alone justifies us in speaking of them as cities? Is there an identical somewhat, say distance or equality, distinct respectively from the particular distances and the particular equalities we have been considering? If there are such "identities," *what are they?*

In view of the more than twenty-three centuries of inconclusive debate in which many of the world's keenest minds have taken part, not always with arguments alone but also with angry anathemas, he would be a foolhardy philosopher who would dare to propound a brand-new answer. Not having such an answer, nor the requisite foolhardihood even if I had, I content myself with suggesting and, so far as this brief occasion permits, with elaborating a tentative solution that is in some respects similar to previous solutions and, so far as I know, somewhat different from any of them. I crave your indulgence when I call this proposed solution "our theory of universals." It is ours for the nonce and ours for discussion; but being all of us of equal temper of kindly hearts, it is not ours, I hope, to be used as ground for excommunication by bell, book, and candle.

Let us begin with some remarks of David Hume's that bear directly on our problem. He presents us with

> a globe of white marble. . . . But observing afterwards a globe of black marble and a cube of white, and comparing them with our former object, we find two separate resemblances, in what formerly

seem'd, and really is, perfectly inseparable. After a little more practice of this kind, we begin to distinguish the figure from the colour by a *distinction of reason*; that is, we consider the figure and colour together, (since they are in effect the same and undistinguishable;) but still view them in different aspects, according to the resemblances, of which they are susceptible.

A little earlier he had said:

'Tis certain that the mind wou'd never have dream'd of distinguishing a figure from the body figured, (as being in reality neither distinguishable nor different . . .) did it not observe, that *even in this simplicity there might be contain'd many different resemblances and relations.*[6]

I have enclosed in parentheses some words thus quoted, and have italicized the concluding clause. The parentheses mark off what our theory rejects. The italics emphasize what, except for the word "simplicity," our theory accepts as fundamental. There is no simplicity in any concrete thing, if by "simplicity" we mean absence of distinguishable constituents. And the diversity of what we can distinguish is as real as the concrete thing itself. Our distinguishing does not make the discovered diversity; it is a discovery of what is there. Our theory, being realistic, does not recognize any more creative power in the so-called "act" of distinguishing what is inseparable than there is in the "act" of perceiving what actually exists.

Hume's "distinction of reason," whereby reason distinguishes what is "in reality neither distinguishable, nor different," becomes for us "reason's ability to discover by comparison what would never have been discovered save by comparison." The discovery of similarities and differences by comparison is "analysis."[7] It is

---

[6] *A Treatise of Human Nature,* the last two paragraphs of Sect. VII, Part I, Book I; p. 25 in Selby-Bigge's edition, Oxford, 1888. Hume's treatment of the subject is, as we all know, extremely confused because of his italicized insistence that *"all ideas, which are different, are separable"* (p. 24).

[7] Cf. William James, *The Principles of Psychology,* New York, 1893, Vol. I, Chapter XIII. Our theory of universals may be regarded as carrying out to their logical conclusion the views James expressed in his psychological writings and in his debate with F. H. Bradley (*Mind,* N.S., Vol. II, 1893), together with his later insistence that *"any kind of relation experienced must be accounted as 'real' as anything else in the system"* (*Essays in Radical Empiricism,* New York, 1912,

by this method that we have learned to distinguish between terms and relations in relational complexes, which without comparison we should never have recognized as such; and without comparison of various relations recognized in different complexes we should never have discovered that there are different kinds of relations. The mind—whatever "mind" by analysis may be found to be—has no "innate ideas," whether of relations or of anything else. The mind's equipment, other than its physiological basis, begins with the beginning of its experiences, and grows with the growth of its experiences.

Comparisons follow upon comparisons. In comparing the results of analysis we find that there are two different kinds of constituents in what is analyzed. In some cases the constituents are separable, and on separation each has a separate career of its own, a different "world-line" in space-time. Such constituents are "components"; that of which they are constituents are "compounds"; and the analysis by which they are discovered is in the first instance "physical" or "chemical" analysis. When this analysis has gone as far, for the time being, as it can, the provisionally ultimate components are for that time "atoms."

But there are other constituents that are not separable from that within which they are discovered. For instance, when we compare three suitably selected color patches, *A, B,* and *C,* we find *A* and *B* two similar hues, *one in each,* but a dissimilar hue in *C;* whereas we find in *A* and *C* two similar brilliances, one in each, but a dissimilar brilliance in *B.* Moreover, whether in *A* or *B* or *C,* the color, the hue, and the brilliance are inseparable. Each hue is the hue of some brilliance, and each brilliance is the brilliance of some hue; and hue and brilliance are the hue and the brilliance of the color of the patch. Ignoring whatever else may be found, we have in each of the patches a trinity, *one* in three, and *three* in one: one because inseparable, and three because distinguishable. Let us

---

p. 42). James was a superlative genius in his flair for fact, but his logic was wanting in finesse and finish. For this reason the debate with Bradley ended with Bradley as the apparent victor.

call such analysis into distinguishable but inseparable constituents "abstraction," the constituents thus discriminated "abstracts" or "properties" or "characters," and the whole thus analyzed a "synthetic whole." In this chapter the name "character" will generally be used.

It must be emphasized that in our theory a character is abstracted, not *from*, but *within* its synthetic whole. In being abstracted it does not lose the particularity it has as a character of just that whole and not of any other whole, neither does its observed similarity to the character of some other whole reveal or imply any literal identity between the two characters; the two characters are no more identical than the wholes they characterize. If a synthetic whole is an event its characters are likewise events. Taking the liberty of wresting three splendid sentences from the context of Bradley's philosophy, we can say of any synthetic whole and its characters:

> Synthesis here has ceased to be mere synthesis and has become self-completion, and analysis, no longer mere analysis, is self-explication. And the question how or why the many are one and the one is many here loses its meaning. There is no why or how beside the self-evident process, and towards its own differences this whole is at once their how and their why, their being, substance and system, their reason, ground, and principle of diversity and unity.[8]

In addition to (1) sensuously qualitative characters, such as hues and brilliances, there are two other kinds of characters that need to be listed here. (2) There are non-sensuous characters that concrete objects have by virtue of the relations in which they stand to other objects; e.g., a man may have the character of being a father, and a rung the character of being a part of a ladder or of a chair. These overtly relative characters we may call "roles."[9] (3) There are characters that *relations* have; these are also non-

---

[8] F. H. Bradley, *Appearance and Reality*, 2nd ed., London and New York, 1897, p. 568. I should like to substitute "fact" for "process," and add that neither a synthetic whole nor its characters can claim logical precedence, one over the other.

[9] For the view that even sense-qualities belong to objects, not absolutely, but relatively to other objects, see my paper, "Perceptual and Memory Perspectives," in the *Journal of Philosophy*, Vol. XXX (1933), pp. 318 ff.

sensuous characters, such as symmetry and transitivity, whereby relations are assimilated and differentiated among themselves. In what follows, what is said of characters, unless otherwise indicated, is to be taken as applying to characters of all the three kinds just now mentioned.

Since the exclusive particularity of characters has been denied by Platonic and Aristotelian realists, and since we are not interested here in proving that our theory is the sole tenable one, but are merely presenting it as a candidate for tenability, let us expressly acknowledge that underlying what we have been saying is an assumption which we now number

Postulate 11. Every character has the exclusive particularity of the particular synthetic whole that it characterizes. ("Exclusive" here excludes the view that a character, while capable of particularization or while always particularized, nevertheless has a "being" that maintains its identity in transcending each of the particulars it characterizes.)

Since in logic *de postulatis non disputandum* except in regard to their mutual compatibility, it is hoped that, by the avowal that Postulate 11 *is* a postulate, the field of dispute may have been narrowed; and also that Platonists and Aristotelians will play fair in likewise admitting that *they too operate,* each school on a *postulate* contrary to ours. Neither they nor we can properly claim self-evidence or apriority for what we respectively say, unless perchance they have some privileged insight that we others do not have and do not miss. If the issue could be placed on a postulational basis there would be no quarrel; it could be decided by each for himself, determined by tradition, by temperament, or by preference for the use of Occam's razor, itself a postulate. (Occam himself, as we know, used this razor to shave off as superfluous what Platonists and Aristotelians insisted upon letting grow just here.)

It is a commonplace that similarity of concrete objects is non-transitive. On the other hand, what has been said of abstraction would suggest that similarity of *characters* is transitive. We therefore lay down

Postulate 12. If A, B, and C are characters, A is similar to C, whenever A is similar to B, and B is similar to C.

Here, according to our previous postulates, there are four particular similarities and four particular relational complexes. The complexes we may symbolize by $r_1(AB)$, $r_2(BC)$, $r_3(AC)$, and $r_4(ABC)$, where r_1, r_2, r_3, and r_4 symbolize the four particular similarities. The first three complexes are parts of the fourth, and the first three particular similarities are parts of the fourth particular similarity.[10]

A "class of characters" is a relational complex whose terms are characters and whose constituent relation is similarity. In other words, it is a set of similar characters. A character that is a term of such a relational complex is a "member" of that class.

An "entire class of characters" is a class of characters whose members are whatever characters (past, present, or future, whether real, imaginary, or conceived[11]) are similar to each other. If by "all characters that are similar to each other" we agree to mean "whatever characters are similar to each other," then an entire class of characters is a class of all characters that are similar to each other. Such a class, while not necessarily finite in its extension, is entire, wanting nothing called for in its definition.[12]

That similarities of objects and of their relations are of fundamental importance has been generally recognized. Without such similarities life as we know it would be impossible. Tropisms, reflex actions, habits, emotions, volitions, and thought, all pre-

---

[10] On the relational view of space, which is, to say the least, logically tenable, the distance (which is a relation) between any two points P_1 and P_2 is *part* of the distance (also a relation) between P_1 and point P_3, if P_1, P_2, and P_3 lie in this order on a straight line. Now if a particular spatial relation can be a part of another particular spatial relation, why may not a particular *similarity* be a part of another particular similarity?

[11] A character is "conceived" when in any intellectual treatment of it its particularity, real or imaginary, is ignored. Conception is an instance of selective attention, which has as its polar correlate an ignoring of what is not selected. That what is ignored is "not there" can only be a postulate; and our theory declines to make that postulate.

[12] See Appendix to this chapter.

suppose similarities of objects. Professor Cohen understates the truth when he says: "Thus it ought to be obvious that the application of laws to phenomena presupposes the existence of real classes, that many things and processes are really alike. If there were no real likeness . . . the formulation of scientific laws would be without any possible application."[13] But similarities of phenomena and of their relations presuppose similarities of their respective characters, since objects and relations are similar so far, and only so far, as their respective characters are similar. In more technical language, any similarity of things that are not characters is a function of the similarity of their respective characters. But once we recognize any class of similar characters, there is no limit to the size of the class except such as is imposed by the number of similar characters. Hence the importance of logical universals, for a *logical universal is an entire class of characters.*

The "identity" of any universal is not the identity of a *character,* but of the entire class of characters which is that universal, and this identity is the identity of a *particular,* namely, of the particular universal as *other* than any other universal. The fact that any universal is a universal does not preclude it from being a particular, any more than the fact that a horse is a horse keeps it from being a particular horse. (It would seem as if this statement should hold good of a universal, *however* defined, whether as *ante rem, in re* or otherwise.)

A universal is "real" if and in so far as it has real instances, whatever "real" may be taken to mean. (If it means empirically or scientifically verifiable, there are innumerable real universals.) A universal is "imaginary" if its instances are imaginary. (Fairy qua universal is presumably exclusively imaginary.) With the exception of exclusively imaginary universals all universals are probably partly real and partly imaginary. A universal is "conceived" if, in an intellectual treatment of it, the particularity of

---

[13] Morris R. Cohen, *Reason and Nature,* New York, (copyright 1931), p. 153. The omission indicated by the spaced periods reads: "no examples of identity in different instances." This omitted phrase we will discuss later.

its instances is ignored. (See footnote 11, above.) A universal is "null" if its instances are absences or lacks. (Some of its instances are found by comparing an empty pocketbook or dinner pail, the truancies of Johnny from school, the millions of cases of unemployment under Franklin Delano Roosevelt's administration, the grin of the Cheshire Cat, and the lack of a kiss in the smile of your girl.) A universal is "merely nominal" or "logically absurd" if its instances are verbal combinations of incompatible characters, e.g., "round square." The logician deals with it by recognition with a snub and by avoidance which is eschewal and not exculpation.

Let us now compare our theory of universals with some others, and first with two of the three that have had the longest and widest currency, viz., with what have historically been known as "Platonic realism" and "Aristotelian realism." Until further notice we shall call the respective advocates of these views "Platonists" and "Aristotelians," without wishing to be understood as implying that all who call themselves Platonists would subscribe to "Platonic realism," or all Aristotelians to "Aristotelian realism," or even to suggest that "Platonic realism" was Plato's own considered view.

We agree with both Platonists and Aristotelians that *there are universals*. What is thoroughly sound in the theories of these two schools is the recognition that experienced similarities between *concrete* things fail to furnish, without more ado, an adequate basis for logical thinking. Abstraction is needed, and when abstraction discovers characters in concrete things, there is *ipso facto* also the discovery that it is by virtue of the similarity of their characters that concrete things are similar. But neither Platonists nor Aristotelians are satisfied that these discoveries reveal all that is to be known in the matter. Just as the similarity of characters is needed to account for the similarity of concrete things, so, they contend, there must be *something* that accounts for the similarity of *characters*. This something they find in *one* character for each entire set of similar characters. Plato and Aristotle called this something εἶδος, and their Latin followers called it *universale*. In

English "universal" is perhaps a better translation than "idea," because the latter word has acquired other meanings much more familiar. For Plato, at least when he wrote the *Phaedrus*, the universal was pure, without alloy or admixture from characters that appear in time, unchanging, absolute. Every temporal character "participates" in its universal (ἐκείνου μετέχει) without thereby adulterating that universal. In Aristotle, if not in the more mature Plato, the universals lost their aloofness from things in time without losing therewith their timelessness. Each universal is one identical character, changeless in many concrete changing things. But in spite of whatever difference there may be between these two theories, they agree that there can be no similarity between two objects except as there is an *identical* character that authorizes and authenticates the similarity. The relation of similarity cannot *by itself* relate anything; but fortunately it can and does operate under charter from some universal.[14]

If in our theory we are unwilling to follow Platonists and Aristotelians in going beyond the empirical fact that characters are actually related by similarities, it is because we do not feel the need nor even the urge to multiply entities beyond necessity by bringing in non-empirical universals to validate empirical findings. However, we do not claim such omniscience as alone could justify us in denying outright that there are universals of the Platonic or of the Aristotelian stripe. There may be such entities, for all we do *not* know, just as there may be an unnumbered multitude of angels in this room, dancing on invisible needle points. But if there are, we do not "hear the flutter of their wings." This may be due to an obtuseness on our part. Hence it is not only in the spirit of tolerance, but also of meet humility that we are willing to let those who need them have their "eternal essences" keeping state either in a realm of their own or in an invisible extension of

---

[14] We are all familiar with F. H. Bradley's treatment of relations on the similar principle that relations are powerless to relate; but instead of recognizing any effective commission they might have from some higher source, he challenged their jurisdiction as being apparent and not real, and finally overwhelmed them in the mystic unity of his totalitarian Absolute (*op. cit.*, chapters III and XXVI).

the realm of experience; willing even to let them have their "Pure Potentials for the Specific Determination of Fact," envisaged in the "Primordial Nature of God." If there be such a Primordial Nature of God, that Nature needs, God knows, something to envisage, and Professor Whitehead knows it too. Our needs are less exacting, and we decline to stop reasoning as best we can and talking about reasoning as much as we must, just because we have no delegated warrant.

Our universals are not characters. For instance, the universal "blue" or "blueness" is not *blue*.[15] As our definition has asserted, it is the entire class of blues, which is no more blue than an asylum for the insane is itself literally insane: it is "insane" only by metonymy (or is it by synecdoche? I always have to look up in the dictionary to learn again which is which; and just now I don't care). Likewise the entire class of blues, "blue" or "blueness," the *universal,* is blue only by whatever that figure of speech is. Each universal by the idiom of our language takes the name of its instances. It is bootless to kick against the pricks of idiom, but it does profit us to beware of its deceptiveness.

An argument based on idiom has frequently been urged with supposedly devastating effect against such theories as ours. How, it is asked, can Smith and Jones be alike in (respect to) breadth— of beam—note well the *singular* "breadth"—if there be no *single*

---

[15] The difference between "blue" and "blueness," when both are used literally, is one of grammatical syntax and not of logic; and grammar has its vagaries. We speak indifferently of the "blue" or the "blueness" of my lady's dress, but hardly of the "orangeness" of your lady's hat. We speak indifferently of a "man of valor" or of a "brave man"; but I do not remember ever having heard of a "man of whiteness." Caesar wrote of *vir magnae auctoritatis,* but never, if Gildersleeve is right, of *vir auctoritatis.* Apuleius, however, some two hundred years later, could have done so; and in English we say a "man of influence" or an "influential" man. Examples could be multiplied indefinitely: a "tower of strength," etc. Issue, therefore, must be taken with J. S. Mill when he says: "The word white, denotes all white things, as snow, paper . . ., and implies, or . . . connotes, the attribute *whiteness*" (*A System of Logic,* 8th ed., London, 1872, Vol. I, p. 31 [Book I, Ch. II, § 5]). But when adjectives are used as nouns the case is different: "None but the brave deserve the fair," "Blessed are the meek." The denotation of common nouns varies with the context. Generally they denote concrete objects and connote characters; but when we say, "he is a *man,*" we mean, but with more emphasis, "he is *manly.*"

identical breadth of beam belonging to them *in common?* The reply is brief and to us it seems adequate: Smith and Jones are alike in being *severally* broad (i.e., alike by virtue of their *respective* breadths) of beam.[16] Every concrete thing "shares" with every other similar concrete thing *membership in the class* of their respective similar characters, but there are as many memberships as there are members. There is nothing mystical in such "participation." It finds its adequate logical explanation in the experienced or postulated relations of similarity between the experienced or postulated characters involved. At least I do not feel a mystic thrill in belonging with Professor X to the class of the superannuated, and so far as I can learn neither does he. If there be myth or mystery here, there is myth or mystery everywhere. If *everywhere,* what's the *difference?*

Once we have made it clear to ourselves and to others that according to our theory there is no character that is literally and identically *common* to two or more things, there is no more objection to our speaking of "common characters" than there is in speaking of sunrise and sunset in connection with the Copernican theory. *The avoidance of idiom is pedantic.*

My long experience in teaching philosophy has led me to the conclusion that *mens naturaliter Platonica* is as mythical as any myth in Plato. That blue things are alike in being blue, students have readily admitted, but with some surprise at being asked to admit a tautology. It was a rare bird, however, that could be coached and coaxed into saying that he believed in a blueness *ante rem.* And when finally he did say it, I cannot now but wonder whether he meant and believed what I then tried to make him admit and what I now vainly try to mean. My present state of mind on this matter reminds me of a brilliant college classmate.

---

[16] "There is one glory of the sun, and another glory of the moon, and another glory of the stars: for one star differeth from another star in glory." If we were captious we might ask how one star can differ in grammatically singular glory when each has its own distinctive glory. But this would be only to cavil *ad hominem.* What apparently St. Paul meant is that every star is glorious, but not all stars are equally brilliant. But if he had said it in this way, what a loss of beauty!

He had become a professor of English in a university, when I sent him a reprint of my doctor's thesis on Hegel. I was immensely flattered when he replied that he understood "every last word of it." Here was praise indeed! But alas! he closed his letter with the curt remark that he did not know what it was all about.

The intimacy between the universal and the particular in the Aristotelian theory is brought out by Professor Sheldon when he says:

> In a very true sense the sameness between the parts of reality permits us to say that one part does what it is, as an individual, very far from doing. This is not poetry—at least in the anti-logical connotation of that term—but is in accord with the strictest logic. And so, to return to our absurd second instance above: if my hat has been around Cape Horn then the identical qualities in yours have indeed had that same experience. If it suits your purpose to consider my particular hat representative of yours, you may consider that yours has had the benefit of the experiences which mine has suffered. The absurdity of the illustration lies in the fact that we can hardly consider any good practical reason why one hat should thus represent another; but there is nothing in the logic of the matter to prevent it. In so far as you *separate* the individual marks of your hat from those of mine, so far yours has done otherwise than mine; in so far as you identify them, the one has done what the other has done. There are two different points of view about the matter, that is all; and neither denies the other. There is no *reductio*; the one object does what the other object does, and it does also much that the other object does not do.[17]

I have quoted this passage *in extenso,* italics and all, so as not to do injustice to the author, but without any intention of suggesting that all Aristotelian realists would subscribe to every or any part of it. It is for them to say. But what Mr. Sheldon says does pose a problem which all of them should face. To his honor, Mr. Sheldon faces it squarely, and solves it to his satisfaction by appealing to "good practical reasons." But apparently not all Aristotelian realists, when dealing with *logic*, think much of "good practical reasons," nor do they seem to think much on the problem Mr. Sheldon faces.

---

[17] Wilmon Henry Sheldon, *Strife of Systems and Productive Duality,* Cambridge [Mass.], 1918, pp. 502–503.

One of the most distinguished advocates of Aristotelian realism at the present time is Professor Morris R. Cohen, and it gives me great satisfaction that in most of what in his important work he says of universals I can agree heartily.[18] The nub of my difference from him is found in what I omitted in my previous quotation from him.[19] Let us now quote in full the sentence from which this omission was made, and in so doing italicize what was then omitted: "If there were no real likeness, *no examples of identity in different instances,* the formulation of scientific laws would be without any possible application." What is meant by "identity in different instances" is brought out in a later sentence in the same paragraph: "The scientific pursuit of rational connection presupposes that things do have certain common natures and relations." Again, we are told that the progress of any science "depends upon our ability to see things . . . only as the embodiments of those universals which are relevant to our inquiry . . . Without some perception of the abstract or universal traits which the new shares with the old, we cannot recognize or discover new truths. In the most elementary kind of inference . . . some perception of the universal or abstract element of identity is involved" (pp. 124-125). In another passage we are told that neither universals nor particulars are what we definitely recognize as such at the start: "the actual growth of knowledge . . . is mainly a progress not from the particular to the universal but from the vague to the definite. The distinction between the particular and the universal is generally implicit and only comes to explicit or clear consciousness in the higher stages of knowledge. . . . The process of reflection is necessary to make the universal clear and distinct, but as the discriminating element in observation it aids us to recognize the individual" (p. 124). I bring our quotations from Mr. Cohen's work to a close with these last three sentences, not because I disagree on this point (if I am

---

[18] The Index to Cohen's *Reason and Nature* lists the most significant passages bearing on universals. The page references in my text, where I deal with Cohen's view, are to that volume. [This chapter was written by Professor McGilvary some years before Morris Cohen's death in 1947.—Ed.]

[19] See p. 236.

allowed to give my own interpretation to "universal"), but in order to present a fairly complete statement of his view, and to confess that if by "universal" is meant literally an "abstract element of identity" "in different instances," such reflection as I have been able to make does not make explicit any such universals. "The higher stages of knowledge" where this revelation is vouchsafed lie beyond my present reach. Such knowledge is too wonderful for me; it is high, I cannot attain unto it. In the meantime I should like to know why *our* universals will not serve all the logical purposes that *his* are said to serve. If they do that, then like all other nominalists I will not attempt further heights. If they do not . . . But let me wait till it is shown that they do not.

Having now discussed the relation of our theory to the Platonic and Aristotelian thesis, we pass on to nominalism. But what is nominalism? Many have been the definitions given of it, and many have been the views of those who have called themselves nominalists or have been so called by others. From "a certain John"[20] and his successor Roscelin, through some eight hundred years to John Stuart Mill and Roy Wood Sellars, there has been an infinite variety of nominalisms rivalling that of Cleopatra. A casual survey of the theories presented by these thinkers reveals only two articles in their common creed. They all agree (1) in disallowing Platonic and Aristotelian universals, and (2) in maintaining that whatever is, is particular. It seems therefore proper to characterize as nominalistic any thinker who subscribes to these two articles. *In this sense* our theory is nominalistic. But a common creed does not secure agreement on other important points.

A comparison of our nominalism with that of Professor Sellars is timely, since his theory is fully presented in a volume[21] the recency of which, together with its importance as a contribution to the philosophy of critical realism, justifies me in assuming that it is familiar to all philosophers. Therefore it is not necessary to go

---

[20] See Maurice De Wulf's *History of Mediaeval Philosophy*, tr. by Ernest C. Messenger, London, 1926, Vol. I, p. 110.

[21] Roy Wood Sellars, *The Philosophy of Physical Realism*, New York, 1932. The page references, when we are dealing with Mr. Sellars, are to this volume.

into details. The fundamental difference of his theory from ours is that Mr. Sellars as a critical realist builds his theory on the position "that any factor distinguishable in a perceptual experience is *given*. . . . It is only the external thing, which is the object of the perceiving, which is *not* given, that is, not a factor in the individual's field of experience. And this view . . . holds equally for conception and judgment. 'Given' means a factor in an individual's experience" (p. 148). Hence universals present to Sellars a double problem: (1) what are universals in the individual's experience, in the mind that makes "categorial interpretations" (p. 406)? and (2) what are universals in the physical world? His solution of the first problem is his "logical conceptualism," that of the second is his "ontological nominalism." "The position which I shall defend," says he, "may be called logical conceptualism and ontological nominalism" (p. 155).

What then is Mr. Sellars's logical conceptualism? "Suppose that I am dealing with sense-data and suppose these are to be regarded as particulars. What, then, do I mean when I apply the concept 'red' to two sense-data? Clearly, I am not denying their particularity, but I am saying that with respect to a feature of the one I can rightly apply the concept red and that with respect to a feature of the other I can likewise apply the concept red. Each feature is an instance of red. But do we mean more by the expression, 'instance of red,' than we mean by the expression, 'the concept applies'? I doubt it. May it not be, then, that the identity of the concept is carried over to the qualities? [Yes.] . . . We think two particulars in terms of the same concept; but does this epistemic unity justify the assumption of a factor literally common to the two particulars?" [No.] (p. 161). The answers which I have supplied in brackets to these two questions constitute Mr. Sellars's logical conceptualism when "identity of the concept" is taken to mean repetition of "the same meaning *as content*" (p. 163).

Mr. Sellars's ontological nominalism is the thesis "that the very mode of working of our minds through concepts as instruments leads us to *project* the recurrence of the same meanings in our minds into the things we are thinking of. Logical identity [i.e., 'identity of the concept'] is transformed into universals in things" (p. 158). "In the strict sense," however, "the only universals are concepts. But the controlled correspondence and revelatory capacity of these concepts make it seem to us *as though* there were universals in nature" (p. 168). A similar distinction to that between actual universals as concepts and *als ob* objective universals also holds between classes. "In the strict sense, classes do not exist in nature. There are only similar things. Classes express a way of thinking things together by means of a logical connotation which corresponds to and applies to actual things" (p. 173).

These quotations, which of course are not to be considered as giving a complete view of Mr. Sellars's theory, indicate the main points of difference between his theory and ours.

Mr. Sellars's view in regard to classes reminds us of the treatment of classes in the *Principia,* where they are introduced as "merely symbolic or linguistic conveniences, not genuine objects as their members are if they are individuals."[22] This means that classes as genuine objects are not needed in the *Principia*; whether there are such classes is not a problem that belongs to mathematical logic. As against this noncommittal attitude our theory takes an affirmative position, not dogmatically but under the postulate that similarities are as "genuine" as the terms they relate, and that a relational complex of "genuinely" similar terms that are themselves "genuine" is itself a "genuine" object. The *Principia* claims the merit of doing justice to the advocates of intensions and those of extensions "by showing that an extension (which is the same as a class) is an incomplete symbol, whose use always acquires its meaning through a reference to intension" (*PM*, p. 72). Our theory can claim the same merit, since any universal of ours is an extension whose members are particular intensions. Furthermore, since according to our theory every character is abstracted within

---

[22] Whitehead and Russell, *Principia Mathematica, Cambridge,* Vol. I., 2nd ed. (1925), p. 72. In the page references given in this and the following paragraph of the text, this volume will appear as "*PM.*"

a synthetic unity of characters, i.e., within an "object," any class of characters is coextensive with the class of objects of which they are the respective characters. The two classes are indeed not equivalent, since their members are not the same; but there is a one-to-one correlation between the two classes, and there is also an inseparability of the one-to-one correlates.

There is another difference between our view and that of the *Principia,* since the latter defines an "individual" or a "particular" as "anything that can be the subject of an atomic proposition" (*PM,* p. xix), while no predicable character and no relation, i.e., no "universals," can be subjects of any propositions. Universals, thus defined, of course differ from our universals; but this is not the difference that I wish to emphasize, for I agree with Ramsey when he says:

> Now it seems to me as clear as anything can be in philosophy [and I would add, in any logic except the logic of the *Principia*] that the two sentences "Socrates is wise," "Wisdom is a characteristic of Socrates," assert the same fact and express the same proposition. They are not, of course, the same sentence, but they have the same meaning, just as two sentences in two different languages can have the same meaning. Which sentence we use is a matter either of literary style, or of the point of view from which we approach the fact."[23]

The paper from which the above quotation is taken had as its purpose "to consider whether there is a fundamental division of objects into two classes, particulars and universals" (p. 113). The first conclusion he reaches after some discussion is

---

[23] Frank Plumpton Ramsey, *The Foundations of Mathematics,* New York and London, 1931, p. 116. As the first footnote in the second edition of the *Principia* tells us, Ramsey "read the whole" of that volume "in MS and contributed valuable criticisms and suggestions" (*PM,* p. xiii). If the view we have just quoted was one of the suggestions Ramsey made it was not adopted, either because the authors of the *Principia* did not agree with the view, or because it did not fit into the technique adopted in their treatment of propositions. The paper from which our quotation is made first appeared in *Mind* in 1925, the year of the publication of the second edition of the *Principia.* In a short Note (1926) Ramsey says that he is very doubtful about what he had been sure of when he wrote that paper, viz., that it is "impossible to discover atomic propositions by actual analysis" (*Foundations,* p. 135). This change of attitude, however, does not affect the general course or force of the arguments in the original paper. The page references in the next two paragraphs of our text are to Ramsey's *Foundations,* unless otherwise indicated.

that, *as regards incomplete symbols,* the fundamental distinction is not between substantive and adjective but between primary and secondary occurrence; and that a substantive is simply a logical construction between whose primary and secondary occurrences we fail to distinguish [p. 128, but without italics].

But, he tells us, this "is not the conclusion which I want most to stress . . . the real question at issue is the possibility of dividing not logical constructions but genuine objects into particulars and universals" (p. 128). This question, of course, is one of the problems which the *Principia* declines to discuss, since they "belong to the philosophical part of logic, and are not amenable (at any rate at present) to mathematical treatment" (*PM,* p. xv). Ramsey's conclusion is that this question should belong to symbolic logic:

> Any one who was interested not only in classes of things, but also in their qualities, would want to distinguish from among the others those functions which were names; and if we called the objects of which they are names qualities . . . the difference analogous to that between "Socrates" and "wisdom" would have disappeared. We should have complete symmetry between qualities and individuals. . . . So were it not for the mathematician's biassed interest he would invent a symbolism which was completely symmetrical as regards individuals and qualities; and it becomes clear that there is no sense in the words individual and quality; all we are talking about is two different types of objects, such that two objects, one of each type, could be the sole constituents of an atomic fact [p. 132].

What interests us is that for Ramsey there *are* "two different types of objects," viz., "things" and "their qualities," and that an example of neither type is an "individual," i.e., a "particular," in any sense in which an example of the other type is not. Any adequate symbolism would be "completely symmetrical" as regards these two types. In the terminology of our theory, the instances of the two types are respectively "characters" and "synthetic unities." The demand for a symbolism more adequate than that employed in the *Principia* is made by the fact that characters as well as their synthetic unities should be treated as values of the subjects of relevant propositional functions. Until we have a symbolism in which this can be done, symbolic logic is not the whole of logic.

Because of the importance and the wide currency of the logic of instrumentalism, a comparison of our theory with Professor Dewey's seems called for, but it is with misgiving that I undertake to make it. Time was when I was sure that I understood what Mr. Dewey meant, and with more zeal than caution I entered the fray, "knowing what I was up against." But the years have brought a more sophisticated mind. How then can I with confidence compare our theory with his? If I remember aright, Mr. Dewey once characterized the mind of George Herbert Mead as "seminal." May I apply the same characterization to Mr. Dewey's own mind? And having on another occasion expressed my great debt to him for the seeds I have picked up from his abundant sowing, I hope he will forgive me if I point out that what is seminal not only promises a future harvest but also is, while it is still seminal, exceedingly puzzling—as The Preacher once observed—because it fails to tell us exactly what is going on or where it is going. Mr. Dewey has found, and found truly, so much that is not right in the philosophical thinking of our time, and has always been so much interested in averting the disastrous practical consequences of this wrong thinking, that he has not taken time off to gather into a conspectus all that he would have us substitute for what he deplores. This is as it should be with a seminal mind. Its business is to produce seed and plant it, not to gather the harvest into well-ordered bins. Mr. Dewey seeds and plants (none better), controversy waters, and time will give the increase. But meanwhile *what is his theory of universals with which we may compare ours?* Let us see:

> To assert that knowledge is classification is to assert in effect that kind, character, has overlaid and overridden bare occurrence and existence. To say that to know is to define is to recognize that wherever there is knowledge there is explicitly present a universal. To hold that cognition is recognition is to concede that likeness, a relation, rather than existence, is central. And to be acquainted with anything is to be aware what it is *like*, in what *sort* of ways it is likely to behave. These features, character, kind, sort, universal, likeness, fall within the universe of meaning.[24]

[24] John Dewey, *Experience and Nature*, Chicago, London, 1926, p. 330. The other page references, given in the text that deals with Mr. Dewey, are to this

I am tempted to say: "This is our theory in a nutshell. All that is needed is to take it out of the shell and let it expand." And I am inclined to think that *after all* this would be a correct appraisal. I say "after all"; and an instance of this "all" is found in the following quotation:

> It would be difficult to imagine any doctrine more absurd than the theory that general ideas or meanings arise by the comparison of a number of particulars, eventuating in the recognition of something common to them all (p. 188).

I should like to think that what is here criticized is "the recognition of something *common* to them all," in the sense of an identical abstract embodied in each. But unfortunately nowhere has Mr. Dewey given a complete formulation of his views on universals. He evidently dislikes regimenting his views according to the technique usually adopted by logicians.

But Mr. Dewey could urge against my formulation of our theory that I have constantly spoken of what is "meant" without telling what I mean by "meaning." This is true. But for the purpose of this chapter I do not care what theory of the meaning of meaning is the correct theory. Take any theory you choose; it probably will presuppose that there is such a thing as meaning. *How* we come to mean does not matter *for the present*. We all *do* mean, and what our theory maintains is that something real is "meant" by "universal," and that analysis reveals that that something is an entire class of characters, each character in any class being as particular as anything can be. For any one who experiences a character it is "consummatory," and it is "evanescent." "Such immediate qualities as red and blue, sweet and sour, tone, the pleasant and unpleasant, . . . are evanescent" (p. 115). As Mr. Dewey has repeatedly said, the very evanescence of the consummatory leaves something to be desired: we not only enjoy, but we wish to conserve and increase our values. This would be impossible

---

volume. When this text was written I had not seen Mr. Dewey's recent volume, *Logic: The Theory of Inquiry*, where I hope to find the conspectus I now miss.

were there not classes of the consummatory and of relations, available for us in our rational effort to secure the good life.

Any one who has critically followed the exposition now given of our theory of universals will probably have asked whether there is a universal "similarity" to be so called from the names of all its instances: can there be a similarity of *all* similarities, as there is, let us say, a similarity of all distances? The answer is negative. Whatever universals there are, are constituted each by the similarity of the characters that are its instances. Thus there are as many comprehensive similarities as there are universals. *These* similarities are themselves similar; and the (1) *similarity* of (2) these similarities is itself similar to these similarities; there is then (3) the similarity of similarity (1) and similarities (2), and so on *ad infin.* Each of these similarities is the particular similarity of the particular terms it relates, but there is no single similarity of *all* similarities. Beginning with the similarity of all the similarities that constitute each a universal, there is a hierarchy of similarities each constituting an entire class of *the* similarities it relates; and somewhere in this infinite series of similarities and of the classes they constitute will be found a class whose members are *any* two similarities you may have previously selected. But in selecting your two similarities, you did not select *their* similarity. Without selection, this latter similarity comes with what you have selected, just as when you have married a woman of your selection, you find that you have acquired, along with her, "in-laws" that you did not choose. Using "type" in the sense it has in the "theory of types," we must say that in our infinite hierarchy of similarities, each similarity differs in type from the similarities it relates.

Having begun my discussion of universals with quotations from Hume, I wish to close it with a reference to the last paragraph of Book I of his *Treatise.* What Hume said there has scandalized a host of critics, but to me it seems a magnificent final paragraph for any work in philosophy. The fact that the critics were scandalized reminds me of the final line in the limerick about the Rev. Jabez MacCotten: "To the pure all things are rotten." I might wish to alter some words in Hume's paragraph, but in substance it expresses the spirit in which I offer this chapter "to the public." It expresses my "present view of the object" under discussion. The view presented I have entertained for a long time, but the details have been growing clearer with further examination. It is, however, a "tentative" view. What has been said will doubtless require much revision, as it is the result of many past revisions. Any one who has found it necessary to revise and re-revise his philosophical outlook would indeed have a "conceited idea of his own judgment" if he presented his present judgment as definitive either for himself or for others.

Appendix

In the discussion referred to in footnote 1, it was argued that our assumption of the particularity of relations excludes the possibility of entire classes of characters. As I understand the contention, it assumed that there is an incompatibility between what, since that discussion, I have now labelled Postulates 10 and 12; or, to be more specific, that Postulate 10 precludes the assertion that there are any two such particular relations of similarity as r_1 (or r_2 or r^3) and r^4, mentioned on page 235. Apparently this contention was based on the assumption that a particular relation cannot have subordinate particular relations as parts. Even if this was not what was meant, it seems worth while to discuss the point, which has already been touched on in footnote 10.

I will begin by granting (but only for the sake of argument) that Postulates 10 and 12 are incompatible. I maintain that even under this concession it is still possible to define an entire class of characters, and that this newly defined class is equivalent to that defined on page 235: the two classes are equivalent in the sense that they have exactly the same extension. Therefore either definition will serve our purpose as well as the other.

Let us consider a particular monogamic family, consisting of X (the father), Y (the mother), and Z (the only son). This family is a "comprehensive" relational complex, having as its parts the "subordinate" relational complexes, $r_1(XY)$ husband-and-wife, $r_2(XZ)$ father-and-son, and $r_3(YZ)$ mother-and-son. We cannot symbolize the family as a whole by $r_4(XYZ)$, because it is a family only by virtue of the "subordinate" relations r_1, r_2, and r_3, each of which obtains between only two of the three members of the family. These subordinate relations are "interlocked," the interlocking consisting in that either term of any one of the subordinate relations is also a term of one other subordinate relation. For instance, X is the husband of Y, and also the father of Z. Without this interlocking there would not be *one* family. Hence we write the symbol for the family as a whole in this way: $r_4(r_1[XY], r_2[XZ], r_3[YZ])$. Here r_4 is the "comprehensive" *family*-relation, which is not similar to any of the other r's; neither are the latter similar to each other. It is perhaps permissible to call r_4 a Gestalt relation, since embosomed in its character are the other three relations, and yet that character is distinctive, not in spite, but by reason, of this enfoldment. Nor do the included characters lose a whit of their particularities in this embrace. (Here we have an actual instance of what Hegel called *Aufhebung:* the included characters are "taken up" but not "cancelled," as are paid notes at a bank.) It is my guess that no one would object to calling the relation of father to son a "part" of the total family relation of which they are terms. If this guess is correct, we have here another instance in which a relation is part of another relation; this instance differs from that cited in footnote 10 where whole and part were similar relations, whereas here whole and part are dissimilar.

I have limited our chosen family to three members in order that the subordinate relations may have only two terms each. Now let us grant (again for the sake of argument) that any particular *similarity* is exclusively dyadic. Why may not any number of such similarities, *if interlocked,* constitute out of all their respective terms one particular complex? Finding in my experience such complexes, and not finding any reason in logic why I should not find them, I take them at their face value. I take them by postulation if you will not let me have them directly from experience. But by hook or by crook I take them, and I challenge your right in logic to deny me this appropriation. Now I define a "class of characters" as a relational complex whose terms are characters any one of which is similar to every other; and an "entire class of characters" as a class of characters whose members are *all* characters, any one of which is similar to every other. Any entire class of characters falling under this definition is equivalent to an entire class of characters as defined on page 235.

Having thus secured "entire classes of characters" by definition, we find ourselves, however, blocked by our concession from having transitive relations, if by transitivity we mean the character of a relation that, while preserving its identity, passes from term P to term R, taking term Q in its stride. This, however, is not an irreparable loss. If no similarity, which now is by concession dyadic, can be transitive in the sense of having this straddling character which would involve its having at least three terms, it may be "transitive" in another sense equally subservient to the purposes of the logician. Let us begin by saying that transitivity is not in the first instance predicable of any particular relation but only of a *chain* or *network* of relations.

Suppose that Noah, in mobilizing his animals for entrance into the ark, had linked every male by a chain to the female of his species beside him, and also by *another* chain to the female of another species in front of him. Suppose, further, that of two bystanders, surveying as much of the procession as lay within their fields of vision, one assumed that only one chain of indefinite length had been used in securing the concatenation, while the other, examining more closely, had discovered that many chains had been used, one for every two animals directly bound together. Which onlooker would have had an advantage over the other when theorizing about the linkage beyond his ken? In either case there would have been "transitivity" available for theory: in the one case it would have been the transitivity of a *single* long *chain*, in the other the transitivity of the *linkage*. And *it is linkage that counts in generalization,* and both generalizers would have had linkage at their service.

Keeping this in mind, let us now define "transitivity" thus: "If a particular relation r_3 obtains between A and C, whenever two similar particular relations, r_1 *and* r_2, obtain respectively between A and B, and between B and C, the interlocked *chain* or set of the relations r_1, r_2, r_3 is said to be "transitive." Between a transitive set of relations and a transitive relation the difference for logic is a matter of indifference, just as for an operating mathematician the difference between an irrational number, defined as a *single* number at a Dedekind cut is Tweedledum, and defined as "a segment of the series of ratios which has no boundary" is Tweedledee. (For the latter definition, see Russell, *Introduction to Mathematical Philosophy,* New York and London, undated, p. 72, and *Principia Mathematica,* Vol. 2 (1912), pp. 684 ff.) If, however, any one should still insist on transitive *relations* rather than transitive chains or sets of relations, his reasonable requirement, if not his preference, can be met by giving him "transitive" relations defined as members of any transitive chain or set of relations.

CHAPTER VII

FREEDOM AND NECESSITY IN HUMAN AFFAIRS

The problem of human freedom will not down. William James was right when he said that "the juice has not been pressed out of the free-will controversy," and that "no subject is less worn out." It would be hard to find a recent philosophical work in which the subject is not discussed as a live issue. But the discussion is not confined to technical circles. Clarence Darrow, the criminal lawyer, attracted large audiences when he lectured on the bearing of determinism on responsibility and drew the conclusion that since determinism is not compatible with responsibility it is unreasonable to hold criminals responsible for their crimes. C. E. M. Joad, an English philosopher, found a medium in the popular *Harper's Magazine* for the publication of an attack upon current deterministic views in psychology on the ground that they are incompatible with morality. The editor evidently believed that his readers were interested in the question. The appeal of the problem to the general public is not hard to understand. Everyone is interested in morality, whether pro or con; and everyone knows that, at least until very lately, science has operated on the assumption of determinism.

But determinism is charged with dynamite. If everything that happens is determined by what precedes, how can a man act differently from the way in which he does act? And if he cannot act differently, why should he be held responsible for what he does? These questions become more important now that they are divorced from theology. So long as a theologically authoritarian morality was accepted, the bearing of determinism upon morality was a conundrum and not a practical problem. Learned men of leisure could exercise their wits upon it, but their solutions were purely academic. No matter what one thought about it, there stood the Ten Commandments, fixed and unalterable even though the tables of stone on which they were graven be broken.

Of late the whole scene has changed. There has been a growing spirit of rebellion against moral dictation. Authoritarian morality has been denounced and renounced, and in its stead in many circles has been set up a golden calf, molten in the flames of hot desires; and in its presence the people sit down to eat and drink and rise up to play. Declining to be driven as slaves by an external taskmaster, many have surrendered themselves to the mastery of their own compelling instincts and justify themselves on the plea that necessity knows no law. Stark determinism is then pleaded as a warrant for the "innocent" career of immoral larks.

Now if morality is inconsistent with determinism, either determinism or morality must go by the board. We thus have before us a question no longer academic but one fraught with the issues of life and death to morality itself. My contact with university students for more than four decades has convinced me that with many of them the deterministic attitude has become an intellectual habit. Their training in the various sciences has disposed them to look at every event as caused; and when faced with the seeming necessity of giving up either determinism or morality, not all of them are inclined to give up determinism. Not a small part of the moral unrest among the brilliant youth of our day, so much discussed and so much deplored by their elders, is to be traced to the prevalence of this deterministic attitude coupled with the belief that determinism is inconsistent with morality. I decline to join in the hysteric hue and cry against the "viciousness" of modern youth. In every generation youth is modern and age is antiquated; this is as it should be. There is no more viciousness in the youth of this day than of any preceding era. On the contrary, confronted with appalling problems, young men and young women are now forced to do more thinking than perhaps has ever before been done by those of their years. And they are doing it fearlessly and honestly. But fearless and honest thinking is not always clear thinking. It is my purpose here to argue the thesis that the irreconcilability of determinism with morality is a pernicious mistake. Let us look at the logic of the question.

But first let us define determinism. It is the theory that every natural event is caused by preceding natural events, and that in its turn it is the cause of later events. Take for instance the striking of a billiard ball with a cue. Given the exact conditions under which this is done, the ball, so far as we can discover, will move in just one way; and if during its motion it strikes another ball, that ball, under the exact conditions under which it is struck, will then move in just one way. Generalizing, the determinist says that under the exact conditions under which any event takes place, that event is the only one that in the order of nature is going to occur under those conditions. Thus determinism is the assumption or postulate that every natural event is unambiguously determined by preceding natural events. Without the belief in determinism on the part of scientists, the achievements won by science up to within the last few years would never have been undertaken. Believing that events have causes, the scientist has proceeded to try to discover what the causes were of events that interested him.

Now volition, being an event, is by the determinist assumed to be determined; and being an event, it is assumed to be in its turn a cause of some following events. It is strange that in many arguments on determinism it is taken for granted (both by determinists and indeterminists) that, if the will is determined, it is not effective. Nobody argues in this way about other things. Lightning, earthquakes, and cyclones lose none of their potency by reason of the fact that they are themselves effects. In the physical world effects are in their turn causes; there is no logical reason why this should not be true also in the world of mind.

The failure to recognize this has led to the confusion of determinism with fatalism, which is the view that, whatever the future may bring, our wills have no part in determining the outcome. For instance, the fatalist says that the hour of his death is fixed; therefore it makes no difference what he does in the meantime. At the fated hour die he shall. If at that time he is engaged in battle his death is not hastened; if at that time he sits peacefully at home his death is not postponed. If a warrior's sword does not dispatch him Fate has at its disposal numberless ways of achieving the destiny decreed; there is many a pestilence that walketh in darkness as well as the destruction that wasteth at noonday. To change to a familiar figure, Fate is an invincible chess player. I have before me any number of moves, and I am at liberty to select any one I wish; but whichever I select, checkmated I shall be when the time comes for my undoing. I may indeed be the master of my will, but I am not the captain of my fate. This is Milton's "fixed fate." It should always be borne in mind that fatalism is not belief in the determinedness of the will, but in the ineffectiveness, the utter futility, of the will, whereas determinism is consistent with belief in the power of the will to determine consequences.

For this reason there is either muddle-headedness or intellectual dishonesty shown by anyone who attributes fatalism to a determinist just because he is a determinist. Words of ill fame are always powerful weapons to use in argument. I am afraid that those who call determinists fatalists have not been unmindful of the fact that the word "fatalism" carries a fatal virus. Now a word is not immediately disinfected by redefinition. In this respect fatalism belongs to the same class of words as atheism, socialism, and materialism. These words are most powerful means of prejudicing the hearer against an opponent. They enable one to obtain all the advantages of bearing false witness against one's neighbor without literally telling a lie. I assume that honest thinkers do not wish to obtain this unfair advantage, and therefore I insist that determinists should be called determinists and not fatalists.

There is still another view to be distinguished from both determinism and fatalism. I refer to predestination, whose advocates maintain that from all eternity God decreed every event that was to occur, but in so doing also decreed the natural means whereby in the time-order that event was to be brought about. Among these means are wills. Thus wills are effective and were predestined because of their effectiveness. Predestination is deterministic, but it is determinism *plus;* as deterministic it is naturalistic, but the surplus is supernaturalism.

> Ere suns and moons could wax and wane,
> Ere stars were thundergirt, or piled
> The heavens, God thought on me his child;
> Ordained a life for me, arrayed
> Its circumstances every one
> To the minutest.

This is Milton's "foreknowledge absolute." The difficulty with this view is not its determinism, but the theodicy it involves. Those who assert Eternal Providence have always felt it incumbent on them to "justify the ways of God to men." I leave the defense to those who have wished to undertake it. Here it is sufficient to say that what is more than determinism in this view is not logically implied in determinism, and therefore does not concern us.

Opposed to all these three theories is that of the indeterminist, who maintains that, whatever may be the case with purely physical events, the will at least is not always determined by preceding natural events. However much it may be "influenced" by what has gone before, it has the power to run counter to all such influences and start on an effective career that is causally disconnected with its past. The will, according to the indeterminist, makes a difference in the world, and in this he agrees with the determinist as I have defined the latter; but he goes on to say that in order to make this difference the will may not be the determined outcome of preceding conditions: In order to be a cause it must not be subject to the reign of causality.

We may sum up the distinction between the four views we have been considering by saying that the indeterminist believes that the will counts but is not to be accounted for; the determinist, that the will counts and is to be accounted for naturally; the predestinationist, that the will counts and is to be accounted for both naturally and supernaturally; and the fatalist, that the will does not count and therefore it makes no difference whether it be accounted for or not.

I shall not refer to predestination again; so far as it goes with determinism, what will be said of the latter may be said of the former. Its theological accretions will not concern us now. Neither will I say anything more of fatalism. Our present interest is in the issue between determinism and indeterminism, and in its bearing upon morality. In other words, our problem is whether "free will" is the monopoly of the indeterminist. But in view of the present vogue of the physical theory of indeterminacy, it is necessary to point out its irrelevance to our problem, which is *not* whether determinism is true, but *whether it is prejudicial to moral interests*. Heisenberg and perhaps most younger physicists maintain that the smallest events in the physical world are matters of chance in the literal sense of the word. The exact movements of an electron can no more be predicted by the physicist than the exact date of a man's death can be foretold by an actuary. The best that can be done by either is to ascertain statistical averages. But since physics is an experimental and mathematical science, what in the nature of the case is not capable of discovery by experiment or by mathematics is by these physicists not considered physical. Now the statistical averages in physics rest upon unimaginably large numbers. How large these numbers are is forcibly brought out by Eddington. "If an army of monkeys were strumming on typewriters," he tells us, "they *might* write all the books in the British Museum. The chance of their doing so is decidedly more favorable" than the chance of a violation of a classical law of physics. "If I put *a* saucepan . . . on *a* fire, will the water boil? ... It may boil; it may freeze; it may do pretty well anything. The details given are insufficient to exclude any result as impossible." Eddington's answer is: "But it will boil because it is too improbable that it will do anything else."[1] Now apply this to the actions of your body, which is a terribly large number of electrons, protons, and (I believe, now) of neutrons; and what your body will do in any of its movements is a statistical average of the random movements of these electric charges and electrically neutral entities. On this theory the probability of your doing anything else than what you do at any time is decidedly less favorable than the probability that the aforesaid monkeys should hammer out at random the contents of all the books in the British Museum. I submit that the difference between determinism and indeterminacy under these circumstances is the difference, not between Tweedledum and Tweedledee, but between Tweedledu ... m and Tweedledu ... m, when these words are spelt out with British quadrillions of u's, for some one of which an e replaces a u in one of the words. I rather suspect that on the theory of indeterminacy, without some further assumption *ad hoc*,[2] the chances against there having been a single violation of any classical law of physics by any single human being in action, ever since some anthropoids began to vary into men, are decidedly more unfavorable than that monkeys should at random type out all the books and papers that have ever appeared on the physical theory of indeterminacy. At any rate the difference between determinism and indeterminacy in the case of any human act is so negligible that for practical purposes it is just nil.

We are now, I hope, in a position to examine the main moral argument against determinism, and we can find no better brief statement of it than that found in Mr. Joad's paper: "The possibility of ethics is clearly dependent on the existence of free will. ... If then morality is to be saved, it is essential that we should be able to praise them [i.e., men] for doing good and

---

[1] *The Nature of the Physical World*, pp. 72, 76.
[2] Such as Eddington makes, pp. 311 ff.

blame them for doing evil; and, in order to do this with good conscience, we must feel assured that they are free to perform the actions which we praise and blame. Otherwise moral judgment is an impertinent irrelevance."[3] As against this thesis my argument is that morality needs to be saved from the kind of thinking on the subject instanced in this quotation from one of its friends.

"Free to perform." But what is freedom? Like all the other eulogistic words in the moral vocabulary, it is a word for which every man of good will claims a place in his outlook upon life. But apart from the glow of it and our pride in it, what does it mean? I maintain that when I say I am free I mean that there is no obstacle to my doing what I will, and especially that I am not coerced *against* my wishes. Coercion apart, I am free, not when there is nothing that causes me to will, but when there is nothing that stands in the way of my doing what I will.[4] For instance, certain physiological conditions cause me from time to time to will to eat. The fact that my will is caused does not prejudice my freedom; I surely do not feel any the less free in willing to eat because my will is the result of a physiological hunger; it is only when, desiring to eat, I have no food, or having food am prevented from eating it, that I am not free to eat. Freedom is not freedom from causes but freedom for causes. This is but to paraphrase one of Nietzsche's glorious epigrams: "Free, dost thou call thyself? Thy ruling thought would I hear of, and not that thou hast escaped from a yoke.... Free from what? What doth that matter to Zarathustra! Clearly, however, shall thine eye show unto me: free *for what?*"[5] In this sense the determinist believes as much as the indeterminist in whatever freedom there is afoot among men. We all, determinists and

---

[3] *Harper's Magazine*, August 1927.
[4] Cf. Hume: "By liberty, then, we can only mean *a power of acting or not acting, according to the determination of the will.*" *An Enquiry Concerning Human Understanding*, Sec. VIII, Part I; p. 95 in Selby-Bigge's edition, Clarendon Press, 1894.
[5] *Thus Spake Zarathustra*, I, 17.

indeterminists alike, have this kind of freedom at times and at other times have it not. Each man has as much as his intelligence and the conditions of his life allow. It is only in this sense that freedom has any relevance to morality.

The indeterminist will reply that I have argued beside the point; that he has never meant to imply that, in this sense of freedom, determinism is inconsistent with freedom; that the kind of freedom with which determinism is inconsistent is the kind of freedom that consists in making choices. In short, the question is whether there is such a thing as choice in human affairs. Now if previous conditions determine a man to choose, the indeterminist claims that he has no choice at all; for choice to be real choice must be free choice. Here it is necessary to be on guard against entering upon a merely verbal dispute. If you arbitrarily define free choice as undetermined choice, then by *that* definition free choice is inconsistent with determinism. But perhaps the correct way to set about defining terms that designate what appears in experience is to take what such terms are applied to and ascertain the characters that distinguish it from what these terms are not used to designate. For example the correct way to define "cow" is to examine the things called cows, and discover the characters by virtue of which they are so called. If on the contrary you arbitrarily define "cow" as "a seven-legged animal that flies," you can, of course, easily prove that on this planet at least there are apparently no "cows," but you have not proved that what are ordinarily called cows do not exist. Now the question is whether in defining "free choice" as undetermined choice, you are not just as arbitrary. Let us use this denotative approach to our definition of "free choice."

Of course, choice is always between competing possibilities. Unless there are at least two possibilities to choose from, there is no choice. But the word "possibility" is ambiguous, and we must clear up the ambiguity. Let us suppose that four of us are playing a game of bridge, and that a perfect pack of cards has been honestly shuffled and dealt. There they lie on the table, thirteen before each one of us players. What are the possibilities? Any one player has before him one of 635,013,559,600 "possibilities," and yet in another sense he has only one "possibility." The many "possibilities" are compatibilities with known conditions and the one "possibility" is compatibility with all the conditions, known and unknown. Each player knows that there are fifty-two cards in the pack, and that any one of these may be one of the thirteen lying before him; and, honestly, that is all that he does know. Logically, i.e., consistently with what is known, his hand is some one of more than six hundred thousand million. The actual conditions of the deal have eliminated all but one of this number; but since many of the determining factors of the deal are unknown, the player has before him very many logical possibilities, and since the determining factors have already operated they have left only one actual possibility. We must remember that there is no logic relevant to *anything* unless *something* is known about that thing, and the logic relevant to it depends upon how much is known; and anything that logic, working with what is known, still leaves undecided about the thing is logically possible. But this does not mean that what is logically possible is *actually* possible.

Now what has been said of the cards is to be said about any past state of affairs with the details of which one is not acquainted. The student who in an examination wrote that Christianity was introduced into Britain by the Jews in 325 B.C. presumably stated what was for him a possibility, which for some unknown reason he chose as the most probable; but of course he did not know much about Christianity, Jews, or dates; he was presumably not a Phi Beta Kappa nor likely to become one. Historians, geologists, astronomers, and detectives are all constantly engaged in the task of reducing the number of logical possibilities with the aim of arriving at the one factual possibility. They hope to do this by ascertaining more of the relevant conditions. If we knew the answer to any problems about the past there would be for us no competing logical possibilities; but when we do not know the answer there are as many logical possibilities as our partial knowledge leaves open.

What is thus true of the present and of the past is true also for at least much of the future. Any scientist in performing for the first time a crucial experiment is facing at least two logical possibilities, and is trying to eliminate one of them; in his endeavors he may even discover a fact not previously conceived as possible. Thus Michelson and Morley, who were both at that time physical determinists, devised an experiment to discover the one actual out of the many conceivably possible shifts of interference rings expected to be caused by the motion of the earth through the ether; and they discovered to their surprise what they had not previously dreamed of as possible, namely that there is no appreciable shift: the future belied *all* the previously computed possibilities.

Now for the determinist there are as many conceivable possibilities as for the indeterminist with the same knowledge. The determinist faces an unknown future just as the indeterminist does, and it is this fact that makes room for choice in his theory. When he chooses from among various possible courses of action, he is choosing from what, relatively to his knowledge, are possible courses. And for both determinist and indeterminist what at the moment of choice is thus possible often turns out to be actually impossible. The actual impossibility does not prove that the choice was not a genuine choice at the time it was made. The brilliant lad who chooses a career and starts promisingly upon it only to fall a victim to an assassin's bullet, none the less *did* choose. The best laid plans of mice and men gang aft agley. If choice, to be choice, has to be choice from actual possibilities, one who knows all the relevant conditions could alone make a chioce; but who among choosers ever does know all the conditions that may affect the course of events upon which he choosingly embarks?

Having thus seen that determinism provides amply for competing possibilities from which choice is made, the question remains whether, if the selection from these possibilities is determined, such selection is the kind of choice that morality requires. To answer this question we must ask another. Why deliberate before choosing? Is it not in order to have before us as clearly as possible the consequences that so far as we can discover would follow from the various courses between which choice is to be made? Now, if the final choice is not to be determined by the results of this deliberation, why waste time in deliberating? Deliberation is a process consisting of two factors working hand in hand. On the one side there is, as just suggested, the attempt to forecast the consequences of the various conceivably possible courses open. This is the intellectual side of deliberation; but there is also the emotional side, the desiderative responses to the expected issues. Foreseen outcomes become advantages to be gained and disadvantages to be shunned when our interests take part in the deliberation. It is these advantages and disadvantages that determine our choice. The value of deliberation is that it opens up larger vistas on whose horizons there appear ends, beckoning or rebuffing. If after deliberation one is not determined by resulting expectations and valuations, deliberation would be a futile process. And sometimes it is: One drifts until some irrelevant circumstance cuts short the suspense and decides the issue. Even weariness over the indecision may determine one to toss a penny and abide by its fall. This is the confession of the vanity of the preceding deliberation, but it is also a hint that no choice is made until some factor, no matter how trivial, tips the beam of the balance; for deliberation is just what its etymology suggests: it is a weighing of values; and if, after weighing, the weights do not count, something is the matter—perhaps the scales are stuck.

This does not mean that I am determined by foreseen consequences without respect to what I am. When I am determined by my interests, I am not determined by some outside power; my interests are mine and are among the most important factors of myself. Had I different interests, I should act differently. Being what I am, I respond as I do to what appeals to me as it does.

But whence come my interests? Are they spontaneous in the sense in which the indeterminist uses the word? The determinist assumes that they are not. He does not claim to be able to lay his finger in every case upon all the determining factors, but he can point to many powerful ones. For instance, there is hereditary bent. Had we been born tigers or catfish our interests would be those of tigers or catfish; but being born of human parents our interests play within human bounds of ordinance, and geneticists are seeking to unravel the skeins that go to make up the warp and woof of the original equipment with which we start upon the adventure of life. Men do not gather grapes of thorns or figs of thistles. But native bent is modified by environment. Interests are contagious. I am likely to get interested in what my associates find interesting. Whether for good or for ill there is an unmistakable tendency in most persons to "get on the band wagon," and this not necessarily for the plums that follow, but because the band wagon is an expression of a widely shared interest in which it is natural to participate. An impartial spectator of a football game is not unlikely to find himself warming up to the side whose partisans surround him. It is only the rabidly intellectualistic college professor who does not feel the thrill of a lively interest when he witnesses a contest over which his temporary neighbors are so wildly excited.

This fact, that interests are determined by associates, is used by all wise parents, instructors, and leaders of men. What father does not try to have his son belong to a gang whose interests are what he wishes the boy to have? What religious teacher does not know the importance of early association in determining the religious interests of the young? The Roman Catholic Church, that wisest and shrewdest of all institutions in its dealings with men, is expressing the result of the experience of centuries when it insists on determining the environment of its children in order to determine once for all their subsequent interests. But it is not only children whose interests can be determined. Salesmanship is a cunning employment of means known to be effective in arousing interests that previously have not been operative, and salesmen know that nothing arouses interests more effectively than the dissemination of the information, true or false, that thousands are rushing to get what nobody before ever thought of wanting. What is called "gregariousness" is not merely the desire to belong to a herd, but the fact that in herds desires and interests are infectious.

Thus the determinist in dealing with human actions sees a chain of causes and effects: interests are due to native bent and social environment, choice is determined by interests in anticipated consequences, efforts are determined by choices, and achievement is determined by effort. (Of course when anything is spoken of as a cause, it must not be supposed that it alone will bring about what is said to be its effect; there are always other factors contributing to the result.)

It now remains to ask whether determinism as we have defined it is consistent with responsibility. Can anyone who believes that whatever a man does is determined by preceding conditions, partly external to the agent, partly in the very character of the agent, reasonably hold such a man responsible for what he has done? Here again as in our previous discussion it is important to define the meaning of our terms. What do we mean by holding any man responsible? If a part of our meaning is holding a belief that, under the precise circumstances under which the man acted, he could actually have done otherwise, then by our very definition we have said that a determinist cannot consistently hold anyone responsible. But is this the only meaning of responsibility? Let us again apply the method of defining by examining instances of what we are trying to define. What actually do we do when we hold persons responsible? We praise and blame, reward and punish, threaten and promise. So far Mr. Joad is correct in calling praise and blame "the twin pillars upon which the structure of morality is built."

Now the question is, whether it is reasonable to praise or

blame a man when at the same time we believe that the act we praise or blame was determined; i.e., that under the exact conditions under which the act was performed no other act was naturally possible. This raises another question. When is it reasonable to do anything? So far as I can see, the only good reason we can give for any act is that it forwards some interest, and the only good reason we can give for not doing an act is that it is either antagonistic or irrelevant to some interest. It is reasonable to build dams if building them advances the interests concerned; it is unreasonable to build them if building prejudices those interests. The life of reason is not a life of *abstract* reason, pure and undefiled and unspotted from the world. Without interests no action is either reasonable or unreasonable. In action reason is not something that lifts itself up by its bootstraps; it rests upon given interests that are present, or on the likelihood of future interests that may meanwhile bestir themselves. Any single interest, considered entirely apart from other interests, is neither reasonable nor unreasonable. It simply *is*. An act can be justified as leading to the satisfaction of an interest, but the interest itself is either there or not there as a fact. Were there no interests to be met, reason, if it spoke at all, would not speak in the imperative mood. In short, were there no life with interests there would be no life of reason. Interests are not interests because they are reasonable, but any interest is reasonable only because there are other interests with which it is compatible. At times Kant thought of interests as subject to the despotic mastery of reason. Reason was then for him a Hohenzollern king and interests had to obey the categorical imperative of the All-Highest. At such times for Kant desires were pathological, and reason alone was sane. This is the modern version of the ancient doctrine that the natural man is conceived in sin and born in iniquity, thus inheriting a carnal mind at enmity with God.

A contemporary of Kant took another view: *Am Anfang war die That*. This other view, which was also Kantian (for Kant was not so narrow as to be consistent and to stick to any one view), is that reason is a republican organization of interests. The practical demands that reason makes on any interest are the demands that other interests make in the republic in which every interest has a voice in determining the policy of the commonwealth. Now, among the ways in which the interests of human beings express themselves in this commonwealth is the way of praising and blaming, of rewarding and punishing. We dislike and then speak out our dislike in blame, or act it out more drastically in punishment. We like and speak out our liking in praise, or more emphatically in favors bestowed. Why should we not? The only reason why we should not is to be found, if found at all, in the injury to other interests that may follow from this instinctive behavior. Other interests interpose their veto when such behavior affects them adversely. The whole history of the practice of responsibility is the history of these effective vetoes. The old maxim, "An eye for an eye, a tooth for a tooth, and a life for a life," was not the demand of reason in its own name; it was a demand, *in the name of other interests,* that instinctive vindictiveness should put bounds to its expression and confine itself to rendering no more than like for like; that instead of exacting the payment of a life for a tooth, the price of a tooth should be just another tooth. The *lex talionis* was not a justification of retaliation; it was the repression of something more severe. It is impossible here to follow the steps by which the expression of instinctive vindictiveness has been further restricted. But there are two steps which we may not here pass over entirely. As everyone knows, in primitive communities responsibility was a tribal and not an individual affair, and at least in many communities no distinction was made between intentional and unintentional injury. What brought about a change from these rude beginnings? As historians have shown, probably various motives were at work. But it is not, perhaps, an overstatement to say that each of these motives represented some interest that was defeated by the prevailing practice. Christianity (and here I mean historical Christianity and not the teachings of Jesus), following the lead of previous decadent thought, gave prevalence to the idea that vindictiveness is not an interest to be tolerated in human beings. Not indeed that it is not a moral interest, for God himself, whose perfection was the standard for human morality, was not without vindictiveness, visiting the iniquities of the fathers upon the children to the third and fourth generation. "Vengeance is mine, I will repay, saith the Lord." The Kingdom of Heaven had a king whose royal prerogative it was to mete out vengeance, just as earthly rulers had begun to claim similar prerogative within their own domain. It was a heavenly instance of the encroachment of the crown upon the previous rights of subjects. It is interesting to note that many modern thinkers, like Mr. Darrow, who in their condemnation of vindictiveness as a proper human motive are loudest in boasting of their worldliness, fail to recognize that in this respect they have inherited an other-worldly tradition. Now that all the other instincts are recognized as having their proper place in a well-ordered life, there is no more reason why vindictiveness should be absolutely taboo than there is to frown upon sex when sex is kept within the limits laid down by regard to other interests. One does not need to justify a hostile indignant reaction to harm done, any more than one has to justify any other natural reaction, unless the justification be in showing that it is exercised in a measure that does not jeopardize other important interests. Interest for interest, vindictiveness is just as natural as any other impulse, and it is only in some such atmosphere as the mid-Victorian age in which Dr. Martineau lived that one can find explanation for the ruling-out of vengeance as a motive unworthy of a moral man. Perhaps this saying will offend less if instead of vindictiveness I euphemistically speak of "righteous indignation." And what has been said of vindictiveness in act can be said of vindictiveness in speech, or blame.

But more can be said in behalf of vindictiveness in act or in speech than has above been said. Not only is it natural to be vindictive, but it is helpful to other interests, provided it be restricted within its proper place in the community of human interests. Within such bounds blame and punishment have a deterrent effect. Men naturally like to be praised and rewarded, they dislike to be blamed and punished. And here we ascend from the purely instinctive level to a higher level. Praise and blame, reward and punishment, threat and promise—in short, holding a person responsible—has efficacy as means to ends, because it has a determining effect upon human wills. The reasonableness of holding men responsible is to be found, not in the undeterminedness of their wills, but in the fact that experience has shown that *their wills can be determined by holding them responsible.* It is in this fact that blame and punishment as moral measures differ from vindictiveness as instinctive.

Mr. Joad wants a reason to salve his conscience when he blames people. What better reason could he have than that when blame is wisely administered it is a powerful agent in upholding morality? It has ceased to be the wayward reaction to present stimulus and has become an instrument for securing the moral order; and it can be this only if wills can be determined by its use. The reasonable man blames his neighbor, not because the latter could have done differently under the circumstances under which he did act, but in order that he as well as others may do differently in the future. When we regard reasonable blame or reasonable punishment as deterrent, and where possible as reformatory, we do not have to look backward to see whether the person involved could have done differently, but we look forward to see whether we can help him by blame or by punishment to do differently in the future. Blame and punishment become tools in the hands of men who are seeking to upbuild a nobler social order. It was not just for rhetoric that I hinted a little while ago that moral responsibility is no more incompatible with the belief in determinism than the building of power-dams is incompatible with the belief that dams impound water. In building a dam the hydraulic engineer looks forward and uses means that experience has shown to be effective for accomplishing his end. Likewise in blaming and punishing, a reasonable man looks forward, using the means he believes to promise efficacy toward securing what he desires. But this of course carries with it the reasonableness of fitting means to end. Where experience has shown that blame or punishment is not likely to accomplish its purpose, it is the part of wisdom to look for other means.

We are now in a position to see why the definition of freedom given earlier in this chapter is relevant to the question of responsibility. If there is some obstacle to the performance of an act demanded, other than the unwillingness of the agent to perform the act, we shall not secure the performance by bringing about the willingness. We shall have to use the appropriate means to remove the obstacle. The kind of freedom that reasonable responsibility presupposes is the lack of external impediments to the carrying out of the willed act demanded, not the exemption of the will from determination. If, and in so far as, a will is not capable of being determined by blame and punishment, blame and punishment are futile and can be looked upon only as impulsive, not as reasonable.

Perhaps the main thesis of this chapter can best be expressed in the proposition that *responsibility presupposes responsiveness to being held responsible*. A door may instinctively be damned but it may not reasonably be blamed for being bumped into in the dark; for blame, blaming never so wisely, will not make it behave differently in the future. Similarly a madman is not to be held responsible in so far as he is not responsive to being held responsible. In such cases we may prevent by physical means, but we cannot influence by such moral means as blame and punishment. It is only where we are dealing with what can be determined by our blamings and our punishings that these moral measures are reasonable.

What we need at the present day is not belief in the undetermined will; we need clearer thinking on the dynamics of morality and more dynamics in our morality. Too much mawkish sentimentality, too much pity for the poor devil who in view of his upbringing could not help murdering and raping, and too little intelligence in the use of means for preventing crimes, are the crying evils of our day. In saying this I do not mean that attention should not be directed toward the improvement of general social conditions. They are of course in many ways bad, and all of us who can in any way help to correct them should be blamed for not doing it; this may spur us to attempt the correction. These things we should do, but not leave the other things undone. When the blame for crime is laid on society alone, and not on the criminal also, we are acting like the man who tried to cut with only one blade of a pair of shears; and of course we make matters worse when, instead of blaming a criminal, we give him flattering indulgence for following the lead of his criminal nature.

Not the least of the reasons for this state of affairs is the promulgation by indeterminists and determinists alike of the doctrine that if an act is determined the agent may not reasonably be held responsible. Those who reason this way do their bit toward undermining morality.

CHAPTER VIII

THE WARFARE OF MORAL IDEALS[1]

Is there some indubitable and invariable standard which determines at all times and in all places what is right and what is wrong? Is morality something eternal and immutable, and can we assume that every intelligent man needs only to have the right pointed out to him to secure his acquiescence in it as right, in much the same way as intelligent children need only to have their attention called to simpler number relations embodied in concrete instances to make doubt of the truth of the multiplication table impossible? The history of ethics has been largely that of attempts to set forth some incontrovertible principle or principles which must be used to decide in the individual case what is moral and what is immoral. The number of these alleged principles has been great, and it would be impossible to give offhand a complete enumeration of them. Ranging all the way from Paley's notorious dictum that virtue is "the doing good to mankind, in obedience to the will of God, and for the sake of everlasting happiness"—how this must have thrilled some of his readers as the definitive definition!—to Kant's "Act only on that maxim whereby thou canst at the same time will that it should become a universal law," we find almost every conceivable way tried of justifying moral judgments and moral conduct. Whatever differences there may have been in what was found, there was seldom any doubt or disagreement in what was sought: the quest was for demonstrable certainty. One writer has exactly expressed the prevailing spirit of ethical inquiry

[1] This was a paper read before the Madison (Wis.) Literary Club, June 9, 1913, and is now reprinted without change from the *Hibbert Journal*, Vol. XIV, 1915–1916. For comments on it see the postscript to this chapter.

when he says: "What the moralist wants is such a distinction between right and wrong as does not depend on any mere accident of reality, even upon the accidental existence of a moral sense. He wants to find the eternal ethical truth. We must insist then that one of the first questions of the moralist must be, *why conscience in any given case is right*. Or, to put the case otherwise, ethical doctrine must tell us why, if the devil's conscience approves of the devil's acts, as well it may do, the devil's conscience is nevertheless in the wrong." The devil, forsooth, must be made to believe—and tremble!

It would seem that where so many principles are put forward, each alleged to be beyond peradventure but each conflicting with the others, the natural conclusion should be that there are no infallible principles and that morality is relative. This conclusion would doubtless have been more frequently drawn had not Fear stood in the way—fear that the relativity of morality would prove the death of morality, or at least its hopeless debilitation. "If there is nothing good or bad but thinking makes it so—why! thinking as we jolly-well please, let us eat, drink, and be merry, and gaily let morality go hang." This is the invariable retort made to the suggestion that morality is not immutable and eternal.

There is still another motive, allied to Fear, that has blocked the path to the acceptance of the relativity of morality. A spokesman of ethical orthodoxy—the same spokesman already quoted —has expressed it: "A minor power for good is not enough. It will not suffice that one bit of reality fights for our moral needs while another bit of reality fights against them, unless we can in some way harmonize these conflicting aspects, or unless we can show that they that be with us are not only more important or more significant than they that be against us, but are really the deepest truth of things. Else we shall be left face to face with a gloomy world of conflict, where good and bad are mingled in hopeless confusion." This writer, like many another man, wants, before committing himself to a battle for his ideals, to know that the universe is with him. He would prefer not to play an uncertain game. He calls for loaded dice, for stacked cards. Unless he holds the trumps he does not relish the idea of letting the game go on. "Let us throw the cards on the table and have a new deal."

William James, the gallant adventurer in all new enterprises of the spirit, felt and recognized the occasional force of this appeal. There are times when in our conflict for our ideals we grow weary. Flesh and blood cannot stand the strain of unintermittent struggle; sometime we must lay our weapons aside and take a rest. At such times it is a comfort to know that our temporary withdrawal does not give the enemy an advantage. It is necessary, if we are to rest in peace, that we should be assured that the fight is going on and that our cause is being pushed to victory. An absolute ideal which condemns the wrong even when our vocal cords are too weak to echo its judgment, stands guard over the cause in which we are enlisted; a power not ourselves that makes for righteousness gives us the privilege of a "moral holiday." The Absolute is the warrior's lullaby, the hum of assurance in the ears of the exhausted man that He that keepeth Israel shall neither slumber nor sleep.

The problem of this chapter is not to disprove the absoluteness of morality. It is a very wise man—or a fool—who *knows* that there is no Absolute. Most of us can do no more than wonder with varying degrees of credulity or incredulity, of interest or indifference. We are not certain. But we must act. Is the only way open to the man of action the way of "The Will to Believe"? Must we cry, "Lord, I believe, help thou my unbelief"? I shall try to show that, however it may be with the Absolute and his standards, we mortals, having no natural access thereunto, can make right and wrong out of such materials as are at our disposal and can very well make shift with the result. But before we take up this problem, let us examine the motives that, as we have seen, have stood in the way of the acceptance of the relativity of morality, and see whether they are definitive.

The fear that morality would be compromised by a recognition of its relativity is groundless—unless morality be something disconnected with our interests. It is usually assumed in such reasonings as are urged against ethical relativism that no one can be enthusiastically interested in a cause unless he be convinced that it is a cause that appeals to all men—at least to all reasonable men. This assumption is directly opposed to all experience. Fighting for a cause against those who fail to recognize its value often gives added value to it—witness the present conflict! Championship in the face of opposition may enhance the charm of that for which we battle. The knowledge that our efforts are needed to make the cause prevail may add to our loyalty. If we really have ideals, the fact that these ideals are not shared by all and the fact that they are attacked and endangered may make us rally with greater zest to their defence. Opposition whets the edge of fealty in most human affairs. Why should morality be the sole exception? Of course, it is a fact that devotion may breed the illusion that the object of devotion is intrinsically precious; but it is perverse to explain the devotion by the illusion rather than the illusion by the devotion. What we want with our whole heart assumes for us by a sympathetic fallacy a cosmic importance; what we long for is likewise the World's Desire. But it is not because the red rose cries and the white rose weeps, the larkspur listens and the lily whispers, that Maud is the lover's dove and dear and life and fate. So when one asks, as our aforequoted orthodoxologist asks: "To the unsympathetic man, how shall you demonstrate the ideals you found upon the feeling of sympathy?" he should be answered Yankeewise by the question: "How to the unenamored man shall you demonstrate the charm and beauty that you found upon your feeling of love?" Suppose that, foolishly, you wished to arouse the same passion in another man's breast that you feel in your own, what would you do? You would tell off the qualities that fascinate you; if they left him unresponsive, little would it boot to search for some intellectually self-evident premise upon which you could rear a syllogism whose conclusion should be amorous rapture.

An ideal is not a cold idea; it is heated in the flame of passion, else it were no *ideal*. It is what we yearn for, not what we passively contemplate. A moral ideal is a glowing vision of conduct and of social life, such as we burn to see realized. It is our ardor for it that converts it from what it would otherwise be, an idle reverie, into a dynamic force. There is no more danger for my moral ideal—provided it be my *ideal*—in the recognition that it is *my* ideal, than there is jeopardy for my love in the knowledge that if I had Mr. Robinson's nervous system I should love Mr. Robinson's wife instead of loving my own. It so happens that my nervous system is my own and not Mr. Robinson's, and therefore the relativity of my love is not relativity to nothing in particular, but a relativity that ties it down hard and fast to given fact. People argue about relativity as if relativity were something up in the air; as if to be in relation were not precisely to be in some definite relation to some definite thing. The fact that the New York Subways would be valueless in Manunkachunk or Sun Prairie does not make them the less valuable in New York. So the fact that our moral ideals would not fit the primitive conditions in Australia does not make them any the less compelling or the less enticing to us, being what we are and where we are.

As to the uncertainty of the realization of our ideals, a hint has already been given as to what seems the proper attitude to take toward this objection. It is cowardly not to make an effort to get what we want, if the failure is due merely to the fact that we are not sure of success. When human nature shall have lost its venturesomeness, when only certainties attract and all uncertainties leave us unnerved, then indeed it will be time to fear a view that makes the realization of our moral ideals problematic. Meanwhile, there is zest in the very fact that something precious is at stake and may be lost or won. The objects most eagerly worked for, the games most strenuously contested, the wars most bitterly fought, are those in the balance. All we need is *not* to know that the end is unattainable, and to believe that there is a chance for success. Fighting for an ideal is subject to all the hazards of war: we may win or we may lose; but if the thing is worth fighting for, it surely does not lose its value just because we are not sure of getting it. Let us take the spirit of adventure into our moral life. In our quest for the moral ideal it may be that the gulfs will wash us down; it *may be* we shall touch the Happy Isles; but the uncertainty should not mar the temper of heroic hearts.

But here again Nature is generous to us. She does not ask us to venture for those causes alone that are sure to prevail; but she often does grant us the comfort of believing, when we have hoisted sail and reached the deep, that our quest will reach the goal. The certainty comes from our committing ourselves; we are not called upon to commit ourselves because we are certain. It is not logic and reason that bring conviction here; it is action and enthusiasm. This assurance will have no scientifically evidentiary value; it is merely Nature's earnest to the earnest. If the pledge is to be redeemed it is we who must exact the redemption.

Having thus put our moral ideals on a par with our other preferences so far as their source[2] and their outcome are concerned, having made them spring from our likes and dislikes and depend for their achievement upon our efforts, we have now to consider the problem of the conflict among moral ideals and the methods by which this conflict is resolved. The title of this chapter indicates the answer we shall give to this problem. The adjudication of differences here is not made by appeal to some *a priori* canon; it is the result of an actual fight eventuating in victory of one ideal over another. Where the appearances point to a contrary conclusion the standard by which the difference is settled is itself one that has come to be accepted after being in dispute. This can be seen in concrete instances. In civilized countries there is now general acceptance of the principle that with certain limitations private revenge is immoral. Lynch law

---

[2] There is another source for moral ideals. Some of our ideals are not autonomous, and perhaps for most men most ideals are not so. But into this matter we cannot enter here.

and the vendetta are regarded with well-nigh universal detestation, except when mob passions are burning hot, or where isolated communities have succeeded in maintaining as survivals what have long ago become obsolete in the wider field of common practice. An historical study of the gradual elimination of the blood feud gives something more than color to the view propounded by Thrasymachus in Plato's *Republic* that justice is the interest of the stronger. In ancient Palestine and in modern England, to mention only two cases, we can trace the process by which governmental punishment of crime was substituted for the older practice of clan revenge. When the British government first took the control of criminal law into its own hands public sentiment was against the usurpation. The clan system had been in vogue for countless generations, and what thus had the sanction of immemorial usage was naturally regarded as just and moral. The encroachments of the Crown were resented as unwarranted interference, and a struggle was precipitated as soon as the centralized power undertook to administer what had always been in the hands of the smaller social units. It was the strength of the Crown as compared with the growing weakness of the clan that gave victory to the principle of State control. The will of the stronger formed the basis of the new justice. In the course of time the sentiments of the community became adjusted to the new order of things; ideas of what was right were moulded upon the practice which had come to prevail; and what a short time before was fought as an intolerable infringement is now regarded by most people as a self-evidencing right.

In this struggle, of course, economic conditions played a most prominent part; but it must be remembered that the part they played was the part of a might—they lent their weight to turn the scales in favor of the Crown. It was victory of the Crown, by whatever means gained and with whatever allies, that resulted in the newer conception of justice in criminal law. The matter was not decided by appeal to the abstract principle that contending parties are by their very interests not fit to pass upon the points in dispute, and that only an impartial tribunal can render the true decision. The tribunal, not always impartial, was first established and maintained by force, and the abstract principle was literally an abstraction from accomplished fact.

Any number of instances could be recited to point the same moral. In the American Civil War one of the issues was slavery. The two parties to the conflict had sprung from the same racial stock; they had much the same traditions behind them; they shared a common heritage of European and Christian ideals. But they differed in certain political and economic practices, and the prevalence of these practices gave rise to divergent ideals in the matter then at issue. From the same Bible the North and South drew different conclusions. The reason was that there was always a suppressed uncanonical premise—inspired indeed, but with an inspiration not of God but of gold. The conflict was at bottom, then, a conflict between different desires springing from different conditions of life. It is often said that this conflict settled the question of slavery for all time. At any rate it settled the question of one kind of slavery for our time and in our country. But this settlement, be it noted, was by force of arms. Slavery was proved to be wrong because its advocates did not prove to be strong. Might made right.

The doctrine that might is right is often regarded as a thoroughly immoral doctrine, a pernicious perversity of view, a damnable heresy. And so it is if taken in a narrow sense. The triumph of a cause by force of arms does not decide the issue of rightness immediately. It did not with the generation of slave-holders in the South. The defeated party, though cast down, did not straightway bow to the justice of the decision. But time completed the work which military victory began. The ideals of the victors gradually became the ideals of the defeated, and before two generations have passed many of the very descendants of those who were loudest in asserting the right of the eventually doomed cause look back upon the conflict as one for a mistaken principle. It is so regarded because the defeat established a new order of things, and to this established order the sentiments have gradually adjusted themselves. The sons of those who fought the Union in the early sixties were found fighting most loyally for the Union before the close of the century. The slavery which had been regarded as an institution ordained of God came to be looked upon with critical eye as condemned of God; and many of the children of those who gave their blood to defend it now look upon that blood as nobly offered in a wrong service.

The adjustments of sentiments and emotions to what has become the established order is one of the most powerful factors in moral history. Mohammedanism fought its way into Africa by the sword. In a few generations it flourished there by the devoted acceptance of those who sprang from its deadliest enemies. Tradition as well as trade follows the flag. This is what gives extreme significance to the world's greatest battles. Had the Persians won at Marathon or the Turks at Lepanto and Vienna, and had they followed up their victory, the moral history of Europe, with its accompanying *ideals*, would have been incalculably different. Might long enough continued wins recognition as right until overthrown by a greater might meanwhile gathering strength. If we, looking back upon the course of history, decline to acknowledge that in any particular case might was right, it is because another might *has* meanwhile arisen and brought our sentiments into accord with its sway; and from the point of view of the new ideals that have thus triumphed we condemn what was once victorious. Naturally we use our own ideals in our judgments; but we are likely to forget that these ideals are in great measure the outcome of just the kind of victory which in the case we condemn we deplore as the triumph of might over right. Such a judgment is nothing but the shadow of a new might cast back over what formerly stood bathed in the light of another ideal.

Between the older and the newer right who is to decide? The

decision *now* is *ours,* and of course we make it in the only way we can, with our standards to control it. But we should not mistake our decision for the utterance of eternal and immutable truth. Having our ideals, however we came by them, we properly use them for what they are, as sources of standards not only for our conduct but also for our judgments. What diverges from our standards is wrong—when measured by these standards; and it is false modesty not to insist on our standards because forsooth there are other standards which have the same footing in the world as ours. Different moral standards, being what they are, namely, dynamic principles, are of course in conflict. It is as unreasonable to demand in the name of theoretical unity or of tolerance that one of them shall fail to energize, as it would be absurd to ask that gravitation should decline to pull upon a marble block which is rising to its place in the dome of a Capitol. If the issue between moral ideals is to be decided *by the issue* why should one ideal politely, nay ignominiously, withdraw from the scene of conflict? And who is to fight for *my* ideals but myself and those who share them with me? The very recognition that might makes right should hearten us to fight with might and main for our ideals and thus make them right. If we fail to champion what we love, our cause is doomed, and some other ideal will prevail. Hegel's dictum, *Die Weltgeschichte ist das Weltgericht,* is no cold-blooded statement of fatalistic fact; it is to any man with backbone and red blood a challenge to make history, that little history that lies within his reach, so as to have the world verdict handed down in his favor.

If after having fought our good fight we lose, we shall be tempted to complain:

> I found Him in the shining of the stars,
> I mark'd Him in the flowering of His fields,
> But in His ways with men I find Him not.
> I waged His wars, and now I pass and die.

Happy shall we be if before the end we have the grace to see:

> The old order changeth, yielding place to new;
> And God fulfils Himself in many ways,
> Lest one good custom should corrupt the world.
> . . . .
> For so the whole round earth is every way
> Bound by gold chains about the feet of God.[3]

Every way—the way of might as well as the way of gentleness—the way of defeat as well as the way of victory.

This leads me to correct the one-sidedness of my previous statements. Heretofore I have argued as if the only might that counts is the might of the sword and of the forty-two centimetre gun; as if God were only on the side of the heavy battalions. But the weapons of the moral warfare are not all carnal, carnal though many of them assuredly are. In the moral armory we find along with material instruments tools of another temper. Every virile moral judgment is itself such a weapon. When we condemn an alien ideal, or an act which embodies such an ideal, we are not merely stating an objective variance between two ideals or between an ideal and an act. We are using powerful insidious means of gaining victory for our own ideal. It is true that praise and blame are not first uttered with self-conscious intention to defeat an opposing ideal; but neither are tooth and claw first used with self-conscious intention to rout the foe. We first react instinctively to the situation that confronts us, and only later and by slow degrees do we come to see clearly the relation of means and end. We first eat not to sustain life but because we are hungry. It is only the sophisticated man who eats to live. Our first loves are not directed to the propagation of an ever-improving race. It is only the eugenist who has achieved as a vision what the sex instinct has blindly and passionately groped after in the form of act. And so our scoldings and beratings and chidings and lambastings are at the outset unenlightened expressions of instinctive anger and hate, nature's offensive weapons. It is the deterministic moralist who comes to see that moral disapprobation

---
[3] Tennyson, "The Passing of Arthur," "Morte d'Arthur."

and censure and reprimand are means to be used for the protection of one's ideal and the annihilation of his rivals. Moral indignation is chastened anger, moral blame is chastened scolding, and moral vengeance is chastened vindictiveness; just as moral love is chastened sexuality subdued to the useful and the good and ennobled by the vision of larger and more comprehensive ends.

Regarded thus, not as *ex post facto* pronouncements presupposing the indetermination of the culprits' acts but as directed to the determination of their future conduct and that of others, blame is seen to be a weapon used in the warfare of moral ideals. I attack opposing ideals by condemning them. I seek by expressing my disgust to produce similar disgust in others. I show myself nauseated so that by the contagion of nausea others shall spue out the abomination. The moral ideals that have conquered in the course of history have had at their service a full equipment of such implements. Read the Hebrew prophets and note how effectively they wielded the lashing tongue. Jeremiah succinctly summarized the mission of his order in these words: "Howbeit I sent unto you all my servants the prophets, rising early and sending them, saying, Oh, do not this abominable thing that I hate." Saul of Tarsus, protagonist of a moral ideal which has been one of the most potent forces of history, well understood the power of this weapon. How did he treat the now unnamable practices which many of the best Greeks and Romans looked upon not only as innocent but as highly praiseworthy? His method was disgust; he aroused esthetic repugnance. Mark his vocabulary: "Uncleanness," "vile affections," "a reprobate mind," "professing themselves to be wise they became fools, and changed the glory of the incorruptible God into an image made like to corruptible man, and to birds, and four-footed beasts, and creeping things." The author of the Revelation of St. John the Divine adopted the same means against the same enemy: "So hast thou also them that hold the doctrine of the Nicolaitanes, which thing I hate." It is he from whom I just borrowed the metaphor which is rather an almost literal description of moral condemnation: "So then because thou art lukewarm, and neither cold nor hot, I will spue thee out of my mouth." It was not by reasoning—for the wisdom of this world was to these men foolishness—it was by denunciation and by the *argumentum ad nauseam*—a sanctified Billingsgate—reinforced by "the expulsive power of a new affection," that Christianity waged its relentless war against conduct that it abhorred and the world idealized. The terminology of morality is and always has been and always must be unlike the impartial terminology of objective science. The word, thief, for instance, does not simply connote the taking of another man's property without his knowledge and consent. It stirs up all the age-long passions that center about the institution of property and hallow it. The moral judgment injects poison into the winged words it lets fly. It does not describe—it damns.

Another blade used in moral warfare is punishment, forged of an alloy of condemnation and force. Antagonistic emotion there must be if punishment is a moral reaction. Punishment administered without emotion is a purely mechanical process, similar to the digging of weeds out of a garden, the use of disinfectants, or the employment of a stomach-pump. What distinguishes or should distinguish punishment, or the damaging treatment of the morally responsible offender, from the treatment of the irresponsible, is just this element of passion directed against one who is believed to be practically *responsive* to the emotions of his fellows. We do not—or should not—punish the kleptomaniac. Why? Because the passion of taking another's goods is so strong in him that it cannot be overcome by considerations of what may be done to him or felt against him in consequence of his act. If he is not responsive to our indignant reaction, such indignation should be withheld in just the same way in which, when we have arrived at years of self-inhibition, we decline to rage against a stone that has caused us to stumble or a door into which we have run in the dark. Such rage, we have learned, does no good, and we have learned to call it foolish. In the case of the normally responsive man, on the other hand, society's displeasure is a mighty preventive, and that society is mawkishly sentimental which declines to make use of this effective weapon. The judge and the jury, in trying the case, are agents of society in seeking to discover impartially what has been done. In pronouncing a sentence, however, the judge is no longer the representative of the inquisitive instincts of society—he is not only the representative of society in determining what shall be done to the convict on the basis of the findings of fact: he is also the mouthpiece of society in expressing abhorrence of the crime committed and of the criminal.

I shall probably be accused of pressing analogies too far when I now pass to the consideration of another instrumentality used in moral warfare. But all war is struggle for ideals, and when this is recognized, what may otherwise be regarded as superficial resemblance will come to be seen as fundamental affinities between species of the same genus. Moral praise, and rewards of a more material kind than praise, are comparable to honorable mention, to the Victoria or the Iron Cross, or to a dukedom with estates conferred upon some successful commander. In war it is not only necessary to disable the enemy, but also to keep up the spirits of one's own forces; and the prospect of glory is recognizedly one of the most effective incentives to deeds of heroism. No less effective in moral warfare than in national conflicts is the desire for glory. Every conquering moral ideal has made use of this motive. "He that is slow to anger is better than the mighty, and he that ruleth his spirit than he that taketh a city." "Ye which have followed me, in the regeneration when the Son of man shall sit in the throne of his glory, ye also shall sit upon twelve thrones, judging the twelve tribes of Israel." In moral education we are constantly using praise and reward, if not directly given to the one whom we wish to encourage, then indirectly by lauding those whom we hold up as examples, thus suggesting that those who follow in the footsteps of these worthies may expect the same meed of honor. But the strait-laced theorist strangely enough insists that love of praise is not a moral motive.

Any motive is a moral motive that supports a moral ideal, and the soldier of the moral ideal who refuses to use all the weapons that make for victory is as stupid as a general who should decline to appeal to his men in the name of glory, insisting that devotion to the cause is the only motive to be tolerated.

The recognition that the confrontation of diverse moral ideals is warfare enables us to understand what at first sight is so puzzling a paradox in moral struggles, namely, the improper employment of physical force by men of otherwise high principles. In this very description of what we find puzzling we are using terms that show our alignment in the struggle; we are not giving expression to impartial judgments. Moral conflicts are actual warfare, and no wonder if those who find the organized might of society arrayed against them resort to extreme methods. The Nihilist of Russia, the Fenian of Ireland, the Kuklux of the South, the militant suffragette, the structural iron worker, the Industrial Worker of the World, and the Syndicalist, all these on occasion use methods we strongly disapprove. The means they adopt, judged by the law of the land or by the ideals of those opposed to them, are viciously immoral. But all these men and women are engaged in a fight, and when met by force they naturally use force in return, and use it not too nicely. I am not justifying the wisdom of their procedure, nor am I expressing my acquiescence in their methods. Our question is now not one of expediency but of understanding. There are causes that cannot be submitted to arbitration, and what these causes are it is only for their adherents to decide. When a cause has become so precious that its value is felt to be greater than that of the continuance for the time being of the ordinary forms of peaceful intercourse, or of international law, then war is the only arbiter. And such causes may divide not only nation from nation, but also classes from classes within the same nation. Civil war, in the latter case, is the result, often a guerilla war rather than open battle.

How then shall I judge them? There are two answers, both

of which must be given if we are to do justice to all the facts. One answer is that these disturbers of the peace, these rebels against the present organization of society, are justified by their ideals in fighting for their ideals. There is no one ideal that can be used unimpassionedly for the measuring of all others. The ideal expressed in some form of civilized government is only *one* ideal, and when it is used to condemn those who fight against the government there is a most lamentable *petitio principii*. The ideal of settling disputes by appeal to the ballot or to the court —or to international usage—is just one ideal, and is not the decisive ideal *when it is itself in dispute*. But this is not the sole answer. What is a begging of the question when construed in terms of logic becomes *in practice* a demand that the question be settled in accordance with *our* ideals when the question comes up to *us* for a hearing. While, therefore, we may theoretically admit the right of anyone to fight for his ideals in any way his ideals allow, we as partisans practically must deny this right when his manner of fighting clashes with our ideals. In other words, we do not solve the moral problems here presented in an impartial manner: we come to them with a prejudice, a prejudice to which we are just as much entitled as those whom we condemn are entitled to theirs. In our judgments upon violence in labor and suffrage conflicts, or upon "frightfulness" in military operations, we take sides. The fiction that we are impartial is itself one of the means we employ to give victory to our ideal. Having elected our ideal, we seek to hypnotize others against the seductiveness or even the possibility of other ideals by claiming for our ideals the sole right. Herein we are wise—but the wisdom is the wisdom of action. When, however, we seek to see with open eye and to understand with open mind, we should recognize that our noblest impartialities are partialities eulogized. Their nobility is derived by patent from our fundamental preferences; similarly the partialities of others to whom we are opposed hold patents of equal temporary validity. Such patents are merely licenses to "make good" against all rivals.

Our view, thus presented, leaves us engaged in a "world of conflict where good and bad *are* mingled in confusion." But the world of conflict is not gloomy to one who has an interest in the struggle, and the confusion is not hopeless. We have indicated some of the agencies which are always at work to secure victory for some ideal, and victory has actually been achieved time and again by successive ideals. If the devil's conscience approves of the devil's acts, as well it may, the question for us is whether we shall let the devil's conscience become *our* standard. And as for the devil himself, first we must defeat him, and then, if he has the adaptability he is rightly credited with, his case may not be desperate. Moral warfare is always a struggle between God and devil; but which is God and which the devil can be answered only by the touchstone of our own ideals. Your God may be my devil; the Kaiser's God is Sir Edward's devil, and Sir Edward's is the Kaiser's. Prior to trying the spirits whether they be of God, we have first to choose which God we shall serve. God is, in fact, the title of homage and fealty we apply to the personification, whether real or imaginary, that embodies for us what is morally most precious. God is the Lord whom *we* have elected to serve; the devil is the devil because he is His enemy and ours. This explains the present dismemberment of God among the present nations of Europe. Only a decisive and overwhelming victory of one side can accomplish the task of Isis for this Osiris.

We shall close our discussion by glancing at the bearing of our view upon the question of moral progress. Such a theory as we have been upholding recognizes change, but does it give the basis for any recognition of progress? Is it true that progress is, as Bernard Shaw maintains, an illusion? Are we on a higher plane of morality than our forefathers? Have we been moving forward in the meantime, or just moving *about*? The answer to this question requires the singling out of some goal, approximation to which or recession from which determines progress or retrogression. As a matter of fact, we all do in our judgments of progress more or less clearly single out some goal. But the question is whether such a selection is anything more than an expression of our preferences. Has the replacement of the Indian tribes by the white civilization of America been a step upward or downward? Upward, of course! But upward—*nobis judicibus*. The Indian may judge differently.

Is there then no perfect judgment of all-seeing Jove which shall settle *this* difference? Even if there be, it still remains a matter of preference, Jove's preference instead of ours or the Indian's. If we deliberately confine ourselves to the question whether a larger number of human beings share in a fuller satisfaction as the result of the Indian's displacement, whatever answer we give, that answer will be what on the face of it it purports to be, namely, a statement that a growing number of men do or do not find an increasing satisfaction as the result of the direction taken by history's movement. And it can only be the nature of these men's desires and aversions that finds expression in such satisfaction. To make the matter clearer by another reference, suppose that industrial progress shall one day make possible that a large majority of men live in Sybaritic idleness; suppose that medical science shall by that time have solved the problem of the removal of all infectious diseases; suppose that the family as we now know it shall then have become obsolete, being replaced by sterilized free love on the one hand and by state-controlled parentage on the other. Would the attainment of such a state be an achievement of progress, or would it be a deplorable retrogression? The majority of the judges contemporary with such a civilization would undoubtedly call it progress. But would it be? There is no doubt that many of the things we now value would have been lost; but suppose the loss were no more felt than we in general feel the loss of the gladiatorial sports that once delighted the Roman populace, not having ourselves been brought up to the habit. Would the loss, unfelt, of our present values, however precious to *us*, counteract the gains appreciated by those who then should have free opportunity of enjoyment along the lines of habits meanwhile established? Such a question admits of no impartial answer. We can answer only in accordance with the standards set by *our* ideals. Those who cherish our institutions because they embody what they hold dear must unreservedly say that any civilization that comes to be built upon the wreck of these institutions would for them be a lapse from a higher state. There would be a sorry exchange of spirituality for sensuality. But the children of that supposed generation would give a different rating of the direction that had led to what they should find good. Spirituality and sensuality are names given to different things at different times and places. The exercise of what at any time are regarded as the higher functions of man is for that time spirituality, provided that exercise be controlled by the highest accepted standards; the exercise of the lower functions is sensuality. With changing evaluations of the higher and the lower, there would come about a "transvaluation" of the spiritual and the sensual. A notable instance of such a change is seen in the spread of the ascetic ideal in the early centuries of our era, resulting in the disparagement of marriage as an unholy state.

But suppose we forestall such a "weak kneed" defense of our present ideals by saying with John Stuart Mill that it is better to be a Socrates dissatisfied than a pig satisfied. Would not this end discussion by making the quality of pleasure the ultimate criterion? Alas, not. It is better to be a Socrates unsatisfied—better for whom? For Socrates or for the pig? But a pig! Who would be a pig? Is he not loathly? Assuredly he is—*to us;* but *to himself* not so assuredly. Who knows what preciousness there may not be to pigs in unadulterated piggery? Who then shall decide? To what arbiter shall we appeal?

It is strange that when such a question is asked, the fact is overlooked that it is not thrown out to the universe in general. It is we men and women who are asking the question; we are asking it of ourselves; why not answer it for ourselves? We are not particularly interested in the question whether pigs like to be pigs. It matters not if they do. We are concerned with the question what *we* should like to be, what we should like to help our children to become, what kind of civilization we shall lend our efforts to build up for the future. The fundamental question to be answered before any question about progress can be answered is the most momentous question in the world for us as moral agents. The question is, *what do we really want?* This is not a question to be answered lightly. Knowledge of all sorts is of help in answering it, especially knowledge of the consequences of getting what we want. But when all the knowledge is got that can be got, when we have obtained as clear vision as with our human limitations we can obtain, still we shall find ourselves passively contemplating a wan and colorless future unless our desires rise up to seize some envisaged possibility and invest it with the charm of the ideal. That which we prefer above all else when we know all that we can know about it, that for us is best. Movement in the direction of this our enlightened preference is progress; movement away from it is retrogression. To a man with active preferences, progress is not an illusion, because his preferences are indubitable fact. The only illusion is in supposing that a preference of his own is the universe's choice, that a fact here and now is a revelation of what the universe is at bottom and at all times.

The evolution that has given birth to us men is an evolution upward, because it is we men who are now assessing its value. The moral evolution that has given birth to our ideals has been progress, because it is we with these ideals who are at present the court of last resort. In this asserted humanization and temporalization of our judgments of progress we have a fact analogous to the terrestrialization of judgments of up and down which took place when modern astronomy ousted the Ptolemaic-Aristotelian conception. For Aristotle there was an absolute up and an absolute down; what was above was aboriginally and intrinsically and eternally above—above yesterday, to-day, and forever; above here, there, and everywhere. Students of history know the confusion that the enforced surrender of this view brought about in the world of established thought. It turned everything topsy-turvy.

The dialectical arguments pressed against the new view were the outcry of a muddleheadedness caused by practical disorientation. But for all that, men did get adjusted to the new view; and when they did they found that they had not lost the practical advantages that went with the old, and that they had gained much from the change. The relativity of the spatially up and the spatially down does not divest us of our sense of direction or of its significance, for our semicircular canals do not have to adjust themselves to the bottom of the universe. The center of gravity of our little planet is all that they have to keep in mind. We are terrestrial beings, each for a time in a definite place where the direction of gravitation is a definite fact; and from this place we get our bearings. In the same way the mere thought that there are many antipodal ups and downs in moral matters may and undoubtedly will and must introduce confusion. Accustomed as we are to believe that we cannot be right without being eternally and everlastingly right, we argue with impeccable logic to the conclusion that the denial of absoluteness in moral standards is a denial of morality altogether. But we must not mistake a faultless syllogism for the ascertainment of truth. New facts may give us new premises, and from these new premises we may still defend a vigorous moral thesis. The ever new fact that every vital moral judgment has to reckon with is the new place in the moral economy which the new judge occupies. Just as the pull of gravitation tells the traveler which way is down and which is up for whatever place he may for the moment occupy, in like manner, but inversely, it is the pull of our system of desires that determines which way is up and which way is down in moral movements. "Heaven [is] the vision of fulfilled desire."

The moral to be drawn from the relativity of the moral ideal is an old one. "Keep thy heart with all diligence, for out of it are the issues of life." But this moral must be reinterpreted, interpreted not in the spirit of asceticism but of aspiration toward a fullness of life. To keep one's heart with all diligence is to keep the fountains of desire ever flowing. The larger the number of springs that well up within it, the stronger will the current be that finally courses forth. But let the incoming jets become confluent in the central basin, mixing their waters there first; what shall then issue from the common reservoir will be a homogeneous stream. The direction of progress for that stream will not be a matter of doubt; it will be marked out for it by the particular configuration of the land it will have to traverse. As it flows forward it will be joined by other streams from other springs; the mingled waters will with ever more majestic sweep press forward till at last they reach the ocean. But even there there will be no rest: there are currents in the sea as well as in the rivers, and from the sea will be drawn that which is to feed new springs whose turn it will be to keep the ocean full.[4]

---

[4] [In the footnote at the beginning of this chapter Mr. McGilvary promised to add a postscript. The postscript was never written. From some remarks that he had made to a colleague it may be surmised that he was concerned lest his advocacy of "might makes right" be misinterpreted. He is not saying either that there is an antecedent objective right and that might proves what it is, or that right is to be equated with physical power, as though a bully—or even a nation—proves that demands are right by bringing an opponent to his knees. An ideal is right relative to the persons, times, and circumstances in which it is held if, by its inspiration and approval, it can enlist the strength to prevail against ideals with which it is in conflict. And this it may do even though many a physical battle is lost. But the careful reader will not, I think, misread Mr. McGilvary on this point, so, perhaps neither his postscript nor my further comment is necessary. —A.G.R.]

Chapter IX

THE LORENTZ TRANSFORMATION AND "SPACE-TIME"

In this chapter I offer a new derivation of the Lorentz transformation as it is used in the special theory of relativity. This derivation has a certain advantage for my purpose: it brings out more directly the significance of a certain expression which has been exploited by those who give a mystic meaning to "space-time." I employ the same postulates as those laid down by Einstein,[1] but I add two others which appear as implications or theorems in his derivation; however, this divergence makes no relevant difference,[2] even if it should be claimed that my postulates are redundant. These two postulates will be labelled "Postulate

---

[1] Einstein's two postulates are:
"1. The laws by which the states of physical systems undergo change are not affected, whether these changes of state be referred to the one or to the other of two systems of coördinates in uniform translatory motion.
"2. Any ray of light moves in the 'stationary' system of coördinates with the determined velocity c, whether the ray be emitted by a stationary or by a moving body. Hence

velocity = (light path)/(time interval)."

"Zur Elektrodynamik bewegter Körper," reprinted in *Das Relativitätsprinzip: eine Sammlung von Abhandlungen*, 5te Aufl., Leipzig, Berlin, 1923, p. 29. English translation by W. Perrett and G. B. Jeffery, London, 1923, p. 41. This translation was made from the 4th German edition of the collection, under the title, *The Principle of Relativity*. Hereafter the German edition will be referred to as "R" and the reference will be followed by "Eng." to denote the English translation.

[2] *Cf. Lectures on Fundamental Concepts of Algebra and Geometry*, by John Wesley Young, New York, 1911, pp. 52–53: "The choice of a set of assumptions is very much like the election of men to office. There is no logical reason why we should not choose the more complex propositions; but as a matter of fact we usually choose the simpler, because it is easier to work with them . . . They are elected for their fitness to serve, and their fitness is very largely determined by their simplicity, by the ease with which the other propositions may be derived from them."

1" and "Postulate 2"; and Einstein's postulate 2 will be labelled "Postulate 3." But first a definition is necessary.

By a "normal plane" in either of two systems in relative motion of translation is meant a plane that is perpendicular to the relative motion of the two systems.

Postulate 1. Planes that are normal in either system are normal also in the other.

Postulate 2. Lengths in normal planes in either system, measured in units of that system, have the same value when measured in units of the other system.[3]

Postulate 3. Any ray of light is propagated with constant velocity c in each of two systems that are in relative uniform translatory motion.

"Velocity c" here has the meaning given by Einstein in the passage quoted in footnote 1, and in each system c is to be reckoned in units of this system.

Let S and S' be two systems of rectangular Cartesian coördinates in relative uniform motion of translation, their XY-planes and X-axes being respectively in continuous coincidence. Therefore, by Postulate 2,

$$y' = y, \text{ and } z' = z. \tag{1}$$

Let S' have in S the velocity v in the positive X-direction, v being measured in S units. Symmetrically, S is to have in S' the velocity $-v$, measured in S' units. In all our subsequent discussion, v thus is to have positive value.

Each system is to be provided with measuring rods, and with clocks that are physically alike. Thus the clocks that are in the same system have equal periods, and those that are in different systems would have equal periods if they were relatively at rest. One of such clocks is to be stationed at each point in either system to which attention may be directed. The measuring rods are such

---

[3] Einstein, after discussing a ray of light emitted along the X-axis of one system says: "An analogous consideration—applied to the axes of Y and Z—it being borne in mind that light is always propagated along these axes, when viewed from the stationary system, with velocity $\sqrt{(c^2 - v^2)}$ . . ." (R, p. 32, Eng., p. 44). This implies both of our preceding postulates.

The Lorentz Transformation 299

that, if or when they are at rest, they have exactly the same length. (By Postulate 2, any two such rods, one in S and the other in S', have equal length if they lie in normal planes.)

The clocks in each system are to be synchronized with each other by means of the same light wave emitted at O and O', the respective origins of S and S', when these origins come into coincidence, this coincidence being taken as zero time in both systems.[4] The clocks at O and O' are then to be set at zero reading, and each is to be the master clock in its own system. The readings of other clocks in S, when synchronized with their master clock, are to be designated by t; those of other clocks in S', when synchronized with their master clock, are to be designated by t'. The spatial coördinates of any point referred to S are to be designated by x, y, z; those of any point referred to S' are to be designated by x', y', z'.

Hereafter by the words "the light" is to be meant the light

---

[4] This proposal to synchronize all the clocks in each system by means of the same light wave implies a proposition that I should have liked to lay down as a postulate, rather than have it turn up as a theorem. I refer to the proposition that v is less than c. Readers beginning the study of relativity feel, when reaching this theorem, as if they had been imposed upon by a magician who takes out of a hat a rabbit that is not there. This puzzlement could have been avoided if by a postulate their attention had been directed to the fact that the rabbit had been put there at the very start. Only a little reflection is needed to convince any one, whose attention is called to it, that this proposition is implied by the present proposal:

Suppose $v = c$. Then the front of the light ray emitted at O in the positive X-direction will remain constantly fixed at O'. Thus the S' clock at O' will remain permanently stopped if it is to be synchronous with itself. Furthermore, no clock in S' that lies in the positive X-direction from O' will ever be reached by the light ray by which it is proposed to synchronize it. On the other hand, the front of the light ray emitted at O' in the negative X direction will remain constantly fixed at O, and no S clock that lies in the negative X-direction from O will ever be reached by that light ray. But this is only half of the story, the other half being told by the ray emitted from O in the negative X-direction, and by that emitted from O' in the positive X-direction. I leave it to the reader to hear for himself what these rays have to say. But it is only fair to call attention to the plight in which the famous twins, Peter and Paul, would find themselves under the supposed circumstances. They would not have to return from joyrides through space to find themselves in a most awkward fix. I use the word "fix" in its literal sense, for each would be fixed in perpetual heat-death and yet living a normal life. Each would be a Siamese twin all by himself, one of him living a death at absolute zero, and the other of him enjoying such life as the conditions could permit. And the conditions would be even worse if v were greater than c. But I leave them to the reader, myself preferring to have nothing more to do with them. They do not even have the merit of being funny. Lewis Carroll might have been able to invest Peter and Paul in these roles with charm to delight us, but unfortunately Lewis Carroll is dead.

emitted from O and O' at zero time. The event of the coincidence of any two points, one in S and the other in S', will be identified by the names of the coinciding points. Thus the event "OO'" will mean the coming into coincidence of the points O and O', and will include in its meaning any other event taking place at this coincidence; for instance, the emission of light there.

The light arrives at any S point P (x, y, z) after having traversed in S the distance $\sqrt{(x^2+y^2+z^2)}$, measured in S, with velocity c; therefore the S time of this arrival is

$$t = \sqrt{(x^2+y^2+z^2)}/c. \qquad (2)$$

Let the clock at P be set at this reading.

It is to be noted that the time of arrival of the light at P is that given in equation (2), *not* because the clock is set to have this reading. On the contrary, the clock is set at this reading *because that is the correct time* by Postulate 3. The clock, when set, continues to give the correct time because it is a good clock.

At S time given in equation (2), point P is coincident with an S' point P' (x', y', z'), and the light arrives at P' after having traversed the distance $\sqrt{(x'^2+y'^2+z'^2)}$, measured in S', with velocity c; therefore the S' time of this arrival is

$$t' = \sqrt{(x'^2+y'^2+z'^2)}/c. \qquad (3)$$

Let the clock at P' be set at this reading. What was said above as to the relation between the correct time and the reading of the clock at P holds also of the clock at P'.

From (2) we get
$$ct = \sqrt{(x^2+y^2+z^2)}, \qquad (4)$$
$$c^2t^2 - x^2 - y^2 - z^2 = 0. \qquad (5)$$

From (3) we get
$$ct' = \sqrt{(x'^2+y'^2+z'^2)}, \qquad (6)$$
$$c^2t'^2 - x'^2 - y'^2 - z'^2 = 0. \qquad (7)$$

From (7) and (5) we get
$$c^2t'^2 - x'^2 - y'^2 - z'^2 = c^2t^2 - x^2 - y^2 - z^2. \qquad (8)$$

From (8) and (1) we get
$$c^2t'^2 - x'^2 = c^2t^2 - x^2. \qquad (9)$$

This equation holds, it is to be remembered, of *any* point P and of the momentarily coincident point P'. But there are two special cases that require special consideration.

Special Case 1. Let us consider (9) in the special case where P' is in the YZ-plane of S'. Here $x' = 0$; and since this plane has been moving in S with velocity v from zero S time till S time t given in equations (2) and (9), at that time t of its arrival at the S normal plane (x), $x = vt$.

By substituting these values of x' and x in (9) we get
$$c^2 t'^2 = c^2 t^2 - v^2 t^2$$
$$t' = t/\beta, \tag{10}$$
where (and always hereafter in this discussion)
$$\beta \equiv c/\sqrt{(c^2 - v^2)}. \tag{11}$$

Special Case 2. Let us next consider (9) in the special case where P is in the YZ-plane of S. Here $x = 0$; and since this plane has been moving in S' with velocity $-v$ from zero S' time till the S' time t' given in equation (3), at that time t' of its arrival at the S' normal plane (x'), $x' = -vt'$. By substituting these values of x and x' in (9) we get
$$c^2 t^2 = c^2 t'^2 - v^2 t'^2$$
$$t = t'/\beta. \tag{12}$$

Since (9) holds for any case of coincident P and P', and since in the special cases we have been considering there is a factor β in the expression of the relation between t and t', we must introduce this factor into (9) in order that the roots in t and t' of (9) shall satisfy these special cases as well as any other case. This we do by expressing unity in terms of β in equation (11), from which we get
$$\beta^2 (1 - v^2/c^2) = 1. \tag{13}$$

Substituting from (13) into (9) we get
$$c^2 t'^2 - x'^2 = \beta^2 (c^2 t^2 + v^2 x^2/c^2) - \beta^2 (x^2 + v^2 t^2).$$
By subtracting and then adding $2\beta^2 xvt$ on the right side of this equation we get
$$c^2 t'^2 - x'^2 = \beta^2 (ct - vx/c)^2 - \beta^2 (x - vt)^2.$$

The only roots in x' and t' of this equation that will satisfy the conditions in Special Case 1 where $x' = 0$ and $x = vt$, and thus accord with equation (10) are

$$x' = \beta(x - vt) \tag{14}$$

and

$$t' = \beta(t - vx/c^2). \tag{15}$$

Returning again to equation (9), and this time substituting from (13) into the left side, we proceed as before with the exception that we now first add and then subtract $2\beta^2 x' vt'$, and that we must satisfy the conditions in Special Case 2, when $x = 0$ and $x' = -vt'$, thus getting

$$x = \beta(x' + vt'), \tag{16}$$
$$t = \beta(t' + vx'/c^2). \tag{17}$$

The last four equations, together with equations (1) and (11), constitute the "Lorentz Transformation." Equations (16) and (17) are usually omitted from the roster of this transformation for the reason that they can be obtained from (14) and (15) by simple algebraic operations and may therefore be treated as redundant. But we have shown that they may be obtained independently by the same chain of reasoning by which (14) and (15) were obtained. However that may be, the inclusion of them in a table with the others furnishes a convenient reference group for the use of any one who deals with the problems involved in the special theory of relativity.

An observant reader will have noticed that the Lorentz transformation, secured as it has been by ascertaining the times of the arrival of light rays at coinciding points, is apparently applicable only to events which can be *reached* by light rays emitted at O and O'. The proposition which I have treated as Postulate 1 above, even if considered as a theorem, is nevertheless an integral part of the special theory of relativity; and a corollary of this proposition is that there is an infinite number of events that are accurately timed with the help of the light from event OO' although that light cannot have reached them. This light first

The Lorentz Transformation

reaches any normal plane (other than the YZ-plane) in the system S at a point P_1 $(x, y = z = 0)$, i.e., at the point where that normal plane is intersected by the X-axis. The time of this arrival is $t = x/c$; and at that time P_1 is coincident with point P'_1 $(x', y' = z' = 0)$. But by the corollary just mentioned, any other point Q in the normal plane (x) in which P_1 lies, comes into coincidence with point Q' in the normal plane (x') in which p'_1 lies, at the *same* time $t = x/c$. (Otherwise the two normal planes *intersect* each other, and this contradicts our Postulate 1.) Thus, however remote Q and Q' are from the X-axis, their coincidence is *timable* as soon as the light reaches P_1 and P'_1, which are on the X-axis; and the clocks at Q and Q', then set properly, will continue to run synchronously with their respective master clocks, and the clock at either point will be showing the correct time when later the light actually arrives at that point. (Of course by that time Q and Q' will no longer be in coincidence.)[5]

We here have instances in which "simultaneity at a distance" is ascertainable without the use of light signals *between the points involved*. The only light signal needed is that from OO' to $P_1P'_1$. None is needed between $P_1P'_1$ and QQ'. This fact is mathematically indicated by the absence of the y and z coördinates from equations (14) to (17) inclusive. Let us call all the events that

---

[5] It might be objected that observers at Q and Q' cannot know what the times t and t' are when the light arrives at P_1 and P'_1, even though *we* know. The light has not yet reached *them*. This objection cannot be sustained. The setup under which all derivations of the Lorentz transformation are secured assumes that observers at O and O' can each recognize the zero abscissal value of the point coincident with his own point. If *these* two observers have this competence, there is no *logical* reason why observers at Q and Q' should not have the competence for each to recognize the abscissal value of any point coming into coincidence with his own point. Nor is there any reason why these observers should not know all the postulates under which the synchronization of clocks is proceeding. It should be remembered that the whole process takes place under the assumption of *ideal* conditions, as for instance that one can actually observe the instant of the arrival of a light ray at one's station. As Einstein puts it, we have the "help of certain (ideal) physical experiences" (*Zuhilfenahme gewisser (gedachter) physikalischer Erfahrungen*, R, p. 29, Eng., p. 40, where the translators use the word "imaginary" where I have preferred the word "ideal"). The assumption that our observers know the postulates under which the setup has been made is surely not more extravagantly ideal than that they can identify points and instants.

are timable *when* they occur but *before* the light can have reached them, "Group 1."[6]

But there is another group of events, which I shall call "Group 2." These events occur before the light can yet have reached the *normal planes* in which they occur, and are *not* timable *when* they occur. They can be timed only *ex post facto*.[7] If an event occurs in the normal S plane (x, positive) or ($-x$), and if the retrospective date of the event is $t = n$ (positive), and if n is less than x/c and greater than $-x/c$, the event belongs to Group 2.

Events in Group 1 and those in Group 2 are end-terms of so-called "space-like" intervals. As we shall see, all so-called "space-time intervals," whether "space-like," "time-like," or "null," are *space* intervals—*only* that and nothing more.

It is to be noted, however, that what has been said of Group 2 holds only with respect to the two systems S and S'. Let there be a third system S'', moving at right angles to the relative motion of S and S', with its origin O'' coincident with O and O' when these two points are coincident. Events forming Group 2 with respect to S and S' are in Group 1 with respect to S, S' and S'' in combination, and every event in any normal plane in S'' is timed as soon as the light reaches any point in that plane. This carries with it the timing of points in S and S' at which these events occur. It follows that the three systems in coöperation succeed in eliminating Group 2 altogether.

---

[6] The existence of Group 1 seems to have some bearing upon Minkowski's "light cones," and especially upon "the one-sheeted hyperboloidal figures" that fill "the territory between the cones" (*R*, p. 61, Eng., pp. 83–84). But the limits of this chapter make it impossible to discuss the problem here.

[7] This retrospective assignment of dates is analogous to the procedure of the historian in determining the date in our calendar of events before the establishment of our calendar. Where events already have dates in one calendar the transformation from that calendar into another is made by use of transformation equations, as when the Gregorian was substituted for the Julian reckoning. (In an article published in 1928 I gave a transformation correlating Newtonian time with Einsteinian time. See "Times, New and Old," in the *University of California Publications in Philosophy*, Vol. 6, No. 4, p. 241.) But often the problem of dating an event is not so easily solved. A striking instance of a solution by use of an astronomical clue is mentioned in *A History of Greece*, by J. B. Bury, London, 1929, p. 222, where it is shown how a previously undated battle can be dated to an exact day, May 28, 585 B. C.

Let us now interpret our equations, beginning for the present with (4). In kinematics "unit velocity" means, as is well known, a velocity that covers a unit of (spatial) distance during a unit lapse of time. Of course there is no special "privilege" appertaining to any particular unit velocity. Convenience or convention usually determines what unit is to be adopted. Astronomers often use "light year per year," but American motorists would find that very inconvenient and prefer "mile a minute." But whatever unit velocity is adopted, it remains a unit *velocity*. There is no logical difference between a unit velocity and an army unit of company or division except that one is a velocity and the other a company or a division. Neither is *unity;* i.e., neither is the number 1. Thus, just because a unit velocity and an army division are both of them units, we may not equate a unit velocity with an army unit and ignore the fact that they are units *of different sorts*. (The reader will please be patient with me while I indulge in commonplaces: commonplaces become important when they are ignored.)

Having selected whatever unit velocity we please, we have therewith selected a correlated unit of spatial length and a correlated unit of time. And now we can multiply *any* velocity by the number of units of *time* during which that velocity has been operating, and get as product the number of units of *distance* covered by that velocity during that time. Thus with mile per hour as unit velocity, a velocity of 40 miles per hour multiplied by 10 hours gives us the *distance* of 400 miles as covered by that velocity. Speaking in general and no longer in specific terms, we say that *velocity multiplied by time gives space*. Applying this fundamental kinematic principle to equation (4), we find that the right side of the equation gives ct as the number of units of spatial length covered by light with velocity c during a measure of time t. The product ct in equation (4) is not a velocity measure nor a temporal measure but a *spatial measure*. The equation equates two spatial measures, one obtained by the application of the fundamental principle just stated, and the other by the use of the spatial coördinates, x, y, z, and the Pythagorean theorem. To speak in terms of vectors, ct is the *spatial* vector traced by the light in going from O to P, and the expression on the right is the *same* spatial vector obtained by the addition of the spatial vectors, x, y, z, in accordance with the principles of vector analysis.

And what is true of ct is also true of c^2t^2, of ct' and of $c^2t'^2$, of vt and v^2t^2, of vt', and $v^2t'^2$ wherever they occur in equations of the special theory of relativity. That is the reason why there is any sense in subtracting vt from x. You can subtract one spatial measure number from another, say three yards from four yards, but see what sense you get in subtracting three years from four yards, or even from four *light* years for that matter. "It isn't done"; it cannot be done except perhaps in the realm of the mystic, over the portals of which are inscribed the words: "Abandon logic all ye who enter here."

This being so, the left side of equation (5) is the expression of a *spatial* measure, not a space-*time* measure, even though it has a time measure as one of its terms. It is to be noted that this equation is one that could have been written by any orthodox Newtonian. What distinguishes relativity from Newtonianism is not equation (5). Even equation (7) could have been written by a Newtonian as an exclusive alternative to equation (5). What distinguishes relativity is the acceptance of *both* equations, with the resulting equation (8). But this distinction does not alter the fact that both sides of (8) are spatial measures. On the right side we have the square of the distance from O to P, minus the square of the same distance; and on the left, the square of the distance from O' to P', minus the square of the same distance. And the square of a spatial distance, minus the square of the same distance, is not the square of a "space-*time* interval," as the *mysticizing* relativists would have us believe.

And what holds of (8) also holds if the respective y and z coördinates of Q and Q' (discussed on page 303, above) are substituted for the respective y and z coördinates of P_1 and P'_1. Such a substitution does not prejudice the truth of the resulting equation, since by Postulate 2 the respective y and z coördinates of Q and Q' are equal; and yet the substitution gives each of the two sides of the resulting equation a value less than zero, since the length of OQ is greater than that of OP_1, and that of $O'Q'$ is greater than that of $O'P'_1$. Thus what our mysticizing relativists call an "imaginary space-time interval" is only an imaginary *spatial* vector. And what is true of Group 1 is also true in Group 2, the only difference being that the t and t' in the latter group are retrospective values.

Now let us with the mysticizers adopt, as they have a perfect right to adopt, the velocity of light as the unit velocity. If we do this, we *should* write

$$\text{unit velocity } c = (1 \text{ light second})/(1 \text{ second}), \quad (18)$$

where "light second" $= 300{,}000$ kilometers, in round numbers. *This* equation is entirely different from the equation used by Minkowski, Sir Arthur Eddington, and others.[8] Their equation is

$$c = 1. \quad (19)$$

Equation (19) treats *unit velocity* as *unity* (i.e., the pure number 1), and not as unit *velocity*. When c is treated as a pure number, our equation (2) becomes

$$t \text{ seconds} = \sqrt{(x^2 + y^2 + z^2)} \text{ } light \text{ seconds}, \quad (20)$$

thus equating the *temporal* measure number on the left with the *spatial* measure number on the right. Writing equation (20) is like writing

$$4 \text{ ladies} = 4 \text{ skirts}, \quad (21)$$

when we see 4 ladies each wearing a skirt, and take 1 lady as unit lady, and 1 skirt as unit skirt. When our mysticizers go on to say that equation (20) assimilates space to time,[9] their logic would

---

[8] R, p. 64, Eng., p. 88. *The Mathematical Theory of Relativity*, by A. S. Eddington, Cambridge, 2nd ed., 1924, p. 35. This latter work will hereafter be referred to as "*MTR.*"

[9] Cf. *The Principle of Relativity*, by A. N. Whitehead, Cambridge, 1922: "My whole course of thought presupposes the magnificent stroke of genius by which Einstein and Minkowski assimilated time and space" (p. 88). Whether Einstein should here be coupled with Minkowski I would gravely question. The "magnificent stroke of genius" was Einstein's when he developed the special theory of relativity, using the "relativity postulate" (viz., his postulate 1 quoted in my first footnote above). It will be remembered that Minkowski called this name "very

allow us to assimilate lady to skirt in equation (21). No wonder that Sir Arthur Eddington said:

> The most natural connection between the measure of time and length is given by the fact that light travels 300,000 kilometres in 1 second. For the four-dimensional world we shall accordingly regard 1 second as the equivalent of 300,000 kilometres, and measure lengths and times in seconds or kilometres indiscriminately; in other words we make the velocity of light the unit of velocity.[10]

And he said this even after having just said:

> An important point arises here. It was, of course, assumed that the same scale was used for measuring x and y and z. But how are we to use the same scale for measuring t? We cannot use a scale at all; some kind of clock is needed.

Time may not be assimilated to space any more than a clock may be assimilated to a scale or a lady to a skirt. Or shall we adopt the jargon of the underworld and call a lady a "skirt"?

If, on the contrary, we adopt equation (18) instead of equation (19), in substituting for c in any of our equations from (2) to (17), we find, as any one can verify, that time remains time and space remains space. There is no more assimilation of them in relativity than there is in "classical mechanics." For instance equation (4), with (18) as our source for substitution, becomes, or rather it *remains*,

ct light seconds, or units of length $= \sqrt{(x^2 + y^2 + z^2)}$ light seconds, or units of length.

And equation (9) tells us that the squared *spatial* vector on the left side of the equation, expressed in S' units, is equal to the squared *spatial* vector on the right side of the equation, expressed in S units.

But if time may not be assimilated to space by the adoption of the velocity of light as our unit velocity, perchance it may be thus assimilated by the use of "the mysterious factor $\sqrt{-1}$, which

---

feeble," and proposed as substitute "the *postulate of the absolute world* (or briefly, the world postulate)" (R, p. 60, Eng., p. 83).

[10] *Space, Time and Gravitation*, by A. S. Eddington, Cambridge, 1929, p. 46. This work is hereafter to be referred to as "*STG*."

The Lorentz Transformation

seems to have the property of turning time into space," as Sir Arthur suggests.[11] Let us see.

In mathematics there is nothing mysterious in this "factor" which we shall call by its usual name "i," whether used in algebra or geometry.[12] Thus if we write $ct' = ics'$, and $ct = ics$, equation (8) becomes

$$-c^2 s'^2 - x'^2 - y'^2 - z'^2 = -c^2 s^2 - x^2 - y^2 - z^2. \quad (22)$$

This corresponds to Minkowski's expression in differential geometry, from which he gets "the mystic formula

$$3.10^5 \ km = \sqrt{-1} \ \text{sec."}[13]$$

We may interpret equation (22) as one in four-dimensional geometry; but even then we have not turned time into space, since ct was already a spatial measure. The feat of turning time into space can be accomplished only by substituting from equation (19) into (8), which would give us

$$t'^2 - x'^2 - y'^2 - z'^2 = t^2 - x^2 - y^2 - z^2. \quad (23)$$

Thus the factor i only "*seems* to have the property of turning time into space." It is the spurious equation (19) that does the trick.

Are we then debarred from obtaining the equation (23) without which there is no passage from the special to the general theory of relativity?[14]

---

[11] *STG*, p. 48. In *MTR* Sir Arthur admits on p. 13 that y_4, which on the next page is to be transformed into time t, "clearly must involve the time ... but we must not too hastily identify it with the time t." Just what is meant by the assertion that a coördinate "must involve the time," without being "too hastily identified with the time t" into which it is transformed, is not itself "clear." Is time, the rabbit, here put into the hat *before* the "analytical device," $i = \sqrt{-1}$, is employed to bring it out? Or does the *device* accomplish the transubstantiation of space into time, and when reversed does it transubstantiate time into space? In the realm of miracles any miracle of course may happen if it does happen. But is relativistic mathematical physics in the realm of *miracles*?

[12] *Cf.* John Wesley Young, *op. cit.*, chapter XII. The meaning of i is even taught to freshmen in colleges; see *Elementary Mathematical Analysis: a Text Book for First Year College Students*, by Charles S. Slichter, 2nd ed., New York, London, 1918. "So, as (-1) may be defined as the symbol which operates to turn a straight line through an angle of 180°, in a similar way *we may define the expression* $\sqrt{-1}$ *as a symbol which denotes the operation of turning a straight line through an angle of 90°.*" (p. 362).

[13] *R*, p. 64, Eng., p. 88.

[14] See Einstein, *R*, p. 87, Eng., p. 119, where his equation (1) is another way of writing our equation (23). For Sir Arthur, see *MTR*, p. 37.

By no means, for while we may not add 4 unit horses to 4 unit snakes and get 8 unit horses or 8 unit snakes or even 8 unit *snake-horses,* we may, however, get 8 *units,* of which 4 still remain horses and 4 still remain snakes. Of such disparate units added together, each retains the classificatory denomination it had before the addition. Now, a corollary of the definition of unit velocity is that *during any lapse of time a unit velocity covers as many units of space as there are units of time in that time lapse.* But in the customary mathematical notation this fact, when c, the velocity of light, is the adopted unit velocity, is not expressed by the equation

$$1 \text{ sec.} = 1 \text{ light second,}$$

any more than the equality of the number of snakes with the number of horses in the collection mentioned a moment ago is expressed by the equation 4 snakes $=$ 4 horses. But we may say in this latter case that (the *number* of snakes) $=$ (the *number* of horses), since the number of snakes is not 4 *snakes* but 4, a pure number. So we may say, when c is the unit velocity, that (the *number* of seconds) $=$ (the *number* of light seconds); and since in all our equations t is not only the time of the arrival of light at any point designated (say P), but may also be taken as the *measure of the time lapse,* i.e. as the *number* of seconds in the lapse, between the emission of the light at zero time and its arrival at P, t as such a *number* may be substituted for ct as an equal *number* in any purely numerical equation, without prejudice either to the validity of the resulting equation or to the characteristic difference between a second and a light second, i.e., between *time* and *space.* Thus in *our* four-dimensional world of time and space, we do *not* "measure lengths and times in seconds or kilometers indiscriminately." To do what Sir Arthur does is by implication to go the way of the mystic for whom logical distinctions disappear in a "night in which all cows are black." If literally the world postulate may by Minkowski "be clothed mathematically in a very pregnant manner in the mystic formula

$$3.10^5 km = \sqrt{-1} \text{ sec.,"}$$

the shame of its nakedness is ill-concealed; and it is also worthy of note that "Space-Time" was born of that pregnancy.

Minkowski had been correct when he had previously said: "The objects of our perception invariably include places and times in combination. Nobody has ever noticed a place except at a time, or a time expect at a place."[15] This has always been recognized in physics. In Aristotle time, place, and motion were interconnected, and time was defined as "the number (ἀριθμός) of motion": it was not "time by itself." But so far as is known he did not use equations, and this of course was a serious shortcoming, made good at the beginning of modern physics by Galileo, "the father of modern mechanics." The famous equation that bears Galileo's name, $x' = x - vt$, also bears witness to the fact that more than three centuries before 1908, "time by itself" and "space by itself" had already ceased to have "independent reality" in physics, and that even then time and space had their being "only in a kind of union." The name of that union is *motion*. What had not occurred to any physicist till 1908 was to clothe that union "mathematically in a very pregnant manner in the mystic formula

$$3.10^5 \, km = \sqrt{-1} \, sec."$$

Of course it was fitting that the belated bride should wear a veil.

It is perhaps too late to object to the idiom, "Space-Time." The statute of limitations runs in language as well as in law, and there is seemingly a magic in a hyphen which the homely word "and" does not possess, as is abundantly shown in the *Social Register* and the *Peerage*. And yet somehow, "George VI, by the Grace of God, King of Great Britain *and* Ireland *and* of the British Dominions Beyond the Seas," has a ring of dignity that would not be greatly enhanced by the substitution of hyphens for the two "ands." And besides, Eire would probably object to being "doomed to fade away into a mere shadow."

---

[15] *R*, p. 55, Eng., p. 76.

CHAPTER X

"THE PARADOX OF THE TIME-RETARDING JOURNEY"

Professor Lovejoy's article in *The Philosophical Review* (Vol. XL, pp. 48–68, 152–167) calls for extended discussion, more extended indeed than is possible within the limits of a single chapter.[1] I therefore shall confine myself mainly to what he says about the retardation of clocks and of senescence in the Special Theory of Relativity. This theory has to do only with systems in relative motion with constant velocity. With such motion there is of course no return journey. But I must touch here and there upon the problem of a return journey, since Lovejoy mixes this problem up with that involved in unaccelerated motion, as will be seen from the first quotation below. Some scrambled eggs have to be unscrambled—if we are to get live eggs out of the scramble.

In speaking of the return journey he says:

> It is assumed (in the Special Theory) that the only motion in question *is* the relative motion between the two systems, and also that any effects . . . of the acceleration (if there are any such effects) will be due solely to the change in this relative motion, viz., to the change of the direction of the motion of each system with respect to each other. Any *such* effect, then, resulting from the acceleration should be the same on both systems (p. 62).

It cannot be too strongly emphasized that the Special Theory has *logically nothing to say* on retardation involved in a journey *to and*

---

[1] Since in that article Lovejoy makes no reference to another which he recently published in the *Journal of Philosophy* (Vol. XXVII, Nos. 23 and 24), I assume that in the former he is not building upon conclusions he thinks he has established in the latter. The two articles seem to be logically independent. All page-references in this chapter are to the article in *The Philosophical Review*.

The Time Retarding Journey

fro. It makes no assumptions whatever as to the effects of acceleration. It deals only with journeys to an undiscovered country from whose bourne no traveller returns. Einstein did, indeed, in 1905 draw a conclusion from the Special Theory as to what would happen if a traveller did get back therefrom. But there was nothing in his equations at that time to warrant this conclusion, and this is now generally recognized by those who are familiar with them. But let us continue our quotation:

> There is, it is true, a tendency among physicists, even when expounding the Special Theory, to drag in a third (and essentially an absolute) reference-body, as an explanation of the postulated absoluteness of acceleration. [This shows the danger a critic of the Special Theory incurs when he relies on non-mathematical expositions of that theory, instead of going back to its equations.] This conception, however, has a place—if anywhere—only in the General Theory; its use in that theory will be considered later. Until such a conception is explicitly introduced and justified, we are concerned only with the motion which is a private affair between Peter and Paul;

the latter having made a stellar journey and returned (with physiological complications, so Lovejoy thinks) to his twin brother. Until the General Theory is introduced, I must repeat, or until we explicitly make some further assumption, we are *not* concerned (except perhaps emotionally) with this private affair between principals dealing with each other under conditions for which the Special Theory makes no provision. But if we do interfere, Lovejoy is more correct than he realizes when he goes on to say,

> and from this point of view, i.e., that of the Special Theory, we must still conclude (*a*) that no comparative retardation whatever can be deduced for the case of a journey in which there is a reversal of direction.

He is correct because no conclusion whatever, either about comparative retardation, or about comparative *non*-retardation, on reversal of direction, can be deduced from the Special Theory alone. But he commits a fallacy and arrives at a false conclusion when he goes on to say, but (*b*) that if there *were* any retardation—i.e., if the acceleration in question were treated as theoretically negligible—the comparative retardation inferrible would necessarily be reciprocal (p. 62).

Here he reaches a result that is comparable with that of a critic who should argue that, *if* Lovejoy were, along with all his present views, also an epistemological monist, he would be a most self-contradictory philosopher. Obviously this conclusion would be false, but no more so than Lovejoy's, as will be shown before this discussion is concluded.

But the contention that I wish especially to discuss is put forth in the following passage, which I must quote quite at length. "The paradox of the twins—in its symmetrical form—arises even though no reversal of Paul's motion, and no acceleration whatever, is supposed to occur." We are to

> imagine Peter to be on a flat platform extending as far as we please in either direction, and Paul to be on a similar platform immediately adjacent to Peter's and in uniform unaccelerated motion relative to it and parallel with it. If, *while the two were at rest, synchronized clocks* and automatic cameras were placed at intervals along the inner edges of both platforms, the event of any reading of any one of Peter's clocks will be simultaneous with the reading of any clock of Paul's which may be passing, for both clocks will be in this case virtually in the same place.

Now, "in order to avoid any complication involved in getting the motion started," we are to make a further supposition:

> Peter and Paul, not now brothers, must be supposed to have been born simultaneously at points A and A' when these points on the two platforms were passing each other, and each remains throughout at the place of his birth on his own platform. In both directions from A and A', on both platforms, observation-posts are placed at wide intervals; at each of these, assistant observers are stationed, duly provided with *clocks originally synchronized*. It is the law on each platform that no one can be appointed an assistant observer unless he was born *at the same time as Peter and Paul*. Assume that 70 years have elapsed on Peter's platform up to the moment when he passes observation-post P' on Paul's platform. Given sufficient velocity, he, an old man of 70 gazing at his *coeval*, the assistant-observer at P', will seem to that observer to be a young man of 21; and assuming, as is done in the customary story, that *a retardation*

observed from one system is a physical fact on the other, Peter will be [Lovejoy's italics] twenty-one as well as seventy. At the same time his *coeval* at P' will appear to Peter to be 21, and will therefore be of that age, as well as of the age of seventy. We thus eliminate any acceleration, and therewith all attempts to evade the symmetrical form of the paradox by invoking accelerations (pp. 63–64).

The reason why I have italicized certain words in this passage is that in one case they are ambiguous and in the others they signalize the points at which Lovejoy introduces into the problem features that do not appear in it as it is faced in relativity-physics. *They insinuate into the relativistic problem a Newtonian postulate.* Reasoning from this Newtonian postulate, innocently smuggled among the relativistic assumptions that are left intact, it is no wonder that Lovejoy gets a result that is neither Newtonian nor relativistic, but a jumble of contradictions.

The statement that "a retardation observed from one system is a physical fact on the other" is at best ambiguous. Any retardation of a clock on its platform is of course a physical fact, and this clock's retardation as measured on the other platform is a physical fact. But if the clock is a good Einsteinian one its retardation is not a retardation with respect to the time-system of its own platform; its being a good clock is a guarantee against that. Its retardation is with respect to the time-system of the platform relatively to which it is in motion. The kind of retardation under consideration is analogous to largeness. A man of average size may be large. His largeness is a largeness where he happens to be; he could not well be large where he was not, any more than he could be of average size where he was not. But just as his being of average size is a characteristic he has with respect to the standard size of his own people, so his being large is a characteristic he has with respect, let us say, to the standard size of a race of pigmies. Retardation, like largeness, is always a relative (or, if Lovejoy prefers, a respective) characteristic. Anything that changes too slowly changes too slowly (*where it is*) in comparison with some *other* change (*where that is*) which is used as the measure of the rate. But this retardation is not a physical fact *where that other change is occurring.*

The first italicized words, and the word "originally" next italicized, show that Lovejoy wishes to have had the clocks on the two platforms synchronized while they were relatively at rest. If this is done and the clocks are afterwards left untouched, acceleration is introduced into the transaction, for when the platforms are eventually set in motion there is of course acceleration. *The clocks in the Special Theory can be properly synchronized only when the relatively moving systems are moving with unaccelerated velocity.*

The word "coeval," appearing twice, and the phrase "born at the same time as Peter and Paul," taken in the context in which they appear, seem to indicate that simultaneity of birth is tested by clocks synchronized while the platforms were relatively at rest. But leaving this aside, a relativist would call attention to the fact that in relativity-physics any babies born (at different places along the line of relative motion) at the same time (by Paul's clocks) as Peter and Paul, are not "coeval" with any babies born (at different places along the line of relative motion) at the same time (by Peter's clocks) as Peter and Paul. Here then the problem is set by Lovejoy in terms of a *universal simultaneity,* which is directly at variance with the relativistic application of the conception of simultaneity to events at a distance from each other. This is as if a critic, after surreptitiously introducing a Euclidean postulate among those of Riemann, were to show that from all the postulates now on hand contradictory conclusions followed.

The fact that a philosopher with Lovejoy's reputation for carefulness can fall into such fundamental mistakes about a theory he is criticizing makes it desirable to go somewhat into detail in stating just what the Special Theory maintains with regard to the retardations of clocks and of other physical processes. In order to give an accurate picture of what we are to consider, it will be necessary to introduce measure-numbers into our discussion. In doing this, I shall give the results of calculations in the text, putting the calculations into footnotes. In this way a reader who is interested only in the picture need not bother about the calculations upon which the picture is based; and the more exacting reader can check up the calculations. Any one who has had a few weeks of high-school algebra can easily follow them. One who has never used the Lorentz transformation can, by reading the footnotes, get some idea of the technique of its employment.

Let us take Lovejoy's general setup, consisting of two straight platforms of indefinite length, moving relatively to each other and always keeping a constant clearance between them sufficient to prevent disaster; for they are to have the uniform speed of 177,425 miles per second.[2] Peter's platform is to move relatively to Paul's in what we shall take to be the positive direction—let us say eastward. Hence Peter's velocity v is positive, i.e., $v = 177,425$. All the clocks on the two platforms are to be such that, *if* they were relatively at rest, they would run at exactly the same rate, and of course that rate would be such that light *in vacuo* would have the velocity $c = 186,000$ miles per second.

Distributed as they are in our set-up, the clocks on each platform are to be synchronized by light-signals in the well-known way, while the platforms have the constant relative speed v. Any reading of "Paul's clocks" (i.e., clocks on Paul's platform) we shall designate by t. Any reading of "Peter's clocks" (i.e., clocks on Peter's platform) we shall designate by t'. On either platform every point with which we shall deal is to have, not only a clock, but also a milestone, marking its distance, measured on that platform, from the "origin" of that platform, i.e., from the point on that platform from which all distances on that platform are to be measured. The origin of Paul's platform we shall designate as A, that of Peter's platform as A'. The reading of any of Paul's

---

[2] The reason why this speed is selected is that we wish the β of the Lorentz transformation to have the value $\beta = 10/3$, since Lovejoy uses the ages 70 and 21 in his story. In that transformation β is defined as $\beta = c/\sqrt{(c_2 - v_2)}$, where c is the velocity of light and v the relative speed of the moving systems. When $\beta = 10/3$, we write $c/\sqrt{(c^2 - v^2)} = 10/3$; and by solving for v we get $v = c\sqrt{91}/10$. Now $\sqrt{91}$, to three decimal places, is 9.539. Hence $v = 177,425$ miles per second, if we take the velocity of light as $c = 186,000$ miles per second. Our units from now on, till further notice, will be miles and seconds.

milestones we shall designate as x, that of any of Peter's milestones as x'. When one of Peter's milestones is directly opposite one of Paul's, we shall for brevity say that the milestones "coincide," since the small distance between them at that instant is at right angles to the relative motion of the platforms and is therefore not relevant to our present problem. Thus the two milestones are for that instant considered as "virtually in the same place"; and any events that occur, one at one milestone and the other at the coincident milestone, we shall consider as occurring "at the same place." The importance of emphasizing this is that, in relativity-physics, any two events that occur "at the same place," if simultaneous in any system, are simultaneous in all systems moving perpendicularly to the direction between the two points at which they occur. Therefore events that occur simultaneously at coincident points on our two platforms are simultaneous on both platforms. The reader knows that in relativity there is an important difference between "simultaneity at the same place" and "simultaneity at a distance." This difference, however, is not in the connotation of "simultaneity," but in its denotation; just as "father" has the same connotation for all English-speaking peoples, but different persons apply the word to different individuals, you to one man and I to another.

We shall lift the embargo Lovejoy places on observation by any one who is not "coeval" with both Peter and Paul. This is necessary because we shall need legitimate observers, and cannot get them under Lovejoy's law; that law, as we have seen and shall see more clearly as we go on, is unconstitutional within the domain of relativity. Besides, we shall need witnesses to the births of Peter, Paul, and sundry other babies: we do not wish to get so far away from plausibility as to allow babies to date their own births without assistance. Therefore we station two ideally competent observers, one at each of any momentarily coincident points upon which our attention may fall. This competence consists in the possession of vision so keen and alert that each observer can see at any time at least six things: (1) the coincidence of his milestone with a milestone on the other platform, (2) the reading of the latter milestone (he is supposed to have learned by heart the constant reading of his own), (3) the reading of the clock beside the milestone on the other platform, (4) the reading of his own clock, (5) any other fact of interest, such as the birth of a baby or the exact physiological age of any one, at any momentarily coincident station of the other platform, and (6) any such fact at his own station. Having seen, he is to make a true and complete record. It is to be especially emphasized that the reading of *each* of any two coincident clocks is to be witnessed and recorded by *two* observers, one on *each* platform.

A and A' are to coincide on January 1, 1900, exactly at noon, which is to be the zero hour for both systems; thus Paul's clock at A has then the reading $t = 0$, and Peter's clock at A' the reading $t' = 0$. At exactly this time Paul is to be born at A and Peter at A'. Here we have simultaneity at the same place (and therefore simultaneity shared by the two platforms) of five events, viz., the coincidence of A and A', the two clock-readings, and the two births.

Needing more babies we call for the birth of a cousin of Paul's at P on Paul's platform of time $t = 0$ by Paul's *clock* there. P is $7\sqrt{91}$ ($= 66.773$) light-seconds—a light-second being the distance light travels in a second—or $7c\sqrt{91}$ miles from A, as measured on Paul's platform, and its direction from A is that in which Peter's platform is moving relatively to Paul's. Peter will therefore in due course pass this baby. To even matters up, a cousin of Peter's is to be born at P' on Peter's platform, P' being the point coincident with P when Paul's cousin is born at P; and the birth of Peter's cousin is to occur simultaneously with the coincidence of P' with P, and consequently simultaneously with the birth of Paul's cousin at P. Here again we have simultaneity of five events at the same place, viz., the coincidence of P with P', two births, and two clock-readings. One of these readings, that of Paul's clock, is $t = 0$. But the reading of *Peter's* clock is *not* zero; it is [3] $t' = -212\frac{1}{3}$. Thus

---

[3] This result is obtained in the following way. We have four known values: the reading of the milestone at P is $x = 7c\sqrt{91}$; the reading of Paul's clock at P is

this clock of Peter's at P' is at this time slower by 212⅓ seconds than Paul's coincident clock at P. This means that, since on Peter's platform the clocks at A' and P' are synchronous, the five events at P and P' that we have just been considering occur earlier by 212⅓ seconds, by Peter's time-system, than the other five events we considered previously, viz., those at A and A' when these points were coincident; since the events at coincident P and P' occur at time $t' = -212⅓$ by Peter's clocks, whereas the events at coincident A and A' occur at time $t' = 0$ by Peter's clocks. (The reader will bear in mind that although *we* have had to calculate in order to get this result, the two *observers* at P and P' do *not have to calculate*. Being competent observers, both of them *see* the readings of both clocks.)

There is nothing in this that the logical reader need boggle at. He is already familiar with the fact that two witnesses may agree that two events take place *at the same time,* and yet may disagree as to *what* that time is, and thus may not give *the same time* to the double occurrence. In other words, the expression "the same time" is ambiguous. Your clock and mine at the same time may not give the same time. To say "at the same time" may be to assert (1) undated simultaneity, i.e., simultaneity without reference to any time-system or "calendar." (In relativity this is possible only of events at the same place.) On the other hand, it may be to assert (2) an agreement (congruence) between two clocks or calendars as to the dates of events at the same place, or (3) an equal dating of events at different places by synchronous clocks, i.e., by the same calendar. In the case before us, to say that the events at coincident

---

$t = 0$; and the constant values in our problem are $\beta = 10/3$ and $v = c\sqrt{91}/10$. We wish to ascertain the value of t' (the clock-reading at P') simultaneous with t and "at the same place" with x. We look among the Lorentz transformation-equations for one that has as its terms our five values, x, t, β, v, t'; and by substituting into it the four given values we obtain the fifth desired. The Lorentz equation that has these five terms is

$$t' = \beta(t - vx/c^2).$$

By making the indicated substitutions we get

$$t' = 10/3 \times (0 - [c\sqrt{91}/10 \times 7c\sqrt{91}]/c^2) = -(7 \times 91)/3 = -212⅓.$$

The minus sign tells us that the time t', when P and P' are coincident, is before twelve o'clock.

A and *A'*, or (*not* and) those at coincident *P* and *P'*, occur at the same time on *either* platform is to make assertion (1). To deny that the events at coincident *P* and *P'* occur at the same time on *both* platforms is to deny assertion (2). To deny that the events at coincident *A* and *A'*, and those at coincident *P* and *P'*, occur at the same time on Peter's platform is to deny assertion (3).

Lovejoy's initial mistake, *fons et origo malorum*, in his misconception of the retardation of clocks in the Special Theory, is his assumption, entirely at variance with the doctrine he is criticizing, that *because by Paul's clocks* all the four births we have been considering are simultaneous, *therefore* they are simultaneous *without qualification*, and *therefore* simultaneous *on Peter's platform*. (If I remember aright, this would be called in the Aristotelian logic a fallacy of accident. Or is it a *petitio?*) By *Paul's calendar* all four babies are "coeval" in the sense that they are "born at the same time." In this sense, the babies born at *P* and *P'* are *not* "coeval" by *Peter's calendar* with those born at *A* and *A'*. But to be "coeval" may mean to be "continuously of the same age"; in this sense, only Paul and Paul's cousin at *P* are relativistically "coeval," and they are "coeval" only by Paul's clocks. In Newtonian time these two meanings of "coeval" are exactly convertible, but they are not exactly convertible in relativity. This difference will be made clear later on in this chapter.

Meanwhile let us follow Peter as he speeds along Paul's platform until he comes directly opposite Paul's cousin at *P*. By *Paul's* clock there, this event occurs at time $t = 70$, i.e., at 70 seconds past twelve o'clock.[4] But this is not the time as given by *Peter's* clock, which on his arrival at *P* has [5] the reading $t' = 21$.

---

[4] This result is obtained thus: Peter, who was born opposite *A* at time $t = 0$ by Paul's clock there, and who travels with velocity $v = c\sqrt{91}/10$, measured on Paul's platform, covers the distance $7c\sqrt{91}$, measured on Paul's platform, by time $t = 70$ by Paul's clock at *P*, since the time taken is equal to the distance covered divided by the velocity.

[5] This result is obtained thus: We have the four known values: $x = 7c\sqrt{91}$, $t = 70$, $\beta = 10/3$, and $v = c\sqrt{91}/10$; and we wish to obtain the value of t'. The Lorentz transformation-equation that contains these five terms, viz., x, t, β, v, and t', is the one we used in footnote 3, viz., $t' = \beta(t - vx/c^2)$. By substituting into this

Now let us turn our attention to point M' on Peter's platform *west* of A' and distant from A' by $7c\sqrt{91}$, as measured on that platform. Let M be the point on Paul's platform coincident with M' at time $t' = 0$ by *Peter's* clock at M', i.e., at the same time by *Peter's* clocks as the coincidence of A with A' and the births of Peter and Paul. This coincidence does not occur at time $t = 0$ by *Paul's* clock at M; it occurs [6] at time $t = -212\frac{1}{3}$. Thus, whereas by *Peter's* clocks the coincidence of M with M' is simultaneous with the coincidence of A with A', and therefore simultaneous with the births of Peter and Paul, by *Paul's* clocks the former coincidence was earlier by $212\frac{1}{3}$ seconds than the latter coincidence and the births at A and A'. Please note again that *we* have had to calculate to find the reading of Paul's clock at M when it was coincident with M', but that the two *observers* at these points do not have to calculate; they *see* the reading.

Note also the chiastic symmetry between the readings, on the one hand, of Paul's clock at P and Peter's clock at P' when these points are coincident, and the readings, on the other hand, of Peter's clock at M' and of Paul's clock at M when these latter points are coincident. In the former case, where P and P' are in the positive direction from A and A', Paul's clock at P has the reading $t = 0$, and Peter's clock at P' has the reading $t' = -212\frac{1}{3}$. In the latter case, where M' and M lie in the *negative* direction from A' and A, and M' is as far from A' as P is from A, it is *Peter's* clock (not Paul's) that has the reading $t' = 0$, and it is *Paul's* clock (not

---

equation from the equations giving us the known values, we get the desired value $t' = 21$. What *we* here get by calculation, the two *observers* at A' and P get by looking and *seeing*.

[6] This result is obtained from a Lorentz transformation-equation, but not from the one we used in footnotes 3 and 5. That equation contained the five terms, t', t, x, β, and v. Now we have the following values as given: $x' = -7c\sqrt{91}$ (the minus sign because M' lies in the negative direction from A'), $t' = 0$, $\beta = 10/3$, and $v = c\sqrt{91}/10$; and we wish to obtain the value of t. Thus we have a term x' not found in that Lorentz equation, and that equation has a term x which we do not have as given in our present problem. But there is a Lorentz transformation-equation that does have our five terms, t', t, x', β and v. That equation is
$$t = \beta(t' + vx'/c^2).$$
We substitute into this transformation-equation the given values of t', x', β and v, and we get
$$t = 10/3 \times (0 - [c\sqrt{91}/10 \times 7c\sqrt{91}]/c^2) = -212\frac{1}{3}.$$

Peter's) that has the reading $t = -212\frac{1}{3}$. The "reciprocity" of clock-readings on the two platforms is *not* mutual reversibility of readings of clocks "at the same place"; it is symmetry with respect to similar *kinematic* conditions. The point M, going westward, is at a distance from A', measured on Peter's platform, equal to the distance, measured on Paul's platform, at which the point P', going eastward, is from A. Hence Paul's clock at M and Peter's clock at P' (M and P' *not* coincident) have *equal readings under similar kinematic conditions,* just as Paul's clock at P and Peter's clock at M' have equal readings under similar kinematic conditions. But this equality of readings is not simultaneity of readings, since the clocks with these equal readings are not on the same platform, and therefore are not synchronous.

Now, just as we followed Peter till he was passing Paul's cousin at P, let us follow Paul till he passes Peter's cousin at M'. Having passed A' at time $t' = 0$ by Peter's clock there, and having travelled with speed $c\sqrt{91}/10$ over a distance $7c\sqrt{91}$, as measured on Peter's platform, he arrives at M' at time $t' = 70$, by Peter's clock at M'. But *Paul's* clock at A, then coincident with M', does not have this reading; it has [7] the reading $t = 21$.

Here we have another example of the chiastic "reciprocity" of clock-readings on the two platforms. Since Peter and Paul both started from kinematic scratch, viz., from coincident A ($x = 0$) and A' ($x = 0$) respectively, at time $t = t' = 0$, the ratio between the readings of Peter's clock at A' and Paul's coincident clock at P, after Peter has traversed a scalar distance *eastward,* is equal to the ratio between the readings of Paul's (not Peter's) clock at A and Peter's (not Paul's) clock at M', after Paul has traversed an equal scalar distance *westward.* The symmetry does not consist in the mutual inversion of *coincident* clock-readings, as Lovejoy supposes when he makes Peter attribute to Paul's "coeval," whom he is

---

[7] Here we have the given values $t' = 70$, $x' = -7c\sqrt{91}$, $\beta = 10/3$, and $v = c\sqrt{91}/10$, and we wish to determine the value of t. The Lorentz transformation-equation that has these five terms is the one we used in footnote 6, viz., $t = \beta(t' + vx'/c^2)$. By substituting our known values into this equation we get $t = 21$.

passing, the age that the latter attributes to Peter. In relativity there is no such mutual inversion of unequal coincident clock-readings. *The relativistic reciprocity is symmetry with respect to kinematic scratch.* Here then we have another fundamental misunderstanding under which Lovejoy labors in seeking to criticize relativity.

So far we have been dealing chiefly with clock-readings "simultaneous at the same place." If relativity is true, observers, such as we have assumed, *consentiently* see, record, and report all the facts we have recorded in the text. The computations we have made in the footnotes are *ours,* not theirs. We have had to make them because we were not bodily present to witness the occurrences. It is impossible to over-emphasize the fact that there is no disagreement as to what is directly observed by competent observers at any two coincident points. If there were any, observations under similar conditions would have to be repeated till agreement should be reached. If such agreement were unobtainable we should have on our hands "a condition and not a theory." But there is no such disagreement; we have in each case, at the mouth of two witnesses, reliable data consisting of statements such as that the two coincident clocks at such and such points had severally such and such readings, and then such and such events occurred there. Where then does the "disagreement" come in?

We are all familiar with the difference between the reading of a clock and the "correct time" when the clock has this reading. In general practice we get "correct time" second-hand from Washington by consulting local Western Union clocks, intermittently synchronized by electro-magnetic impulses. But *if* every *identical* electro-magnetic impulse is to have constant velocity on each, and equal velocity on both, of our relatively moving platforms, the clocks synchronized on Peter's platform cannot have the same synchronism as those synchronized on Paul's.

Synchronism is a relation between clocks, and it consists in the fact that they (*a*) run at the same rate, and (*b*) are so set that any reading of any one of them is simultaneous with the equal reading of any other of them. If (*b*) is true (*a*) is also true, and therefore our definition is reduntant. Still, it is important to distinguish (*a*) and (*b*), for the reason that (*a*) may be true and yet (*b*) may be false. But what for our present purpose is more important is that the asynchronism of Peter's clocks as tested by Paul's, and of Paul's as tested by Peter's, cannot be understood without this distinction. According to the current Newtonian conception, we may have two groups, each consisting of clocks running at the same rate and set together, the rates, however, of the two groups not being the same. In such a case, says the Newtonian, *any observer will see that the equal readings of the clocks of either group are simultaneous,* but that readings of the clocks of one group are not, in general, simultaneous with equal readings of the clocks of the *other*. The clocks of one group will lose time as compared with those of the other; and all observers will agree which group is the loser. Any one who thinks only in terms of this conception will find the relative asynchronism of Peter's and Paul's relativistic clocks contradictory— but the contradiction will be with the terms in which he thinks, not an internal contradiction in relativity.

In order to understand relativistic time, we must not *start* with the idea that the clocks of either platform run slowly with respect to those of the other; we must start with the fact that *at no time, registered by the clocks of either platform, does any one of the clocks of the other have a reading equal to the reading of any other clock of that other platform* (unless the two latter clocks lie in a plane perpendicular to the relative motion of the platforms). In other words, the italicized statement of the preceding paragraph, which is true of Newtonian time, is not, in general, true of Einsteinian times. This is the basic difference between relativity and Newtonianism. The fact that the clocks of either platform run slowly, as measured by the synchronism of the other, is *a logical consequence* of the italicized statement of this paragraph. The relative retardation of clocks is a corollary of the intersystemic asynchronism of intrasystemically synchronous clocks, i.e., of the fact that *simultaneity* is not in general shared by the two platforms. The popular expositions of the Special Theory, being popular, fail to bring out this logical relationship between "retardation" and the fact that two relatively moving systems have disparate simultaneities. This logical relationship can be made clear only by following the *reasoning* of relativists as they proceed from the Lorentz transformation which they have derived, to the "paradoxical" conclusions which they deduce. Let us see how this reasoning runs. In this chapter it is obviously impossible to consider the *deduction* of the Lorentz transformation from the relativistic postulates. Those postulates, *if* accepted, compel the acceptance of the transformation.

To distinguish between the data involved in the acceptance of the Lorentz transformation, and the logical conclusions that follow, we shall now impose a hard law upon our "observers." *They* shall not *think* at all, in the sense of comparing any observation they may make at any time with those they may make at any other time, or with those which other observers may make "at other places." They are to do nothing but attend strictly to the six things their "competence" enables them to do; they are merely to observe and record and report—like private soldiers, theirs is not to reason why. All the records thus made on Paul's platform are to be sent to the Office of the Register of Physical Deeds at A, and all the records made on Peter's platform are to be sent to a similar office at A'. At each office is to be an intelligent accountant, whose task it is to scan all reports and to make what he can out of them. He is an ideal statistician with no axe to grind; he is impartial between the clocks of the two systems, knowing that on each platform the clocks have been properly synchronized. Of course he must begin somewhere, and we let each accountant begin with the known fact that the clocks *on his own platform* are synchronous. We are now to look over the shoulder of the accountant on Paul's platform as he works. He writes the following memoranda:

"(1) *Paul's clocks are synchronous.* At time $t = 0$ *by Paul's clock* at A, A' was at A, and at that time *Peter's* clock at A' had the reading $t' = 0$. At time $t = 70$ by Paul's clock at P, A', having meanwhile travelled eastward, was at *P*, and at that time that identical clock of *Peter's* at *A'* had the reading $t' = 21$. Thus during a time-interval of 70 seconds (i.e., the interval between $t = 0$ and $t = 70$), *as measured by Paul's synchronous clocks at A and P,* that identical clock of *Peter's* at *A'* advanced its reading by only 21 seconds. Therefore that clock of Peter's lost 49 seconds during a time-interval of 70 seconds, as measured by Paul's synchronous clocks at *A* and *P*; i.e. it lost time at the rate of 7 seconds in every 10."

Now the same accountant, knowing that *Peter's* clocks also had been properly synchronized, goes on to write as follows:

"(2) *Peter's clocks are synchronous.* At time $t' = -212\frac{1}{3}$ by *Peter's* clock at *P'*, *P* was at *P'*, and at that time *Paul's* clock at *P* had the reading $t = 0$. At time $t' = 21$ by Peter's clock at *A'*, *P*, having meanwhile travelled westward, was at *A'*, and that identical clock of Paul's at *P* had the reading $t = 70$. Thus during a time-interval of $233\frac{1}{3}$ seconds (i.e., the interval between $t' = -212\frac{1}{3}$ and $t' = 21$), *as measured by Peter's synchronous clocks at P' and A'*, that identical clock of *Paul's* at *P* advanced its reading by only 70 seconds. Therefore that clock of Paul's lost $163\frac{1}{3}$ seconds during a time-interval of $233\frac{1}{3}$ seconds, as measured by Peter's synchronous clocks at *P'* and *A'*; i.e., it lost time at the rate of 7 seconds in every 10."

Resorting to algebraic instead of arithmetical numbers,[8] and being an impartial accountant, who desires to avoid the appearance of making statistics lie by failing to tell the whole truth, he writes:

"*Measured by the synchronism of Paul's clocks,*[9] any one of

---

[8] Let us call Paul's platform *S*, and Peter's *S'*. At *any* point *P* ($x = n$) on *S* at *any* time $t = a$, the *S'* clock at *P'*, then coincident with *P*, has the reading $t' = \beta(t - vx/c^2) = \beta(a - vn/c^2)$. *P'*, moving with constant velocity v in the positive *x*-direction of *S*, arrives at any point $Q(x = n + m)$ at time $t = a + m/v$. At that time the clock at *P'* has the reading $t' = \beta(t - vx/c^2) = \beta(a + m/v - v[n + m]/c^2)$. Thus during the time-interval which has the measure m/v by the *S* clocks at *P* and *Q*, synchronous on *S*, the clock at *P'* on *S'* advances its reading by $\beta(m/v - vm/c^2) = m/\beta v$. Thus whatever clock on *S'* is coincident with *any* clock on *S* at *any* time, will, after traversing *any* distance, have lost time, as measured by synchronous clocks in *S*, at the rate of $(\beta - 1)$ seconds in every second. A symmetrical result is obtained for any clock in *S*, as measured by synchronous clocks in *S'*, by using the transformation-equation $t = \beta(t' + vx'/c^2)$.

[9] It is to be observed that our accountant uses the word "measured" instead of

Peter's clocks loses time, in going from any point to any other point on Paul's platform, at the rate of 7 seconds in every 10; i.e., it runs only 3/10 as fast as Paul's clocks." Then he adds as a footnote: "*Measured by the synchronism of Peter's clocks,* any one of *Paul's* clocks loses time, in going from any point to any other point of Peter's platform, at the rate of 7 seconds in every 10, i.e., it runs only 3/10 as fast as Peter's clocks."

If we now look over the shoulder of Peter's accountant we shall find that the only difference between what he writes and what Paul's wrote is that the memorandum which Paul's accountant numbered (2) Peter's accountant numbers (1), and *vice versa;* and that what Paul's accountant put into a footnote Peter's accountant puts into the text, and *vice versa.* Such unanimity among accountants is surprising—at any rate it is refreshing—but what are we to expect from impartial and competent accountants who have exactly the same data to interpret?

Let us review carefully what each accountant has done. He compares (*a*) the reading of a clock on one platform with the reading of a coincident clock on the other platform, and (*b*) a later reading of the former clock with the reading of the then coincident clock on the other platform; and he treats the clocks on that other platform as synchronous, since they have been synchronized on their platform. Each of these comparisons gives the same result for both accountants. The only difference that can arise is a difference of *preference;* each naturally prefers to use the synchronism of the clocks on his own platform—it is more convenient, and in fact the convenience amounts to a physical necessity for *observers,* since an observing physicist has at his disposal only his *own* instruments, including chronometers. Our set-up with "competent" observers is an ideal one. A physicist would be decidedly

---

the word "judged," frequently employed by other accountants. In this connection they mean the same thing; but the latter is often misinterpreted as if the "judgment" were not necessary in view of the numerical data furnished and of the fact that the clocks in each system have been physically synchronized. There is nothing subjective in our accountant's statement, any more than if he were to say, "Measured by this meter-stick, this bar of iron is 2 meters long."

embarrassed if, with chronometers flying by him at every conceivable speed short of the velocity of light and in every direction, *he had to read every one.* He uses his own synchronism for the same reason that the terrestrial astronomer uses as *the* astronomical year the time-interval that is required for the *earth* to complete a revolution around the sun, although he is aware that *each planet has its own year.* Which is *the* true, *the* absolute, *the* cosmic year? The answer to *this* question is in principle the relativistic answer to the question: Which is *the* correct time-system? It happens that the transformation from the terrestrial year into the Martian year is not the same as that from Paul's synchronism into Peter's, but the latter is not necessarily "subjective" for that reason.

If we have followed the reasoning of the accountants, we have seen that the reciprocal retardation of the clocks on the two platforms is not reciprocal inversion of *coincident* clock-readings. It is *because* there is *no such* reciprocity, e.g., it is *because* the clocks at coincident P and P', and at coincident A' and P, have unequal and noninterchangeable readings when these points are respectively coincident, that the relativist concludes that the clocks of either system run slowly as measured by the synchronism of the other. If the readings of coincident clocks *were* interchangeable, as Lovejoy supposes, there would be no reciprocal retardation—there would be temporal chaos. Just try it out.

Now let us suppose that Peter's heart and the hearts of all his cousins beat once every second *by his clocks,* and that Paul's heart and the hearts of all his cousins beat once every second *by his clocks.* Let us further suppose that all the other physiological processes of each of these babies run at a normal rate as measured by his heartbeats. In accordance with this assumption, Peter is 21 seconds old *physiologically* when he arrives at P, since his clocks have ticked off 21 seconds since his birth. On the other hand Paul's cousin at P is 70 seconds old physiologically when Peter arrives at P, since Paul's clocks have ticked off 70 seconds since this cousin's birth. The two competent observers at A'' and P agree in recording these respective physiological ages. Neither observer attributes to Paul's cousin the physiological age that the other attributes to Peter, nor *vice versa*. Our observers have to do only with clock readings and with events and facts simultaneous with these readings at the same place with these readings. The automatic relative motion of the platforms and the automatic movements of the clocks and of physiological processes furnish them with events and facts to be observed.

But the *accountants,* when they receive and examine the reports sent them, *compute the time-intervals involved,* and in doing this they discover that they must *distinguish between physiological and calendar ages.* Before they became relativists they had been familiar with this distinction. For instance, a child born in Moscow on January 1, 1800, O.S., was one year old by the Russian calendar on January 1, 1801, O.S. But by the calendar used elsewhere in Europe he was one year and one day old. The fact that the child had two calendar ages did not give him two physiological ages. Where two different calendars are employed, the same physiological age is compatible with two calendar ages. In relativity each of two relatively moving systems has its own distinctive calendar. By the supposition made in the preceding paragraph, the calendar age of any person, by the calendar of his *own* system, is equal to his physiological age. But his calendar age by the calendar of another system, which we shall for short call his "heterochronic age," is not equal to his physiological age. We now let our accountants work out the problem.

"*Paul's clocks are synchronous.* Peter, having been born at time $t = 0$ by Paul's clocks, arrived (21 seconds old physiologically) at P at time $t = 70$ by Paul's clocks. Hence on Peter's arrival at P his heterochronic age by Paul's calendar (i.e., the *measure* of the interval between Peter's birth and his arrival at P, as given by Paul's clocks) was 70 seconds, and this heterochronic age was $3\frac{1}{3}$ times his physiological age.

"*Peter's clocks are synchronous.* Paul's cousin at P, having been born at time $t' = -212\frac{1}{3}$ by Peter's clocks, arrived (70 seconds old physiologically) at A' at time $t' = 21$ by Peter's clocks. Hence on

Paul's cousin's arrival at A' his heterochronic age by Peter's calendar (i.e., the *measure* of the interval between Paul's cousin's birth and his arrival at A', as given by Peter's clocks) was $233\frac{1}{3}$ seconds, and this heterochronic age was $3\frac{1}{3}$ times his physiological age."

Note that neither the heterochronic nor the physiological ages of Peter and of Paul's cousin are respectively interchangeable. It is true that Peter's heterochronic age is equal to Paul's cousin's physiological age, but the reverse is not true. The "reciprocity" involved here is in the *ratio* of heterochronic to physiological age. Each has a heterochronic age 10/3 his physiological age. We may not like the calendars the relativist employs on his platforms, and therefore may not choose to run with him on them. But this does not justify us in misrepresenting the facts on his platform and then accusing him of contradiction—unless we choose to adopt the kind of logic that Lovejoy (or for that matter any of us at times, unless we are very careful) employs in dealing with those he criticizes.

Lovejoy thinks (pp. 155-156) that since "number (of discrete individuals) is an absolute quantity," the Special Theory is committed to an absurdity in treating durational lengths as respective. But the absurdity is in his imagination, not in relativity. All the *numerical* data involved, in the case of Peter and Paul, are agreed upon by both our accountants; just as you and I, travelling together, may agree that we passed 10 milestones while your watch was ticking off 15 minutes and mine 14. We agree on the count of everything we count, when we count the *same* things: milestones, your watch-ticks and my watch-ticks. We might under these circumstances dispute as to *how long* it took us to pass those milestones, unless we agreed that it took 15 minutes by your watch and 14 by mine. So far as the analogy holds, this is just what happens in relativity. The physiological ages of Peter and Paul, counted by heartbeats, are analogous to the milestones, and their heterochronic ages to your 15 minutes and my 14. All observers agree on the count of everything they count. It is agreed by all relativists that Peter's clock at A' ticked, and Peter's heart beat, 21 times from his birth till his arrival at P; and that the heart of Paul's cousin beat, and Paul's clock at P ticked, 70 times from *this* cousin's birth till Peter's arrival at P. The "discrete individuals" here are these clockticks and these heartbeats. Their number is "absolute" in the sense that *all* agree on the count. But when the question arises *how long* it took for these two sets of heartbeats and clockticks to run off, there is a double answer, depending upon the synchronism used. By Paul's synchronism, Peter and Paul's cousin were born at the same time; therefore, since Peter's heart, 70 seconds later by Paul's clock, had beat only 21 times, and that of Paul's cousin had beat 70 times, Peter was growing old physiologically only 3/10 as fast as Paul's cousin. By Peter's synchronism, Paul's cousin was born $212\frac{1}{3}$ seconds before Peter; therefore, since Paul's cousin's heart, $233\frac{1}{3}$ seconds later by Peter's clock, had beat only 70 times, and that of Peter $233\frac{1}{3}$ times, Paul's cousin was growing old only 3/10 as fast as Peter. There is no difference as to any count; there is difference only as to the *dates* at which the counting begins and ends; and on the two platforms the dates are different because different calendars are used. Again, the idea that Paul should have eaten only 365 and also 25,550 breakfasts during a certain trip is of course absurd, but it is Lovejoy's idea (p. 155) attributed to the relativist. There is surely no absurdity in the idea that the number of hours taken to eat 365 breakfasts varies with the clocks used to measure the time-factor of the breakfast-eating process. The number of breakfasts any one on a relativist platform eats in making a trip is "absolute." The *time* it takes to make the trip, *when measured,* gives different measure-numbers according to the different clocks used in measuring. Lovejoy himself admits this when he says that "even this [lack of 'accord' in 'time-measurements'] would not amount to a contradiction" (p. 51). The correctness of his article lies mainly in his verbal insistence on thinking straight.

We are now ready to answer the question, What would happen if Peter were to *reverse his direction* and return to Paul, and "if the acceleration in the reversal were treated as theoretically negligible"? We shall treat "theoretically negligible" as synonymous with "having no physical effects." Let us add another platform to our set-up and call it "John's platform." It is to be parallel to the other two and in unaccelerated motion relatively to them. It moves relatively to Paul's platform in the direction opposite to that in which Peter's moves; and its speed relative to Paul's is 177,425 miles per second. It is equipped as the others, i.e., with clocks properly synchronized with milestones, and with observers. We designate as A'' the point on it that is coincident with A and A' when these points are coincident with each other; at that time John's clock at A'' is to have the reading $t'' = 0$. We designate as K'' the point on John's platform coincident with P and A', when these points are coincident with each other, i.e., at time $t = 70$ and $t' = 21$. Thus on Peter's arrival at P, K'' is passing P going the other way.

This set-up is in accord with the Special Theory of Relativity. We now introduce a new assumption, not contemplated in that theory: we imagine both Peter and his clock at A' to be instantaneously transferred to K'' when directly opposite K''. This transfer thus takes place when Peter is 21 seconds old physiologically, and when his clock has the reading $t' = 21$. The transfer is to have no disturbing effects on Peter's physiological processes or upon Peter's clock other than that after it both Peter and his clock are to carry on just at the same rate as if they had been indigenous to John's platform. (This is of course a most violent supposition, as the transfer is a most violent transfer; but we are not responsible for either. We are following Lovejoy's supposition, and merely wish to see whether his inference from it is correct.) Peter's heart continues to beat with his clockticks, and his clock now runs at the same rate as the clock originally at K''; the difference between its reading and that of the original clock at K'' is to remain constant. Now that original clock at K'' has the reading[10] $t'' = 445\frac{2}{3}$ when the transfer is made, and Peter's transferred clock has the reading $t' = 21$. Hence after the transfer Peter's clock is to be constantly slower than John's at K'' by $424\frac{2}{3}$ seconds. Peter, now retracing his movement with the same speed back as he had on his outbound journey, reaches A at time $t = 140$ by Paul's clock at A, at which time John's clock at K'' has the reading[10] $t'' = 466\frac{2}{3}$. Hence Peter's transferred clock has then the reading 42, and Peter's physiological age, which has been advancing in the rhythm of his clock, is 42 seconds. There is no "reciprocal" retardation of clocks after the return journey has been completed. *It is the clock that reversed its direction that is slow.* Lovejoy desires that, since relative motion is relative and reciprocal, reversal of relative motion shall be reciprocal in its effects upon clock-readings and physiological processes. But we are dealing with *Einstein's relativity;* and when dealing with Einstein's relativity, we must use his relativity-*equations*. The physical theory of relativity is not just the classical theory of the relativity of motion dressed up in mathematical clothes. The only *logical* consistency that any theory is required to have is consistency *with itself*, not consistency with some one's preconceived notion, or even with some one else's internally consistent notions.

Now let us see what the comparative ages of Peter and Paul would be when they met, if *each* were to be transferred instantaneously to the other's platform, on the assumption that the transfers are to have no disturbing effects, and that they are made under similar kinematic conditions. Peter is to be transferred after he has travelled a given distance along Paul's platform, and Paul after he has travelled an equal distance along Peter's. Let Peter be transferred when he has arrived at P, and Paul when he has arrived at M'. Each is thus transferred to the other's platform when he is 21 seconds old physiologically. When they meet, each

---

[10] This result is obtained by using for John's clock at K'' the Lorentz transformation-equation $t'' = \beta(t + vx/c^2)$. Into this we first substitute $x = 7c\sqrt{91}$, and $t = 70$, and the constant values for β and v, getting $t'' = 1337/3 = 445\frac{2}{3}$ for the reading of John's clock at K'' at the time of the transfer; and then we substitute $x = 0$, $t = 140$, and the constant values for β and v, into the same transformation-equation and get $t'' = 1400/3 = 466\frac{2}{3}$ for the reading of John's clock at K'' when it arrives at A. Thus John's clock has advanced its reading by 21 seconds in going from P to A. Peter's clock, having the reading 21 on the transfer, and advancing its reading *pari passu* thereafter with John's, has the reading 42 on Peter's return to A.

is 42 seconds old physiologically.[11] Thus the equal accelerations undergone by the two babies under similar kinematic conditions, and under the assumption that these accelerations have no disturbing effects, bring them back to each other with equal physiological ages.

* * * * * *

Let us now in terms of years instead of seconds tell the story of Peter and Paul moving relatively at the furious speeds of 177,425 miles a second on their unaccelerated platforms.

Peter at the physiological age of 21 years, on January 1, 1921 (by his calendar), was passing one of Paul's "coeval" cousins at Q (born simultaneously with Paul by Paul's calendar). This man was at that time 70 years old physiologically; for he was born on January 1, 1900, by Paul's calendar, and his heart had been beating once every second by Paul's clocks; and now it was January 1, 1970, by Paul's calendar. Peter had been told some ten years and nine months ago[12] that news had been received of the birth of this cousin of Paul's as having occurred on September 1, 1687, by Peter's calendar. This man therefore was 233⅓ years old by Peter's calendar when Peter was passing him. Peter was astonished to see this man still alive, in spite of his nearly twelve-score years—he surely looked like a mighty fine specimen of a super-bicentenarian. Peter could not understand it, for in the lifetime of this prospective Methuselah the fountains

---

[11] Let us work out the answer algebraically, and then apply the answer to our arithmetical setup. Let v be any positive constant less than c, and let n be any positive constant. Peter, having been at $A(x=0)$ at time $t=0$, reaches point $D(x=n)$ at time $t=n/v$ by Paul's clock there, and Peter's clock has then the reading $t' = \beta(t - vx/c^2) = \beta(n/v - vn/c^2) = n/\beta v$. His clock is therefore at that time slower than Paul's clock at D by $n/v - n/\beta v = n(\beta - 1)/\beta v$.

Paul, having been at A' at time $t'=0$, reaches $E'(x'=-n)$ at time $t'=n/v$ by Peter's clock there, and Paul's clock then reads $t = \beta(t' + vx'/c^2) = \beta(n/v - vn/c^2) = n/\beta v$. His clock is therefore slower than Peter's clock at that time by $n(\beta - 1)/\beta v$.

The points D and E' pass each other at time $t = t' = n(\beta + 1)/\beta v$, this being the reading of the *indigenous* clocks at D and E'. We get this result by substituting $x = n$ and $x' = -n$ into the Lorentz equation $x' = \beta(x - vt)$, and solving for t; and then into the Lorentz equation $x = \beta(x' + vt')$, and solving for t'.

Since the transferred clocks are slower, each than the indigenous clock beside it, by $n(\beta - 1)/\beta v$, both, on passing each other, have the reading $n(\beta + 1)/\beta v - n(\beta - 1)/\beta v = 2n/\beta v$. Since the heart-beats of Peter and Paul have been running off in the rhythm of their clocks, they are both $2n/\beta v$ seconds old in passing each other.

If now we substitute for n the value $7c\sqrt{91}$ and for v and β their respective numerical values in our set-up, we get the readings of the transferred clocks, on their passing each other, as being 42.

[12] The reader is now probably able to work this out for himself.

of youth had run completely dry. There was something devilishly queer about it all; for now that he came to think of it, he had passed several other men who were said to be very old but looked quite otherwise. He began to wish that he knew the secret of living two and one-third centuries without showing the ravages of labor and sorrow; he even had the passing wish that he had been born on the other platform, where age sits so lightly on the sons of men. However, being 21 and in love, he gave these matters only a moment's thought; there were other things more important.

Paul's cousin, on his side of the anti-friction clearance, was likewise puzzled. He had learned, some three years and three months ago,[12] of the birth of Peter as having occurred when he himself was born, and he had lately been kept informed by the *Daily Platform* of Peter's rapid approach. When Peter did whirl by, he could not believe his eyes. Instead of being a septuagenarian like himself, Peter proved to be a remarkably handsome lad, not more than 21; he must have resorted to goat glands or hormones or whatever it was that in 1970 had long been noised abroad as effective antidotes for old age. Whatever it was, he himself had not found it effective in his own case; the practitioners had taken his money and left him his years. Perhaps he had been born on the wrong platform; on the other, youth preservers must be more potent! Having heard of relativity but not knowing more about it than that it proposed rapid travel as the way to keep from growing old, he now suspected that it must be true. Finally in a mood, mixed of high resolve and desperation, he jumped over to the other platform, where under the ministration of relativists he might get the benefit of speed for the rest of his days.—And that was the last seen or directly heard of that cousin of Paul's. Neither hide nor hair of him could be found.

Peter, however, soon thereafter got word by wireless that there had been a terrific platform-quake some way down the line. Coming so soon after the passing of Paul's cousin, so old and yet so spry, this news set him a-wondering whether there might not be some connection between the strange events that were taking place in his neighborhood. The miracle that had transformed a man over 233 years old into a sprightly though gray-haired buck might account for anything else. He bethought him of the accountant he had heard of as a very learned man, and betook himself to him and introduced himself as Paul's "coeval." He now remembered that word, and one thing leading to another he asked for news of Paul. He was told that Paul was probably getting along splendidly; he must now be getting his first molars, for he must be over six years and three and a half months old.[12] This completely bowled him over; he was done with this accountant and all his ilk. He set out hot-foot for Hannah, who soothed him by promising to keep her world-line always as close to his as possible in this new Space-Time, which people were beginning to talk so much about.

This is the authentic story of the Paradox of the Time-Retarding Journey in the Special Theory of Relativity, as told by relativists in the privacy of their nurseries. All my relativistic friends tell me that at bedtime their children cry for it, and when they get it they "just lap it up." Like all children, they know by heart the stories repeatedly told them; and when a father, just to tease his little ones, mixes up the ages of Peter and Paul's cousin, they shout the correction in unison of protest. I am afraid that in any of these nurseries Lovejoy's story would provoke a storm of derision. Just where he picked it up I do not know. He is certainly correct in speaking of it as "pleasing"; but why did he call it a "pleasing *relativistic Märchen*"?

Chapter XI

SPACE-TIME, SIMPLE LOCATION, AND PREHENSION IN WHITEHEAD'S PHILOSOPHY

In retrospect we can now see that the publication of Mr. Whitehead's *Organisation of Thought* in 1917 was the herald of the coming of an important protagonist into the arena of philosophy. He was already well known in mathematical circles, but only a few philosophers, at least on this side of the water, had ever heard of him. Within three years we were all reading *The Principles of Natural Knowledge* and *The Concept of Nature* greatly to our profit and enlightenment. And we needed the enlightenment. There had been a rumor for some time bruited about among us of a new theory in physics called the theory of relativity; but most of us had a vague idea that it was of concern only to physicists, that somehow it solved problems in that field by proving that space by itself and time by itself were only shadows cast by space-time, which alone had independent reality. But the theory, so we were told, could be understood only by adepts in higher mathematics, mathematics so high as to be utterly out of reach of a pedestrian philosopher. We even heard that not more than a dozen mathematicians could master the elements of the theory. No wonder that we had all become defeatists and drew into our own shells, where we might hope to withstand the assaults of the mystical giant Abracadabra, who could make the less appear the greater length.

Such was the general situation when along came Mr. Whitehead, speaking a language that for the most part we could understand and employing equations that after considerable brushing up we could follow. There might be some sense in relativity after all. At least it became evident that, for better or for worse, relativity had been plunked down right within our very shells by one who showed himself a philosopher. We could no longer ignore it. But it took some of us a long time to come to terms with it, and some of us apparently still regard it as an enemy of clear thought. But there it is, and there it bids fair to stay. And Mr. Whitehead is largely responsible for its being there in our own bailiwick.

For one I am very grateful to him for what he has done. But he not only has forced relativity upon our recognition, if not upon our acceptance. After he had rewritten relativity to his own liking in *The Principle of Relativity,* he proceeded to use it as a building stone in a new philosophical structure which he called "the philosophy of organism" or "organic mechanism," and beguiled us into reading it by writing some of the choicest prose ever used in a brief outline of the development of modern thought. This he did in the first two-thirds of *Science and the Modern World.* And when he had us thoroughly charmed, he thrust upon us his "prehensions" and his "fallacy of simple location," his God as "the ultimate limitation, and His existence" as "the ultimate irrationality." Mr. Whitehead is a master of propaedeutics: he would not have his disciples cross their bridges till they came to them, but when they did come, what staggeringly steep bridges! We had hardly caught our breaths before he displayed to us reality in process in *Process and Reality.* And most of us have not yet done with catching our breaths. There we have again, after years of dormancy, philosophy in the grand manner. It is truly a great work; few have ever been greater.

In my copy of it I put under my name the date of its purchase, "1929." I see that it is also the date of its publication. Ever since that date it has been the subject of recurrent study, both in privacy and in the fellowship of other students. The time thus spent has been repaid with usury, leaving me greatly in debt. There is much that I still do not understand, as will appear in sequel. But even where I cannot understand the solutions Mr. Whitehead offers for the problems he discusses, I have come to realize more keenly the significance of the problems and the necessity of grappling with them afresh. And oddly enough, the failure to understand has often not had the result such failures usually have. I have in many cases the vague feeling that if I only could get the right hold on his solutions I should see that they are tenable. Each item in his philosophy leaves on me the impression the famous "flower in the crannied wall" left on Tennyson. Or shall I make a more homely comparison? An attempt to get my teeth into Mr. Whitehead's philosophy reminds me of the struggle of a squirrel with a cocoanut. He knows that there is something inside that would satisfy could he but get at it; but all that he can do is to roll it around; his jaws are too small, or to put it the other way about, the nut is too big and too round.[1] But even a cocoanut has "eyes" through which teeth lucky enough to find them may get at the meat inside. Sometimes I think that I have hit upon such eyes, but still there is meat beyond my reach.

Another difficulty in understanding Mr. Whitehead is what one should expect of any philosopher whose publications range through more than a score of years, during which his views have been developing. One has no right to expect him publicly to retract every sentence he has written that he now would not write again. Henry James tried to do this in part by rewriting some of his novels, but the result has not been such as to tempt a philosopher to follow his example. In studying Mr. Whitehead's earlier works,

---

[1] Some years ago a story was circulated here in Madison, and I got it from one of the participants in the events narrated. A distinguished dean and several other equally distinguished biologists, all of them enthusiastic investigators, decided on a novel experiment. A cocoanut was placed on the flat roof of a porch overhung by a branch of a tree frequented by squirrels; and the issue was eagerly awaited, with notebooks out and pencils poised, ready to record every item with split-second date. It was not long before things began to happen. A squirrel jumped down to the roof, squirrel enough to know a nut when he saw and smelt it. For minutes, long to the spectators and doubtless long also to the squirrel, the nut was pushed hither and yon, till it finally rolled off the roof and smashed the skull of a dog that happened to be strolling by. The tale has a moral: Had the nut been less round, the dog's head were now sound.

one is not seldom left wondering whether what one finds there will fit into the later scheme or whether it has been demoded by what follows. Hence it is the part of prudence to raise the question without flatly attributing contradiction to the philosopher. For this reason I will take up some of Mr. Whitehead's works in chronological order, confining my attention to five. Of these five *The Principles of Natural Knowledge, The Concept of Nature,* and *The Principle of Relativity,* all published within the course of three years, evidently constitute an integrated group. One important thought running through the three is that the universe consists in part of "contingent" facts and relations and in part of "systematic relatedness," and that any definiteness of character "is gained through the relatedness and not the relatedness through the character."[2] This idea controls Whitehead's "explosion of an alternative rendering of the theory of relativity." "My whole course of thought," he tells us, "presupposes the magnificent stroke of genius by which Einstein and Minkowski assimilated time and space."[3] But he does not accept Einstein's philosophy of nature.

> The metrical formulae finally arrived at are those of the earlier theory [of Einstein], but the meanings ascribed to the algebraic symbols are entirely different. As the result of a consideration of the character of our knowledge in general, and of our knowledge of nature in particular, undertaken in Part I of this book and in my two previous works on this subject, I deduce that our experience requires and exhibits a basis of uniformity, and that in the case of nature this basis exhibits itself as the uniformity of spatio-temporal relations. This conclusion entirely cuts away the casual heterogeneity of these relations which is the essential of Einstein's later theory. . . . It is inherent in my theory to maintain the old division between physics and geometry. Physics is the science of the contingent relations of nature, and geometry expresses its uniform relatedness.[4]

Apparently results obtainable only by experiments exhibit "contingent relations of nature," whereas results obtained by purely logical processes are alone expressive of nature's "uniform related-

---
[2] Whitehead, *The Principle of Relativity,* p. 19.
[3] *Ibid.,* p. 88.
[4] *Ibid.,* p. v-vi.

ness." With this distinction in mind, let us review Mr. Whitehead's criticism of Einstein's special theory of relativity.

> The reason why the velocity of light has been adopted as the standard velocity in the definition of simultaneity is because the negative results of the experiments to determine the earth's motion require that this velocity, which is the "c" of Maxwell's equations, should have this property. Also light signals are after all our only way of detecting distant events. . . .
> But there are certain objections to the acceptance of Einstein's definition of simultaneity, the "signal-theory" as we will call it. In the first place, light signals are very important elements in our lives, but still we cannot but feel that the signal-theory somewhat exaggerates their position. The very meaning of simultaneity is made to depend on them. There are blind people and dark cloudy nights, and neither blind people nor people in the dark are deficient in a sense of simultaneity. They know quite well what it means to bark both their shins at the same instant. In fact the determination of simultaneity in this way is never made, and if it could be made would not be accurate; for we live in air and not *in vacuo*.[5]

This passage calls for several comments. In the first place, Mr. Whitehead must have been aware of the fact that Einstein makes a fundamental distinction between simultaneity *at the same place* and simultaneity *at a distance*. Any man's two shins are (of course not precisely) in the same place, and so are my watch and a train I see arriving at a station. And yet of watch and train Einstein says:

> If, for instance, I say, "That train arrives here at 7 o'clock," I mean something like this: "The pointing of the small hand of my watch to 7 and the arrival of the train are simultaneous events."

And he expressly says the simultaneity thus defined

> is satisfactory when we are concerned with defining a time exclusively for the place where the watch is located; but it is no longer satisfactory when we have to connect in time series of events occurring at different places, or—what comes to the same thing—to evaluate the times of events occurring at places remote from the watch.[6]

---
[5] Whitehead, *The Principles of Natural Knowledge*, p. 53. Until further notice subsequent quotations are to the immediately following passages.
[6] "Zur Elektrodynamik bewegter Körper," in *Das Relativitätsprinzip*. Hereafter I shall, as in Chapter IX, refer to the German edition as "*R*" and to the English translated as "Eng." I shall include the name of the author of the paper referred to. In this way confusion is avoided between the collection of papers and Mr. Whitehead's volume which bears the same title.

Of course such judgments of simultaneity are never ideally precise, not even, as we have seen, in the case of the barking of one's two shins. But without such direct experiences of simultaneity we probably should never have got any idea of simultaneity. Mr. Whitehead is thus obviously in error when he says of Einstein's definition of simultaneity: "The very meaning of simultaneity is made to depend on light signals." He is also in error when he says: "In fact the determination of simultaneity in this way [i.e., by electromagnetic signals] is never made." Any one who checks his clocks by radio is determining simultaneity at a distance in this way; and if it be objected that when this statement was made radio was not in very general use, the reply is that "Western Union clocks" have been in use in America for many years.

But is the telegraphic transmission of signals transmission *in vacuo?* Of course not. As Mr. Whitehead says, "we live in air and not *in vacuo,*" and telegraphy lives in metal wires. But it is of course not bringing news to him when it is pointed out that absolute precision is never attained in experimental physics. Einstein's problem was to "define" some method whereby we can determine with as great precision as possible what events at a distance from each other are simultaneous, since the extrapolation of the felt simultaneity of barked shins, without more ado, did not seem to him to be satisfactory. Such a fact as that "we live in air and not *in vacuo*" has never in modern physics been regarded as a valid objection against the assumption in physics that there are physical constants. Physics obtains its "constants" by devious methods of successive approximations, and the velocity of light *in vacuo* and in the absence of gravitational fields is one of these constants. These constants are indeed "contingent" facts, and therefore for the present we admit that Mr. Whitehead has scored a point—but we will return to this point later.

Also there are other physical messages from place to place. There is the transmission of material bodies, the transmission of sound, the transmission of waves and ripples on the surface of water, the transmission of nerve excitation through the body, and innumerable other forms which enter into habitual experience. The transmission of light is only one form among many.

But there has never been any evidence offered that these other innumerable forms of transmission have the character that the prevalent interpretation of innumerable experiments gives to the propagation of light *in vacuo,* namely, the character of having the same velocity in both of two systems in relative motion, a character that Mr. Whitehead grants to it "as an approximation."[7]

One of the most surprising objections that Mr. Whitehead makes to the "signal theory" is given next:

> Furthermore local time does not concern one material particle only. The same definition of simultaneity holds throughout the whole space of a consentient set in the Newtonian group. The message theory does not account for the consentience in time-reckoning which characterises a consentient set, nor does it account for the fundamental position of the Newtonian group.

The first of these sentences surely is not meant to imply that Einstein held to Lorentz's view with regard to "local time." It has been very generally recognized that Einstein did away with local time that concerned "one material particle only." He organized Lorentz's "local times" into time systems each extending throughout a whole system at rest. He did not call these time systems "consentient sets," but this at worst can only be regarded as failure to hit upon a felicitous terminology. He did not account for "the fundamental position of the Newtonian group" because he did not recognize that fundamental position. On the contrary, he denied that the Newtonian group is fundamental. This group is for him a limiting group but not a fundamental group. To charge him with failure to account for "the fundamental position of the Newtonian group" is to beg the question: *Is* the Newtonian group fundamental? It is difficult to see how this question can be answered dogmatically in view of the fact that all pure geometries

---

[7] Whitehead, *The Concept of Nature,* p. 195.

—Euclidean, Riemannian, and others—rest on postulates and not on self-evident axioms, whereas all physical geometries involve what Mr. Whitehead calls "contingent factors." *As a matter of fact and not of logic*, is physical space Euclidean, Riemannian, or other? It would seem as if the only way to answer this question is to go to the laboratory, and the results of laboratory experiments are "contingent." They are what they are, but they might conceivably have been otherwise.

This raises the whole question as to the relation between physics and mathematics in the construction of the philosophy of nature. Is the physicist required to dig into the foundations of mathematics and work out a satisfactory logical theory as to these foundations before he has a right to make use of whatever extant mathematics is available for his purpose? Is not the relation between physicist and mathematician one of co-operation, in which the physicist is entitled to depend on the mathematician for the mathematics he uses, just as the mathematician may follow the lead of the physicist in deciding what further developments in pure mathematics are in order to meet the demands of the physicist? "Once in the bluest of blue moons," a physicist may arise who is also a mathematical genius and who, in order to solve his physical problem, establishes a new branch of mathematics on a secure logical basis. Being an ignorant layman in the history of mathematics, I have to depend on hearsay evidence that Newton was such a genius. What Einstein did in working out his special theory was to accept from mathematics the Euclidean notions of straight lines, parallels and perpendiculars, without asking whether these notions could be defined by assuming families of parallel durations and by subjecting the durations to "the method of extensive abstraction." What Mr. Whitehead has done is to make this assumption and to develop this method, and then to go to the results of the laboratory to find that "within the limits of our inexactitude of observation the velocity of light is an approximation to the critical velocity c which expresses the relation between our space and time units."[8] Mr. Whitehead and Einstein started from the opposite sides of the field of co-operative enterprise; and, when they met in the same equations, Mr. Whitehead seems in effect to have greeted his fellow worker with the charge that there is only one side from which to start in order to secure a philosophy of nature. In philosophy uniform relatedness always must come first (so he insistently asserts), and then find the contingent facts for it to relate—*never* the other way about! In other words, definiteness of character "is gained through the relatedness and not the relatedness through the character." Otherwise you have only "the casual heterogeneity of these relations"!

But before considering whether Einstein's "heterogeneity" of spatio-temporal relations was so hopelessly "casual," let us return to Einstein's definition of simultaneity at a distance. I am not sure whether I have touched upon the real nerve center controlling Mr. Whitehead's reaction to this definition. Other critics of this definition at any rate have argued that it is arbitrary; and the argument is so important that it is worth while here to discuss it, whether Mr. Whitehead would underwrite it or not. Let us quote the passage in which this definition is given:

> If at the point A of space there is a clock, an observer at A can determine the time values of events in the immediate proximity of A by finding the positions of the hands which are simultaneous with these events. [The reader will observe here that Einstein repeats that something similar to the felt simultaneity of barked shins is the basis of his further discussion.] If there is at the point B of space another clock in all respects resembling the one at A, it is possible for an observer at B to determine the time values of events in the immediate neighborhood of B. But it is not possible without further assumption [*Festsetzung*] to compare, in respect of time, an event at A with an event at B. We have so far defined only an "A time" and a "B time." We have not defined a common "time" for A and B, for the latter cannot be defined at all unless we establish *by definition* [*man durch Definition festsetzt*] that the "time" required by light to travel from A to B equals the "time" it requires to travel from B to A. Let a ray of light start at the "A time" t_A from A toward B, let it at the "B time" t_B be reflected at B in the

---
[8] *Ibid.*, p. 195.

Space-Time, Simple Location and Prehension 347

direction of A, and arrive again at A at the "A time" t'_A. In accordance with definition the two clocks synchronize if

$$t_B - t_A = t'_A - t_B.[9]$$

This passage requires especial attention. In the first place, it is to be noted that, beginning with the fourth sentence, the word "time" appears eight times, and every time it is enclosed in quotation marks. The reason should be obvious. The reason is that "time" is here used in three different senses. "A time" and "B time" are separate *dates* as given by the respective clocks on the occasions of the respective events mentioned; whereas in the clause "that the 'time' required by light to travel from A to B equals the 'time' it requires to travel from B to A," the word "time" means *time interval*. And there is a third "time," namely "a common 'time' for A and B."

In the second place, it is to be noted that what one *"durch Definition festsetzt"* is *not* the meaning of *simultaneity*, but the *equality of the two time intervals* here mentioned. And it should be obvious that the equality of two time intervals is not the same thing as the simultaneity of two events.

In the third place, we shall have to discover what is meant by the expression *"durch Definition festsetzt."* Whatever be the meaning, it is natural that we should interpret the meaning of the verb *festsetzen* in the same way in which we interpret that of the noun *Festsetzung* used in the previous sentence.

In the fourth place, the paragraph we have quoted does not stand alone. There are six others following it in the same section, which is entitled "Definition of Simultaneity"; and in the third paragraph of the next section there is a reference back to our paragraph. I suggest that we take the whole context into consideration; and since those who have worked forward have so sadly failed to see what Einstein was doing in the way of "defining" simultaneity of events at a distance, I suggest that we work backward. I therefore quote from the second section:

---

[9] Einstein, *The Principle of Relativity*, R, p. 28, Eng., pp. 39–40.

The following reflexions are based on the principle of relativity and on the principle of the constancy of the velocity of light. These two principles we define [please note this word "define"] as follows: . . .

2. Any ray of light moves in the "stationary" system of co-ordinates with the determined [*bestimmten*, i.e., definite] velocity c, whether the ray be emitted by a stationary or by a moving body. Hence

$$\text{velocity} = (\text{light path})/(\text{time interval})$$

where time interval is to be taken in the sense of the definition in § I.[10]

I requested the reader to note the use of the word "define" in the second of these quoted sentences. Einstein's two "principles" are what we also call "postulates" or "assumptions," and what he does when he "defines" these postulates is *to lay them down in explicit terms*.

The closing reference to "definition in § 1" given of "time interval," would seem to justify us in suggesting that perhaps "to define a principle or postulate" is another way of saying "to postulate by definition" (*durch Definition festzusetzen*), namely, to lay down a postulate *in explicit terms*. With this interpretation the last sentence of the earlier paragraph is a *sequitur:* "In accordance with what is thus laid down explicitly as a postulate (*definitionsgemäss*), the two clocks run synchronously if $t_B - t_A = t'_A - t_B$." I know of no other interpretation that would not involve a *non sequitur*. Nor do I recognize any arbitrariness in the whole procedure. Any one has a right in his theory of nature to lay down explicit postulates on which he operates—as much right as Mr. Whitehead has to lay down in his later theory his postulate of God in his two natures, "primordial" and "consequent." And it can be said of Einstein's postulate that it is at least subject to experimental test. This is of course to resort to "contingency," but most scientists prefer a theory that admits of such resort.

Now, whether my suggested interpretation of the puzzling "*durch Definition festsetzt*" be accepted or not, one thing is clear: what is "*festgesetzt*" is the *equality* of the two time *intervals*,

---

[10] Einstein, *op. cit., R,* p. 29, Eng., p. 41.

and *not* a definition of simultaneity. And what has been obtained *as a logical consequence* is a clock at A and a clock at B, thus at a distance from each other, and known to be running synchronously. Now by universal acceptance, two clocks are synchronous when they run at the same rate and their equal readings are simultaneous. Hence, after two or three sentences which we need not here quote, Einstein could say:

> We have settled [*festgelegt*] what is to be understood by synchronous stationary clocks located at different places, and have evidently obtained a definition of "simultaneous," or "synchronous," and of "time." The "time" of an event is that which is given simultaneously with the event by a stationary clock located at the place of the event, this clock being synchronous, and indeed synchronous for all time determinations, with a specified stationary clock. . . . The time now defined being appropriate to the stationary system we call it "the time of the stationary system."

Thus, in spite of the conceded uncertainty as to the meaning of a single phrase, it must, I think, be also conceded that there is no uncertainty or ambiguity or arbitrariness in Einstein's method of defining "simultaneity at a distance." First he places two clocks "in all respects resembling" each other, one at A and the other at B, A and B being different points in a stationary system. At A and B he also stations observers. Since the clocks are *clocks* they mark time, and since they resemble each other in all respects their periods are equal, or, in other words, they run at the same rate. He signals by a light flash from A to B, which is reflected back to A. He assumes or postulates that the time intervals in the to and fro trips are equal. On this assumption he has his clocks set so that $t_B - t_A = t'_A - t_B$, where t_A is the reading of the clock at A at the time of sending the signal from A, t_B is the reading of the clock at B on the arrival of the signal at B, and t'_A is the reading of the clock at A on the return of the reflected signal. The clocks thus set are defined as "synchronous," and this definition is the definition of "simultaneity at a distance," since synchronous clocks are those which, having equal periods, have equal *simultaneous* readings. And, because simultaneity is a symmetrical and transitive relation, *other* events occurring at the places and times where and when synchronous clocks have equal readings, are simultaneous with each other. The symmetry and transitivity of synchronism is expressly postulated by Einstein in two sentences (not quoted) in this very connection.

It is to be noted that neither here nor anywhere else in the paper, "The Electrodynamics of Moving Bodies," does Einstein so much as refer to any *actually measured value* of the velocity of light. Had he used such a value, as for instance 300,000 km/sec, basing his argument on such a value, it could be said that he had used a "contingent" fact as a basis of his argument. On the contrary, he based his argument on the "principle of the constancy of the velocity of light," explicitly defined as "light path divided by time interval." What more in the way of "the uniformity of spatio-temporal relations" would Mr. Whitehead exact of a philosophy of nature than such a constancy of the spatio-temporal relation of the velocity of light, when it is borne in mind that it is the *constancy of this relation* and *not* the experimentally measured value of this relation that plays the decisive part in Einstein's special theory?

It is true that in the general theory the velocity of light is not regarded as constant. But the general theory is based on the special theory, and it is by the employment of tensor analysis that the general theory is developed. And tensor analysis deals with nothing but spatio-temporal relations. It is quite true, also, that Einstein says with regard to the requirement of general covariance that it "takes away from space and time the last remnant of physical objectivity."[11] But this is because he had accepted from Minkowski the view that the special theory involved the reduction of space and time to mere shadows of space-time, which alone has independent reality. This view Mr. Whitehead himself in part accepts when he says:

---

[11] *Ibid.*, R, p. 86, Eng., p. 117.

SPACE-TIME, SIMPLE LOCATION AND PREHENSION 351

My whole course of thought presupposes the magnificent stroke of genius by which Einstein and Minkowski assimilated time and space. It also presupposes the general method of seeking tensor or invariant relations as general expressions for the laws of the physical field, a method due to Einstein.[12]

The first sentence of this quotation accepts the assimilation of space and time, while the second accepts the method of tensor analysis adopted by Einstein, which Einstein regarded as depriving space and time of the last remnant of physical objectivity, but which Mr. Whitehead regarded as having no such implication. However, what Mr. Whitehead calls "the modern assimilation of time and space"[13] is, I think, exactly what deprived space and time of physical objectivity.

In Chapter IX I have attempted to show that "the modern assimilation of time and space" was not the work of Einstein but of Minkowski, and that it was accomplished by the use of the spurious equation $c = 1$, where c is the velocity of light, adopted as unit velocity. By substituting from this equation into the Einsteinian equation[14]

$$x^2 + y^2 + z^2 = c^2 t^2,$$

there is obtained the equation

$$x^2 + y^2 + z^2 = t^2.$$

This equation effects the "assimilation" of time and space, since the expression on the left is unquestionably a spatial expression, and that on the right a temporal expression. A mystical turn is given to this assimilation by introducing what Sir Arthur Eddington calls "the mysterious factor $\sqrt{-1}$, which seems to have the property of turning time into space."[15] As the result of this transformation, Minkowski finds Einstein's "relativity postulate" a very feeble word for what has become *"the postulate of the absolute world* (or briefly, the world-postulate)." And "the

---
[12] Whitehead, *The Principle of Relativity*, p. 88.
[13] *Ibid.*, p. 58.
[14] Einstein, *The Principle of Relativity*, R, p. 33, Eng., p. 46.
[15] Eddington, *Space, Time and Gravitation*, Cambridge, 1929, p. 48.

essence of this postulate," he tells us, "may be clothed mathematically in a very pregnant manner in the mystic formula
$$3.10^5 \text{ km} = \sqrt{-1} \text{ sec.}"[16]$$
The equation $c=1$ is spurious because c is a *velocity* unit and *not* unity (i.e., the number 1). The correct equation is
$$c = \text{unit-length/unit-time} = 3.10^5 \text{ km/sec.} \ldots (1)$$

In Chapter IX I gave a new derivation of the Lorentz transformation, in which the expression ct appears early in the process in the equation
$$ct = \sqrt{(x^2 + y^2 + z^2)} \ldots (2)$$
where the expressions on both sides are unquestionably measures of *spatial* length. By substituting from the spurious equation $c = 1$ we get
$$t = \sqrt{(x^2 + y^2 + z^2)} \ldots (3)$$
and thus seem to have converted a *spatial* measure number, ct, into a *temporal* measure number, t, or, to borrow from Sir Arthur Eddington, we seem to have "turned time into space." It is apparently this conversion that Mr. Whitehead calls the "assimilation of time and space." I am not suggesting that anywhere in his mathematical reasoning he actually makes use of the equation $c = 1$. He does, however, adopt "the modern assimilation of time and space," which can be effected only by that use.

But if we substitute in (2) from (1), the left side of (2), where t is the number of time units, becomes
$$(\text{unit-length/unit-time} \times t \text{ units of time} = t \text{ length units (4)},$$
since in authentic kinematics the product of the number of units of velocity by the number of units of time is the number of units of *length*, and *not* the number of units of *time*. Substituting from (4) into (2) we get
$$t \text{ units of length} = \sqrt{(x^2 + y^2 + z^2)} \text{ units of length},$$
a perfectly respectable equation, which asserts that the number of units of a length, measured kinematically, is equal to the number of units of the same length when measured analytically by the

---
[16] Minkowski, *The Principle of Relativity*, R, pp. 60, 64; Eng., pp. 83, 88.

use of co-ordinates. Here there is no turning of time into space, no assimilation of space and time. Time measures *remain* time measures, and space measures *remain* space measures, because unit velocity *remains* unit *velocity,* not having been illegitimately turned into a "pure" number. There is as much difference between a unit of velocity and the number 1 as there is between 1 cow and the number 1. It is the failure to recognize this logical fact that brought "Space-Time" into our world and all the attendant mysticism. Minkowski was correct when he said that his world-postulate "may be clothed mathematically in a very pregnant manner in the mystic formula

$$3.10^5 \text{ km} = \sqrt{-1} \text{ sec.}"$$

If a man's "genius" is to be measured by the influence he has exerted on the thought of his time, Minkowski deserves to be regarded as a genius. But whether his genius was "magnificent" is something else. At any rate, it is of a different sort from that of Einstein. Einstein unhappily was misled by Minkowski into accepting the assimilation of space and time, and therefore into depriving them of objectivity.

It is to Mr. Whitehead's credit that, in spite of his acceptance of the assimilation of time and space, he did not follow many other relativists into the realm of mysticism, but continued to insist on the "heterogeneity of time from space."[17] However, the assimilation of time and space has had one fortunate result, since

> There is some soul of goodness in things evil
> Would men observingly distil it out.

That assimilation has drawn men's observing attention to the sort of real union of time and space which has always prevailed, but the implications of which had been overlooked. For instance, the view that "the progressive advance of nature" consists of a succession of instantaneous presents seems to have been widely held until the present century, although there were notable exceptions, among which Bergson's philosophy occurs to every one. But there

---

[17] Whitehead, *The Principle of Relativity,* p. 68.

was nothing in the accepted equations of motion that implied that time is a succession of self-sufficient instants. Physicists spoke of "velocity at an instant," and apparently some of them regarded this concept as having a meaning even when the "instant" was taken as an isolated point in time. But this view was not universally held before the advent of relativity. I find even in an article on "Calculus" in a popular encyclopedia the following discussion:

> But as this idea of what a differential is is somewhat vague, owing to the difficulty of actually conceiving something that is "infinitely small," the following considerations may be resorted to. Studying the motion of a ball thrown up in the air, we consider infinitely small intervals of time dt merely in order to be able to think of the motion as uniform; for within any finite interval the motion is variable. . . . We may, accordingly, define the differential of distance dl as the distance that *would be* traversed by the ball in an arbitrary finite interval of time, dt, beginning at a given instant, if at the instant the motion became uniform.[18]

It is as unfair to attribute to any scientist or philosopher who has not expressly said that "velocity at an instant" is a manner of speaking the view that there is in actuality such a thing, as it would be unfair to attribute to a scientist who speaks of "acceleration from infinity" in connection with gravitation the view that actually any object ever starts at rest from an infinite distance and on reaching the earth has acquired the assigned "acceleration from infinity." I rather suspect that correct thinking on the union of space and time did not begin in 1908, just as the correct doctrine of "limits" was not initiated then.

Let us now turn to a consideration of what I cannot but regard as a strange denial of a patent fact of experience, when Mr. Whitehead says:

---

[18] *The New International Encyclopedia* (New York, 1902), Vol. III, p. 745d. The author of this article could not have been influenced by either Einstein or Minkowski; and yet I wonder whether those under the influence of "the modern assimilation" could succeed much better in conveying to the lay reader the idea that velocity at an instant is not to be interpreted as something that has any meaning apart from "an *interval* of time *beginning* at an instant."

Space-Time, Simple Location and Prehension 355

> It is an error to ascribe parts to objects, where "part" here means spatial or temporal part. The erroneousness of such ascription immediately follows from the premise that primarily an object is not in space or in time. The absence of temporal parts of objects is a commonplace of thought. No one thinks that part of a stone is at one time and another part of the stone is at another time. The same stone is at both times, in the sense in which the stone is existing at those times (if it be existing). But spatial parts are in a different category, and it is natural to think of various parts of a stone, simultaneously existing. Such a conception confuses the stone as an object with the event which exhibits the actual relations of the stone within nature. . . . The fundamental rule is that events have parts and that —except in a derivative sense, from their relations to events—objects have no parts.[19]

As to temporal parts of a stone, how about the geological theory of the process of sedimentation by which rocks are formed? If they have grown by sedimentary accretion, it would seem as if their parts are in time; or is Mr. Whitehead speaking only of such small stones as we find these days, and not of rocks? But even in this case, any one who has seen a stonecrusher in operation naturally thinks of a part of a stone at one time and another part at another time. A full discussion of the subject would take us over into the question of physical particles; but without entering into this subject, may one not ask whether the "fundamental rule" is not rather dogmatically stated? Mr. Whitehead's position is that of an uncompromising Platonist; and of course any one has a right to be a Platonist. It cannot be proved that Platonism is a false doctrine, but I wonder whether it can be proved that it is a true doctrine. I have discussed this question above in Chapter VI and cannot here go into the matter again. I only venture to remark that a fundamental cleavage within nature between eternal objects and events is as objectionable as a "bifurcation of nature" to which I object as much as does Mr. Whitehead. It seems to result in two mutually contradictory notions about events. The first is expressed in the passage just quoted: "events have parts and . . . —except in a derivative sense, from their relations to

---

[19] Whitehead, *The Principles of Natural Knowledge*, p. 65f.

events—objects have no parts." This makes events distinct terms of a two-term relation of "ingression." The second is expressed when it is said:

> I give the name "event" to a spatio-temporal happening. An event does not in any way imply rapid change; the endurance of a block of marble is an event. Nature presents itself to us as essentially a becoming, and any limited portion of nature which preserves most completely such concreteness as attaches to nature itself is also a becoming and is what I call an event. By this I do not mean a bare portion of space-time. Such a concept is a further abstraction. I mean a part of the becomingness of nature, coloured with all the hues of its content.[20]

How the becomingness of nature can have "a part coloured with all the hues of its content," when all colors and hues have no parts, is beyond my understanding. I can understand when it is said that "there is no such entity as a bare event,"[21] but if this is the case, it seems that a relation of "ingression" is unnecessary for reconstituting an entity which abstraction has torn apart. All that is necessary is to let the event be the entirety it is before we have split it into an "event that has parts" and something else called an "object" which has no parts.

Let us pass to what Mr. Whitehead calls "the fallacy of simple location."

> To say that a bit of matter has *simple location* means that, in expressing its spatio-temporal relations, it is adequate to state that it is where it is, in a definite finite region of space, and throughout a definite finite duration of time, apart from any essential reference of the relations of that bit of matter to other regions of space and to other durations of time. Again, this concept of simple location is independent of the controversy between the absolutist and the relativist views of space and time. So long as any theory of space, or of time, can give a meaning, either absolute or relative, to the idea of a definite region of space, and of a definite duration of time, the idea of simple location has a perfectly definite meaning. . . . I shall argue that among the primary elements of nature as apprehended in our immediate experience, there is no element whatever which possesses this character of simple location.[22]

---

[20] Whitehead, *The Principle of Relativity*, p. 21.
[21] *Ibid.*, p. 26.
[22] Whitehead, *Science and the Modern World*, p. 81. A similar definition of

SPACE-TIME, SIMPLE LOCATION AND PREHENSION 357

Since the relativist theory of space and time maintains that no region of space (or duration of time) has any meaning apart from its spatial relations of distance and direction to other regions (or apart from its relation of before and after to other durations), I find it hard to distinguish the denial of "simple location" from the relativist doctrine, unless we emphasize the words "a bit of matter" at the beginning of the passage just quoted. That this is the intended emphasis is apparent when we consider the context in which the denial of "simple location" is made:

> There will be some fundamental assumptions which adherents of all the variant systems within the epoch unconsciously presuppose. . . . One such assumption underlies the whole philosophy of nature during the modern period. It is embodied in the conception which is supposed to express the most concrete aspect of nature. The Ionian philosophers asked, What is nature made of? The answer is couched in terms of stuff, or matter, or material, . . . which has the property of simple location in space and time, or, if you adopt the more modern ideas, in space-time.[23]

Now Mr. Whitehead's answer substitutes "actual occasions" for stuff, or matter, or material, and it is by "prehensions" that any actual occasion effects its own concretion. What it prehends is, among other things, other actual occasions. These prehended occasions have their "locations" in space and time, and the prehending occasion also has its location. And the denial of "simple location" is the denial of the exclusiveness of these several locations. Each actual occasion is located not only where its own concrescence takes place, but is also in every other location where the prehension of it by other actual occasions occurs.

> In a certain sense, everything is everywhere at all times. For every location involves an aspect of itself in every other location. Thus every spatio-temporal standpoint mirrors the world. If you try to imagine this doctrine in terms of our conventional views of space and time, which presuppose simple location, it is a great paradox. But if you think of it in terms of our naïve experience, it is a mere transcript of the obvious facts. You are in a certain place per-

---

"simple location" is given on pages 69–70. (Page references in this essay to *Science and the Modern World* are to the American edition, 1925.)
[23] *Ibid.*, p. 69.

ceiving things. Your perception takes place where you are, and is entirely dependent on how your body is functioning. But this functioning of the body in one place, exhibits for your cognisance an aspect of the distant environment, fading away into the general knowledge that there are things beyond.[24]

Now this concept of "mirroring" reminds us of Leibniz, and Mr. Whitehead says: "It is evident that I can use Leibniz's language, and say that every volume mirrors in itself every other volume in space."[25] But Leibniz's mirroring monads had, as we all know, no windows through which they could *go out* and through which other monads could *enter*. Their mirroring took place by grace of "pre-established harmony." Not so with Mr. Whitehead's monads. "Each monadic creature [so he tells us] is a mode of the process of 'feeling' the world, of housing the world in one unit of complex feeling. . . . Such a unit is an 'actual occasion'."[26] It is like 'Omer, when he "smote 'is blooming lyre":

An' what he thought 'e might require,
'E went an' took—the same as me.

This taking, which of course is the English for "prehension," is literal taking and bringing home; and, as with 'Omer's taking, what is thus taken is not *dislodged* from where it was; and the reason for this is that "everything is everywhere at all times." The qualification, "in a certain sense," thus is not left vague. The "sense" in which "everything is everywhere at all times" is that, except perhaps in "negative prehension," everything is actually and actively taken up into everything else. Not the *whole* of everything is thus taken up, but only what the prehending monad can use in effecting its concrescence.

The things which are grasped into a realised unity, here and now, are not the castle, the cloud, and the planet simply in themselves; but they are the castle, the cloud, and the planet from the standpoint, in space and time, of the prehensive unification. In other words, it is the perspective of the castle over there from the standpoint of the unification here. It is, therefore, aspects of the castle,

---
[24] *Ibid.*, pp. 128–129.
[25] *Ibid.*, p. 92.
[26] Whitehead, *Process and Reality*, p. 124. (Page references to *Process and Reality* in this essay are to the American edition, 1930.)

Space-Time, Simple Location and Prehension 359

the cloud, and the planet which are grasped into unity here. You will remember that the idea of perspectives is quite familiar in philosophy. It was introduced by Leibniz, in the notion of his monads mirroring perspectives of the universe. I am using the same notion, only I am toning down his monads into the unified events in space and time [i.e., into actual occasions].[27]

Thus we find that Mr. Whitehead's doctrine of denial of "simple location" is intimately connected with his view of "prehension," and that this is likewise intimately connected with his view of "perspectives." This implication of elements in a theory with other elements is, of course, what is to be expected in any truly systematic philosophy. We thus have to examine his doctrine of perspectives to see whether we can get additional light on the assertion that in a certain sense everything is everywhere at all times. Unfortunately, so far as concerns an attempt to discuss Mr. Whitehead's philosophy in a short chapter, the doctrine of perspectives implies his doctrine of "objectification," and that implies other doctrines, and so on till we have come full circle.

But as we have seen, even a cocoanut has "eyes" through which teeth, lucky enough to find them, may possibly get at the meat inside. I suspect that the following "Categories of Explanation" may be such "eyes" in Mr. Whitehead's philosophy of organism, where everything is endowed with ubiquity and sempiternity.

(ii) That in the becoming of an actual entity, the *potential* unity of many entities—actual and non-actual—acquires the *real* unity of the one actual entity; so that the actual entity is the real concrescence of many potentials.

(iv) That the potentiality for being an element in a real concrescence of many entities into one actuality, is the one general metaphysical character attaching to all entities, actual and non-actual; and that every item in its universe is involved in each concrescence. In other words, it belongs to the nature of a 'being" that it is a potential for every "becoming." This is the "principle of relativity."

(v) That no two actual entities originate from an identical universe; though the difference between the two universes only consists in some actual entities, included in one and not in the other.[28]

[27] Whitehead, *Science and the Modern World*, p. 98f.
[28] Whitehead, *Process and Reality*, p. 33f.

Thus each novel entity in its concrescence "includes" within itself other actual entities, which thus become "elements" within its constitution. In this way the novel entity is where and when its concrescence occurs. The other entities are where and when their concrescences occur; but in being included in the constitution of the novel entity, they are also where and when this entity occurs. It is in *this* sense that "everything is everywhere and at all times."

To call this inclusion of other entities within the novel entity a "mirroring"[29] is an understatement by metaphor. A more adequate and more literal expression of what occurs in prehension is found when Mr. Whitehead says that an actual entity "objectifies" what it prehends. "The term 'objectification' refers to the particular mode in which the potentiality of one actual entity is realized in another actual entity."[30]

> Some real component in the objectified entity assumes the role of being how that particular entity is a datum in the experience of the subject. In this case, the objectified contemporaries are only directly relevant to the subject in their character of arising from a datum which is an extensive continuum. . . . They thus exhibit the community of contemporary actualities as a common world with mathematical relations—where the term "mathematical" is used in the sense in which it would have been understood by Plato, Euclid, and Descartes, before the modern discovery of the true definition of pure mathematics.[31]

Thus, an act of experience has an objective scheme of extensive order by reason of the double fact that its own *perspective* stand-

---

[29] "The volumes [*A* and *B*] of space have no independent existence . . . the aspect of *B* from *A* is the *mode* in which *B* enters into the composition of *A*. This is the modal character of space, that the prehensive unity of *A* is the prehension into unity of the aspects of all other volumes from the standpoint of *A*. The shape of a volume is the formula from which the totality of its aspects can be derived. Thus the shape of a volume is more abstract than its aspects. It is evident that I can use Leibniz's language, and say that every volume mirrors in itself every other volume in space." (*Science and the Modern World*, pp. 91–92.) It [the extensive continuum] is not a fact prior to the world; it is the first determination of order—that is, of real potentiality—arising out of the general character of the world. In its full generality beyond the present epoch, it does not involve shapes, dimensions, or measurability; these are additional determinations of real potentiality arising from our cosmic epoch." (*Process and Reality*, p. 103.)
[30] Whitehead, *Process and Reality*, p. 34.
[31] *Ibid.*, p. 97.

Space-Time, Simple Location and Prehension 361

point has extensive content, and that the other actual entities are objectified with the retention of their extensive relationships.[32]

But if we take the doctrine of objectification seriously, the extensive continuum at once becomes the primary factor in objectification. It provides the general scheme of extensive perspective which is exhibited in all the mutual objectifications by which actual entities prehend each other.[33]

This general scheme, as prehended by an actual entity from its own perspective standpoint, is what Mr. Whitehead calls "geometrical perspective relatedness."[34]

I have now singled out a number of passages, taken each from its own context, and put them together in such a way that each forms a part of the context in which the others play a part. Whether in doing this I have done injustice to the author's thought, he alone can say; and, fortunately, he is here with us to say. All that I can claim is that, by doing this, I get into my perspective Mr. Whitehead's theory of perspectives—a perspective which for me at least "makes sense" out of his denial of simple location. I cannot agree with what Lord Russell said of Mr. Whitehead's "fallacy of simple location, when avoided": To his mind, "such a view, if taken seriously, is incompatible with science."[35]

On the contrary, I find a remarkable family resemblance between Mr. Whitehead's view of perspectives and Lord Russell's, with individual differences such as are found in all families except in case of identical twins. The resemblance, no doubt, appears to the two authors to be superficial, and yet it is there, superficial or not. Often it happens that members of the same family dislike and even resent attention called to family characteristics.

We have already seen what Mr. Whitehead's view is, if my

---

[32] *Ibid.*, p. 105 (my italics).
[33] *Ibid.*, p. 118.
[34] *Ibid.*, p. 185.
[35] Russell, *The Analysis of Matter* (New York, London, 1927), p. 340f. He added, "and it involves a mystic pantheism." On this added stricture I reserve my comments, for the reason that I am here considering only Mr. Whitehead's way of avoiding that "fallacy" and not the *other* features of his philosophy with which this avoidance may be implicated.

interpretation of it proves to be correct. Let us look at Lord Russell's:

> It will be observed that *two* places in perspective space are associated with every aspect of a thing: namely, the place where the thing is, and the place which is the perspective of which the aspect in question forms part.[36]

The "two places" will be indefinitely multiplied when it is remembered that there is an indefinite number of places where the perspective is, of which the aspect in question forms part. But *this* resemblance is not what I have in mind, since something like this multiplicity of places associated with every aspect of a thing is found in any theory of perspectives. The resemblance I have in mind is deeper:

> The two places associated with a single aspect correspond to the two ways of classifying it. We may distinguish the two places as that *at* which, and that *from* which, the aspect appears. The "place at which" is the place of the *thing* to which the aspect belongs; the "place from which" is the place of the *perspective* to which the aspect belongs.[37]

Note that the "aspect belongs" both to the thing and to the perspective. Just what this means requires explanation, which can be given by a few more quotations. Imagining that each mind looks out from the world, as in Leibniz's monadology, the author says:

> Each mind sees at each moment an immensely complex three-dimensional world. . . . If two men are sitting in a room, two somewhat similar worlds are perceived by them; if a third man enters and sits between them, a third world, intermediate between the two previous worlds, begins to be perceived. . . . The system consisting of all views of the universe perceived and unperceived, I shall call the system of "perspectives"; I shall confine the expression "private worlds" to such views of the universe as are actually perceived . . . but there may be any number of unperceived perspectives.[38]

---
[36] Russell, *Our Knowledge of the External World as a Field for Scientific Method in Philosophy*, Chicago and London, 1915, p. 92.
[37] *Ibid.*, p. 92. (The last two italics are mine.)
[38] *Ibid.*, p. 87f. The same treatment of perspectives is given in Lecture VII of *The Analysis of Mind* (London, New York, 1921). I have purposely omitted important features of Lord Russell's theory, features that differentiate his theory from

> Perspective space is the system of "points of view" of private spaces (perspectives), or, since "points of view" have not been defined, we may say it is the system of the private spaces themselves. These private spaces will each count as one point, or at any rate as one element, in perspective space.[39]

Thus everything we ever see is at the point, or *is* the point, in perspective space where we are when we see it. This constitutes the point of resemblance between the two theories of perspective we are comparing, since for Mr. Whitehead the concrescent actual occasion in prehending "includes" the prehended datum in its own constitution. If I may use the vernacular, everything we see is, for both our philosophers, where we are when we see it.

But naturally both our philosophers were not content with leaving everything they see in their own physical heads—to speak Lord Russell's language—or in their own concrescent occasions, in Mr. Whitehead's language. The different ways in which they severally avoided such a predicament mark one of the distinctive differences between the two. Lord Russell went to work and constructed an entirely different space from the space in any perspective, called it "perspective space"—later he called it "physical space"—put the different perspectives at different places in this new space, and put the "thing" perceived in a different place in this space from that assigned to any perspective that contains an "aspect" of the "thing." In this way he successfully committed "the fallacy of simple location" as far as the "thing," is concerned. But partially to atone for this commission, he generously allowed the "aspect" to "belong" both to the "thing," now at one place, and to the "perspective," now at another place in the "perspective space." The atonement is only partial, since he did not say that the *same* "aspect" is *at* the two different places where its two owners are. And of course something can belong to two owners, without being where the owners are. Just what "belong-

---

Mr. Whitehead's. An instance is the former's assertion that "there is absolutely nothing which is seen by two minds simultaneously" (*op. cit.*, p. 87). I perpetrated this omission for the reason that I am now interested in pointing out the *resemblance* between the two authors.

[39] *Ibid.*, p. 89f.

ing to" means in Lord Russell's theory we need not ask here, since the answer is part of another story. At any rate, everything has "aspects" scattered "all over the map," so to say. Its "aspects" are everywhere and, if not at all times, at any rate at many times: they are everywhere except, apparently, where the thing is to which they belong.

Mr. Whitehead, as we have seen, avoids the predicament by having declined at the start to commit the "fallacy of simple location." His "concrescent occasion" has therefore the good fortune of being able as it were both to eat its cake and have it. The actual occasion ingests all its cakes into its own "inner constitution" and also leaves them out where they were before.

It is not my purpose here to criticize in detail either of these doctrines of the nature of perspectives. Space will not permit. I can only say that neither seems necessitated by the facts or even plausible. When Mr. Whitehead argues that "among the primary elements of nature as apprehended in our immediate experience, there is no element whatever which possesses this character of simple location," I can only reply that this does not find confirmation in my experience. The very fact that he finds it necessary to relegate all apparently "immediate experience" that contravenes his assertion to the category of "perception in the mode of presentational immediacy," shows that "immediate experience" has to be categorized in order to be used as evidence on the question at issue. He himself has said:

> The verification of a rationalistic scheme is to be sought in its general success, and not in the peculiar certainty, or initial clarity, of its first principles. In this connection the misuse of the *ex absurdo* argument has to be noted; much philosophical reasoning is vitiated by it. . . . In the absence of a well-defined categorial scheme of entities, issuing in a satisfactory metaphysical system, every premise in a philosophical argument is under suspicion. . . . There may be rival schemes, inconsistent among themselves; each with its own merits and its own failures. . . . Metaphysical categories are not dogmatic statements of the obvious; they are tentative formulations of the ultimate generalities.[40]

---

[40] Whitehead, *Process and Reality*, p. 12.

To assert that the doctrine of simple location is a fallacy is a "misuse of the *ex absurdo* argument," since the very essence of a "fallacy" is that it is a logical absurdity, a self-contradiction. To condemn as fallacious rivals whose assumptions do not agree with one's own is not in keeping with the position that one's own categories are *"tentative* formulations of the ultimate generalities."

There is much else in Mr. Whitehead's philosophy of "space-time" on which I should like to have more light. I can mention here only one of the remaining perplexities. It concerns the status of "the extensive continuum" among the "categories of existence."

> An extensive continuum is a complex of entities united by the various allied relationships of whole to part, and of overlapping so as to possess common parts, and of contact, and of other relationships derived from these primary relationships. The notion of a "continuum" involves both the property of indefinite divisibility and the property of unbounded extension. There are always entities beyond entities, because nonentity is no boundary. This extensive continuum expresses the solidarity of all possible standpoints throughout the whole process of the world. It is not a fact prior to the world; it is the first determination of order—that is, of real potentiality—arising out of the general character of the world. . . . This extensive continuum is "real," because it expresses a fact derived from the actual world and concerning the contemporary actual world. All actual entities are related according to the determination of this continuum; and all possible actual entities in the future must exemplify these determinations in their relations with the already actual world. The reality of the future is bound up with the reality of this continuum. It is the reality of what is potential, in its character of a real component of what is actual. Such a real component must be interpreted in terms of the relatedness of prehensions.[41]

This passage, when compared with that quoted in footnote 29 above, suggests that any volume of space in this extensive continuum is to be interpreted as "the prehension into unity of the aspects of all other volumes from the standpoint" of that volume. Does that volume itself prehend into unity all other volumes? If it does, then it is itself an *actual entity*, since Mr. Whitehead has said: "I have adopted the term 'prehension', to express the

---
[41] *Ibid.*, p. 103f.

activity whereby an actual entity effects its own concretion of other things."[42]

But in an earlier work Mr. Whitehead had said that "a bare portion of space-time" is an "abstraction," and "any limited portion of nature which preserves most completely such concreteness as attaches to nature itself," is "a part of the becomingness of nature, coloured with all the hues of its content."[43] Can an "abstraction" be "an actual entity" which "effects its own concretion of other things" through the "activity" of "prehension"? I therefore repeat my former question, Where among the categories of existence does the extensive continuum find a place? Is it an "eternal object"?

All philosophers have much to look forward to, when a philosopher of Mr. Whitehead's eminence consents to elucidate his position in reply to critics. He himself has acknowledged that "the worst homage we can pay to genius is to accept uncritically formulations of truths which we owe to it." He should feel assured that our criticisms are our best expression of homage to his genius.

---

[42] *Ibid.*, p. 81.
[43] Whitehead, *The Principle of Relativity*, p. 21.

Chapter XII

CONCLUSION

Each one of us is an organism with inherited characteristics, that develop in part through growth without the action of environment, and also with acquired characters that are the result of the action of the environment upon us; and a large part of the action of this environment is the action of other human beings. Thus for each of us the physical world, including our own physical organism, is primary and whatever is not physical is secondary as far as time goes. But what is here called secondary is of supreme importance. It would not occur where there is no consciousness, and consciousness according to the view here presented is a relation of its own kind that arises between an organism and something else called the object of consciousness when the brain of the organism is activated in certain ways, as has been explained in preceding chapters. And mind is an organism *as and when conscious.* Thus mind is of a twofold nature, on the one side it is physical and on the other side is not physical; although what is not physical is the result of the physical. Such a view as this is perhaps abhorrent to many persons brought up under the influence of tradition. It is often said that the mind is a prisoner of the body; according to our view, without body no mind, but not all bodies are minds; or, as the saying usually goes, not all bodies have minds.

Abhorrent as this view may be especially to those with strong religious feeling, it is interesting to note that perhaps the fundamental doctrine of Christianity is *the resurrection of the body.* Without the resurrection of the body there would be no immortality. It is true that the resurrected body in the Christian view is not physical. St. Paul says there's a natural body and there's a spiritual body. However, the spiritual body apparently is a transformed and glorified natural body. What sort of a world these glorified bodies live in and respond to is not made clear. Whatever may be the interpretation of the theologians on this matter, the new Jerusalem within which these transfigured bodies live is described as similar to the physical world in which we in this dispensation are living. Consult what the author of the Book of Revelation says about the characteristics of the New Jerusalem.

The perspective realist offers no opinion on these matters. He is dealing with this world, and in this world he accepts the fact that the physical is such as the physicists of the present generation describe it to be. And he finds nothing derogatory in the assumption that mind is a physical organism when it is conscious. He agrees with the late Sir Charles Sherrington, who regards what mind contributes as "all that counts in life: desire, zest, truth, love, knowledge, 'values,' and, seeking metaphor to eke out expression, hell's depth and heaven's utmost height."[1]

It is only as there is mind to value the world that there is any value in it. There is no evidence that the inorganic, physical world appraises itself. In what stage of the evolutionary development of the organic world values occur it is not possible to say, but at any rate we human beings do value, and what we value is what makes life worth living.

Let us examine this view that has been briefly sketched above. What shall be said here is to a large extent a repetition of what has been said in previous chapters, but it is worth while to repeat in order to bring together the evidence and its bearing upon the whole problem of what a person is: What is referred to by the word "I" when one says, "I am tired, I have pain, I hurt myself"; or in a happier vein when one says, "I am succeeding; I have friends who are precious and they make my life worth living."

---

[1] *Man on His Nature*, New York, 1941, p. 357.

Take away the body which gives utterance to all this, what is left of anything that can be called an "I"? Is it not the continuity of the body over the gaps occurring in sleep that gives continuity to what each one of us speaks of as "I"? There are temporal gaps in the course of everyone's consciousness but there is no gap in the continuity of any organism from start to finish. A mind does not demean itself by identifying itself with a certain organism when it is functioning consciously.

* * * * * *

[These few pages of a concluding chapter appear to have been written before the last rewriting of Chapter V. The script breaks off after another page in which a discussion of the liaison between physical energy and mind is introduced with the quotation from Sir Charles Sherrington which appears above on p. 198, and the Penfield and Rasmussen book, *The Cerebral Cortex of Man,* is referred to as though it were being mentioned for the first time. Evidently this book, published in 1950, motivated Mr. McGilvary to recast the long chapter on "Perspectives" so as to utilize the best recent scientific evidence in the field of neurophysiology in support of his thesis that sensations are epiphysical events dependent upon specific brain processes. Mr. McGilvary died before he could revise and complete the concluding chapter that he had begun some years earlier. It is perhaps not altogether unfitting that his philosophy is left without a definite terminus. In the perspectives of circumstances yet to be fulfilled and times yet to be occupied by some living organism there will be a new look upon the face of nature, and it may well be that McGilvary's philosophy will itself provide a part of the perspective without which that new look would neither be actualized nor understood. For a Perspective Realist the world is never finished, nor is any philosophy about it the last word. —A. G. R.]

INDEX

INDEX

INDEX

Absolute, 2, 22, 25, 277, 294. *See also* Space, absolute, *and* Time, absolute.
Absolutism, 5, 22
Abstraction, 233, 237, 366
Act, action, 42, 43n, 45-6; reasonableness of, 269; retroactive, 113, 186
Actual occasions, 357-8, 364
Aerial perspective, 179
Affects, 97, 98
Afferent and efferent mechanisms, 175, 210
Ages, 329-331
Alexander, Samuel, 8
Analysis, 231; abstractive, 55; tensor, 351
Appearance, 139-148
Appearing, 55, 71; an additive relation, 142, 147, 148; relation of, 47, 135, 142-8, 154
Apuleius, 239n
Aristophanes, 21
Aristotle, 22, 32, 59n-60n, 237-8, 242, 294, 311; logic of, 4
Aspect of a thing, 362, 363
Assumptions, 5, 73, 194, 348. *See also* Postulates.
Atomic proposition, 246
Attention, physiology of, 67
Authoritarianism, 256
Automatism, 90
Awareness, 108, 115, 123. *See also* Sense-awareness.
Axioms, 5

Begging the question, 27, 290
Bergson, Henri, 7, 94, 119, 185, 353
Berkeley, George, 12
Bible, 194-5
Bifurcation of nature, 35, 107, 355
Biology, 73, 80, 100, 204
Biser, Irwin, 8n
Body and self, 130. *See also* Mind and body.
Bradley, F. H., 40, 231n, 233, 238n
Bradley, James, 157
Brain, 50, 77, 98, 115, 164; frontal lobe of, 190, 209; neurology of, 171-5
Broad, C. D., 92, 214, 218, 219
"Buzzing confusion," 99

Caesar, Julius, 239n
Calendar, 304n; age, 330
Calvinism, 207
Camera and vision, 161, 170
Carlson, A. J., and Johnson, V., 163n, 165n
Carus Lectures: (Dewey), 138, 143, 147; (Lovejoy), 195; (McGilvary), ix, 2
Categorial interpretations, 244
Categorial scheme, 364
Causal condition, 145
Causal theory of perception, 6, 43
Causality, 203, 204, 207
Cause, 202, 257; and effect, 205
Cells, chemistry of, 73
Cerebellum, 98
Cerebral cortex. *See* Cortex, cerebral.
Certainty, and scepticism, 6; quest for, 4
Change, experience of, 129; sense of, 222
Characters, 36-40, 233-5; classes of, 235-6, 245-6, 251, 253; real, 224; relational, 17, 30, 40; transient, 33
Chemistry, 80; of cells, 73
Chimpanzees, 167, 209
Choice, 263, 265
Christianity, 270, 367
Classes, 235, 236, 245
Clay, E. R., 214
Clocks, retardation of, 315, 325, 329; synchronism of, 299, 316, 324, 349
Coeval, 316, 318, 321, 323, 336. *See also* Simultaneity.
Cohen, Morris R., 236, 242
Color blindness, 37
Common sense, 46, 52, 59, 60n, 79, 181, 190, 205, 220
Communication, 10, 12
Components, 37, 232
Conation, 192
Conceived characters, 235
Conceived universals, 236
Conceptualism, 244
Concrescence, 359-360, 363-4
Condemnation, moral, 286
Conditioned reflex, 200, 201
Conflict of ideals, 280, 284
Conscience, 276

Consciousness, 41-72, 100, 117, 185, 209, 211, 212, 367; epiphysical, 199, 201; in other philosophies, 123-153; nature of, 134, 136-8; not a dynamic relation, 154; of brutes, 90; of consciousness, 63-5; theories of, 138
Conservation of energy, 199, 203
Consistency, 121
Context, 14-18, 38, 126
Contingency, 341, 343, 345, 348
Continuants, 33
Continuum, 59, 61; extensive, 365, 366
Copernican theory, 193-4, 240
Cortex, cerebral, 165-175, 192, 205; motor, 208; temporal, 180, 182, 185
Craniotomy, 171, 172
Creative evolution, 94. See also Bergson, Henri.
Crime, 274

Dalton, John, 37
Darrow, Clarence, 255, 271
Darwin, Charles, 95
Deliberation, 266
Descartes, René, 4
Desires, 192, 295
Determinism, 206, 257; and free will, 255-274; in biology, 204
Dewey, John, 5-6, 7, 10, 13-4, 19-20, 29, 31, 37, 121, 129n, 137-153, 159, 188, 206-7, 248-9
Diencephalon, 174-5, 208, 209, 211, 212
Directions, 158, 294; temporal, 220
Distinguishability, 231
Dreams, 181, 183, 184
Dualism, 195
Duration, 187, 213-9, 357
Dynamic characters, 33
Dynamic events, 86-9, 102
Dynamic factor, 82, 114
Dynamic processes, 118
Dynamics, 87, 89

Eddington, Sir Arthur S., 30n, 111n, 211, 260-1, 307-10, 351-2
Einstein, Alfred, 14, 22, 23, 24, 36, 88, 199, 297-8, 307n, 313, 341-353. See also Postulates, of Einstein, and Relativity, Theory of.
Einsteinian time, 304n, 325
Elan vital, 94
Embryo, 200
Emergence, 76, 94
Emerson, R. W., 207
Emotion, 98, 117
Empedocles, 153
Empiricism, 64, 179; immediate, 138; radical, 127, 132, 137, 146

Energy, 43n, 69, 76, 77; and mass, 198, 204; closed to mind, 84; conservation of, 199, 203
Energy-scheme, 86, 96, 102, 114
Epidynamicism, 89, 91, 92, 96, 100, 113, 114
Epileptic discharge, 179, 180, 183, 191, 209, 211
Epiphenomenalism, 89-92
Epiphysical, 173, 177; consciousness is, 199, 201; sensations are, 369
Epiphysical relation, 170, 176
Essences, eternal, 238
Ethics, 275. See also Morality.
Euclid, 87; geometry of, 4, 87, 345
Events, 19, 355. See also Dynamic events.
Evolution, 76, 93, 101, 294; creative, 94; innovative, 95
Experience, 14, 78, 148; defined, 82-3; primary, 150-3; pure, 17n, 125-133, 147. See also Sense-experience.
Experiencing, 82, 89, 127
Extension, 245
Extensive abstraction, 219, 345
Extensive continuum, 365, 366

Fact and theory, 78
Fallacy, of accident, 225, 321; psychologist's, 65, 127, 128. See also Simple location, Whitehead's fallacy of.
Fatalism, 258
Field of consciousness, 70
First principles, 4
Freedom and necessity, 255-274
Froude, James Anthony, 207
Functionalism, 138
Fundamentalism, 117, 194

Galileo, 311
Genealogy, 136
Geometry, 4, 87, 341, 344-5; non-Euclidean, 88
Gesell, Arnold, 165n, 166-8
Gildersleeve, 239n
God, 194-5, 239, 283, 348; and devil, 291; and morality, 271
Green, Thomas Hill, 61
Gyrectomy, 191

Habit, physiological basis of, 201
Hallucination, 180, 181, 183
Harrison, George Russell, 103n
Hegel, G. W. F., 7, 36, 252, 284
Heisenberg, 260
Heterochronic age, 330-1
Heterogeneity of space-time, 346
History, 148

INDEX

Humanism, 137
Hume, David, 230-1, 250-1, 262n
Huxley, Thomas Henry, 89, 90
Hypotheses, 35. *See also* Postulates.

Idealism, 2, 195, 197
Idealist theory of consciousness, 138
Ideals, 1, 278-280
Identity, 230, 242; conceptual, 244; numerical, 27-8; of character, 233; of events, 111; of self, 66
Illusions, 180, 181, 183
Imaginary characters, 235
Imaginary universals, 236
Immediacy, 19, 29, 364; of qualities, 37, 139
Immediate experience of time, 223
Immortality, 367-8
Indeterminacy, physical theory of, 260
Indeterminism, 259, 265
Indignation, 287
Individual, 74, 246
Infinite regress, 63
Infinity, 61
Ingredience. *See* Ingression.
Ingression of objects in nature, 109, 110, 356
Innate ideas, 232
Innovative evolution, 95
Insects, memory of, 98
Instant, 219
Instrumentalism, 248
Integration, neural, 58, 182, 208, 210-12; of sensory processes, 175; temporal, 63
Intellectual perspectives, 193
Intension, 245
Interests as causes and as caused, 266-270
Ivins, William M., Jr., 160, 163n

James, Henry, 340
James, William, 14, 17n, 40, 55, 56-8, 64-6, 99, 113n, 146, 148, 155, 172, 181, 184-5, 188, 201, 213-9, 223, 226, 231n, 255, 277; his view of consciousness, 124-132
Jeremiah, 286
Joad, C. E. M., 255, 261, 268, 272
Judgment, moral, as weapon, 285
Jurisprudence, 117-8

Kant, Immanuel, 4, 269, 275
Kierkegaard, 113n
Kinematics, 87, 305
Knowing, 123, 125; appearance not, 141
Knowledge, 43, 190, 243, 248; and progress, 294

Kronecker, 28

Languages, 48
Laplace, P. S. de, 206
Laue, 112
Laws of nature, 203
Leibniz, G. W. von, 158, 163, 164, 358, 362
Lewis, C. I., 7
Lex talionis, 270
Liberty, 262n. *See also* Determinism and free will.
Life, 80, 148
Light, velocity of, 112, 157, 298, 342, 345, 350; wave theory of, 160
Linear perspective, 178-9
Lobectomy and lobotomy, 190
Localization, 176; of function, 171, 180, 193
Logic, 4, 48, 245; symbolic, 247
Logical universals, 236
Lorentz, "local time" of, 344
Lorentz transformation, 23, 297-311, 317, 322n, 326, 334n, 352; equations of, 302
Lovejoy, Arthur O., 195, 312-18, 321, 323, 324, 331-4, 337

McGilvary, Evander Bradley, ix, 296n, 369
Margenau, Henry, 203-5, 207
Martineau, James, 271
Mass, and energy, 198, 204; of consciouness, 70-2
Mathematics and natural science, 88, 345
Matter, 84
Mead, George Herbert, 8, 187, 248
Meaning, 115-6, 138, 249; relation of, 135-7
Means and end, 285
Mechanics, 86, 203, 308. *See also* Quantum mechanics.
Mechanisms, 86; afferent and efferent, 175, 210; of the body, 74
Mechanists, 80
Memory, 98, 113, 117, 137, 175, 179-190; reproductive, 215, 219
Mental experience, 98
Mental functions, 181
Mental processes, 43n
Mesencephalon, 174-5, 208, 212
Metaphysics, 104, 108-9
Michelson and Morley experiment, 22, 105, 265
Might makes right, 281, 282, 284
Mill, John Stuart, 239n, 243, 293
Milton, John, 258, 259

Mind, 51, 197; an organism, 67, 72, 82, 199; and body, 73, 77, 79-80, 83, 91, 101-2, 121, 198, 199, 221n, 367; evolution of, 76; excluded from nature, 109; recognizable, 75; world of, 178
Minkowski, H., 23n, 24, 25, 307, 310, 311, 341, 350, 351, 353
Mirroring, 357-8, 360
Mohammedanism, 283
Moment, 219, 221
Monads, 158, 358
Monism of nature, 40
Montreal Neurological Institute of Investigation, 171
Moore, G. E., 123-4
Morality, chaps. VII and VIII, 255-296
Morgan, C. Lloyd, 94n, 115
Motion, 212; sensation of, 176
Motivation, moral, 289
Münsterberg, Hugo, 181

Names, magic of, 20
Natural science, 80, 84, 88
Nature, closed to mind, 84-7; concept of, 104, 107; monism of, 40; Whitehead's definition of, 105, 106n; world of, 30, 34, 177. See also Laws of nature.
Nervous system, 134
Neuronal patterns, 182, 185, 201
Newton, Isaac, 345; Absolute Space of, 5, 52, 162; physics of, 193
Newtonian group, 344
Newtonian time, 304n, 325
Nietzsche, Friedrich, 112, 262
Nominal universals, 237
Nominalism, 54, 243-4
Nonphysical quality, 156, 177. See also Epiphysical.
Normal plane, 298
Normality, 184
Null universals, 237
Number, 27-8

Objectification, 360
Objectivity, 23-6, 350
Objects, and events, 355; attained in reflection, 151; eternal, 109; of consciousness, 50; physical, 156. See also Sense-objects, *and* Thought, objects of.
Occam's razor, 234
Occasions, actual, 357-8, 364; concrescent, 363-4
Ockham, William of, 52. See also Occam.

Omar Khayyam quoted, 186, 196
One and many, 233
Organism, 15, 47, 66; biological, 50, 73, 199; conscious, 134-7; dynamic, 120; human, 155, 367; philosophy of, 8, 339, 359; physical, 71, 72
Orthodoxy, 11

Pain, 174, 201
Painting and perspective, 163-4, 179
Paley, William, 275
Paradox of the twins, 314. See also Time-retarding journey, Parodox of.
Particular and particularity, 17, 228-230, 234, 246
Pavlov, I. P., 121, 201
Penfield, Wilder, 207n-212; and Rasmussen, Theodore, 171n-176, 179-180, 182-3, 191-2, 205, 369
Perceiving, act of, 81
Perception, 78, 155, 182, 184; theory of, 6, 43, 114-7. See also Sense-perception.
Percepts, 44
Percipient event, 108
Percipient organism, 115, 116
Perry, Ralph Barton, 125n, 146
Perspectives, 1, 154-225, 359, 360; aerial, 179; linear, 178-9; temporal, 161, 220. See also Realism, perspective, *and* Space, perspective, *and* Sense-perspectives.
Peter and Paul, twins, 313. See also Time-retarding journey, Paradox of.
Petitio principii, 290, 321
Philosophy of science, 105, 109-110
Physics, 80, 86, 87, 341
Physiological age, 329-31, 335
Physiology, 42; of attention, 67; of perception, 116; of the brain, 98
Picture theory of vision, 16
Plato, 3, 21, 22, 237-8, 281; metaphysics of, 109-10
Platonism, 355
Polarized pattern, 115
Possibility, 263-4
Postulates, 5, 8, 14, 23, 35, 154, 194, 223.—*No. 1*, 15; *2*, 17, 26, 36, 48; *3*, 30; *4*, 39; *5*, 47; *6*, 75, 80; *7*, 102; *8*, 113; *9*, 158; *10*, 228, 229, 251; *11*, 234; *12*, 235, 251.—Of Einstein, 23, 297-8, 302, 348; of Newton, 315
Potentiality, 67
Pragmatism, 81, 137
Praise and blame, 268, 272, 285
Predestination, 259
Predication, 48
Preference, 294

INDEX

Prehension, 339, 357-360, 365, 366
Prejudice, 290
Present vs. past, 186, 187. *See also* Specious present.
Presentations, 141. *See also* Appearance.
Principium individuationis, 229
Probability, 88, 199, 261
Progress, 291, 294
Projection, 115, 175, 244
Propositional functions, 26
Protagoras, 3, 21
Psychologist's fallacy, 65, 127, 128
Punishment, 268, 270, 272, 287

Qualities, 19, 31; irreducible, 29; secondary, 176, 178. *See also* Sense-qualities.
Quantum mechanics, 75, 86, 105

Ramsey, Frank Plumpton, 246-7
Rasmussen, Theodore, 207n. *See also* Penfield, Wilder.
Real characters, 235
Real universals, 236
Realism, Aristotelian, 237-8, 242; perspective, 2-8, 169, 193, 195, 225, 369; physical, 114; Platonic, 237-8
Realist theory of consciousness, 138
Reality, 9, 12
Reese, Hans H., 171n
Relations, 17-8, 27, 36-40, 45, 49, 62, 127, 129, 135, 226-254; additive, 142, 147, 148, 149; conscious, 47, 50, 51, 93, 118, 132, 135-7, 199-200; contingent, 341; dynamic, 34, 132; logical, 134; particularity of, 228-30; physical, 143; spatial, 228; temporal, 111, 228; transitive, 254. *See also* Appearing, relation of, *and* Characters, relational, *and* Meaning, relation of.
Relativism, 5, 36
Relativity, 318, 320, 324, 325, 330, 331, 341; of direction, 295; of morality, 276-9; of perspectivism, 194; of size and mass, 193; physical, 61, 86; Whitehead's principle of, 359
Relativity, Theory of, 23, 105, 112, 334; made intelligible, 338-9; General Theory of, 25, 26, 88, 309, 313, 350; Special Theory of, 14, 22, 24, 26, 297, 302, 306, 309, 312, 313, 316, 321, 326, 331, 333, 337, 342, 350
Remembering, 82. *See also* Memory.
Responsibility, 268, 270, 273
Resurrection, 367-8
Retardation of clocks, 315, 325, 329
Retinal images, 164, 170
Retroaction, 113, 186

Retrospection, 186
Riemannian geometry, 88, 345
Riesen, Austin H., 168n
Right and wrong, 275
Roman Catholic Church, 267
Römer, Ole, 157-8
Roscelin, Jean, 243
Royce, Josiah, 14, 223
Russell, Bertrand, 5, 6, 7, 16-18, 26n, 28, 30, 43-4, 46, 254, 361-4. *See also* Whitehead and Russell, *Principia Mathematica.*

St. Augustine, 213
St. Paul, 368. *See also* Saul of Tarsus.
Santayana, George, 5, 11, 13, 52-3, 89, 91-2, 170-1, 222-3
Satisfaction, 292
Saul of Tarsus, 286. *See also* St. Paul
Scepticism, 5, 6
Seeing, 15, 42, 43n, 54n, 59, 63, 81, 170. *See also* Vision.
Self, 64, 66, 77, 129, 149, 150, 197, 368
Sellars, Roy Wood, 33n, 114-7, 243-5
Sensation, 123, 155, 212; auditory and visual, 205; epiphysical, 369; of movement, 176
Sense-awareness, 105-8
Sense-data, 114-6
Sense-experience, 13, 15
Sense-objects, 109, 110
Sense-organs, 134
Sense-perception, 85, 107; physiology of, 96
Sense-perspectives, 223-4
Sense-qualities, 96, 97, 156, 223
Sensing, 160
Sensory processes, 208
Sensuality, 293
Separability, 231
Shaw, George Bernard, 291
Sheldon, Wilmon Henry, 241
Sherrington, Sir Charles S., 58, 68n, 73-86, 93-99, 102, 104, 118n, 134, 193, 198, 207-8, 211-12, 216n, 368
Sight. *See* Vision.
Similarity, 28, 49, 235-240, 245, 250, 251
Simple location, Whitehead's fallacy of, 339, 356, 357, 359, 361, 363, 364, 365
Simultaneity, 303, 316, 318, 320, 342-9
Slavery, 282, 283
Smuts, 36
Socrates, 21
Solipsism, 11
Sommerfeld, 112
Soul, 197. *See also* Self.

INDEX

Space, 23, 25, 220, 235n, 308; absolute, 5, 52, 162; and time, 53, 158, 310, 357; perspective, 362-3
Space-time, 24-6, 44, 297, 306, 311, 353, 356, 357, 365, 366; heterogeneity of, 346; intervals, 26, 304, 306; reality of, 350
Spatial measure, 305-7
Specious present, 213-5, 223
Spectator theory of vision, 16
Spinoza, Benedictus de, 4, 32, 144
Spirit, 52-3, 196-7
Spirituality, 293
Statistical averages, 260
Subject, 152
Substance, 32-4
Supernaturalism, 259
Survival value, 101
Swift, Jonathan, 63
Symbols, incomplete, 245, 247
Synaptic record, 180, 185
Synchronism of clocks, 299, 316, 324, 349
Synthetic whole, 233, 234

Tennyson, Sir Alfred, 16, 69, 196, 285
Tensor analysis, 351
Terms, 36-40, 45, 62
Thalamus, 174, 209-11
Theology, 255
Theory and fact, 78
Things, 30, 32, 37, 362, 363; physical, 177, 188
Thinking, 82
Thought, 77, 99, 107, 110, 117, 137, 150; objects of, 144-5
Thrasymachus, 21, 281
Time, 23, 25, 111, 118, 305, 308, 324; absolute, 5, 329; as sensed, 213-223; coincident, 302; intervals, 347, 348; local, 344; relativistic, 325; sense of, 188. *See also* Space-time.
Time-retarding journey, paradox of, 312-337
"Time's Arrow," 111

Transcendentalism, 64-5
Transient characters, 33
Transitive verb, 44
Transitivity, 234, 235, 253-4
Transmission of signals, 343
Tweedledum and Tweedledee, 254, 261

Understanding, 212
Units, 305
Universals, 230, 236-250; classes of, 236-7
Ushenko, Andrew, 8n

Values, 78, 368
Velocity, at an instant, 354; relative, 317. *See also* Light, velocity of.
Vindictiveness, 270-1
Virtue, 275
Vision, 16, 137, 159-174; not an act, 169; of infants, 165-7. *See also* Seeing.
Vitalists, 80
Vivas, Eliseo, 92n
Volition, 192, 213, 257. *See also* Will.

Wald, George, 161, 165, 170
Ward, James, 90
Warfare of moral ideals, 275-296
Watrous, James S., 164n
Whitehead, Alfred North, 5n, 8, 36, 85n, 86, 88, 104-10, 158, 177, 219, 239, 307n, 338-366
Whitehead and Russell, *Principia Mathematica*, 245n, 254
Wiener, Norbert, 216n
Will, 212, 257; determination of, 272. *See also* Volition.
Woodbridge, Frederick J. E., 41, 60-1, 132-7, 146
World, of mind, 178; of nature, 30, 34, 177; physical, 22-6, 177; postulate, 23, 351
Wulf, Maurice de, 243n
Yerkes Laboratories of Primate Biology, 167